GW01374629

Power and Protest

To Roy and Joy Williamson

With love

POWER AND PROTEST

Frances Power Cobbe and Victorian Society

Lori Williamson

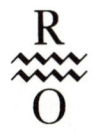

Rivers Oram Press
London, New York, Sydney

First published in 2005 by
Rivers Oram Press
144 Hemingford Road, London N1 1DE

Distributed in the USA by
Independent Publishers Group,
814 North Franklin Street, Chicago, IL 60610

Distributed in Australia and New Zealand by
UNIReps
University of New South Wales
Sydney, NSW 2052

Set in Baskerville by
NJ Design Associates and
printed in Great Britain by
T.J. International Ltd
Trecerus Industrial Estate, Padstow, Cornwall

Lori Williamson asserts the moral right to be identified as the author of this work

This edition copyright © Lori Williamson, 2005

No part of this book may be produced in any form, except for the
quotation of brief passages in criticism, without the written permission
of the publishers

British Library Cataloguing in Publication Data
A catalogue record for this book is available from the British Library

ISBN 1 85489 100-6 (cloth)
ISBN 1 85489 101-4 (paper)

Contents

List of illustrations	vi
Acknowledgements	vii
Introduction	1
1. Early Years	7
2. The Grand Tour and Work in Bristol	36
3. The Claims of Women and Life in London	70
4. 'The Rights of Man and the Claims of Brutes'	97
5. From Restriction to Abolition and Beyond	120
6. 'Health and Holiness'	157
7. Controversy and Retirement to Wales	177
8. *Fin de Siècle*	197
9. A Matter of Conscience	213
Notes	221
Bibliography	254
Index	267

List of Illustrations

1. The Cobbe family tree — 9
2. Newbridge House, Co. Dublin. The Cobbe family seat — 18
3. Newbridge, sketch by Frances Power Cobbe — 27
4. Portrait of Charles Cobbe (Irish School) — 33
5. Charles Cobbe, 1857 — 33
6. Florence, 1863, from Villa Giglioni, sketch by Frances Power Cobbe — 43
7. Frances Power Cobbe in a sedan chair at Aix-les-Bains, 1863 — 98
8. Experiment for testing the time required for injected poisons to traverse the circulation, from Bernard's *Physiologie Opératoire* — 139
9 & 10. Claude Bernard's 'apparatus for the study of the Mechanism of Death by Heat' — 139
11. Method for exposing the salivary glands of a dog — 140
12. Claude Bernard's method for catheterism of the blood vessels, to obtain blood samples and temperature recordings, from his *Physiologie Opératoire* — 140
13. Frances Power Cobbe, age 20 — 214
14. Frances Power Cobbe, age 55 — 214
15. Frances Power Cobbe, age 72 — 214

Acknowledgements

There are many people to thank for their support and encouragement throughout the years that I spent researching and writing this book.

This biography began as a doctoral dissertation at the University of Toronto, and it is those who supported me in Toronto whom I wish to acknowledge first: my dissertation supervisors, Ann Robson, Richard Helmstadter and Michael Bliss, who watched the transformation of this study from research proposal to completed dissertation; also to Jeanne Peterson, who offered constructive criticism as my external examiner and who encouraged me to think about approaching publishers in the summer of 1994. I have had many entertaining and encouraging discussions with John McLeod and Mary Hora first in Toronto and later in numerous cross-Atlantic emails. Special mention must be made of the tireless efforts of the interlibrary loan librarians at Robarts Library, University of Toronto who for several years fielded seemingly never-ending requests from me for books and articles, many of which proved time-consuming to track down. Thanks are also due to the archivists and staff at the following British libraries who showed great tact and patience when dealing with a post-graduate student on a research trip in the autumn of 1990: Dr. Williams's Library, the Bodleian Library, the Fawcett Library (now the Women's Library), The British Library, Colindale Newspaper Library, the University of Southampton and The British Library of Political and Economic Science. Julie Roxburgh, who was the Information Officer at the British Union for the Abolition of Vivisection when I began this research, was very supportive and helpful in providing me with access to the Union's archives. Ellen Slack, formerly at the Historical Society of Pennsylvania and archivists at the Huntington Library San Marino, California, the National Library of Wales and the

Manchester Public Library must be thanked for dealing with my requests for material by post. To this list must be added the following who have assisted my research since I moved to England in 1995: staff at Girton College, Cambridge, Brynmor Jones Library at the University of Hull, the Bristol Record Office, and Emma Hopley at the BUAV.

The School of Humanities at Oxford Brookes University, where I took up a post in British social history in the autumn of 1995, provided me with a vibrant scholarly environment in which to test my ideas. Financial assistance to complete my research for the book was forthcoming from a School of Humanities Quality Research Grant. Richard Wrigley and the Humanities Research Centre gave me the opportunity very early on in my appointment to present my work on Cobbe at a lunch-time seminar. Several colleagues deserve mention: John Stewart and Donal Lowry for their interest shown, Anne Digby and David Nash for assisting with book proposals, and the late Jeanne Sheehy for suggesting that I look at Gifford Lewis's biography of Esther Roper and Eva Gore Booth. Aspects of my work on Cobbe have been presented over the past three years at various conferences and seminars in England, the United States and Canada; all who attended are thanked. Your comments gave me further food for thought. Thanks also are offered to: Caroline Lazar and Anna Davin; to the Reverend Professor Andrew Linzey for permission to quote from 'Making Peace With Creation'; to Lady Shaftesbury for permission to quote from letters held at the Shaftesbury Estates, Dorset; to the Trustees of the Broadlands Archives; to Alec Cobbe for permission to reproduce material from the Cobbe archives; and to Hugh Cobbe.

Many thanks to Michael and Elizabeth Lloyd for their generous hospitality and assistance during the final stages of publication. To Laura, Adam and Aidan for so much entertainment during visits to Toronto. And, of course, to Allan for so much. There are three more people who deserve special mention, and they are my parents and my brother, Mark; your support, encouragement and patience has been amazing. You withstood many temper tantrums and much frustration as I researched and wrote and revised chapter after chapter and dealt with far too many computer disasters. You have lived with Frances Power Cobbe for as long as I have, and I hope that you will now share with me the sense of achievement that comes with publishing *Power and Protest*.

Introduction

In a November 1866 newspaper article the American author Louisa May Alcott reminisced about her introduction in June to a 41-year-old Anglo-Irish women's rights campaigner named Frances Power Cobbe. Alcott had left her New England home for Europe the previous summer to act as travelling companion to the invalided Anna Weld. Cobbe, who had moved to South Kensington in 1864 and who, by the power of her pen and her oratorical skill, was rapidly proving herself an asset to 'the cause', was just one of 'many interesting persons' whom Alcott met during her stay at Aubrey House, the London home of the radicals Peter and Clementia Taylor. Like others who met Cobbe, Alcott was overwhelmed:

> As I sat poring over Gustave Doré's *Illustrations of Dante* one morning, the door suddenly flew open, and in rolled an immensely stout lady, with skirts kilted up, a cane in her hand, a fly-away green bonnet on her head, and a loud laugh issuing from her lips, as she cast herself upon a sofa, exclaiming breathlessly;
> 'Me dear creature, if ye love me, a glass of sherry!'
> The wine being ordered, I was called from my nook, and introduced to Miss Cobbe. I had imagined the author of *Intuitive Morals* [a religious book that Cobbe had written in 1855] to be a serious, severe lady, of the 'Cornelia Blimber' school, and was much surprised to see this merry, witty, Falstaffian personage. For half an hour she entertained us with all manner of droll sayings, as full of sense of humor, one minute talking earnestly and gravely on the suffrage question, which just then absorbed the circle in which I found myself, the next criticising an amateur poem in a way that convulsed her hearers, and in the middle of it jumping up to admire

a picture, or trot about the room, enthusiastically applauding some welcome bit of news about 'our petition'. Cheery, sensible, kindly, and keen she seemed; and when she went away talking hard till out of the gate, and vanishing with a hearty laugh, it was as if a great sunbeam had left the room, so genial and friendly was the impression she made. I saw her several times afterward, and always found her the same wherever she was, people gathered about her, as if she was a social fire, and everyone seemed to find warmth and pleasure in the attractive circle which surrounded her. It was truly delightful to see a woman so useful, happy, wise, and beloved; and it confirmed still more my belief that single women are a valuable and honorable portion of the human race, in spite of the sneers at 'old maids' and lamentations over their unhappy lot.[1]

Old maids had been 'sneered at' with particular enthusiasm by William Rathbone Greg in his 1862 essay, 'Why Are Women Redundant?', wherein he argued that women who did not marry were freaks and that England could rid herself of these unnatural burdens by enforced emigration. His recommendations earned him criticism from several feminists, Cobbe included, who jumped to the defence of the unmarried. Spinsterhood was not something over which Cobbe lamented; it was to be celebrated. She never found the prospect of marriage and maternity alluring: as a young woman she had been frustrated by the expectation that she submit herself to men, whom in general she considered tedious and domineering. She preferred an independent life, and the ability to make free choices. Cobbe was not very good at compromise, she was stubborn and inflexible in her views and could not understand people's inability to 'get ahead' when she herself, as an unnatural, 'redundant' woman with few rights and many wrongs, forged a useful public life. Cobbe judged others by her own high standards and was often frustrated to discover people unwilling to meet them. She was intolerant of those who tried her patience and did not hesitate to break with old friends, for example, Charles Darwin, Emily Davies and Stephen Coleridge, if she felt betrayed. Yet she also proved herself to be steadfastly loyal to those who shared her beliefs.

These beliefs were grounded in conservatism and Theism and they formed the ethical foundations from which Cobbe debated Poor Law reform, animal and later human vivisection, and women's rights, the issue which first brought her to the widespread attention of her peers. She was a witty commentator, fired repartee with lightning speed, and thwarted many opponents with her cutting remarks. Cobbe was not a man-hater, despite her vitriolic condemnation of matrimony. She cooperated with several leading male figures, including Lord Shaftesbury and John Stuart Mill, whom she idolised as a stalwart supporter of the woman's cause. Although an outspoken critic on various issues connected with powerlessness and exploitation, Cobbe never advocated revolutionary change of society; it could only be modified. She was a product of the Victorian age and as such could never completely reject it. She did, however, reject an unspoken right of the powerful to exploit the powerless. Her insistence on women's moral autonomy and self-development sat comfortably beside her conviction that women were different from men, and she used every advantage her sex and society offered her to become one of Victorian England's most visible and vocal women, denouncing established religion, working with Bristol's 'perishing and dangerous' classes, reforming workhouses and defending the claims of both women and animals.

In 1908, four years after Cobbe's death, one Mrs S. Woolcott Browne unveiled a plaque at Harris Manchester College, Oxford, commemorating Cobbe's achievements.[2] The inscription reads: 'Writer on philosophy and religion and a pioneer in social reform'. Andrew Linzey, who holds the International Fund for Animal Welfare senior research fellowship at Mansfield College, Oxford, noted in a paper he gave that, 'to students who pass by the austere marbled countenance of this Victorian woman, I fear she appears a relic of a bygone age'.[3] Nothing, according to Linzey, could be further from the truth. Cobbe's theorising on power hierarchies and exploitation are relevant to issues still being discussed today, including welfare, women's rights and animal rights, and her critique of the medical profession is strikingly similar to recent denunciations of what can be seen as a potentially abusive medical system.[4] Is it too much of a stretch of the imagination to suggest that in this respect Cobbe was ahead of her time?

In her book *Victorian Feminists* Barbara Caine claims that although Cobbe was one of the nineteenth century's most influential feminist theorists, she was not a great activist, and it is for this reason that she has not been the subject of a biography.[5] This is a flawed excuse. She was an original thinker and a skilled polemicist who goaded her adversaries to debate, which she often won through rhetorical talent and logic. True, she had an aversion to working within formally constituted organisations, yet this did not compromise her role as agent provocateur for women's rights and anti-vivisection. She co-ordinated the anti-vivisection offensive first from London and, from 1884, from her home in Wales, and founded two societies that are still active today, the Society for the Protection of Animals Liable to Vivisection (now the National Anti-Vivisection Society) in 1875 and the British Union for the Abolition of Vivisection in 1898.

Cobbe simultaneously represented and rejected much of Victorian life and thought and was herself full of contradictions. She was an elitist who supported the status quo, yet demanded that the exploitative inequality that underpinned it be removed and remodelled along more just, loving and equitable lines. She had little faith in democracy which she believed undermined the civilising process.[6] She supported equal opportunities for men and women (as long as the latter were single or without family responsibilities), but not for classes. She was emphatic that women not sacrifice themselves for others, but remonstrated against those who refused to renounce their aspirations in order to care for ageing parents. She backed Elizabeth Garrett's demand for a medical education in 1862, yet twenty years later she said that only the callous and hard-hearted would be attracted to the medical arts. She rejected much medical progress as immoral and demanded that people endure their pains virtuously; but when her companion Mary Lloyd was in agony from rheumatism Cobbe asked her American friend Sarah Wister if her physician husband could recommend any medication. Cobbe wrote extensively about religious tolerance, yet was prejudiced against Jews, Catholics and mystics. In theory she believed in fair play and just treatment for all, yet she resorted to unscrupulous means to oust her rivals from the anti-vivisection movement. Cobbe proved herself an able and credible campaigner for workhouse reform and women's suffrage, but a headstrong, insensitive figure where anti-vivisection was concerned. She often distorted fact to prove her point and fostered internecine conflict by clashing with several colleagues. She was considered by some a megalomaniac crank; many, however, continued to support her. 'No candid mind', the author Elizabeth Eastlake wrote to Cobbe after more than a decade of anti-vivisection struggle, 'can fail to be struck with the moral ingenuity as well as humanity and rectitude of your pleas [for animals].'[7]

Cobbe's abundant optimism was sapped by the forty-year-long battle she fought to convince her contemporaries that a society which exploited the powerless was neither Christian nor just. That the government, the preserve of privileged, powerful men, did not defend the rights of the weak, did not strive to protect them, but endorsed their victimisation by the strong, galled her. Like many of her feminist counterparts, Cobbe realised that this was because parliament only dealt with issues behind which was a politically powerful voice; laws were made by those in power, consequently protection was offered to those who least needed it. Life was a Darwinian struggle for survival.

Cobbe's efforts on behalf of human and animal welfare brought about limited change. Reformers such as Louisa Twining and Ellice Hopkins bemoaned the absence of a 'womanly' influence in workhouses. 'Men, men, everywhere; til I cry, where are the women? where are the mothers in this family of the state?...[what little female activity there is], finds itself a shrill female voice crying in the wilderness, with about as much influence on the masculine decisions as the wind piping through the keyhole of the committee-room' wrote Hopkins in 1882.[8] Workhouse hospitals continued to be burdened with second-rate caregivers, many of whom were still paupers and, although the training given to both doctors and nurses improved, disparities continued in the care provided by metropolitan and rural workhouse infirmaries. Into the 1930s long-term bedridden patients continued to be removed from voluntary hospitals to a Poor Law hospital to free up beds for less chronic cases. Boarding out pauper and workhouse children never caught on, and the numbers of aged inmates, especially of men, continued to increase. In theory the 1878 Matrimonial Causes Act, which Cobbe had directly influenced, gave abused wives easier access to separation, rights to their children and enforced maintenance payments by their estranged spouses; in practice, however, magistrates often did not follow its guidelines. And the anti-vivisection battle continues to this day.

This biography of Frances Power Cobbe, which appears on the centenary of her death, is one of which she probably would not approve. The biographer's task, she believed, was to elevate both subject and reader to a higher plane of moral worth . If it were necessary to leave information out to achieve these ends, then so be it. 'Can he [the biographer] retain what he ought to retain', she asked in 1864, 'and exclude what he ought to exclude, with regard at once to the interests of the living and the sacredness of the dead?'[9] Cobbe wrote her autobiography in 1894; in it she retained what she wanted to retain and excluded what she wanted to exclude. The result: an incomplete, often inaccurate, although as she intended, moral piece of literature. The 'self' that Cobbe constructed and which she allowed her readers to see was not entirely typical of other 'selves' created and made public by her female contemporaries who published their memoirs, such as Fanny Kemble and Josephine Butler. Social convention demanded that women appear modest and self-abnegating, especially in public, and many women who wrote their life stories negotiated an autobiographical path for themselves which allowed for 'covert' public displays of achievement.[10] Cobbe, however, did not hide behind false modesty. Her autobiographical self is conflated to a great extent with the movements to which she devoted her life, and yet it is very much independent of them. She was a force to be reckoned with; distinct and highly visible.

This biography, which is as much about ideology and protest as it is about an individual, aims to fill in the gaps and rectify the inconsistencies that exist in Cobbe's life as told both by herself and by individuals who have studied her since her death in 1904. Included are many of the personal and public crises that do not appear in her reminiscences. Her numerous conflicts with individuals show that power and control were highly influential and often detrimental forces throughout her life, while her thoughts and activities serve as a catalyst for exploring the wider issues of protest, reform, hierarchy, power and gender, and for recognising that protest is a cultural and ideological expression of dissatisfaction with the status quo. Finally, *Power and Protest* is the life story of an Anglo-Irish woman whose life spanned the Victorian age; her reforming career, her involvement in controversy and her descent into obscurity and old age.

1

Early Years

Frances Power Cobbe, the woman who was to lead the charge against vivisection, was born in 1822, the year in which Richard (Humanitarian Dick) Martin's bill outlawing cruelty to cattle and horses became law, offering domestic animals limited protection from mistreatment for the first time. Over fifty years later Cobbe in turn became a pioneer in the realm of animal welfare. She lived a productive and at times controversial life, dying in 1904 at 81 years of age. Her childhood was spent in Ireland; the prime of her life was played out in London; and she declined into old age with her female companion in remote north Wales.

Newbridge was the Cobbe family seat. It had been built in 1737 by Cobbe's great-great-grandfather, Charles Cobbe, the Archbishop of Dublin, who had come to Ireland in 1717 as Chaplain to the Duke of Bolton, the Lord Lieutenant. Newbridge was often full of people, especially at Christmas and in the summer, when Cobbe's brothers would return from university and an assortment of relatives from Bath would descend and crowd around the massive fireplace and dinner table. The family could be traced back to the fifteenth century and William Cobbe of Steventon, near Southampton. Charles Cobbe's great grandson, the future father of Frances Power, also named Charles, was born in 1781, the eldest of five sons all of whom would eventually have military or religious connections. He obtained a Lieutenant's commission in the 19th Light Dragoons, served under Wellesley during the second (India) Maratha War (1803–5), contracted ague, sold his commission, and returned to his mother's house in Bath, where the Cobbe clan had retired *en masse* in the early 1780s. Here Charles awaited the day when he would inherit Newbridge from his grandfather, his own father having died some years before. It was in Bath that Charles met and married

Frances Conway, only daughter of Captain Thomas Conway of Morden Park, Surrey. After their marriage in 1809 he took possession of Newbridge and began to refurbish it and the dilapidated outbuildings. In 1821 he became High Sheriff of Dublin.[1]

Newbridge lay between the villages of Malahid and Rush in Donabate north of Dublin. Charles Cobbe and his neighbour Lord Trimleston were the chief proprietors of the immediate area, charging a rent to their tenants of between £1 10s. and £2 per acre, and paying 6–8s. per week wages to the approximately 160 labourers who worked the land. The only time Charles became an absentee landlord was in 1822 when he moved his family to Bower Hill Lodge in Melksham for four years to be near to his sons' school.

In 1826 Charles resumed his country duties. He rebuilt the thatched tenant cottages on his land with slate and stone, and sold off a number of the family paintings to raise money for the project after he found the tenants' rents would not cover the cost. Frances Power Cobbe later realised that her father's selfless sacrifice made him somewhat of an anomaly amongst his Anglo-Irish landowning peers, such as their absentee neighbour Lord Trimleston of Turvey, who often neglected their land and tenants. No English landlord, Cobbe believed, could match her father's generosity. But this did not render him immune from attack: 'Those hopeless Irish subscribed to buy pikes to kill him! Subscribed out of the money I had given them,'[2] she later told the women's rights activist Millicent Garrett Fawcett in horrified disgust.

While Charles was the model English landlord, Frances was the model wife: a competent mistress of a large house, and equally successful in her reproductive duties. Four sons were born in six years: Charles in 1811; Thomas in 1813; William in 1816; and Henry in 1817. By this time Frances Cobbe was forty-two, and Henry was considered the final addition to the family. Yet on 4 December 1822 in Dublin, at the age of forty-seven, she gave birth to her only daughter, named Frances Power in honour of herself and her husband's mother, Anne Power Trench, sister of the first Earl of Clancarty. Frances Power later commented that although her arrival was not welcome, she was never made to feel unwanted. She liked being the centre of fraternal attention during the all too brief vacation periods, and recollected sadly in her autobiography that the 'rest of the year…the place [Newbridge] was singularly quiet, and my life strangely solitary for a child'.[3]

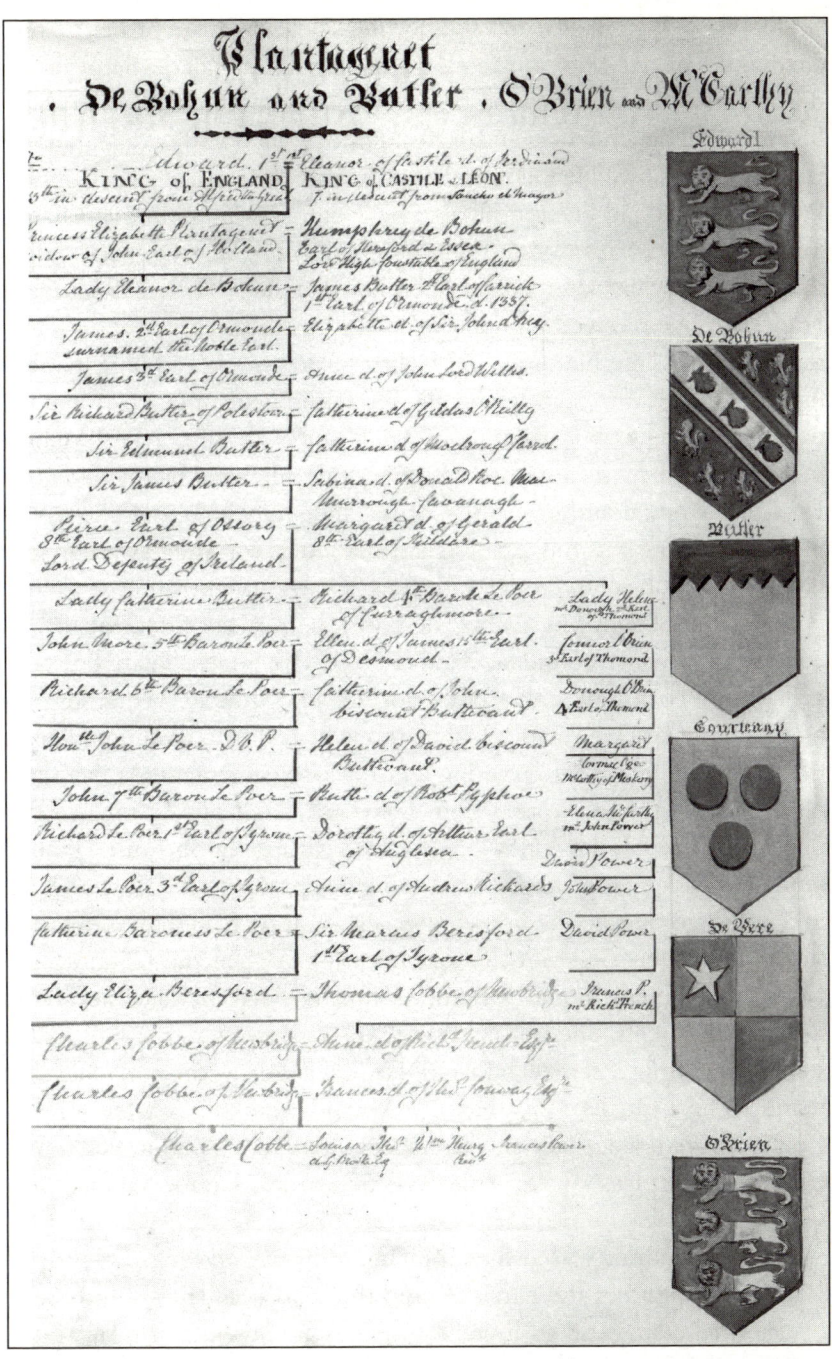

1. The Cobbe family tree (FPC's book of genealogy). The Cobbe Archive.

Cobbe's independence and stubbornness developed out of her solitary childhood. In her book on female autobiography, Valerie Sanders has discovered a direct correlation between isolation and loneliness in childhood and independence and self-sufficiency in adulthood, a pattern which Cobbe's own life followed.[4] Shortly after the birth of her daughter, Frances Cobbe had been mistreated by doctors for an injured ankle; this initiated bouts of invalidism that worsened as the years passed—a fate that was, ironically, later visited upon her daughter. The treatment that Frances Cobbe received was later to colour her daughter's opinion of the medical profession; but as a child Cobbe could understand only that her mother's health was delicate and allowed for limited contact between the two. The young Cobbe spent most of her time with nurse Mary Malone in a large nursery, 'so distant from the regions inhabited by my parents'.[5] Far from parental authority, the Cobbes' little daughter could do as she pleased and make as much noise as she wanted. For an active four year old who was subject to temper tantrums, it was very liberating.

In her autobiography Cobbe describes herself as 'a typical sort of Saxon child'[6] with a round face and fair hair. Her angelic form, however, belied a precociousness that often got her into trouble. When given a new winter coat by a relative Cobbe threw herself into a mud puddle so that she could go back to wearing a favourite old garment. At five years of age she wandered a mile from home in search of her now retired nurse, who lived at the end of Newbridge's shrubbery. She once climbed onto Newbridge's roof and walked along one parapet after she had been told not to go outside the house; after all, 'on top of' and 'outside' were surely completely different things. One winter, when the Cobbes were visiting St James's Square, Bath, Cobbe decided to take her hoop through the streets. She was discovered by the Town Crier in a muddied state not befitting a genteel little girl. He 'cried' her, as she made her way home alone.[7] On her way back to Ireland from this winter sojourn Cobbe was handed a box of Shrewsbury cakes to pass on to her cousin Charley. 'I was pleased to give the cakes to Charley,' Cobbe remembered,

> but then Charley was at the moment far away, and the cakes were always at hand in the carriage; and the road was tedious and the cakes delicious; and so it came to pass somehow that I broke off first a little bit, and then another day a larger bit, till cake after

cake vanished, and with sorrow and shame I was obliged to present the empty box to Charley on my arrival. Greediness, alas! has been a besetting sin of mine all my life.[8]

All was forgiven, however, and before long the two children were amusing themselves by pulling hairs out of a bull's tail; not what one might expect from a future animal welfare advocate.

The freedom Cobbe experienced for the first seven years of her life ceased with the arrival in 1830 of the first of four governesses who replaced informal lessons in reading and writing with a curriculum designed to promote feminine passivity. Cobbe struggled against this from the start. Frances Cobbe had sent her sons to boarding school with the expectation of a place at university, but for her daughter she quite naturally harboured no such grandiose plans.

On her twelfth birthday Cobbe was liberated from her governesses' control by the family doctor's recommendation that lessons be avoided after noon. Most medical men at this time advised that girls approaching puberty should reserve their energies for the development of their reproductive organs, not of their minds, for it was around the former and not the latter that their adult lives would revolve. Cobbe took advantage of the restrictions placed upon her by entering into a concordat with each successive governess: she could do as she pleased after morning lessons were over. By the time Cobbe entered her teens she enforced privacy by taking possession of two garrets in the house, and carefully hid the keys. Thus she had what Virginia Woolf believed every woman should have— a room of her own. It was here that Cobbe studied astronomy and carpentry, wrote poetry, and learned to appreciate her assertiveness.

Cobbe's control over her life ended in 1836, when her father sent her to boarding school and where she would be taught the graces that would help to make her a social success in Dublin. Most girls of Cobbe's age and background spent a couple of years at finishing school before their debut; Charles and Frances chose an establishment in fashionable Brighton, 32 Brunswick Terrace.[9]

Frances Cobbe sailed with her daughter to Bristol and then travelled for three days by postchaises to Brighton, where both marvelled at the recently installed gas lamps that lit their way. On the fourth day mother and daughter arrived at the school, and Frances Cobbe was satisfied that her daughter would have her own room. However, Cobbe recollected many years later that this was not to be.

> When I went to it [her bedroom] next night, heart broken after her [mother's] departure, I found that another bed had been put up, and a school fellow was already asleep in it. I flung myself down on my knees by my own and cried my heart out, and was accordingly reprimanded next morning before the whole school for having been seen to cry at my prayers.[10]

Cobbe weathered this early public humiliation, although the experience did not bode well for her future at the institution. Yet during her two-year stay in Brighton, Cobbe was treated far better than many who attended less élite boarding schools where insanitary conditions, poor food, harsh discipline and cramped conditions prevailed.

It was the tuition which was cramped at Brunswick Terrace and it was unfortunate that Cobbe's foray into education coincided with the height of useless and pretentious female schooling. The headmistresses, Miss Runciman and Miss Roberts, offered a curriculum from which the 27 pupils and seven teachers were not allowed to waver, and Cobbe found herself confined to the shallow rote learning which characterised nineteenth-century female education. Religiously instructive texts, *Daily Bread*, were left in the girls' bedrooms, and they were expected to recite the appropriate day's passages to each other before classes began. Cobbe found herself playing music she did not like on the piano and harp. She was taught to dance, with the encouragement of Madame Michaud and her husband, all of the popular dances in vogue and every national dance in Europe. Calisthenic exercises were given each week by a 'Capitaine', who put the girls through routines with poles and dumbells. English classes consisted of memorising lengthy passages. Sundays consisted of Bible reading and attendance at Christ Church with the Evangelical Mr Vaughan as preacher. 'The din of our large double schoolrooms was something frightful,' Cobbe later wrote,

> Sitting in either of them, four pianos might be heard going at once in rooms above and around us, while at numerous tables scattered about the rooms there were girls reading aloud to the governesses

and reciting lessons in English, French, German, and Italian. This hideous clatter continued the entire day till we went to bed at night, there being no time whatever allowed for recreation, unless the dreary hour of walking with our teachers (when we recited our verbs) could be so described by a fantastic imagination. In the midst of the uproar we were obliged to write our exercises, to compose our themes, and to commit to memory whole pages of prose.[11]

Cobbe had little desire to reach the heights of feminine accomplishment in dancing, singing and sewing, and bewailed the fate of her bright and potentially useful classmates. All of them seemed content to measure success by the extent of their uselessness and their suitability for marriage. Cobbe had her own definition of female achievement. All of 'this fine human material [at Brunswick Terrace] was deplorably wasted,' she critically reminisced 60 years later:

> Nobody dreamed that any one of us could in later life be more or less than an 'Ornament of Society'. That a pupil in that school should ever become an artist, or authoress, would have been looked upon by Miss Runciman and Miss Roberts as a deplorable dereliction. Not that which was good in itself or useful to the community, or even that which would be delightful to ourselves, but that which would make us admired in society, was the *raison d'être* of each requirement. Everything was taught us in the inverse ratio of its true importance. At the bottom of the scale were Morals and Religion, and at the top were Music and Dancing; miserably poor music, too, of the Italian school then in vogue, and generally performed in a showy and tasteless manner on harp or piano.[12]

Cobbe's own recitals must have been painful both for herself and for those within earshot. Partly out of respect for her parents, who were paying £500 per annum to make their daughter a social success, and partly to gain control of the uncontrollable, she set out to 'conquer' Beethoven. She did not succeed.

Cobbe's autobiography is full of contradictions and inconsistencies, and her rendition of her emancipation from Brunswick Terrace in 1838 is one example. After spending a number of pages rejecting the standards set by the schoolmistresses, Cobbe breathed a sigh of relief that she was allowed home; not because she was free from puerile exercises, but because she assumed that she had been taught all that was required of a genteel lady. A few pages earlier she was dissatisfied; now she accepted what she described as a rather vacuous future—an unmarried daughter from Ireland's landed gentry. One of her brothers, probably Charles, accompanied her to Bristol on the Brighton coach, the Red Rover; he mounted the box, she rode inside, content to be alone. From Bristol she sailed to Ireland.

Cobbe spent the first few months of her return to Newbridge immersed in her own regime of leisurely pursuits and novel reading. It did not take long for her to realise that she was as ignorant now as she had been upon her entry at 32 Brunswick Terrace, and like other dissatisfied young women she began to educate herself.[13] Over the next four years she taught herself history and read extensively the works of Milton, the *Iliad*, the *Odyssey*, the *Aeneid*, Pharsalia, Herodotus, Thucydides, Dryden and Pope. According to Cobbe, Newbridge was not blessed with an abundance of literature. The library had been well stocked with religious books by Charles's brother Henry, rector of Templeton, but received little secular reading material apart from the single-sheet *Dublin Evening Mail*, three times a week on the day after publication. None of her neighbours took *The Times* or any other English paper, although *Blackwoods* and the *Quarterly* appeared regularly. To compensate, Cobbe subscribed to Dublin's circulating library, which offered a good many French books, but the literary tastes of the Irish gentry she found narrow and uninspiring.

Despite the poor quality of readily available material, and with a great deal of effort tracking down appropriate texts, Cobbe expanded her studies to include astronomy, architecture and heraldry. She read about Greek and Alexandrian philosophers and constructed highly organised tables detailing their life histories and ethics. She arranged to learn Greek and geometry from the parson of her parish, who, she proudly related many years later, 'was able to teach me in one lesson as many propositions as he habitually taught the undergraduates of Dublin College in two'.[14]

On reflection, Cobbe believed she received an education at her own hands more satisfying than that she would have received fifty years later at Girton or Newnham, where conformity, set standards and competition were encouraged. Cobbe believed that education should satisfy *individual* thirst for knowledge, not incite rivalry amongst students for academic prizes.

> When I came across a reference to a matter which I did not understand, it was not then necessary, as it seems to be to young students now, to hasten over it, leaving the unknown name, or event, or doctrine, like an enemy's fortress on the road of an advancing army. I stopped and sat down before it, perhaps for days and weeks, but I conquered it at last, and then went on my way strengthened by the victory.[15]

Cobbe's self-confidence grew with each intellectual victory, and her mother did not try to stop her personal development. Frances Cobbe, unlike other Victorian mothers with intellectually active daughters, did not appear particularly distraught at her child's unimpressive show in Brighton. Charles Cobbe, however, was not so tolerant of a daughter who had cost him a considerable sum at a girls' school, only to prove a failure in the feminine arts. In matters of their children's education, pursuits, marriages and careers, Victorian fathers held sway, and Cobbe was well aware that she was subject to paternal authority. It was with a sense of duty, therefore, that she found herself propelled, at the age of eighteen, into Dublin society. Charles Cobbe probably hoped that social interaction with eligible bachelors and her genteel female peers would control her intellect and awaken in her those feminine instincts which had refused to surface at Brighton.

The Cobbes enjoyed an active social life in Dublin, of which Frances was very much a part from an early age. In her autobiography, she recalls the boisterous family dinners and visits to neighbours, such as Harriet St Leger who lived at Ardgillan Castle, with great fondness. But public events when she was 'on show' were another matter. She was often escorted to dances and parties by her father or her uncle, and there is no indication in her reminiscences that any other escort was forthcoming. Because her mother was now virtually bedridden Frances Cobbe never accompanied her daughter to social functions. Cobbe felt abandoned without any maternal figure to cling to during the social events. Alone and awkward, she began to dread evenings out and longed to avoid them.

A picture of Cobbe two years after she entered society shows her as a rather large young woman; the corpulency she was to blame on mistreatment by doctors in the 1860s was already evident. A solid-looking neck supports a long, full, intelligent face. Her large, rather sad eyes look upwards as if in answer to some silent question she has posed to her Maker from her unsmiling, thin lips, perhaps the only physical attribute she inherited from her delicate mother. Her long dark hair is drawn back from her face; her simple dress allows only minor concessions to feminine fashion; a lace collar, braid and a pin.[16] One can assume from this photograph that Cobbe presented herself in an orthodox manner when attending dances and dinners. She was far from the 'round and fat...Turkish sultana, with yellow hair, and face mature & pulpy'[17] that Arthur Munby described meeting in the 1860s. However, she belied the albeit dowdy debutante image she presented: she enjoyed dancing because it was physical activity (throughout her life Cobbe was a very active woman), even so, indifference quickly set in because of 'the extraordinary inanity of the men whom I met'.[18] Cobbe wanted and needed intellectual stimulation which the sexual politics of male dominance/female submission courtship patterns did not allow. Her inability to absorb her mother's example and the Misses Runciman's and Roberts's lessons in etiquette, coupled with the dearth of animated company, made her feel uneasy and awkward at the social functions she was obliged to attend. She failed her father—again.

By the time she was nineteen, Cobbe begged her parents to allow her to stay home and attend only local dinner parties. 'With some regret my parents yielded the point, and except for a few weeks of sightseeing and one or two trips in Ireland to houses of our relations, my life, for a long time, was perfectly secluded'.[19] Now that she was freed from parental expectation and social obligation, Cobbe discovered that a multitude of potentially liberating activities awaited her. She turned from society back to books, ministered to the needs of her father's tenants and also, because of her mother's worsening invalidism, took on the responsibility for the day-to-day management of Newbridge. Cobbe slipped into this new role with ease; lessons in housekeeping had been a pleasure to learn, and now she was able to put them to practical use. For the first time she was voluntarily pursuing 'womanly' activities. This undoubtedly pleased her father; his experience with her had taught him to appreciate small mercies. Each morning she would compose menus for the family and staff; pay regular visits to the kitchen, arrange the rooms, attend to visitors, pay the servants their wages and supervise their activities. She did not glory in usurping her mother's role, but found rewarding the responsibility that control over the household and its staff required; by all accounts she was proficient at her task.

By the 1840s, Frances Power seems to have settled down into a life according to her desires. She had replaced the inanity of Dublin society with the onus of running a large family home, and in her seclusion she discovered, and was able to exercise, a certain amount of independence in thought and action. In theory, her life should have been as well ordered as she made Newbridge. Yet in practice, the self-education which liberated her from convention led to one of the most important crises of her life. She was tossed from religious stability into flux, and for her sins was banished from the family home.

The Cobbes had figured prominently in established religion for hundreds of years as rectors, bishops and archbishops and it was within the orthodox bounds of the Irish Church that Charles Cobbe placed his family. He was attracted to the Evangelical Clapham Sect, and with patriarchal proddings he ensured that his family would embrace the spirit of William Wilberforce's *Practical View* and engage in intense introspection and the ceaseless activity that defined evangelical moral worth. Evangelicals did not just follow the Gospel, they were inspired with and lived their lives by its spirit. They emphasised the sense of sin, the weakness of man without God, the experience of conversion and dedication to service.

Individuals within and outside of the established church, such as Hannah More and William Wilberforce, reinforced, through an explosion of missionary activity and conversion, the concept of Christianity as the guide to human conduct. Evangelicals' perpetual fear of being found wanting on the Day of Judgement led to intense self examination and criticism in the fear that they were wasting their talents and neglecting the opportunity of doing good. Evangelicals judged all men by their standards: a man might be good, but was he useful?

Evangelicalism was never as strong in Ireland as it was in England,

2. Newbridge House, Co. Dublin. The Cobbe family seat. The Cobbe Archive.

mainly because of the presence of the Roman Catholic church. The 1861 Census indicated that members of the Church of Ireland were concentrated in Dublin, they were still predominately of the landowning class, and comprised only 11.9 per cent of the population. In the parish of Donabate where the Cobbes lived, 337 of the 405 residents were Roman Catholic.[20]

Cobbe's earliest recollection of religious ritual in which she was trained to participate was of repeating the Lord's Prayer at her mother's knee, and the Collects and Church catechism to her father in his study on Sunday mornings. In strict evangelical fashion, no books except those of a pious nature were allowed in Newbridge on Sundays, nor was there any amusement, apart from a leisurely walk after a visit to the parish church with its neat interior, marble monument to Charles Cobbe the Archbishop who had died in 1765, and 'handsomely stuccoed ceiling...[above a gallery] appropriated for Mr Cobbe's family'.[22] The Reverend Mr Hamilton provided inspiration for the Cobbes' Sunday rituals that Charles reinforced with his own evening sermons attended by the entire Cobbe household. This rather stifling religious atmosphere was a normal environment in which pious Victorians enveloped themselves, and formed what the historian W. L. Burn calls the closely guarded, authoritarian, almost sealed community of the mid-Victorian family. Cobbe had very little trouble structuring her life around it, and liked the isolation that introspection required.

The duty and devotion stressed by evangelical Christianity formed a strong theme in Cobbe's childhood religious lessons, and its impact was profound:

> God was always to me the All-seeing Judge. His eye looking into my heart and beholding all its naughtiness and little duplicities...was so familiar a conception that I might be said to live and move in the sense of it...I think my mother was aware of something of the kind and looked with a little wonder, blended with her tenderness, at my violent outbursts of penitence, and at my strange fancy for reading the most serious books in my play-hours. My brothers had not exhibited any such symptoms, but then they were healthy schoolboys, always engaged eagerly in their natural sports and pursuits; while I was a lonely, dreaming girl.[22]

Because Cobbe was such a lonely child and was part of a family which took religious ritual and the Bible very seriously, it was natural that she should immerse herself in religious tomes. She was, as she herself admits, 'devout beyond what was normal at my age'.[23] Ironically, this highly structured and introspective religious life that gave many children security and purpose also contributed to personal rebellion and conflict during their adolescence.[24] At eleven years of age the tremors leading up to what Cobbe would later describe as her moral earthquake began. The image of the Cobbe family and their servants seated around the fire on a Sunday, listening to Charles read the evening sermon, is an ideal picture of a devout family. However, on a winter's evening in 1834 Cobbe's unconditional acceptance of her father's sermon wavered. She did the unthinkable—she questioned the Bible, the miracle of the Loaves and Fishes:

> 'How did it happen exactly?' I began cheerfully to think, quite imagining I was doing the right thing to try to understand it all. 'Well! first there were the fishes and the loaves. But what was done to them? Did the fish grow and grow as they were eaten and broken? And the bread the same? No! that is nonsense. And then the twelve basketsful taken up at the end, when there was not nearly so much at the beginning. It is not possible!' O Heavens! (was the next thought) *I am doubting the Bible!* God forgive me! I must never think of it again.[25]

But Cobbe regularly thought of it over the next six years, and what began as a simple dilemma over the Loaves and Fishes, escalated into doubts about the Atonement and Heaven and Biblical veracity itself.

Religious crises were not unusual for young girls of Cobbe's age; for many they took the form of rites of passage, or routes to self-awareness and the realisation of a purpose in life outside marriage and domesticity. For example, in February 1837, just before her seventeenth birthday, Florence Nightingale experienced a mystical revelation whereby God called her to His service. Mary Ann Evans (later George Eliot) began to think seriously about evangelicalism after reading Bulwer Lytton's *Devereux* in which an amiable atheist lived and died virtuously: she was 'considerably shaken by the impression that religion was not a requisite to moral excellence'.[26] At the age of fifteen, Evans underwent a religious crisis during which time she neglected her appearance and abstained from simple pleasures to stress her goodness and piety.

Cobbe never abandoned the evangelical outlook that religion was vital, and life was to be participated in, not denied. She was, however, part of a generation of honest doubters, many brought up in evangelical homes, where the strictness and extremes of duty and devotion often led to their abandoning orthodoxy in favour of a more rational, less doctrinal, though by no means less moral, religion. By 1870, Cobbe was able to conclude that children shared their parents' religious feelings, but because of their unformed intellect,

> the awakening to strong spiritual life rarely or never happens under their influence, or that of anyone all together familiar with us. The spark must be kindled by a more distant torch, the pollen brought from a remoter flower. When the mysterious process does not take place wholly spontaneously, it comes from some person who adds a fresh impetus and keener sympathy to elements hitherto dormant in our souls.[27]

Cobbe's distress was exacerbated by the knowledge that she was failing her parents yet again; that faith, the basis of her sacred and secular life, was shaken; and that she was alone.[28] Her companion in solitude had been the literature which was now alienating her from her family's doctrinal allegiance. The more Cobbe thought about the Bible, the more she doubted its authority and truth. This drove her into her state of flux and torment, but also strengthened her emerging independent spirit. Yet in a family where evangelical Christianity had to be accepted or rejected in its entirety, when orthodoxy had not yet been challenged by broad interpretations of the scriptures, by *Essays and Reviews*, Cobbe found herself, by the age of twenty, in a religious quagmire:

> It was not very wonderful, as I think I can recall, my disposition underwent a considerable change for the worse while all these tremendous questions were being debated in my solitary walks in the woods and by the seashore, and in my room at night over my Gibbon or my Bible. I know I was often bitter and morose and selfish; and then came the alternate spell of paroxysms of self-reproach and fanciful self-tormentings.[29]

Early Victorian Britain witnessed many such crises of faith, especially amongst the literati. Like many of them Cobbe no longer believed in human immortality or supernatural revelation. The existence of God was neither denied nor affirmed: she had no means of arriving at any knowledge of Him. By her own account, over thirty years before Huxley first coined the word, she had become an agnostic, an individual whose faith was shaken because of limited knowledge of the unknowable God. In 1883 a more confident Cobbe was able to explain her agnosticism

> as a phase through which many of the most luminous intellects of our time are doomed to pass. It is precisely because the Agnostic fails to find God where he persists in exclusively looking for Him— namely in the order of the physical world—that the darkness has fallen on his soul.[30]

By this time, Cobbe evidently viewed the agnostic as being more inclined towards the secular than the sacred, interested in physical manifestations of God rather than intangible manifestations of faith. The agnostic was in a world of darkness precisely because, as Cobbe understood it, he was not religious and demanded physical rather than metaphysical proof of his existence.

Light came to Cobbe's soul on a spring day in 1842 as she sat alone in the park at Newbridge, abandoned to her misery:

> something stirred within me, and I asked myself, Can I not rise once more, conquer my faults, and live up to my own idea of what is right and good? Even though there be no life after death, I may yet deserve my own respect here and now, and if there be a God He must approve me.[31]

This was a revelation Cobbe could accept. She cast off the remnants of her father's evangelical preachings, and looked to her heart rather than the Bible for confirmation of God's existence. Her understanding of religion was 'transformed...from one of reverence only into one of vivid love for that Infinite Goodness which I then beheld unclouded....God is more perfectly good, more perfectly just, wholly, eternally, universally good'.[32] In agnostic fashion, Cobbe used her reason to sift through the limited information available to her about God's existence, and compensated for its deficiencies by her intuitive faith in Him.

Cynicism and anger at the world around her were to make Cobbe an acerbic woman, yet at twenty years of age she was sensitive to the effects that rebellion would have on other people. So as not to contribute to the family's distress at her mother's worsening invalidism Cobbe decided to keep her revelation to herself, and continued to attend all of the family's religious ritual, except for Communion. Many years later, Cobbe learned from George Eliot's confidante, Caroline Bray, that Eliot had dealt with her religious awakening in a similar manner. Frustrated by the amount of time that it took her to sort out her religious wrestlings, Cobbe later inaccurately claimed that whereas George Eliot's mind had been affected in only one night, it had taken her four years of torment to accept her agnosticism.

Cobbe was happier now that she had discovered God was in her heart, yet she longed to legitimise her findings. She found comfort in Blanco White's *Life*, read works by Deists such as Gibbon and David Hume, discovered more rational explanations for God's existence in William Paley's *Theory* and the *Bridgewater Treatises*, and moved nearer to the agnostics' reverence for natural theology. In 1844 she read James Martineau's *Rationale of Religious Enquiry* and his *Endeavours* and credited them with helping her 'struggle out of the fetters of orthodoxy'.[33] The following year, a notice of a new book entitled *Discourse of Religion* by the American ethicist Theodore Parker appeared in the *Athenaeum*. Cobbe sent away for a copy of the book out of the generous £130 annual allowance her father gave her. Charles Cobbe was, unknowingly, fuelling his daughter's emerging heterodoxy.

The Discourse of Religion had been published in America in 1842, and it outraged Boston, the home of both Parker and of Unitarianism. Many considered *Discourse* a deistical and unChristian work because Parker attacked not only Unitarianism, but the conservative established order that went with it. Strict Unitarians believed in the message of the Bible. But Parker, influenced by the Transcendentalism of Ralph Waldo Emerson, suggested that God's existence was established through intuition as much as reason. No pretence of proving the existence of God could therefore be made. The Bible was a human, not Divine, work and was liable to error. Religion passed through three progressive stages:

fetishism, polytheism and monotheism, the latter being the most civilised expression of worship. Parker placed God in man and permitted inspiration. He did not accept the idea of atonement, but instead believed that each man was his own Christ and was responsible for his own acts. He viewed God as good, and concluded that there could be no Hell, 'for the Infinite Love of God must make the whole of existence a blessing to each man'.[34]

In Parker's *Discourse* Cobbe discovered all for which she had been searching; she was not alone. Parker's words

> threw a flood of light on my difficult way. It was, in the first place infinitely satisfactory to find the ideas which I had hammered out painfully, and often imperfectly, at last welded together, set forth in lucid order, supported by apparently adequate erudition and heart-warmed by fervent piety. But, in the second place, the Discourse helped me to regard Divine Inspiration no longer as a miraculous and therefore incredible thing; but as normal, and in accordance with the natural relations of the infinite and finite spirit; a Divine inflowing of mental Light precisely analogous to that moral influence which divines call Grace.[35]

Cobbe aligned herself totally with Parker's Theistic vision which taught that faith transcended all that could be received from bodily senses, and accepted implicitly the direct Divine teaching of God's holiness and love in the soul: this had been how Cobbe had rediscovered her faith in Newbridge's park on a spring day. Perhaps her beliefs would have evolved with less travail had she been living amongst the Transcendentalists in Boston than amongst the Evangelicals in Ireland.

Within a few months of discovering a religious comrade, Cobbe lost her only female confidante. In 1846, at the age of seventy, Frances Cobbe died, and her daughter once again found herself plunged into an agony, both physical and spiritual, the intensity of which she was still able to recount fifty years after the event. It is interesting to note the emphasis Cobbe placed on her 'perfect' relationship with her mother as being one in which she was dominant:

> The agony I suffered when I realized that she was gone I shall not

try to tell. She was the one being in the world whom I truly loved through all the passionate years of youth and early womanhood; the only one who really loved me...No relationship in all the world, I think, can ever be so perfect as that of mother and daughter under such circumstances, when the strength of youth becomes the support of age, and the sweet dependence of childhood is reversed.

But it was all over—I was alone; no more motherly love and tenderness were ever again to reach my thirsting heart. But this was not, as I recall it, the worst pang in that dreadful agony. I had...ceased to believe in a future life, and therefore I had no choice but to think that that most beautiful soul which was worth all the kingdoms of earth had actually ceased to be. She was a 'Memory;' nothing more.[36]

Cobbe had accepted Parker's explanation for God's presence, but in the days after her mother's death she could not make herself believe that a future life existed. During these years of famine and fever at Donabate and Balisk she buried herself in her household duties and philanthropic endeavours in order to shield herself from her grief and loss of faith, yet neither would go away.

She decided to pour out her heart to her father, fully aware of what his response would be: a mixture of dismay, anger and frustration. He refused to speak to her and a letter conveyed his decision to banish her from his home. Within a few days his daughter left Newbridge and moved to her barrister brother's farm in Donegal.

'I was absolutely lonely,' Cobbe remembered,

my brother, though always very kind to me, had not the least sympathy with my heresies, and thought my father's conduct (as I do) quite natural; and I had not a friend or relative from whom I could look for any sort of comfort. A young cousin to whom I had spoken of them freely, and who had, in a way, adopted my ideas, wrote to me to say she had been shown the error of them, and was shocked to think she had been so misguided. This was the last straw. After I received this letter I wandered out in the dusk as usual down to a favourite nook...and buried my face in the grass. As I did so my lips touched a primrose which had blossomed in that precise spot since I had last been there, and the soft, sweet flower which I had in childhood chosen for my mother's birthday garland seemed actually to kiss my face. No one who has not experienced utter loneliness can perhaps quite imagine how much comfort such an incident can bring.[37]

Despite her pain and loneliness, Cobbe profited by her solitude. The absence of domestic duties allowed her to write her 'Essay on True Religion' and to re-read Parker's *Discourse* in an attempt to discover some answers to her lingering questions about a future life. She found none, so in early April she wrote to him. Theodore Parker's response, on 5 May 1848, laid the groundwork for what was to become one of the strongest and most important relationships in her life, lasting until Parker's death twelve years later. 'My dear friend,' Parker wrote

Your letter of April 2 gave me great delight. I rejoice exceedingly at being able to smooth the difficulties away which have been thrown in the way of Religion & so your kind letter warmed my heart anew with its thought that I had actually helped one fellow mortal.[38]

He then addressed the issue at hand—the death of Cobbe's mother. 'You speak of the *immortality of the Soul*,' he wrote.

I am a believer in it. I *feel* my immortality & have no more doubt of my eternal life—eternally *conscious*, eternally *progressive*— than of my present mortal condition. But I do not pretend to know any thing about the *form* of that life, or its *conditions*. Since I believe the intense *goodness of god*—which you so beautifully speak of—I have no fear, or desire to know more about the form of the next life, or rather of the next stage of this life. If I had only Reason, which cares little about persons & deals more with Ideas, I should not think I suffer or care about meeting my friends in the next stage of life. But as I have Affections more powerful too than reason, I cannot doubt that I shall see & know my friends in Heaven. Once I did not think so. But at the grave's mouth, as it closed on a Sister, I could not doubt. Where my logic had failed me Nature came in & completed her work.[39]

3. Newbridge with baby carriage, sketch by Frances Power Cobbe. The Cobbe Archive.

Cobbe followed Parker in reaching an understanding of God and immortality through feeling and intuition as much as by reason, and it was his letters and his *Sermon on the Immortal Life*, which he sent to Cobbe, that enabled her to think of her mother as living within God's universe. Her religious reawakening was complete. Cobbe saw immortality as evidence of God's goodness, and like F. W. Newman believed that 'If Man be not immortal, God is not just'.[40]

During her ten-month exile from Newbridge Cobbe received a number of conciliatory letters from her father. If she curbed her religious heresies he would allow her to return home. Cobbe regarded this as moral bribery. She emphatically refused.

Ultimately it was Charles who relented: he was lonely, ageing and needed his daughter's competent housekeeping talents. Cobbe was summoned home to resume duties which, as the only daughter, she knew she was obliged to take up. In *The Duties of Women*, published in 1881, Cobbe stated that women 'are to be Human Beings of the Mother Sex (that is the best definition I can find for them), and their duties must be human, including the whole circle of human virtues, and applying them to the special obligations of daughter, mother, wife'.[41] Cobbe accepted the responsibility to care for her ageing parent, but insisted that she remain morally autonomous and not be expected to participate in family services.[42] Charles Cobbe reluctantly accepted. This experience proved to Cobbe that if in conflict with others she remained committed to a principle and was unflinching and uncompromising in the stand she took, she would emerge victorious.

Once back at Newbridge, Cobbe found herself living in virtual religious isolation that was broken only by the arrival of letters from Theodore Parker, and while this experience may have strengthened her independence, it also initially unsettled her:

> It was an anomalous position, that which I held at Newbridge, from the time of my return from Donegal till my father's death eight years later. I took my place as head of the household at the family table and in welcoming our guests, but I was all the time in a sort of moral Coventry, under a vague atmosphere of disapprobation wherein all I said was listened to cautiously as likely to conceal some poisonous heresy. Everything of this kind, however, wears down and becomes

easier and softer as time goes on, and most so when people are, au fond, just-minded and good-hearted, and the years during which I remained at home till my father's death, though mentally very lonely, were far from unhappy.[43]

At the age of thirty, Cobbe suffered a severe attack of bronchitis from which she nearly died. As she lingered on what she thought was her death bed, waiting to be reunited with her mother, she realised that while she had benefited from 'heterodoxy', she had done nothing to help others who were in an ethical quandary similar to her own. Discovering, with surprise and relief, the reunion with her mother to be postponed, Cobbe began to consider the approach she would take to help others pass from orthodoxy to heterodoxy; she discovered her answer in the works of the Konigsberg philosopher Immanuel Kant. 'God said, Let there be Light!' she later recollected in her autobiography, 'and there was—the Kantian Philosophy'.[44] Inspired thus, Cobbe wrote what was to become the first of many works which championed Theism as the religion of the future, *The Theory of Intuitive Morals*.

Intuitive Morals was not an original work. Cobbe wrote it to popularise Kant and to impress upon her readers that the end of creation was not happiness, but the virtue of rational souls. Her views may have altered somewhat over time, but the theme of disinterested virtue was always central to them. She based this idea on the presence of a universal Moral Law as outlined by Kant, which she knew God expected her to follow and which, throughout her life, she bullied others into following also. The message within *Intuitive Morals* allowed Cobbe to introduce a wide array of thought-provoking subjects into her commentary which foreshadowed her involvement in future controversy—benevolence, women's rights, and animal rights, or a lack thereof: all of these were central to the Moral Law as Cobbe understood it.

Cobbe accepted the Kantian premise that men and women from all walks of life shared a common moral vocation and destiny—the suppression of animal passions and secular desires to morality and the development of a good will. And it was because man lived in two distinct but interconnected worlds, that he was able to work towards that destiny. In the sensible world, man was *Homo phenomenon*, motivated in his actions by instinct. In the supersensible world, man was *Homo noumenon*, governed by moral laws which were derived from objective maxims given by his reason alone. These maxims distinguished what was morally right from what was morally wrong, and allowed for the emergence of a moral code governing individual and collective group behaviour.

As a rational free agent who lived in two distinct but coeval worlds, man was compelled to choose morality over instinct through the exertion of his free will:

> The Free Man, therefore—the *Homo noumenon*—is, *as such*, purely moral. And as this supersensible world is the background and *substans* of the phenomenal world whose laws (though incomprehensible to us) it coacts, the man, in his character of an inhabitant of the supersensible world, is capable of coacting himself in his phenomenal nature, and breaking in upon the chain of instincts and solicitations of the sensory, whereby, if only a *Homo phenomenon*, he would be totally enslaved.[45]

Thus man was free, able to bury his animal desires under that freedom. But what if those impulses continued to resurface, bringing with them the likelihood of moral wrong doing? Where did Cobbe stand on sin, especially as it was explained in the Bible?

Cobbe could not attribute moral lapses to original sin in man or to the influence exerted by God's antithesis, the Devil. She dismissed both as ludicrous twaddle in a fallible book that had replaced the essential goodness of God (a concept straight out of Parker) with hell-fire warnings of eternal perdition and suffering. There could be no devil that dwelt in man, tempting him to choose wrong over right because he had been created by a loving creator for one purpose only: to do what was right and to become virtuous. The commission of sin was something that Cobbe considered part of God's plan and important to man's moral development, not evidence of innate corruption.[46]

Cobbe understood that God would punish sin, but she despised creeds that preached all men to live their lives according to a system of rewards for good behaviour and punishment for bad behaviour. She also questioned why her society deemed the sin of a woman to be so more reprehensible than that of a man. If God planned the same end for both men and women, then why would He allow one sex to live differently from the other? And if God was inherently good, then why would He have created a Hell in which sinners, of both sexes, would burn eternally? Such punishment did nothing to make men more virtuous; it made them fearful of a vengeful God rather than loving of a perfect one.[47] All men and women, Cobbe later told a Unitarian congregation at Clerkenwell in 1873, were 'doomed to be saved' because God was the all-seeing Judge who personified love, not hate, and would not punish eternally sinners who, like saints, were '*destined* to be noble, not base; pure, not unholy, loving, not selfish or malicious'.[48]

Cobbe was emphatic that man act in accordance with the Moral Law not out of fear of retribution or in the quest for personal happiness (private eudaimonism). Men and women, she argued, should act because they took an interest in acting, not because they derived some benefit from their actions. Moral freedom, Cobbe wrote, 'must be the free choice of actions to which we are NOT determined by the instincts of the internal, nor the solicitations of the external world'.[49]

Cobbe was more lenient with public eudaimonism than she was with its private counterpart. She was critical of Jeremy Bentham's philosophising on utilitarianism and 'the greatest happiness of the greatest number' because neither required man to exercise his moral nature.[50] She preferred Kant's suggestion that man could make others happy as he pursued his virtuous and benevolent life, but he could not use anyone to reach a state of personal happiness. Nor should philanthropy pander to public eudaimonism. To do so would place *Homo noumenon*, the free will and moral character in jeopardy. This was one reason why Cobbe disliked indiscriminate charity and embraced, like many a Victorian, the idea of self-help, which encouraged the development of self-reliance and duty to the Moral Law. Benevolence was fine, but it had to make the recipient moral as well as happy. Reason and reflection on practical experience, Cobbe suggested, taught one what was needed by an individual, by society, by charity, but 'the moment Intuition has proved an action to be *Right*, Experience must no longer ask whether it also be *Expedient*. Whether it be so or not, it is still THE RIGHT'.[51]

It took Cobbe three years to write *Intuitive Morals*, primarily because she was preoccupied with domestic responsibilities. She had to direct Newbridge's household, entertain guests, carry on the family's correspondence, and play the role of Lady Bountiful in Donabate and Balisk. To complete her work she often wrote and read into the early hours of the morning, a habit that she continued to her dying day.

It was while she was on holiday with Charles in London that Cobbe took her completed manuscript to the publisher Mr William Longman. According to her account, she argued with him in an eloquently aggressive manner until he agreed to publish her work. She spent the rest of her time in the British Library (her request for a reader's ticket is still there) verifying quotations and correcting proofs. Cobbe returned to Ireland puffed with pride. She was under the impression that her religious ideas not only made her the first 'heretic' in the Cobbe clan, but, incorrectly, that her success in bringing them to the reading public's attention made her the first member of her family to employ a printer and publisher.[52] Charles Cobbe was neither delighted with nor proud of his daughter's effort. The sheets of the manuscript that she left lying around the house almost sent him into fits of apoplexy. 'Don't leave those about,' he warned her, 'you don't know into whose hands they may fall'.[53]

Cobbe's work was brought out in 1855. It was favourably reviewed by a number of critics, and one of Theodore Parker's clerical friends who borrowed the volume asked 'what Man (!) had written so noble a Book!'[54] However, once it became known that a woman had written *Intuitive Morals*, members of the clergy criticised her for stepping outside the bounds of quiescent womanhood: 'The writer' wrote the *Christian Observer*, 'we are told, is a lady, but there is nothing feeble or even feminine in the tone of the work.[55] But Cobbe looked upon her decision to publish as a combination of God's will and an educated woman's nature. And even after her death in 1904, eulogies that celebrated Cobbe's skill emphasised her gender and the disadvantages she faced as a self-educated woman when discussing the contribution of *Intuitive Morals* to mid-nineteenth century ethical debate.[56]

Cobbe was not the only woman publishing her religious ideas in mid-nineteenth-century Britain; indeed, she has been eclipsed historically by other eminent dissenters, such as Eleanor Sidgwick, Marie Louise De la Ramée (Ouida), Mary Ward and Annie Besant. Cobbe read Ward's *Robert Elsmere* with admiration for its author, and told her so. 'I am so glad you like *Robert Elsmere*,' Ward replied. 'You have done so much & fought so well for the cause it tries to further'.[57] The atheist Besant could not agree with Ward's praise, and attacked Cobbe and Theism in a pamphlet

4. Portrait of Charles Cobbe (Irish School). The Cobbe Archive.

5. Charles Cobbe, 1857. The Cobbe Archive.

published by the Freethought Publishing Company in 1885. Thirty years after critics had celebrated Cobbe's analytical abilities, Besant accused her of being an incompetent member of the 'semi-rational school,' with an 'impatient, unbalanced, helter-skelter mind,'[58] overly concerned with feeling, ignorant of fact and blinded by her belief in the presence of a God whose absence, Besant argued, would make man more, not less strong.

Shortly after *Intuitive Morals* was published, Cobbe wrote three more religious books, although the only one she published (a few years later in 1864) was *Religious Duty*, in which she sought to convince her readers of the importance of intuitive faith. She opened her treatise with a definition of the law of religious duty as loving God with all one's heart and soul and strength. She then discussed the religious offences of blasphemy, hypocrisy, perjury against the law, thanklessness, irreverence and worldliness and she concluded her work with six sermons on thanksgiving, adoration, prayer, repentance, faith and self-consecration.

While suffering from an attack of ague in 1857 Charles Cobbe allowed his daughter to read him the manuscript of *Religious Duty*. Cobbe decided not to reveal herself as the author, and Charles was forced to judge objectively the book's content. He seems to have mellowed somewhat since he first was exposed to his daughter's heterodoxy more than a decade earlier, and sympathised with her views. In her autobiography, Cobbe reflected on this precious and rare moment with fondness, yet she emphasised that the cause of their strained relationship was his inflexibility, not hers: 'His mistakes and errors, such as they were, arose solely from a fiery temper and a despotic will, nourished rather than checked by his ideas concerning the rights of parents and husbands, masters and employers; and from his narrow religious creed'.[59]

Charles Cobbe died in November 1857. Frances Power wrote to her friend Harriet St Leger:

> I grieve that I was not more to him, that I did not better win his love and do more to deserve it; but even this sorrow has its comfort. Perhaps he knows now that with all my heart I did feel the deepest tenderness for his sufferings and respect for his great virtues. At all events the wall of creed has fallen down from between our souls forever, and I believe that was the one great obstacle which I could

never overthrow entirely. Forbearing as he proved himself, it was never forgotten. Now all that divided us is over…It seems all very dream-like just now, long as we have thought of it, and I know the waking will be a terrible pang when all is over and I have left everything round which my heart roots have twined in five and thirty years. But I don't fear—how can I, when my utmost hopes could not have pointed to an end so happy as God has given to my poor old father? Everything is merciful about it—even to the time when we were all together here, and when I am neither young enough to need protection, or old enough to feel diminished energies.[60]

Cobbe was not a feeble woman. She had weathered the storm which her early experience with unorthodox religious discovery had caused, and had placed herself outside her family's doctrine when she pledged her allegiance to Theism. She had dared to publish her heretical opinions, and this act, which fanned the flames of parental opprobrium, also sparked self-confidence and independence in Cobbe. She had no intention of being protected any longer, and decided to dissociate herself completely from her dependent life. Three weeks after Charles Cobbe's death, Frances Power set out on a Grand Tour that lasted eleven months. Her decision to travel alone set her further outside convention, and over the following year, liberated from the constraints that had bound her, she began to question that convention even further.

2

THE GRAND TOUR AND WORK IN BRISTOL

Charles Cobbe had left his daughter £200 per year, and fully expected that she should continue living at Newbridge with his eldest son Charles and his wife Louisa. Cobbe had different ideas. The money her father left her she considered 'a narrow provision'[1] in comparison to the £130 annual allowance she had received while living under his roof, and she could not envisage herself being demoted from Charles's housekeeper to her brother's lodger, without any domestic authority or control: 'Such a plan was entirely contrary to my view of what my life should thenceforth become,' she defiantly proclaimed.[2] She accepted her 'poverty cheerfully enough',[3] cut her hair in order to avoid the time-consuming process of dressing it every morning and left Ireland for the Middle East.

Cobbe's trip was comparable in scope and duration to the Grand Tour wealthy young gentlemen took during the eighteenth century, and although her excursion at first might appear anomalous in mid-nineteenth-century female behaviour, she was following in the footsteps of a number of intrepid female travellers, some who accompanied male relatives, some who travelled alone or in groups. Mary Wortley Montagu accompanied her husband to Turkey in 1716 when he was appointed Ambassador; Elizabeth Simcoe travelled to Canada in 1791 with her husband John Graves Simcoe the Lieutenant-Governor of Upper Canada; the sisters Susanna Moodie and Catherine Parr Traill followed their husbands to the backwoods of Canada in the 1830s; and upon her father's death in 1784 Jane Parminter, her invalid sister, an orphaned cousin, Mary, and a London friend embarked on a Grand Tour through France, Italy, Germany, Switzerland, Spain and Portugal, which lasted an astonishing eleven years.

When women travelled they adapted to their surroundings and developed an entrepreneurial spirit which was not expected in England, but only later would Cobbe appreciate the benefits of her odyssey. She spent the night before her departure for France with her friend and neighbour Harriet St Leger at St Leonard's. In despair, Cobbe commented on her fate:

> When I had gone to my room rather late that evening, I opened my window and looked out for the last time before my exile, on an English scene. There was the line of friendly lamps close by, but beyond it the sea, dark as pitch on the December night, was only revealed by the sound of the slow waves breaking sullenly on the beach beneath. It was like a black wall before me; the sea and sky indistinguishable. I thought: 'To-morrow I shall go out into that darkness! How like to death is this!'[4]

Cobbe's choice of words—'death', 'exile'—is paradoxical; she had rejected security in her brother's offer of room and board, yet here she expressed reservations about an 'unknown' future. Perhaps she exaggerated her feelings at this time when reminiscing about them nearly forty years later. Her ambivalence was typical of other women who found themselves uprooted and liberated by traumatic events. Yet like other independent women travellers who came before and after her, it did not take Cobbe long to abandon her identity as the English spinster and replace it with the intrepid nomad. Over a period of eleven months and at an estimated cost of £400 Cobbe travelled from Dublin to Paris, Marseilles, Rome, Naples, Messina, Malta, Alexandria, Cairo, Jaffa, Jerusalem, Bethlehem, Hebron, the Dead Sea, Jordan, Beirut, Lebanon, Baalbec, Cyprus, Corfu, Trieste, Adelsberg, Venice, Florence, Milan, Lucerne, Geneva, Wiesbaden, Antwerp, completing her travels in London.

Cobbe kept a journal, written in pencil and peppered with sketches, of her Grand Tour and recounted her adventures in a series of articles she wrote for *Fraser's Magazine* between 1861 and 1863. Like many mid-Victorians, she considered literature first to be didactic, then entertaining, and her travelogue follows these literary priorities. She often digressed from descriptive accounts of her journey to lecture her readers on God, natural theology, homes for the poor in Britain and the ability of the lower classes to appreciate religion. However, her Irish humour resists the weight of didactic moralising; her words entertain as well as enlighten.

After her arrival in Rome Cobbe was stricken with illness caused, she believed, by the stress and anxiety surrounding her father's death and her decision to leave Newbridge, yet during her three-week long soujourn she managed to visit the Colosseum, the Vatican and Shelley's grave. She found Rome's scenery inspiring—'We may all know that a mountain may be *sublime*; but to learn how *beautiful* it is we must go to Rome'[5]—but Rome itself was a dismal place, with air she later described as being 'foul with the blood and corruption of a thousand years.'[6] She found the Italians dull and lacking in intelligent conversation. The Roman Catholic church swaddled their minds and bodies, especially those of the young men training for the priesthood. 'The result,' Cobbe wrote, 'is that a Roman boy of twelve or fourteen is about the dullest mortal under the sun.'[7]

Things became more lively for Cobbe once she left Italy. *En route* to Egypt from Malta the ship on which Cobbe was travelling was caught in a hurricane. She spent most of the night alone on the floor of her cabin, convinced that she was going to meet her Maker, until she was joined by an American woman with whom she conversed intensely about death and the afterlife. The two bonded during their near-death experience and were inseparable during the next few weeks.[8]

The landing at Alexandria was horrifying. The ship was 'boarded by hordes of half-naked porters and gorgeously attired dragomans, while crowds of wild creatures, black, brown, and white, scuffling, screaming, struggling like maniacs on the quay, seemed to jostle each other into the water,'[9] and Cobbe found herself surrounded by a 'tribe of demented creatures.'[10] Two days at Alexandria were enough. As the group of tourists with whom she journeyed gathered outside their hotel to transfer to Cairo, they were swamped by 300 donkey boys, porters and assorted individuals competing for their attention and money. The hotel servants attempted to clear a path for the tourists by throwing water over the crowd—it landed squarely on Cobbe. Later in the day she almost lost her trunk when she was informed that it was too cumbersome to accompany her any further and was to be sent to Bombay with the luggage of the overland mail passengers instead. It was her newfound American friend who saved the day and retrieved Cobbe's trunk for the journey to Cairo.

These setbacks stiffened Cobbe's Anglo-Irish upper lip, and allowed her to construct a peripatetic identity for herself that drew on all that it meant to be a Briton at a time when the nation was the 'workshop of the world' at the height of economic greatness and world dominance.

> There is an imperiousness in the true English mind rising up immediately against any obstacle in its path to which I believe we owe a vast deal of our national achievements, physical and moral. Assuredly we owe it to the way in which travelling is facilitated in every corner of the world where English people do congregate. One after another we pour on, starting at every delay, insisting on more and more rapid conveyance, fretting, fuming, making ourselves objects of astonishment to the calm Oriental, and of ridicule to our fellow Europeans; but still eventually always conquering, and leaving rough places smooth, and crooked things straight behind us. 'Fag an bealach' is an Anglo-Saxon far more than Celtic war-cry. That sign of a thoroughly healthy constitution, the arising of a slight fever after every wound, is peculiarly our own. No true-born Briton ever takes meekly being stopped, bullied, cheated, and thwarted; but a decided quickening of the blood, with a few other febrile symptoms is sure to ensue![11]

Once they landed in a foreign country, most independent women travellers happily abandoned notions of genteel behaviour that had enveloped them since girlhood. Yet while they were able to remove the layers of gendered convention under which they had been buried back home, they were unable to cast off other cultural baggage, and resolutely clung onto their sense of class, hierarchy and whiteness. Their innate differences from the indigenous population enabled female travellers to exercise a degree of control in their new found foreign surroundings, although Cobbe soon discovered that this could be compromised by a particularly unruly beast. She struggled valiantly to subject to her will the donkey she rode to Cheops. She came to loathe the beast as it often got the upper hand and did not allow her to behave as a 'lady' should:

On horse-back you are a lord (or lady) of creation, with the lower animal subject unto you. On mule-back, or ass-back, you are a bale of goods, borne with contumely at the will of the vilest of beasts, not where you please, but where, when, and how it pleases.[12]

Upon her arrival at Cheops Cobbe met up with an English party who had arrived some time before her. She was glad of their company although she was annoyed that the women within the group did not seem to share her sense of adventure. She asked one of the ladies if she had ventured inside the pyramids. No, the lady replied that she was too afraid of the Arab guides to risk a peek at the pyramids' interior. This feeble excuse did not sit well with Cobbe. Nobody was going to stop her from seeing the burial chambers, especially after the unpleasant donkey ride. Cobbe ordered five Arabs to guide her down to the burial chamber. Upon arrival the men demanded payment for their service, else they would abandon her:

> 'We want baksheesh [payment]!' said all five of the villains in one loud voice.
> ...I suddenly spoke out, angrily and preemptorily—
> 'I'll have no more of this. *You* fellow there, take the light, and go out. *You*, give me your hand. Come, along, all of you.'
> It was a miracle; to my own comprehension, at all events. They one and all suddenly slunk down like so many scolded dogs, and without another syllable, did as I ordered them. The slave habit of mind doubtless resumed its usual sway with them the moment that anyone asserted a claim of command. At all events, it was a fact that five Arabs yielded to a single Anglo-Saxon woman, who was herself quite as much surprised as they could be at the phenomenon.[13]

Surprised Cobbe may have been, but her behaviour was typical rather than unusual. Other women travellers, such as Edith Durham, Alexandra David-Neel and Cobbe's friend Amelia Edwards, also empowered themselves with the lowly status they bestowed upon their racial subordinates; it enabled them to ignore gender, which so often put them at a disadvantage in their homelands, and to focus instead upon their racial superiority. They were *Europeans*, not European *women*, able to see themselves as genderless white explorers. Cobbe shared in the discourse and rhetoric surrounding nineteenth-century cultural imperialism,[14] and was empowered by it. It was not the memory of the pyramid, but her adventurous experience with the five Arabs and her success in asserting her control over them that Cobbe chose to emphasise in her reminiscences.

Cobbe was drawn to danger, to the unusual, the unexpected, and on her way to Jerusalem with a party of Americans and Britons, she convinced her guides, a Jewish physician and a clergyman whom she had met on the way, to take her inside the Mosque of Omar. 'It was a rather dangerous attempt,' she remembered with relish, 'for at that moment the Moslem population were in an unusually excited state, and ingress to any part of the building was strictly forbidden to both Jews and Christians.'[15] Forbidden was not a word Cobbe ever heeded, and she convinced her male companions to sneak through the Mosque's outer gate and onto the roof of a nearby house so that her curiosity could be satisfied. On descent the three were caught by Moslem pilgrims who chased them from the premises and threw stones as they fled. Cobbe was exhilarated.

But her gender would occasionally bar her from sharing the experiences of her male counterparts. On one occasion, for example, Cobbe decided to visit a Coptic Church in Cairo. She found, to her annoyance and frustration, that her plans to go inside were not to be fulfilled: the 'little church, dark and dingy, with a sort of sheep pen at the west end for women, was adorned by no pictures—only by two poor broken and filthy glass chandeliers. The screen closing off the chancel was not to be passed by a woman's unhallowed foot; but looking through it I saw an altar, on which was a small box of burning incense'[16]—an unsatisfactory and anti-climactic excursion.

Cobbe said good-bye to her British and American travelling companions at Jerusalem, and rode alone with an Italian and a muleteer to Jaffa. She then sailed to Beirut where she hired a Turkish dragoman and was able to try out her dozen Arabic words on a Syrian woman whose 'sweet soft face, and...lithesome figure and pretty colours of the graceful dress made her a charming picture.'[17] In her travelogue Cobbe wrote about indigenous populations within the eighteenth-century cult of the picturesque and, like Elizabeth Simcoe before her, Cobbe's tendency to view people and places as picturesque or not influenced her acceptance or rejection of them. Cobbe found the Syrian woman at Beirut and a Jewish woman at Jerusalem who 'might have made as sweet a Madonna as Raphael ever painted'[18] more appealing than the unpicturesque Arab men, the 'scolded dogs' at Cheops.

Cobbe left Beirut for Baalbec with her Turkish dragoman, both on Syrian steeds, while the muleteer and his mule were responsible for her tent, kitchen, cooking and eating utensils, food, drink, bed and bedding, table, stool, bath, carpetbag and leather travelling case that had almost been sent to Bombay. Cobbe had briefly flirted with willow-patterned china when she ate dinner with the English party at Cheops, yet like other women travellers who spent time with European or American tourists, she soon sought a more unconventional existence, and found hers in tents and sharing her dragoman's utensils. At times it was not picturesque, but it was liberating. She brushed off the six-inch long centipedes that had invaded her shelter at the Dead Sea, and withstood with developing fortitude a procession of mules and Arabs who stumbled over her tent pegs in the middle of her first night on the road to Baalbec: 'It was not very pleasant, but courage had come in my long wanderings, and neither that nor many subsequent similar disturbances prevented me from rest.'[19] She rose before dawn and ate, by her standards, a rather sparse breakfast of dry bread, two eggs and a cup of milkless tea in her dragoman's tin mug which retained the odour of the onions that were normally carried in it. After her belongings were strapped onto the mule, she continued to Baalbec where she spent two enjoyable days before returning to Beirut to catch a steamer to Athens.

It was while she was at Athens that Cobbe abandoned the new and took hold of the old. She was glad of the civilised approach to life there compared with the rough-and-ready existence she had encountered in Syria and Egypt, which a few months earlier she had found so liberating. At Athens she could 'enjoy thoroughly those mundane satisfactions of bath and breakfast, which by no means fail to enhance our sense of the merits of either art or nature.'[20] Her impressions of Athens became some of the most passionate of her travelogue.

Cobbe spent one week in Athens before she left for Constantinople and her return trip home through Corfu, Adelsburg, Trieste and Italy, where she spent a number of less than idyllic weeks. The only redeeming feature of Italy was the group of expatriate Britons, Frenchwomen

6. Florence, 1863, from Villa Giglioni, sketch by Frances Power Cobbe. The Cobbe Archive.

and Americans who had formed their own cultural community in Florence, and whom Cobbe visited frequently: Harriet Hosmer, the American actress Charlotte Cushman, Isa Blagden, the French painter Rosa Bonheur, the mathematician Mary Somerville and the Welsh sculptor Mary Lloyd. They furnished the only fond memories of Italy that Cobbe took back home.

Cobbe returned to England in 1858 with some American friends, the Althorps, who had joined her at Montreux. 'The perils and fatigues of my eleven months of solitary wanderings were over,' Cobbe wrote. 'I was stronger and more active in body than I had ever been, and so enriched in mind and heart by the things I had seen and the people I had known that I could afford to smile at the depression and loneliness of my departure.'[21] Cobbe's wanderings proved to her that she could do whatever she put her mind to, and she returned to Ireland with a revitalized faith in the ability of the British as a race, and of women in particular: 'I envy not him who could make a great journey in our day, and not come back proud and thankful to belong to our Saxon race. The trust in our word, the respect for our courage (assumed even in a woman), the belief in the steadfastness of our resolution, is something that does one good to meet.'[22]

Cobbe spent the first three weeks of her return visiting Charles and Louisa at Newbridge, and mulled over what she should do with her time now that both her household duties and nomadic lifestyle had ended. She refused to adopt a 'passive' lifestyle because idleness, 'which is the root of all evil for men, is not particularly suited to be the root of all virtue for women.'[23] Unmarried women from the middle and upper classes, Cobbe believed, needed 'real lives—lives devoted to actual service of father or mother, or to work of some kind for God or man...[in such activity] alone spring up real feelings. Lives of idleness and pleasure have no depth to nourish such plants.'[24]

Biological determinism and notions of gendered spheres relegated the 'ideal' woman to marriage and maternity in hearth and home; this narrow gendered view limited the life choices of women and made those who did not or, because of demographic patterns, could not, conform to the norm into a creature both abnormal and unnatural.[25] Cobbe later criticised the binary fusion of biological and cultural determinants of woman's fate as being particularly unfair to the woman who, through no fault of her own, found herself alone in the world:

It is one of the many perversities of woman's destiny that she is, not only by hereditary instinct a home-making animal, but is encouraged to the uttermost to centre all her interests in her home; every pursuit which would give her anchorage elsewhere (always excepting marriage) being more or less under general disapproval. Yet when the young woman takes thoroughly to this natural home making…then, almost invariable comes to her the order to leave it all, tear herself out of it—and go to make (if she can) some other home elsewhere. Supposing her to have married early, and that she is spared the late uprooting from her father's house at his death, she has usually to bear a similar transition when she survives her husband; and in this case often with the failing health and spirits of old age. I do not know how these heart breaks are to be spared to women of the class of the daughters and wives of country gentlemen or clergymen; but they are hard to bear. Perhaps the most fortunate daughters (harsh as it seems to say so) are those whose fathers die while they are themselves still in full vigor and able to begin a new existence with spirit and make new friends; as was my case.[26]

Cobbe had made a number of new friends on her Grand Tour. Her robust constitution meant that she was 'in full vigor'. She had no one but herself to look after. Yet none of these attributes were of direct help as she mulled over the options available to her. A passage from one of her articles, written many years later, suggests where she thought the origins of her quandary lay.

No man will give his son a stone when he asks for bread; but thousands of men have given their daughters diamonds when they prayed for books, and coiled the serpents of dissipation and vanity round their necks when they needed the wholesome food of beneficent employment.[27]

Cobbe had rejected the 'serpents of dissipation and vanity' which her father had attempted to coil around her neck when she was an adolescent, but had been unable to convince him of the practical wisdom of educating her in the same way as he did her brothers. She did not want to be dependent, yet she had not been educated to be anything else.

Cobbe believed that three distinct categories of employment were open to women of the 'refined' class. They could labour in the True: science, literature, philosophy; the Beautiful: art; the Good: philanthropy. These were the high-born lady's calling, given by God himself. 'The true, the beautiful, and the good,' Cobbe wrote in *Fraser's Magazine* in 1862, 'are all revelations of the Infinite One, and therefore all holy'.[28] Cobbe recognised that because of the inadequate education a woman received, her efforts in the True and Beautiful

> may be...derided as a failure or denounced as an invasion of fields which she can never adequately cultivate; but her pursuit of the Good, her efforts to ameliorate and brighten human life have never been repudiated, and are daily more warmly recognised.[29]

Victorian society revered the benevolent woman. Benevolence was considered an innately female quality, and it offered to many middle-class women the opportunity of forging public lives for themselves. In 'Female Charity—Lay and Monastic', written in 1862, Cobbe argued that whatever else 'may be doubtful respecting woman's "general worth and particular missionariness" it is pretty well conceded that she is in her right place teaching the young, reclaiming the sinful, relieving the poor, and nursing the sick.'[30] As a young woman growing up in rural Ireland, Cobbe had found ample opportunity, especially during the years of the Famine, to exercise her philanthropic talents, and her evangelical background impressed upon her the importance of doing God's work on earth. Later on in *Intuitive Morals*, Cobbe emphasised that disinterested benevolence was essential to the Moral Law. She believed that God had designed women to be particularly benevolent, and that because of their moral superiority they were obliged to first, set up God's kingdom in their hearts; second, to make their homes God's kingdom; third, to try to extend that kingdom throughout the world in useful activity. On a less altruistic note, Cobbe also remarked that philanthropy did wonders for the unmarried woman's self-confidence: 'The "old maid's" life may be as rich, as blessed, as that of the proudest of mothers with her own crown of clustering babes. Nay, she feels that in the power of devoting her whole time and energies to some benevolent task, she is enabled to effect perhaps some greater good than would otherwise have been possible.'[31]

Red Lodge and the Children of the Streets

Soon after her return to Ireland, one of Cobbe's acquaintances, Lady Byron, informed her that the philanthropist Mary Carpenter was looking for a co-worker in her reformatory and ragged school work. Cobbe had read Carpenter's *Juvenile Delinquents*, and felt a sense of attraction to Carpenter as 'a very religious woman, and one so completely outside the pale of orthodoxy that I should be sure to meet from her the sympathy I had never been yet privileged to enjoy; and at all events be able to assist her labors with freedom of conscience.'[32] Introductions were made, and in November 1858 Cobbe, accompanied by her little Pomeranian, travelled to Bristol and moved in with Mary Carpenter at her home, Red Lodge House, close to Red Lodge reformatory and a ragged school in a decrepit lane, St James' Back. Carpenter introduced Cobbe to Red Lodge's fifty 'scholars' on Friday 12 November, and she immediately 'captivated the girls by her bright animated & kind manner.'[33]

At the time Cobbe began her work with Carpenter there were a number of different educational institutions available to the working classes. Day schools were run by the National and British Societies for the respectable working-class children. Those children who, either because of their character or appearance, were unsuitable for the day schools went to the ragged schools which had grown out of the London City Mission in the 1830s. For the 'perishing' classes who had not yet fallen into crime there were the industrial schools, and for juvenile offenders there were reformatories. A number of pauper schools attached to workhouses and factory schools, mandated by the Factory Acts, coexisted alongside private endeavours such as Dame Schools.[34] Mary Carpenter looked after street children in a reformatory and ragged school in Bristol where she strove to educate, rehabilitate, reform and save them from becoming part of the 'dangerous' class involved in crime.

Carpenter became the leading light in rescuing street children in the 1850s. Her work was part of a widespread response to the increased visibility of street children; the ideological transformation of poor child from slave, exploited in a *laissez-faire* economy, to criminally inclined savage; and the increasingly popular idea amongst philanthropists that childhood was a special time distinct from adulthood that needed to be nurtured and protected and, radical suggestion as it was, to be a happy time for all children, not just the privileged.

In her biography of Mary Carpenter, Jo Manton argues that Cobbe's work at Red Lodge was doomed from her arrival: that she wanted to control Carpenter, convert her to Theism, and make her her lover.[35] There is no evidence that Cobbe harboured a 'missionary' agenda, nor that she expected Carpenter to renounce Unitarianism. And the charge of lesbianism, while titillating, cannot be substantiated. As far as Cobbe was concerned there did not appear to be any reason why she and Carpenter would not be compatible co-workers and friends, especially since Carpenter's religious character and philanthropic goals appeared to be so similar to her own. 'First, and above all,' Carpenter wrote in 1851,

> there must be in the minds of those who plan, and of those who carry out the work, a strong faith in the immortality of the human soul, the universal and parental government of God, and the equal value in His sight of each one of these poor perishing young creatures with the most exalted of our race. We must feel even a reverence, blended with that intense pity which can never be separated from love, for these children, coheirs with ourselves of an eternal existence, and be able to discern under the most degraded exterior the impress of God's creative Spirit, one of those for whom Christ died.[36]

Carpenter's emphasis upon love was one component of her three-part plan for transforming Bristol's youthful savages into children. She also argued that children needed to be treated as children, not as adults, and that they had to grow up in a stable family because it was in a comforting domestic setting that emotional security would find its roots for further growth, and where social stability would find its foundations. Cobbe's beliefs in the immortality of the soul, God's ability to love all men equally, her understanding that poor children needed to be loved as children, and the virtues of disinterested charity seemed to complement Carpenter's expectations for a colleague. Each woman believed in a Moral Law and considered it her duty to become part of God's philanthropic army of servants and soldiers and care for His unfortunate children. They saw themselves and each other as moral guides of the Red Lodge inhabitants, and in the early days of Cobbe's stay, their religious compatibility made for a harmonious atmosphere. Cobbe paid Carpenter 30 shillings per week, room and board, while she laboured for God and helped civilise the children of Bristol's streets.

According to Carpenter's journal, Red Lodge seems to have been plagued by unruly children and ineffective teachers who were unable to exert the control and discipline that Carpenter required, and references to obstreperous girls who flew into rages, went absent without permission, stole and sang 'the most improper songs'[37] are plentiful. When the girls behaved badly they had their hair cut, were put on a bread-and-water diet and spent time in the 'cellar'.[38] There appears to have been a steady stream of cropped haired recalcitrants going to and fro between school and cellar. Despite perennial problems with discipline, Carpenter preferred to reason with the girls rather than physically punish them, and the cane was resorted to only in extreme cases. Carpenter believed that punishment should not crush a child's youthful spirits, nor should it humiliate her or take away what little self-worth she possessed. This was quite a radical approach to take when most educational institutions followed the advice implicit in 'spare the rod and spoil the child'. Carpenter stressed moral obedience to God and physical cleanliness as an adjunct to morality: a pure, clean body was visual proof of a pure, clean mind, and Carpenter ensured the Red Lodge children were always visibly pure.[39]

Cobbe approved of Carpenter's approach to redeeming Bristol's wayward children. Like Carpenter she associated moral purity with its physical counterpart.[40] She, too, believed that corporal punishment was wrong; it demoralised the individual who inflicted it as well as the recipient, and led to the possibility of what Cobbe later recognised as *schadenfreude*, or pleasure in the pain of others. She also, like her contemporaries, saw the child as wild and untamed: 'If narrowly watched, at least one child out of two or three will be seen to be abnormally excited by the sight of his brother's Pain,' she wrote in *Hopes of the Human Race*,[41] and heteropathy, she noted, was a hallmark of the morally vacuous savage. Although Cobbe did not want to destroy the children's spirits with punishment, she firmly believed that their unkempt appearance had to be made respectable, and their wild behaviour had to be controlled. She remembered Kant's description of the continual battle between man's brute self and his moral nature, and nowhere did she see this conflict more clearly than at Red Lodge. If children acted like animals, it meant that their animal passions held sway over their undeveloped sense of morality, and this brought into question the level of civilisation from which they came and the level to which they would descend if they were not 'rescued' in time.[42]

Cobbe questioned her didactic influence at Red Lodge and the ragged school because of her perceived communication problems with the children; Mary Carpenter, however, valued her presence. The two women appeared to share a warm relationship based on sound religious beliefs and mutual respect, and Cobbe seemed to fit in as best as she could at the reformatory, causing, when compared with the other teachers, little trouble. Carpenter enjoyed having a co-worker to help her transform the ragged children of Bristol into respectable God-loving individuals and Cobbe enjoyed having a purpose in life. But within a few months the relationship between the two women began to falter.

Carpenter's life revolved around Red Lodge—she was awake early in the morning and was exhausted by night time—and Cobbe began to find this pre-occupation tedious: 'Her absorption in her work always blinded her to the fact that other people might possibly be bored by hearing of it continuously,'[43] Cobbe complained. Carpenter was happy with a colleague who laboured, but Cobbe wanted a companion who conversed. Carpenter's wholly unsatisfactory response to Cobbe's requests for conversation was to recommend that she read her *Meditations*, or her father's works; her views were represented in these, and if Cobbe took the trouble to read them, then Carpenter would not have to waste valuable time in idle chatter.

Nor could Cobbe adapt to Bristol's slums after life at Newbridge. Lewin's Mead was a derelict area ill lit by gas lamps, and which teemed with criminals and drunks; even the police avoided it. St James' Back, where Cobbe taught 'a class of very wild city Arabs',[44] was a filthy, run-down alley; the ragged school was next to a 'tripe and trotter shop', the odours of which hung foetid on the summer air. The street children were rowdy, boisterous, undisciplined and lacking in respect for authority, and taunted Cobbe in the streets shouting 'Cob-web, Cob-web' as she passed through Lewin's Mead one winter's night.[45] Many times during evening classes the boys would ignore their lessons, play marbles, shout and run around the school room and out the door onto the streets. Their attention spans could not last through lectures on such inspirational but abstract topics as 'Thankfulness', whereas Cobbe's talk on the French Revolution, the guillotine and heads being chopped off grabbed their interest, albeit they lost the gist of the moral lesson that Cobbe was hoping to impart.

The lack of physical comfort at Red Lodge House must also have thrown Cobbe's Newbridge years into sharp relief. According to Cobbe, Carpenter 'was an ingrained Stoic, to whom all the minor comforts of life are simply indifferent, and who can scarcely even recognize the fact that other people take heed of them.'[46] Cobbe needed furniture more comfortable than the horse-hair chair in the sitting room, and food more palatable than salt meat. She was a firm believer in making use of the good things God provided and she could not accept Carpenter's spartan way of living.

Want of good food made Cobbe miserable and bad tempered. She believed that God had provided the world with savoury food so that people could enjoy eating it and expand both spiritually and corporeally by the energy it provided. Virtue, she believed, was sustained not only by faith but by a well-fed, content body—cut off sustenance to the latter and the former withered. The one concession Carpenter made to her co-worker's need for tasty fare was to provide six small radishes as a supplement to the evening meal; their appearance rendered Cobbe speechless and did nothing to alleviate Carpenter's neglect of Cobbe's body and mind.

It must be noted that other teachers also suffered at Red Lodge. A Miss Swansbourne left at the end of July 1859 because her health was breaking down under the stress of the regime and the rebelliousness of the students, and a Miss Stuart was also reported to be in bad health.[47] It was during this time also that Cobbe questioned her place at Red Lodge, and she expressed her discontent to Theodore Parker who wrote:

> I wonder if you have found the right niche to place your statue in & if a Ragged School be the place for your work!...
>
> But you know while I only guess & enquire. It is a noble place you seek to fill—but there are disunities of gifts even when there is unity of spirit.[48]

Cobbe probably would have questioned Parker's reference to 'unity of spirit' in reference to her relationship with Red Lodge's matriarch. She could not get much conversation out of Carpenter, let alone a 'decent' meal, and she was finding it increasingly difficult to come to terms with the attention that Carpenter bestowed upon Red Lodge's juvenile inhabitants. Cobbe may have captivated them with her 'bright animated and kind manner', but they did not captivate her, and she began to resent them. In her autobiography Cobbe does not suggest that there were problems between her and the children, yet letters written during this trying time suggest otherwise.

Cobbe left Red Lodge in summer 1859 to regain some of her energy and recover from an attack of rheumatism. During this time, Carpenter and Cobbe wrote to each other; unfortunately, Cobbe's letters have not survived, but one can conclude from the tone of Carpenter's words that Cobbe was becoming increasingly jealous and resentful of those upon whom Carpenter lavished attention.

> Red Lodge House
> Mar. 17 1859—
>
> Dear Friend
> You know me as little as any one else if you think that I shd love you one bit better for being a teetotaler, a delinquent, or one of the others. Be sure I am more grateful for your love than for any external help you can give me.—If you [illegible] desire mine, do not doubt that it will grow, like the seed mysteriously placed in the earth which no *human* effort can cause to germinate, only heaven's sun & dew & rain...I...believe it is unsafe to attempt to look into the *mysteries* of the soul's sanctuary.—So please let it alone.—
>
> I only desire to do the work given me by the loving Father. I mean to take my Easter trip & give you a holiday after you return, if you will keep house for me.
> We shall all be delighted to see you—...
> Ever your truly & afftly
> M. Carpenter[49]

Throughout the summer Carpenter kept Cobbe up to date on the happenings at Red Lodge, and begged Cobbe to return and resume her labours. She constantly tried to reassure Cobbe of her affection for her, even when she was on holiday at Babbiscombe: 'I think of you when drinking in the loveliness of the expanse of blue sea.'[50] Carpenter's reassurances of her admiration for Cobbe as teacher did not assuage the jealousy which made Cobbe say things she otherwise would not. 'Be assured,' Carpenter wrote,

> I have never been hurt by any thing you may have said, because I *know* you mean nothing unkind. I feel increasingly that I never can be a companion to any one, nor give the *inner* sympathy [which] might be reasonably expected....My work & my cause require & must have the devotion of *all* my heart & soul & strength....[51]

It was not the kind of affection Cobbe offered that troubled Carpenter, but the degree. Despite Carpenter's attempts to reason with Cobbe, she continued to demand complete devotion, and refused to compromise or see Carpenter's point of view.

Over the next months, and well into the following year, Cobbe periodically left Red Lodge for the more congenial atmosphere of Italy and her friend Isa Blagden. The comfort of Blagden's villa in Florence compensated for Carpenter's inhospitable demeanour and gave Cobbe the opportunity to recoup her health. She had begun to suffer from fainting fits as well as rheumatism and it is possible that she exaggerated her suffering to garner the attention she believed she deserved.[52] Reports of ill-health certainly provoked a sympathetic response from Carpenter. In one letter Carpenter sent Cobbe in December, she expressed deep concern for her friend's poor health, and suggested that she return to Bristol where her recuperation could be supervised by Carpenter herself. In a moment of sympathy for her friend's suffering Carpenter offered Cobbe *carte blanche* to run her own life and meals: '[you can] be your own mistress! here as much as in the [illegible], & can take your meals at whatever time you like.'[53] Carpenter was at her most empathic when responding to Cobbe's distress, and it is hardly surprising that Cobbe would carry on with behaviour that provided her with the attention that she craved.

Yet the presence of those Red Lodge children continued to prevent Carpenter from devoting her entire self to Cobbe, and Cobbe would not let Carpenter forget this. 'Do not suppose me so cold hearted as to have received you here on simple terms of personal interest!' Carpenter explained as graciously as she could,

> I do not know why you think or feel differently from what you did before. I have always most truly sympathized in your joys & sorrows & in your work. The only hindrance to your comfort which I cannot prevent is my poor child. I feel bound to her, & as it were brought to me by a higher power—I do not feel that it would be right to send her away from me at all, & am longing to bring her under more [illegible]. Still I will do all I can to keep her from annoying you. I really know not what to say more,—except that I hope you will soon come back....[54]

'My poor child' to whom Carpenter refers was Rosanna, a five-year old Carpenter had 'adopted' in September 1858 and whom Cobbe wanted to see disappear. God had told Carpenter to be a mother to Rosanna and she would not disobey His command, even when Rosanna's mother arrived to reclaim her child. Many philanthropic women, given the emphasis they placed upon the concept of the family, felt driven to act as mothers towards those in need of their assistance.[55] Carpenter, however, seems to have been obsessed by children in general and by Rosanna in particular.

Carpenter made some effort to fulfil Cobbe's emotional needs in December 1859 by sending her belated love and best wishes for her birthday; she also let Cobbe know that she was making her a purse as a present. It was in her birthday letter to Cobbe that Carpenter also made clear her reservations about Cobbe's place at Red Lodge:

> I am truly grieved to be the cause of disappointment to you, but, dear friend, I cannot find out that any thing is my fault about it.— Much as I love & admire you, I have long perceived, & I thought you did so too, that your particular gifts & talents have not their true development in the work of these Schools. I am thankful to have your love & am grateful for your exertions & help, but I have always held myself ready to resign that & all other things whenever the Father's orderings remove what has been lent. The injury which my mode of living does to your health is a definite reason why you

should feel it necessary to remove from my roof—when my change of servants will render it undesirable for me to continue the altered arrangements you propose.[56]

In all likelihood, Cobbe continued her pleading, for three days later Carpenter wrote again,

> Dear Friend
> My feelings to you under go no change—As long as you find it suitable to you to remain with me, I shall try to make you happy. I think however that if you find my way of life & meals do not suit you this summer will be the last time for making a change.[57]

Cobbe informed Theodore Parker, who was at this time ill and convalescing in Italy, of her trials and sorrows at Red Lodge, and in January he encouraged her to leave: 'I knew your relation with the Ragged School could not continue: it always seemed to run incongruous, & I am not sorry it should end, for now I think you can betake yourself to work not less philanthropic & needful, far more congenial.'[58] By the spring Cobbe had removed herself to Blagden's Villa Brichieri where she seems to have rallied; she met up with her Grand Tour friends and impressed many more with her wit and brilliant conversation. The contrast between this society and that at Red Lodge convinced Cobbe that when she returned to Bristol, for there was no doubt that she would, it would be wise to look for accommodation away from Carpenter. She headed to Marseilles in June before returning to Bristol in August where she took lodgings alone at Belgrave House, Durdham Down, and continued to work amongst the city's poor.

Workhouse Reform

Cobbe enjoyed her new home on Durdham Down. She walked into Bristol every day to fulfil her teaching duties at Red Lodge because she considered the omnibus fare a luxury she could ill afford. She had her much loved little Pomeranian with her who no longer had to suffer Mary Carpenter's admonitions of being an overly indulged dog because it, like Cobbe, enjoyed good food and comfortable surroundings. Both pet and mistress were happy outside the city for Cobbe had found her old life, one which provided endless opportunities for self indulgence. There were evenings out with Margaret Elliot, Recorder Hill and Lord Lansdowne, afternoon teas with the theologian Benjamin Jowett and stimulating discussions on Toryism with the Dean of Bristol, Margaret Elliot's father. Yet this life of plenty was to soon to be thrown into sharp contrast with the next phase of her philanthropic career that would in retrospect make her work with Bristol's wayward children seem palatable, and the sparse and 'inhuman' conditions within Red Lodge seem sybaritic by comparison.

Carpenter had suggested a number of times to Cobbe that she channel her benevolent energies into Bristol's workhouses, but Cobbe had always resisted. 'The very name [of workhouse]' Cobbe wrote, 'conveyed to me such an impression of dreary hopelessness that I shrank from the thought'[59] of working in them. Her attitude was shared by many of her contemporaries who criticised the workhouses for their degrading punitiveness. Cobbe was finding the Red Lodge work difficult enough, despite its soul-inspiring nature, and had no intention of branching out to less appealing terrain.

Cobbe's attitude changed after she accompanied Margaret Elliot, a fellow teacher at Red Lodge, on a visit to a woman Elliot knew who had been removed to the workhouse. Once Cobbe set eyes on the woman, she found herself being engulfed by a wave of emotions that threatened to drown her. She was appalled by the conditions within St Peter's; she pitied the woman Elliot had come to visit; and she was disgusted with the 1834 New Poor Law and its administrators for treating humans in a most inhuman manner. St Peter's did not embody what Cobbe understood to be charity, nor did she consider it a good example of reform. '[M]y first chance visit to St Peter's in Bristol with Miss Elliot,' Cobbe explained in her autobiography, 'showed me so much to be done, so many claims to sympathy and pity, and the sore lack of somebody, unconnected officially with the place to meet them, that I at once felt that here I must put in my oar'[60] into what was very muddy water. Her mission was to make the water run clear. Elliot shared Cobbe's attitude towards St Peter's, and she soon replaced Mary Carpenter in Cobbe's affections. Cobbe adopted the Elliots as her surrogate family, and their presence assuaged any remaining feelings of abandonment.

Between 1860–2 Cobbe and Elliot visited a number of workhouses in Bristol and London, and discovered very little difference among them, despite the inequitable enforcement of the 1834 Act. It was not the actual idea of housing the indigent in a workhouse that they found distressing, but the conditions within them which appalled their sense of decency. The infirm wards were a disgrace: they were placed in the worst possible locations, windows could not be opened and qualified medical practitioners were almost non-existent. The sick lay on hard wooden beds nursed mostly by pauper women from the lowest class who, Cobbe was convinced, were paid in gin. The children in the workhouses were joyless, spiritless creatures whose faces were often scarred by disease and many were nearly blinded with opthalmia. Husbands, wives and families were often separated. The deaf, dumb, blind and insane cohabited, and fallen women and prostitutes, some with venereal disease and many with bastard children, roamed the wards as did the criminally inclined.[61]

Conditions within the workhouse hospitals were no better. Workhouse doctors were either inexperienced beginners or unqualified incompetents, and many accepted workhouse duties to supplement private practice. They were controlled by the Guardians, had little personal or professional autonomy within the institution and therefore were prohibited from introducing medical reform or even attempting minimal improvement. An 1842 General Medical Order had mandated that doctors in workhouses possess two qualifications, one of which should be from the College of Physicians and Surgeons, while the other might be from a University or the Society of Apothecaries. Improved qualifications did not bring with them improved medical care. Abuses within workhouse hospitals continued. In the absence of an apothecary, inmates sold pills to their less healthy brethren; the sick often did not receive food because it was stolen before it reached them and many nurses continued to come from within the workhouse.[62] Cobbe could not believe that God, her God, would want men, women and children to live like this; she was concerned that the morally 'bad' would infect the 'good' with their vile ways, and was outraged that those in need of compassionate care were being ignored and abused. She spent many a day attempting to understand the approach taken by the 1832 Poor Law Commission, and to discover how workhouse inmates ended up as they did and what she could do to remedy the injustice.

Despite the growing reputation of Louisa Twining and the Workhouse Visiting Society (founded in 1859), women's efforts inside the workhouses were still limited to ameliorative rather than curative measures, and as late as 1898 Twining was still warning her workers that they would probably meet with determined opposition from male-dominated Poor Law Boards.[63] Men, Cobbe believed, had not done well in administering charity within the workhouse and she hardly considered her entrance into its precincts as interference. As a woman she believed herself to have a natural affinity with and a right to help those in distress, and to bring justice where it was needed. The Poor Law, concerned with economic efficiency, encouraged the state to deal impersonally with incurables *en masse*, and not individually and intuitively as would a sympathising woman. Because God dealt with all of His children as individuals, Cobbe surmised that it was only natural that those working in charity deal with their charges in a similar manner. And it was because Cobbe saw combined in God the feminine attributes of love and goodness and justice and the masculine attribute of authority that she was able to argue for her place, and that of all women, in the workhouse.[64]

Due to the constraints placed upon them, Cobbe and Elliot discovered that they were only able to provide limited improvement to the living conditions within St Peter's. For the curable inmates who could not tolerate the hard wooden benches, the two women brought in easy chairs with cushions; hammock-like bed rests allowed patients to sit up in bed; gifts of tea occasionally replaced the undrinkable workhouse brew. Colourful pictures, interesting and often moralistic magazines and the addition of a canary turned St Peter's into a community of happier, if not healthier, curables.

Given Cobbe's understanding of the connection between mental and physical stamina, her appreciation of physical comforts, and her belief that he who was happy was closer to God than he who was not, it is not surprising that she emphasised aesthetic improvement. Given also her priorities for private and public eudaimonism, it was logical that she would attempt to make the sick workhouse inmates happy in preparation for their moral awakening: 'Happiness is a Real End, a Positive Good', she had written in *Intuitive Morals*.

It may indeed be treated by us sometimes as the means to warm and soften human hearts and so prepare them for Virtue; and it is quite possible that it is as such it is bestowed by God who alone can righly [sic] estimate its infinitesimal smallness compared with the glorious realm of Virtue of which man is the heir. But still I apprehend that, deduction made of its power to promote Virtue, Happiness is a true end in itself, and that the law of benevolence commands us to make our neighbour Happy when it is out of our power to conduce to his Virtue.[65]

Like her contemporaries, Cobbe made the distinction between the able bodied and potentially employable poor and those who were not able bodied. She considered curables to be the former, and she argued that it was not economic to provide 'less eligible' care to those who, if they were cured of their disease, could be later released from the workhouse hospital and trained within the workhouse for a useful future. She estimated that it cost £300—£400 per year to support a curable pauper in the workhouse; if a competent doctor could be hired and drugs provided at a cost of £80—£150 per year the parish would save a substantial amount of money; curables would become productive members of society and not remain burdens on the state.[66] Cobbe's recommendations for the able-bodied, curable paupers were simple. She did not take into account the realities of the economic climate, but believed that training alone would ensure employment.

The problems with the incurables, the group Cobbe wrote of as the 'most piteous class of the community,'[67] were not so easy to solve, and they elicited a different response because:

> it is not an accidental misfortune, but a regular descent down the well-worn channels of Poverty, Disease and Death, for men and women to go to one or other of the 270 hospitals for *curable* patients which then existed in England…and after a longer or shorter sojourn, to be pronounced 'incurable', destined perhaps to linger for a year or several years, but to die inevitably from consumption, cancer or some other of the dreadful maladies which afflict human nature. What then becomes of them? Their homes, if they had any before going into the hospital, are almost sure to be too crowded to receive them back, or too poor to supply them with both support

and nursing for months of helplessness. There is no resource for them but the workhouse, and there they sink down, hopeless and miserable; the hospital comforts of good beds and furniture and carefully prepared food and skilled nurses all lost, and only the hard workhouse bed to lie, and *die* upon. The burst of agony with which many a poor creature has told me: 'I am sent here because I am incurable,' remains one of the saddest of my memories.[68]

In the early 1860s, there were only two hospitals in England, two in Scotland and one in Dublin which dealt with incurables. In an 1864 article which criticised the Poor Laws, Cobbe estimated that these hospitals had space for only 500 patients, although 80,000 died annually, half of whom belonged to the working class.[69] Those who did not hold a ticket and were therefore unable to be admitted into a free hospital, and Cobbe estimated this number at thousands, were forced into the workhouse where both curable and incurable inmates were lumped together as a homogenous group, neither of which received adequate medical care.

At the lowest rate of £30 a year, £900,000 per annum would have been required to re-house and maintain the 30,000 incurables whom Cobbe and Elliot estimated needed care outside the workhouse infirmary. Cobbe possessed enough common sense to realise that attempting to raise £900,000 either through private donations or increased poor rates made neither philanthropic nor economic sense: to raise poor rates to meet the need would pauperise the lower strata of rate-payers.[70] Cobbe's solution was to equalise rates over a large area, a suggestion that found political support in her cousin-in-law, John Locke's, bill for equalisation in 1859. The bill's failure did not diminish Cobbe's confidence in her suggestion, but she and Elliot eventually decided to pursue a different course of action.

The two women returned to the original purpose of the Poor Law Amendment Act, which was to differentiate between the deserving and the undeserving and to provide appropriate treatment for each. Cobbe and Elliot abhorred the principle of less eligibility when it was applied to incurables, and it was because of the unnecessary suffering it imposed that they suggested a revision of the care given to workhouse inmates and a reconsideration of the category into which they were slotted:

Surely it lies on us to prevent their enduring the *physical* wants and miseries, if we leave them to the moral sense of degradation inseparable in their minds from an abode in the Workhouse. In other words, I repeat it, if we force them into the Workhouse for want of hospitals, we are bound to treat them there, not as PAUPERS, but as PATIENTS.[71]

Cobbe and Elliot wanted to see the pauper taint removed for incurables. They were not slothful, but they could never be able bodied and they should not be treated as if they were. The incurables' situation was different from other workhouse inmates; for without hospitals specifically designed to deal with their afflictions little choice remained for sufferers, who did not have the economic resources for private care, except entry into a workhouse hospital.

Cobbe and Elliot attempted to mitigate physical distress and the stigma of workhouse residence simultaneously. Their idea was to put acute cases of dropsy, consumption and cancer in male and female wards and substitute for the callous attitude of the Poor Law administration voluntary charity in order to ease the incurables' mental and physical sufferings. Over the bones of the state law, Cobbe believed, 'the flesh and blood of warm free charity should clothe the whole, else it is but a grim and hideous image.'[72] Louisa Twining encouraged Cobbe's plans by informing her of the progress she herself had made with incurables in the metropolis; in 1861 Twining gave Cobbe a tour of St Giles's Schools and the Strand, West London and Holborn Unions and the Hospital for Incurables at Putney.[73]

Cobbe's plan to separate incurables, introduce private charity and replace government administration with loving voluntary workers received widespread support from the press and reading public. Newspapers and journals aided her efforts by publishing leaders and letters supportive of her workhouse plans. Cobbe and Elliot printed circulars and posted them to the 660 Poor Law Unions which existed in England, and in response they received words of encouragement and support from numerous Guardians, fifteen of whom actually implemented the women's plan for segregation of incurables. But it was only after further external pressure from *The Lancet*, Florence Nightingale, Ernest Hart and Edwin Chadwick that the Metropolitan Poor Law

Amendment Act of 1867 segregated the sick poor away from the workhouse—although the stigma of relying on state charity remained.[74]

Cobbe knew that separation of the sick would not improve the care they received unless properly trained doctors and nurses were provided. The greatest shortcoming of Poor Law infirmaries was the lack of competent care givers. It 'is easy to suppose,' Louisa Twining wrote about workhouse hospital care, 'what the result must be during the long hours when, in the nurses' absence, the sick wards are left to their [pauper nurses'] control.'[75] Cobbe provided a more dramatic account of the fate of those left in the hands of pauper nurses in *The Workhouse as an Hospital* published by Emily Faithfull in 1861:

> In the male wards [the pauper nurses] are usually old men, who have been perhaps artisans or labourers, and have come to destitution by vice, calamity, general incapacity and imbecility, or sickness and infirmity. The women's case is worse....It is among the most depraved and abandoned members of the community that the poor decent woman who has come to suffer, and perhaps die, in the Workhouse must find her sole attendant, too often her rough and cruel tyrant. The ways in which a hard unfeeling nurse may torment her wretched patient are beyond enumeration. She moves her roughly when every touch is agony, she neglects every little precaution which might make her bed more comfortable, she gives her food cold, she speaks brutally so as to shake her nerves to misery, she monopolizes for herself, or refuses to use for the patient, the easy chairs, cushions, or bed rests, any kind visitor may have provided. And when the wretched sufferer has reached the last stage, and needs *every* attention in her helplessness, she refuses (as we have witnessed) to give her the cold Workhouse tea she craves for in her agony, to save herself the trouble of the needful arrangements.[76]

The pauper nurse was unable to empathise with the sick because she was morally void; and because she was at the very lowest rung on the ladder of moral development, her ability to sympathise was at its most crude and animal-like. The pauper nurse was only able to express heteropathy, or hatred for the weaknesses of others, and she had to advance through this and the subsequent stage, aversion, before she was able to feel sympathy. What the workhouse hospital needed, Cobbe insisted, was properly trained and morally responsible nurses who would not only provide the sick with the care and attention they deserved, but whose example would encourage women of the higher classes, and amongst whom the numbers of redundant were increasing, to enter a newly respected and remunerative occupation.

Cobbe showed the same degree of tolerance towards aged paupers as she did towards incurables; she also noticed that the aged inmate's situation was often very different from that of his incurable brethren. The majority of aged paupers, Cobbe surmised, must have children who were obviously shirking their filial responsibility by not taking care of their parents as she herself had done. The degree to which families looked after sick or aged relations was one means by which Cobbe measured the existence of sympathy in society and allegiance to the Moral Law. The prevalence of aged workhouse dwellers was a distressing indication to Cobbe of just how many Britons abdicated their responsibility towards their parents and towards that Law. Scores of children, Cobbe speculated, obviously preferred to allow their parents to rot in workhouses while they competed for the wealth and success that was available to them in a *laissez-faire* economy. She was convinced that children and family members would take up their duty to look after aged relatives, and thereby render hospitals virtually obsolete, once they shunned worldly success in favour of self-consecration.[77] She did not seem to understand that most members of the working classes, both male and female, would be forced by economic circumstances to work for their own survival.

Cobbe's blinkered view of poverty and her immutable understanding of parent/child relations and responsibilities led to recommendations that were incongruous with her logic. She proposed that a tax be levied on sons who allowed parents to enter workhouses, and that both sons and daughters be publicly shamed for their unChristian behaviour. In order to avoid paying taxes and suffering public humiliation, Cobbe believed that children would look after parents, space would be freed in the workhouse for those who needed to have their idleness repressed, and poor rates would decrease.[78] Cobbe's suggestion conflicted with her earlier proselytising that behaviour, to be truly virtuous and in harmony with the Moral Law, needed to be disinterested. She never saw any inconsistencies with the position she took, or if she did, she ignored them and continued to impress upon others their duties.

Youth within the workhouses preoccupied her thoughts as much as did the aged. The 1834 New Poor Law required Unions to set up schools with a headmaster and headmistress, but most children remained demoralised and degraded.[79] The conditions in which young workhouse girls were educated Cobbe found particularly liable to be counter productive in helping them become 'womanly'. Because women were seen to be domestic creatures, workhouse girls, who were disadvantaged not only by gender but also class, were encouraged to think of their futures in strict terms of domestic service; placement in service would bring out a pauper girl's best and most womanly qualities, while dulling the 'animal passions' against which her moral self struggled. '[D]omestic matters are of the highest importance from a moral and sanitary point of view,' Louisa Twining argued, and Cobbe agreed.[80] Yet the Poor Law administrators failed in this endeavour because, for the sake of economy, workhouses trained their juvenile inmates *en masse* 'without individual love and care [which] has never yet been other than a grievous failure.'[81]

The domestic training workhouse girls received often proved inadequate by employer's standards; many were considered uncontrollable and were often dismissed. Cobbe held the Poor Law Guardians responsible for the state of affairs. As men they were unable to recognise the necessity of individual attention and love in making workhouse girls God-loving humans; nor did they share the emphasis Cobbe placed on the necessity for a young girl to have someone to care for. 'It will not answer to treat a human being as one of a herd of cattle,' Cobbe told the Social Science Congress in Dublin in 1861,

> however carefully fed and housed and driven from yard to yard. With all reverence let us say it, God Himself does not treat us so, but with individual care and love; and out of our belief in this personal love springs all that is deepest in religion. In like manner, it is the parents' love for the child as an individual by which the germs of affection in her nature are kindled, and through such human love she learns to conceive the existence of the love of God. But the poor workhouse girl is the child of an institution, not of a

mother of flesh and blood. She is nobody's 'Mary' or 'Kate,' to be individually thought of—only one of a dreary flock driven about at certain hours from dormitory to schoolroom and from schoolroom to workhouse yard. The poor child grows up into womanhood, perhaps, without one gleam of affection, and with all her nature crushed down and carelessly trampled on. She has no domestic duties, no care of a little brother or an old grandparent, to soften her; no freedom of any kind to form her moral nature. Even her hideous dress and her cropped hair are not her own! Yet she is expected to go out inspired with respect for the property of her employer, able to check her childish covetousness of the unknown luxury of varied food, and clever enough to guess at a moment how to light a fire, and cook a dinner, and dress a baby, and clean a house, for the first time in her life. What marvel is it, these hapless creatures constantly disgust their employers by their ignorance, thievishness, and folly, and fall, poor friendless children! under the temptations which the first errands in our wicked streets will have sufficed to set before them.[82]

To this same Dublin audience Cobbe set out a practical as well as moral plan by which she and the Elliots (Margaret's sister had joined them in their efforts) sought to alleviate the problems faced by workhouse girls. In anticipation of the aims of the Metropolitan Association for Befriending Young Servants, Cobbe and the Elliots focused their attention on establishing a system of supervision for workhouse girls after they had entered service, usually at the age of sixteen, hopefully preventing them from falling into sin and preparing them for what was generally considered to be their rightful place in society 'able in due time to take her happy and honored place as wife and mother in the great human family!'[83]

The means by which Cobbe and the Elliots supervised the girls was typical for the time. It was part of Cobbe's task to persuade workhouses to provide her with the addresses of every girl sent out to service to whose employer she then duly paid a visit. She prevailed on employers to allow their servants to attend a Sunday afternoon school which the Elliot sisters taught at the Bristol Deanery. Because Cobbe fervently believed in her duty to serve God and to protect the lives of His children and make the perishing classes moral beings, she usually succeeded on her intrusive visits. While at the Deanery the girls participated in morally uplifting exercises: hymns were sung; Cobbe's favourite work, *Pilgrim's Progress*, was read; and those in attendance were encouraged to save a portion of their meagre earnings in a penny banking account. The curriculum at the Sunday School stressed the attributes of a virtuous and responsible person: hard work, honesty, piety, self control, self help and thrift, attributes that, over thirty years after introducing her curriculum, Cobbe told her Philadelphia friend Sarah Wister were still missing from every domestic's education.[84]

It is interesting to note that despite the confidence Cobbe had in her abilities to make good moral servants out of workhouse girls, she apparently never took the opportunity to employ one herself, preferring instead older, more respectful women who knew their place and deferred to their mistresses. And there was one particular kind of servant upon whom Cobbe always could rely and whom she recommended to her friends: 'Try & get Scotch servants,' Cobbe advised Wister in the spring of 1898,

> I am enchanted with the superior class of minds they seem to have & the (perhaps consequent) sense they entertain of the real nature of the difference between their class & ours. I am more glad than I can tell you to have got my new maid (Cameron). She is such a rock to rely upon! She was educated at the school the Queen keeps for her servants' children at Craigie. If you could only pick up the duplicate of her, your peace would be assured.[85]

Of the 100,000 people on indoor relief in 1859, 51,000 were children, 12,000 of whom were orphans.[86] Again, Cobbe was appalled at the scenes she witnessed of indifference and ignorance towards this vulnerable group.

> I have sat in the infants' ward when an entire Board of about two dozen gentlemen tramped through it, for what they considered to be 'inspection', and anything more helpless and absurd than those masculine 'authorities' appeared as they glanced at the little cots (never daring to open one of them) while the awakened babies screamed at them in chorus, it has seldom been my lot to witness.[87]

All children, whether high- or low-born, were innocent and deserved treatment that would make them into morally autonomous adults. No child, Cobbe argued, should be punished just for being born for he was 'a germ of a soul, rather than a soul either burdened with sin or 'trailing' any foreknown light, when he's covered up in a little child's cradle.'[88]

Many of the screaming babies Cobbe came across died in the workhouse. Within days after giving birth in the lying-in ward, the mother would be removed to the able-bodied ward; contact with her baby was lost and it was placed in the hands of the pauper nurses whom Cobbe and Twining so vigorously recommended be denied employment as care givers. Unless the mother removed herself and her child from the workhouse, its fate would almost certainly be sealed. Children who remained and managed to survive at the hands of pauper nurses fared little better since they often succumbed to the 'moral contagion' that swept unchecked throughout the wards of the workhouse.

Living amongst the lowest of low, where guardianship of the children was non-existent, it was obvious that the workhouse child's moral being was in jeopardy. The 'precincts of a workhouse are about as fit for the rearing up of young life as the precincts of a jail'[89] the reformer Ellice Hopkins wrote: morality could not coexist with immorality, therefore a child's residence in the workhouse virtually ensured that he would emulate his evil cohabitants, much as children from bad homes copied their parents' habits.

Most nineteenth-century reformers were concerned, in one way or another, with the environment in which the poor lived. Too many home visitors, workhouse visitors and missionaries failed to fill the morally empty with devout feeling because, according to Cobbe, their misguided efforts ignored environmental causes of distress: 'We have no right to expect any other result from filth than disease, or from corrupting influences than sin'.[90] Godliness could not come before cleanliness, and material improvement had to precede moral improvement. And if, as Cobbe suggested, the workhouse environment could not be restored to an acceptable standard, then she and all who worked towards reclaiming the individual, as moral rather than biological mothers, had a right to remove the object of their concern and replant him or her in foundations that would encourage moral development. The target group for such relocation was often the children.

Mary Carpenter and the working girls' club founder and Poor Law Guardian for St Ann's Soho, Maude Althea Stanley, were convinced that the only way children could be prevented from falling into vice and crime was by distancing them from morally bad homes, so that they would be unable to imitate parental sin.[91] What children needed was a good role model and a healthy atmosphere in which they could flourish and reach their virtuous potential. Carpenter had taught Cobbe that there was no such thing as a pauper child, and that no matter what the faults of his or her parents, he or she should not be forced to suffer. 'If this poor little creature is to be saved from a life of ill-health and helplessness—from a pauper life, in fact—it can only be by giving it the healthiest nurse, the freshest air, and, by-and-by, the wholesomest country food and exercise we can obtain.'[92]

Despite support for boarding out from the likes of Cobbe, Louisa Twining and Florence Hill, one of the strongest advocates of the scheme, it was never widely practised. In 1897 there were only 1,957 children boarded outside union boundaries despite a Poor Law regulation passed in 1870 that allowed unions to board children over two years of age outside their boundaries to rural areas. In 1906, only 6,000 children were boarded out within union boundaries. Dr Barnardo, however, had greater success in boarding out children much further afield, and the emigration enthusiast Jane Stuart-Wortley chortled in one 1893 essay that Maria Rye's efforts to 'export' surplus children had been beneficial not only to over-populated England, but to under-populated Canada.[93]

Cobbe's activities within the workhouses came to an abrupt end some time around 1862, when she lost her footing when getting off the train on which she was travelling (she was returning to Bristol after visiting friends in Bath) and injured her ankle. The numerous physicians she consulted advised her to renounce her life within the workhouse for one of quiet repose and recuperation, with occasional visits to baths on the Continent. Cobbe could barely tolerate confinement at Durdham Down and continual visits from doctors, especially when the medical treatment she received worsened her health. Tight bandaging, baths and herbal poultices caused her to be 'in a most miserable condition, for I could not drop the limb for two minutes without the blood running into it till it became like an ink-bottle, when, if I held it up, it became as white as if dead.'[94] Cobbe found herself suffering a fate similar to that of her mother many years before; she could walk only with great difficulty and a cane, and her health and demeanour began to improve only once she ignored her doctors' advice and resumed an active life a few years later.

It was because of the restraints imposed upon her physical activity that Cobbe exercised her mind; she wrote, and the 1860s became one of her most prolific periods of journalistic activity. Her output was a mixture of religious books and articles, accounts of her European and Middle East adventures, her thoughts about poverty, pauperism and women's potential in social protest and reform, and embryonic considerations of women's place in the political realm. In these articles one can detect Cobbe's increasing concern about and criticism of power hierarchies and exploitation. This is evident in her women's rights pieces, such as *Why Women Desire the Franchise*, published in 1869, and in her first animal rights article, 'The Rights of Man and the Claims of Brutes', published six years earlier. This journalistic activity, much of it written for *Fraser's Magazine*, was punctuated by frequent visits to Italy where she acted as correspondent for the *Daily News*, a position she had secured for herself in the same year as her mishap.

Cobbe's philanthropic work undertaken after she returned from her Grand Tour made her blatantly critical of legislative attempts at dealing with poverty and the poor. She saw, as had Anna Jameson, that the 1834 New Poor Law, hostile and uncaring workhouse Masters, the lack of women visitors, and the stigma attached to poverty because of less eligibility had turned the workhouse into 'a hell upon earth.'[95] What Cobbe did not realise was that as she was making the workhouses more humane, as she was becoming more optimistic of the possibility of a more humane society, there was a greater hell on earth emerging that would prove more disturbing to her and more difficult to combat. Within a few years, Cobbe found herself confronting that hell on earth, the issue of animal experimentation. Before this, however, she defended the rights of women.

3

THE CLAIMS OF WOMEN AND LIFE IN LONDON

Feminism in London

Many nineteenth-century women became involved in feminism after spending time in 'good works' which exposed them to the injustices meted out to working-class women and which made them aware of their own capacity for activity for the public good. Cobbe was drawn to the fledgeling women's rights movement for a number of reasons. She credits the American Reverend J.J. May, whom she met while he was visiting Red Lodge in 1859, with encouraging her to think about women's suffrage, and her own personal experience as an unmarried, 'ornamentally educated' and financially dependent woman made her aware of how unprepared she and many of her counterparts were to lead a life outside domesticity. Through her work in Bristol amongst the so-called 'perishing and dangerous classes' she had learned that she could produce change that would benefit all society, and in December 1861 she explained how valuable women could be in an article for *Macmillan's Magazine*, 'Social Science Congresses and Women's Part in Them'. In February of the following year she wrote 'Celibacy *v.* Marriage' for *Fraser's*, wherein she vindicated the life of the single woman and argued that all women should be provided with an education and skills which would allow those who so wished, to live outside the conventional expectations of marriage and maternity and to contribute to society in some valuable, non-domestic way.

A few weeks after 'Celibacy *v.* Marriage' appeared Cobbe heard that Elizabeth Garrett had been denied permission to sit the matriculation exam required to obtain her medical degree. The barrier that Garrett faced was detrimental to her own future, but also to women everywhere.

Not only was Garrett being denied an education which would qualify her for useful employment (employment, Cobbe concluded, that was suitable for women because of its nurturing qualities), but women with medical problems were being denied the opportunity of seeking medical advice from their own sex. Cobbe believed it was unnatural for young women to consult male physicians, and any girl who spoke 'freely about one of the many ills to which female flesh is heir, would be an odious young woman'.[1] Cobbe assured herself that the majority would, out of modesty, ignore their illnesses, damage their health as future mothers, that of their children *in utero*, and undoubtedly contribute to a premature death. Maternal and national well-being could be guaranteed only if women were able to choose their medical care givers.

Cobbe considered medicine to be one of those inalienable 'Rights of Woman', a right that had been appropriated by male practitioners at the turn of the nineteenth century when the medical community organised itself into professional bodies dominated by men. Cobbe lamented the disappearance of the feminine qualities of empathy, sympathy and intuitiveness that had made medicine a caring occupation and their replacement with competition, discovery, experimentation and observation. These masculine qualities associated the medical profession with greed, power, social advancement and prestige, and rendered the vulnerable patient, especially the female patient, powerless and susceptible to exploitation.

It made Cobbe's blood boil to think of how many women suffered at the hands of male doctors who denied them their rightful place as healers. She reflected on her time spent caring for incurables in the workhouses and concluded that a large number of women would not have succumbed to poor treatment and agonising death had they been able to obtain the advice of a female physician in the initial stages of illness. Cobbe pointed out that women tended to the needs of their immediate families, why, therefore, should they not be offered a medical education to enable them to minister to the extended family of the nation? Inherent female qualities made women 'natural' care givers; it was neither right nor logical to deny them this public role. Cobbe concluded as she mourned the fate of Garrett, that society would improve immeasurably if women were given access to a useful, not necessarily medical, education and welcomed into a chosen profession to which they would bring co-operation not competition. Shame on those who refused.

Cobbe quietly pondered the disabilities and obstacles faced by women such as Garrett, and drafted a conservative argument defending a woman's right to an education and a useful and remunerative life as long as she was either single or a childless wife without family responsibilities. She took her plea to the National Association for the Promotion of Social Science meeting in London where, supported by her crutches and her faith in woman's ratiocinative abilities, she eloquently put forth her case:

> there are purposes in the order of Providence for the lives of single women and childless wives, and they too are meant to have their share of human happiness. Most people prefer to ignore their existence as a class to be contemplated in the education of women, but it is as vain to do so as it is cruel. All of us know enough of those hapless households where the wife, having no children and few home duties, undergoes the most deplorable depreciation of character for want of employment of heart and mind; and her nature, if originally weak and small, shrivels up in petty vanities and contentions; and if strong and high, falls too often blasted by the thunderstorms of passion accumulated in the moveless and unwholesome atmosphere. All of us know those other households, no less hapless, where grown-up daughters, unneeded by their parents, are kept from all usefulness or freedom of action, frittering away the prime of their days in the busy idleness of trivial accomplishments; till, when all energy to begin a new course is gone, the parents die at last, and each one sinks into the typical 'Old Maid,' dividing her life henceforth in her small lodgings, between '*la médisance, le jeu, et la dévotion*'.[2]

Cobbe's was a personal plea; she was not only bemoaning the loss of female potential, but was also mourning her own wasted years at Brighton. She echoed Emily Davies's sentiments when she argued for equal educational opportunities, and like others who demanded the same her defence rested on gender differences. Learning would make a woman feminine, not masculine as so many of those who opposed higher education believed. 'No man can possibly less desire any obliteration of the mental characteristics of the two sexes, than does every woman who has an intelligent care for the welfare of her own,' Cobbe told her NAPSS audience.

> But is such an erasure indeed *possible*? Is it not clear enough that the Creator has endowed men and women with different constitutions of mind as of body? and need we be under the slightest apprehension that any kind of education whatever will efface those differences? Education is, after all, only what its etymology implies—the educing, the drawing out, of the powers of the individual. If we, then, draw out a *woman's* powers to the very uttermost, we shall only educe her *womanliness*. We cannot give her a man's powers any more than we can give a man a woman's brilliancy of intuition, or any other gift. We can only educe her God-given *woman's* nature, and so make her a more perfect woman. These differences will, I affirm, come out in every line of woman's expanding powers—in study, quite as much as in all beside.[3]

Cobbe's words were written and eloquently spoken during the early years of organised activity when Emily Davies and Elizabeth Garrett herself defended a woman's right to an education. It was to be another three years before the Kensington Discussion Society took up the issue and most demands for female education were either ignored or ridiculed, as was Cobbe's the day after she made her speech. Only *The Times* agreed with her. This early neglect spurred Cobbe on to reiterate that women needed to be educated in order to lead productive lives as single women, or as wives or mothers.

Nineteenth-century society, however, did not expect the ideal woman to lead a productive life. She was required only to lead a reproductive life within the domestic sphere. Cobbe found it frustrating that so many women seemed willing to relinquish control over themselves and be shackled to a highly dependent, one-dimensional existence. 'The truth', she told Sarah Wister in the spring of 1874,

> is that if girls & women will submit to be braced up in stays & laden with a stoneweight of petticoats, eat [illegible] & drink tea lemonade instead of beef [illegible] & wine & dance in hot rooms instead of riding swimming & running it is quite clear they will be poor

sickly creatures on whom the additional burden of mental work means destruction. Let them live healthily & that same natural law will only 'renew their strength like the eagles'.[4]

Almost thirty years after writing this letter to Wister, Cobbe was still waiting for women to challenge entrenched stereotypes: 'At bottom most men feel to us as we do to children,' she told her audience at the Ladies Club at Clifton during a suffrage speech; 'and this acts most injuriously on our own characters in making us childish'.[5]

Cobbe agreed with the emphasis that many of her contemporaries placed upon the centrality of 'home' for women, but refused to see women only as domestic creatures. First and foremost they were individuals and they deserved to be treated as such: 'We must not fall into the absurdity of supposing that all women can be adapted to one single type, or that we can talk about 'Woman'...as if the same characteristics were to be found in every individual species, like 'the Lioness' and 'the Pea-Hen'.[6] Nor should a woman's life revolve around serving the interests of men. Women had been created by God as *rational* free agents; yet society circumscribed their identities and activities to the extent that they were being denied the opportunity to use their God-given faculties This was a moral crime which damaged their minds and their bodies: 'There must be work, and there must be freedom for women if they are ever to be really healthful beings,' Cobbe wrote in *Putnam's Magazine*.[7] Girls needed to be educated and, above all, encouraged to think for the only thing that a woman possessed that was her own was her mind, and it was through exercising it that she could be liberated, symbolically and literally, from the artificiality of hot-house femininity and domesticity. And if an education encouraged a girl to choose a celibate life devoted to education and employment rather than to marriage and maternity then she was not abandoning notions of womanhood; she was following her capacity as a morally autonomous being to choose her life course and to be in control of it.[8]

The deplorable state of female education, coupled with Cobbe's observations on the treatment women received in the workhouses, contributed greatly to the development of a feminist conscience as did her decision to move to South Kensington with the Welsh sculptor Mary Lloyd in 1864. Much mid-nineteenth-century feminist activity was centred on Kensington, and Cobbe integrated herself into it with ease. Her *Macmillan's* and *Fraser's* articles had been read by campaigners such as Bessie Rayner Parkes, Barbara Bodichon, Clementia Taylor and Emily Shirreff, and she soon found herself being drawn into their company and onto the various women's rights committees as they were formed. The variety and scope of Cobbe's interests corresponded with the multifarious nature of the nineteenth-century Englishwoman's movement, and she moved within and around the various strands with enthusiasm and a sense of purpose. She was a founding member of the Kensington Discussion Society, and along with Elizabeth Wolstenholme, Sara Armour and Elizabeth Garrett contributed to one evening debate on 'the true basis, and the limits of parental authority' by arguing that a child must recognise his or her obligations towards parents, but should not allow those obligations to degenerate into 'slavery'.[9] She supported the agitation designed to admit girls to Oxbridge local exams, sat on Barbara Bodichon's Married Women's Property Committee, and on the executive of the London National Society for Women's Suffrage, campaigned to get Mrs Grey elected to the London School Board, and in 1870 helped Frances Buss raise £6,000 for her Camden School.

Even before she moved to London, Cobbe's opinions on women's rights, and the best way of promoting them, were solicited by friends and acquaintances. In January 1863 she advised Emily Davies on the *Englishwomen's Journal*, which was suffering from severe financial difficulties, and which was, in Davies's opinion, of little use in the debate on education. 'I had a talk with Miss Cobbe about it,' Davies wrote to Barbara Bodichon.

> Her notions are, that to have a weak, poor, Journal, purporting to represent women, is decidedly worse than nothing. That we ought to put down in black & white what we want to do. That a really vigorous & interesting advocate of women, which should be <u>read</u>, would be a capital thing. That to be interesting we must leave off balancing between parties & take up our decided line of religious thought. That as a matter of policy, the most effective line at this time would be what she calls Broad Church. That to get good writing, we must pay high & that whether we have strength among us to sustain such a Magazine as would be worth having, she is not sure.[10]

Davies wanted Cobbe to write for the *Journal*, but could not afford her services. She considered using Cobbe's writing skills for the *Victoria Magazine*, but realised that excessive demands could not be made on Cobbe because of continuing health problems associated with her mistreated ankle. By the end of the summer in 1863, however, Davies was also suggesting in correspondence to Bodichon that perhaps Cobbe was beginning to suffer from over exposure and that it would be of benefit to the women's movement if Bodichon pushed forward her own work: 'I think it would be to our advantage,' Davies explained in an August letter to Bodichon, 'to have our subject brought forward by a new hand, rather than by Miss Cobbe'.[11]

On the whole, Cobbe seems to have enjoyed amicable relationships with her feminist colleagues, which is evidence of the general sense of comraderie that Philippa Levine has discovered existed within the nineteenth-century feminist movement.[12] Davies thought of Cobbe as a 'thoroughly good woman'[13] and Bessie Rayner Parkes told Barbara Bodichon that she liked Cobbe '*exceedingly*' but also did not agree with her (on what is not made clear, but it may have been religion or the suffrage question) 'as she very well knows'.[14] Cobbe's reputation as a supporter of women's suffrage spread to America within a few years of her arrival at Kensington; she received notes and letters from leading American suffragists, and in 1869 was elected a member of New York's feminist Sorosis Club.

Cobbe did not resist her absorption into the developing women's suffrage agitation in London, although she never chose to lead the organisation of pro-suffrage sentiment. In 1866 she signed the petition for women's suffrage (with over 1,400 other names) that had been drawn up by Barbara Bodichon, Jessie Boucherett and Emily Davies, and which was presented to Parliament by John Stuart Mill on 7 June. In the following year she was in the chair of the London National Society for Women's Suffrage working quite happily alongside branch societies in Bristol, Manchester, Birmingham and Edinburgh. Once confronted with the possibility that the regional societies would be amalgamated, bringing together women whom Cobbe did not know and whose sympathies she did not think she could trust, she threatened to remove herself from the executive committee of the London branch: 'this woman question is precisely the one on which it is hardest and yet most imperative to preserve the strictest dignity and on which I could trust only those I knew most thoroughly to take any steps of importance,'[15] Cobbe explained to John Stuart Mill's step-daughter Helen Taylor in late 1867. When the London, Manchester and Edinburgh societies joined forces at the end of the year, Cobbe was absent from the executive, taking with her Mary Lloyd and fellow suffragist Jane Hampson.

Throughout her life Cobbe had an aversion to taking responsibility for organising protest movements, and only agreed to do so when encouraged by friends or by circumstance. Her preference was to lobby independently on behalf of causes she held dear, and women's rights was no exception. Radicalism had not yet infiltrated the suffrage movement, yet even in 1867 Cobbe was concerned that it eventually might, a possibility from which she wanted to distance herself. She knew about the Hyde Park riots in 1867 and could not understand how the unruly behaviour by the working classes had secured them the vote. Women, as Cobbe reiterated again and again, had to prove their political worth through rational activity to reflect the dignified and morally superior nature of their sex. That was why she was a firm believer in the petition and measured persuasion; to follow any other course would reinforce popular prejudice that women were too nervous, hysterical and mentally and physically unfit to exercise the franchise: 'It is sentiment we have got to contend against not reason' she told Sarah Wister, '& to conquer it we must show ourselves strong & calm & wise—& not pretty & silly & vociferous'.[16] Working-class enfranchisement granted in 1867 spelt disaster for Cobbe. 'England in the midst of calm and prosperity,' she wrote in a letter to Mary Somerville, 'has periled [sic] her whole national existence out of wretched party spirit. Tories and Whigs and radicals outbidding each other with that blessed Working Man—the origin of all evil!'[17] Only women could take England off the dangerous path down which Disraeli's 1867 'Leap in the Dark' had propelled it, and Cobbe warned that by refusing to allocate

> a share in the law-making of a nation to the most law-abiding half of it; to exclude on all largest questions the votes of the most conscientious, temperate, religious, and (above all) most merciful and tender-hearted moiety, is a mistake which cannot fail, and *has* not failed, to entail great evil and loss.[18]

Cobbe's experiences to date had proved to her that women were neglected and unfairly treated; they were disadvantaged socially, educationally, economically and politically, and then were refused the possibility of advancement because of the disadvantages that had been thrust on them by men. Those whom society served were those who framed the laws and possessed political power. Women did neither and it was no surprise that they served society, rather than society serving them.

Cobbe drew inspiration for her first women's rights pamphlet from her new-found, pro-suffrage associations and from the 1867 Reform Act. She had already written a number of papers in the early 1860s defending a woman's fitness to preach, to be philanthropically active, to be single and employed and to receive an education, and her pro-suffrage articles built on these early foundations. 'Criminals, Idiots, Women, and Minors; Is the Classification Sound' was brought out by *Fraser's Magazine* in December 1868 and was published separately as a pamphlet by A. Ireland and Co. in Manchester the following year. Cobbe's paper attacked the inequitable social and legal system that had reduced woman, a rational free agent created by God in His image, to the status of Criminal, Idiot, Minor. Especially biting were her acerbic comments on marriage and the common law that victimised women, destroyed their individuality and potential, while consolidating male power in the private and public spheres.

Abusive Alliances

Whatever Cobbe's criticisms, she was not being anti-male, nor did she condemn the institution of matrimony. When based on God's simple law of love, Cobbe understood marriage to be the best and most natural condition for mankind.[19] However, she noted in another article: 'if anything could have been ingeniously devised to deter one sex from the natural desire of marriage, it would be the conditions arbitrarily attached to it by man-made laws all over the world'.[20] As the eighteenth-century legal expert Sir William Blackstone wrote in his *Commentaries on the Law of England*, the husband and wife were one person and that person was the husband. In the eyes of the law the wife owed to him all duty, obedience and fealty; in return the husband owed his wife very little. In 'Criminals and Idiots', Cobbe drew on the impressions of an 'outsider' to expose inequitable, spousal relations:

> 'Ah,' we can hear him say to his guide, as they pass into a village church, 'What a pretty sight is this! what is happening to that sweet young woman in white, who is giving her hand to the good looking fellow beside her?...She is receiving some great honour, is she not?'...
>
> 'Oh yes,' would reply the friend; 'an honour certainly. She is being Married. After a little further explanation, the visitor would pursue his inquiry.
>
> 'Of course, having entered this honorable state of matrimony, she has some privileges above the women who are not chosen by anybody' I notice her husband has just said, 'with all my worldly goods I thee endow'. Does that mean that she will henceforth have control of his money altogether, or only that he takes her into partnership?...
>
> 'By our law it is her goods and earnings, present and future, which belong to him from this moment'.
>
> 'You don't say? But then of course his goods are hers also?'
>
> 'Oh dear, no! not at all. He is only bound to find her food; and truth to tell, not very strictly or efficaciously bound to do that'.
>
> 'How! do I understand you? Is it possible that here in the most solemn religious act...every husband makes a generous promise, which promise is not only a mockery, but the actual reverse and parody of the real state of the case: the man who promises giving nothing, and the woman who is silent giving all?'
>
> 'Well, yes; I suppose that is something like it, as to the letter of the law'.[21]

Legally, husbands were under no obligation to provide for their wives, who could do very little to support themselves. Power, potential and privilege rested with men. 'The legal act by which a man puts his hand in his wife's pocket, or draws her money out of the savings bank', Cobbe pointed out, 'is perfectly clear, easy, inexpensive. The corresponding process by which the wife can obtain food and clothing from her husband when he neglects to provide it—what may it be? Where is it described?'[22] It was not to be found in the laws made by men, for men.

Nor could wives easily obtain a legal separation from an adulterous or abusive husband. The 1857 Divorce Act had simplified divorce proceedings for men, but had not done the same for women. Cobbe admitted that there were good men who loved their wives but added that 'marriage is meant not for good men only, but for bad' and the lot of a wife with a bad husband was 'all but irremediable. Other servants choose their masters many times, and change them when ill-treated; but 'a woman to whom is denied any lot in life but that of being the body-servant of a despot,' is refused (unless he add adultery to his cruelty) all release from him'.[23]

The often violent way in which husbands treated their vulnerable dependents upset Cobbe. Divorce was time consuming and costly. James Hammerton draws upon work by Gail Savage to show that the costs involved in bringing action against a spouse, while acting as a deterrent to the lower classes, did not actually prevent them from appearing in the Divorce Courts.[24] However, the trend throughout the nineteenth century suggests that justice was out of reach for working-class women, and Cobbe believed it was amongst this pitiable class that spousal violence was most common and help was most needed.[25]

In December 1868 Cobbe was appointed as leader writer for the *Echo*. It did not take her long to learn that if she based her leaders on reports of Coroners' Inquests she could elicit sympathy, and at times monetary support, from the reading public for the victims of injustice, crime and trauma. Before Cobbe composed heart-rending pleas for assistance, she had to satisfy herself of the veracity of the reports, and she would dutifully investigate all of the cases with which she dealt. It was while she was verifying the case of Susanna Palmer, indicted on 14 January 1869 at the Central Criminal Court for wounding her husband in a scuffle, that Cobbe was introduced to the law as it dealt with wife abusers.

Cobbe learned that Susanna Palmer had been married to James Palmer for twelve years, during which time she supported the entire family, which included four children. James Palmer had contributed a paltry five shillings over the twelve years. He had been in prison a number of times for acting violently towards his wife and children, and his prison experiences seemed to make him even more aggressive. In an attempt to retain her own earnings, Susanna had applied to the magistrates at Clerkenwell for a Protection Order. She was refused because her husband had not deserted her. During yet another domestic dispute, Susanna picked up a knife to protect herself from assault; she inadvertently injured James and he brought charges against her. Susannah Palmer ended up in Newgate Prison where Cobbe visited her 'and heard her long tale of wrong and misery.'[26]

The case was a startling example of how differently the legal system dealt with men and women. An offence against a wife was considered an inferior guilt, while that of a wife against her husband was viewed with all the horror of 'petty treason'.[27] Over the next few years Cobbe read about cases similar to that of Susannah Palmer; she began educating the public on the criminality of wife abuse, and canvassed those in political power to introduce and support a bill granting women like Palmer the ability to obtain a Protection Order. She believed that the Order should have the same validity as a judicial separation, that custody of any children should be given to the wife, and that husbands be forced to pay weekly maintenance. Cobbe did not believe that harsher penalties, such as flogging, would be of any use; wives could hesitate to turn in violent husbands for fear that they would be treated even worse when the husband was released. Women were victimised because they were the legal dependents of their spouses, and Cobbe argued that abuse would stop only if women were separated from violent men and provided with the economic support that would enable them to live independently. She believed that the only people who could possibly understand the plight of abused wives and who could legislate for them were women, and until they had political power the female victim would receive scant attention.

Violence against women, and wives in particular, was not confined to the nineteenth century, and Cobbe acknowledged its lengthy lineage. Because the husband was held legally responsible for his wife's conduct, it was his right to use his power to control her behaviour and if this meant physical chastisement, then so be it. Acts 'which would amount to an assault if committed against a stranger, may be legally innocent when committed by a husband against a wife,' a nineteenth-century legal text blithly stated.[28] Even popular entertainment, much of it enjoyed by young children in their formative years of moral development, sanctioned violence against women and encouraged it as something to be laughed at rather than punished. Shakespeare's *Taming of the Shrew* and Punch and Judy shows were two examples that Cobbe cited as being detrimental to the way in which society judged the abuser and abused. After perusing police reports in the mid 1870s Cobbe was not surprised to discover that violence against wives was common amongst labourers, especially those from the North where 'kicking districts' flourished, and where the environment contributed to a violent culture. Cobbe supported common ideas that wife beating was a working-class problem, and instead of bringing a fresh perspective to the issue, her attitude served to reinforce class-based misperceptions of the problem.

There had been a lack-lustre attempt in 1853 to punish abusers of wives and children. The Act for the Better Prevention and Punishment of Aggravated Assaults Upon Women and Children and for Preventing Delay and Expense in the Administration of the Criminal Law made it possible for assaults resulting in bodily harm to women and children to be punished before two Justices of the Peace in Petty Sessions or before any Police or Stipendiary Magistrate. The punishment for the offence was not to exceed six months in jail or a £20 fine. Assaults against wives continued. Individuals such as John Stuart Mill and Harriet Taylor spoke out against wife abuse throughout the 1850s and it aroused considerable discussion in Lydia Becker's *Women's Suffrage Journal* as the 1870s drew to a close. In 1874 Colonel Egerton Leigh criticised the inadequate 1853 Act in Parliament. Six months later there was a Home Office inquiry into brutal assault, which drew on the evidence of various judges, magistrates and recorders to conclude that the Act was indeed next to useless. Cobbe came to the same conclusion.

A couple of weeks after her fifty-fifth birthday Cobbe wrote a letter to the *Spectator*. In it she cited three cases of wife abuse that she had recently read about in a newspaper. One woman had been kicked in the forehead; another had been kicked in the face and had been blinded in one eye; a third had been badly burned when her husband threw a paraffin lamp at her. Cobbe was outraged. She demanded that women be given the political power to protect their sex. 'I beg Sir,' she began,

> to ask solemnly of you and of all my countrymen with *whom* lies the guilt of these never-ceasing, ever-multiplying English 'atrocities'? If we, the women of England, possessed constitutional rights, the very first exercise of our power of political pressure would undoubtedly be to compel the attention of our representatives in the Legislature

to the prevention of these crimes of wife-beating and wife-murder. Can you, men of England, wholly acquit your consciences, while you tie our hands, and never lift your own?[29]

Cobbe put her case most eloquently in a paper for *Fraser's* in April 1878 entitled 'Wife Torture'.[30] She implored her readers to take up the cause of beaten wives, for what began as hits and kicks soon progressed to torture, then to murder. She played upon her readers' aversion to pain and on their sympathy by graphically describing cases where wives were maimed by their socially and legally appointed 'protectors'. She criticised Members of Parliament for ignoring the plight of battered women and caustically commented that Parliament only dealt with issues behind which was an enfranchised voice.

In general, Cobbe did not join forces with others advocating changes in the law as it dealt with wife abusers, but she did collaborate with a Birmingham magistrate, Alfred Hill, the son of one of her oldest friends, Recorder Hill, to draw up a bill to protect abused wives. This initiative, coupled with her graphic renditions of wife abuse cases, coincided with an attempt by Lord Penzance to amend divorce legislation. A clause offering separation orders to wives whose husbands had been convicted of assaulting them was incorporated into the proposed Act to Amend the Matrimonial Causes Act, which passed through the House of Lords and the Commons without debate, and became law on 27 May 1878. Provision was made for mandatory maintenance payments and custody of children under the age of ten was to be given to the wife. All women who had obtained a separation order from their husbands were legally now entitled to maintenance. Jessie Boucherett, a long-time friend and colleague of Cobbe's, called the 1878 Act Cobbe's 'monument' to the women's cause.[31]

Yet what looked impressive and progressive on paper was not so in practice. Only with reluctance would magistrates question a husband's prerogative to chastise his wife and they rarely enforced maintenance payments when separations were granted. Cobbe herself perhaps over simplified the benefits that would come with mandatory maintenance payments. The maximum amount to be paid per week was 5 shillings, too low for working-class women to be economically independent without taking on additional employment. Cobbe told Helen Taylor that magistrates' disinclination to accept the Act and follow its provisions derived in large part 'from High Church superstition about the sanctity of marriage'.[32] James Hammerton believes that magistrates' reluctance to break up families derived from the perception they had of themselves as 'marriage menders'.[33] In cases where magistrates did grant the wife a separation order, custody of the children was routinely given to the husband in order that he could benefit from the tranquillizing effects that it was believed all innocent children had on parents, despite Cobbe's insistence that children in a wife-abuser's home were no more safe than 'in the cage of a wild beast'.[34]

The 1878 Act failed as had its 1853 predecessor, and others had to take up the cause of wife abuse in later years. Matilda Blake, Jeannie Lockett, Mabel Sharman Crawford and Elizabeth Wolstenholme Elmy repeated many of Cobbe's earlier criticisms of marriage. They censured magistrates for the lax sentences they handed out to abusers, which only served to reinforce a husband's right to thrash his wife. In 1895, four years after a highly publicised case of wife abduction (R. v. Jackson), the Summary Jurisdiction Act strengthened the provisions within the 1878 Act. But it was difficult to change ideas about marriage, the claims of wives and the rights of husbands, especially when women continued to live as political subordinates.

Given her feelings about marriage, it is hardly surprising that Cobbe, like a number of her contemporaries, opted for a lifestyle that offered companionship and emotional fulfilment without the political and legal complications of a traditional heterosexual arrangement. Cobbe preferred the company of women over men, and spent a great deal of time observing the social interaction between the sexes. She was convinced that when men were present women had an irritating tendency to conform their behaviour and conversation to what they thought men expected of them. As Cobbe explained, women became 'adjectives'. Once men were absent, the rapport between women took on more liberating dimensions; the flippant and the feeble were weeded out, and the strong minded came to the fore, conversed and grew as people in their own right: they became 'nouns'.[35]

Cobbe had become aware of the benefits of exclusive female company during her Grand Tour when she discovered in Italy a colony of artistic women happily living together. Here the American actress

Charlotte Cushman lived with Matilda Hayes who dressed like a man and later wrote for the *Englishwoman's Journal*; (Emily Davies believed that Hayes gave the publication a bad 'bloomerism' reputation while Cobbe eventually considered her to be a liability to woman's suffrage).[36] The painter Rosa Bonheur, who also dressed in masculine attire (and was to support Cobbe's anti-vivisection efforts in later years), lived with Natalie Mica. Closer to home, Cobbe's Irish neighbour, Harriet St Leger, lived with Dorothy Wilson. Cobbe saw that the dynamics of same-sex relationships seemed to work, whereas those of a heterosexual nature appeared fraught with tension and conflict. She decided to arrange her life along lines similar to those she had discovered in Italy, and it was with great delight that, while on a literary sojourn in Florence in 1863, she convinced one member of this group, the Welsh sculptor Mary Lloyd, to return to London with her and set up house.

Lesbianism and Homosocial Unions

Cobbe's relationship with Lloyd fluctuated between the parental and the spousal, and the intensity of their companionship was drawn from spiritual, if not overt sexual, affinity; spiritual sisterhood defined many a romantic female (lesbian) friendship.[37] One problem historians face when attempting to understand the nature of female relationships in the past is to determine whether or not they were 'lesbian'. Liz Stanley astutely points out in her article 'Romantic Friendship? Some Issues in Researching Lesbian History and Biography' that the debate surrounding women's romantic friendships is part of an attempt to draw lesbian history more fully into feminist scholarship.[38] It could even be suggested that the need to 'legitimate' lesbianism involves attempts to discover and recreate a strong, socially accepted and acceptable lesbian past. Victorian women would not have understood or articulated their relationships with each other in the ways that individuals try to do today. Nineteenth-century society facilitated and accepted female relationships; the intricate network of female ritual and sociability, including time spent at all-girl boarding schools and the experience of childbirth, excluded men.[39] That women 'loved' one another is not to be doubted, yet how can we define what these women meant by the term 'love'?

It is impossible to conclude whether Cobbe's relationship with Lloyd was lesbian or not. Lilian Faderman suggests that women

> generally do not view lesbianism as a sexual phenomenon first and foremost. What romantic friends wanted was to share their lives, to confide in and trust and depend upon each other, to be there always for each other…Almost always they envisioned themselves together forever. In these ways, surely, there is little to distinguish romantic friendship from lesbianism.[40]

Cobbe never doubted that she and Lloyd would be together until death did them part. They cohabited first in London and later in Wales in what can be seen as a 'marriage', and like other women involved in 'romantic friendships' Cobbe wrote about her life with Lloyd in spousal terms.[50] Both women had been part of a lesbian community in Italy and participated in England's feminist movement after their move to South Kensington in 1864, and on Cobbe's part she had an aversion to entering a heterosexual union. According to Emily Hamer these are all reasons for suggesting that the relationship was lesbian.[41]

Cobbe's background also appears to correspond to what various scholars have suggested is 'typical' for lesbians and feminists. They are either only or eldest children whose education and character are moulded by the father with the mother taking a secondary role in her daughter's upbringing. The daughter and father enjoy a close relationship, although the daughter, sensing that her father would have preferred a son, adopts masculine attributes and interests. Their relationship becomes ambivalent; this development sets the daughter at odds with patriarchy. She avoids marriage and establishes herself in public; any companionships that she seeks guarantees freedom, self-development and independence.[42] Cobbe was not an only child nor was she the eldest, but she was a late and not altogether welcome addition to the Cobbe family. She had a close, though often antagonistic, relationship with her father; she displayed 'masculine' characteristics from an early age (her 'mannish' appetite was later commented upon by many dinner partners); as a child she preferred adventures outdoors to passively playing with dolls; she struggled with her father and governesses to be given a useful education; she rebelled against patriarchy in both its sacred and secular manifestations; and she chose to live with a woman.

Cobbe had always been attracted to women. In one letter that she wrote to Sarah Wister, who enjoyed an intense emotional relationship with Jeannie Field Musgrove, she mentioned that she was drawn to the conversation of women as 'somebody with whom we feel the strong cords of sympathy uniting us so as to make us "find in all they do or say Love's own deep charm".'[43] 'Love's own deep charm' was, for Cobbe, a metaphysical rather than physical manifestation: 'Moral sympathies produce Equal Friendship. Intellectual sympathies tend to refined and delightful companionship. Sensual sympathies alone make masters and slaves'.[44] Cobbe's idea of love between women echoed the feminist Margaret Fuller's sentiments. Fuller believed love to be 'purely intellectual and spiritual, unprofaned by any mixture of lower instincts, undisturbed by any need of consulting temporal interests'.[45] For Cobbe, 'love' was emotive and spiritual, and under the 'right circumstances' it was pure and fulfilling for both partners; God-given it was the foundation upon which a long-lasting, mutually beneficial relationship was based. Cobbe had discovered 'Love's own deep charm' in Mary Lloyd, 'my old darling,'[46] 'my dear pet,'[47] but 'such an unmanageable old Welshwoman'[48] when she irritated Cobbe while redecorating their London home. They holidayed each year at Lloyd's estate, Hengwrt in Wales. These vacations together were frequently supplemented by independent travel. Cobbe visited her brothers in Ireland, Bedfordshire and Petersfield and spent time in Broadlands and Aston Clinton. Lloyd spent most of her time in Wales but occasionally ventured further afield. When Lloyd visited the Somervilles one winter, Cobbe told Mary Somerville that 'I am very lonely and sad without her'.[49]

The spiritual and emotional bond between the two women is expressed by Cobbe in a poem that she wrote to Lloyd in 1873; it is a celebratory address to her ideal companion, who was as important to Cobbe as her mother had been. Its emotional intensity is typical of declarations between women involved in romantic female friendships:

> Friend of my life! Whene'er my eyes
> Rest with sudden, glad surprise
> On Nature's scenes of earth and air
> Sublimely grand, or sweetly fair,
>   I want you—Mary.

When men and woman, gifted, free,
Speak their fresh thoughts ungrudgingly,
And springing forth, each kindling mind
Streams like a meteor in the wind,
    I want you—Mary.

When soft the summer's evenings close,
And crimson in the sunset rose,
Our Cader glows, majestic, grand,
The crown of all your lovely land,
    I want you—Mary.

And when the winter might come round,
To our 'ain fireside', cheerily bound,
With our dear Rembrandt Girl, so brown
Smiling serenely on us down,
    I want you—Mary.

Now, while the vigorous pulses leap
Still strong within my spirits deep,
Now, while my yet unwearied brain
Weaves its thick web of thoughts again,
    I want you—Mary.

Hereafter, when slow ebbs the tide,
And age drains out my strength and pride,
And dim-grown eyes and trembling hand
No longer list my soul's command,
    I'll want you—Mary.

In joy and grief, in good and ill,
Friend of my heart! I need you still;
My Playmate, Friend, Companion, Love,
To dwell with here, to clasp above,
    I want you—Mary.

> For O! if past the gates of Death
> To me the Unseen openeth
> Immortal joys to angels given,
> Upon the holy heights of Heaven
>   I'll want you—Mary.[50]

This poem was included in the posthumous edition of Cobbe's autobiography, but elsewhere Cobbe did not go into detail about her relationship with Lloyd. She elaborated on her poetic outpourings in her autobiography by explaining that:

> God has given me two priceless benedictions in life;—in my youth a perfect mother; in my later years a perfect Friend. No other gifts, had I possessed them, Genius, or beauty, or fame, or the wealth of the Indies, would have been worthy to compare with the joy of those affections.[51]

Cobbe mentioned Lloyd continually in letters to Sarah Wister, and to others she referred to her companion as 'my friend'.[52] Lloyd never intimately described their arrangement in her surviving correspondence, and Cobbe refused to elaborate on their relationship: 'of a friendship like this, which has been to my later life what my mother's affection was to my youth, I shall not be expected to say more'.[53]

Intense jealousy of interlopers threatened many a homoerotic relationship, and the insecurity Cobbe had felt with Mary Carpenter resurfaced with Lloyd. Cobbe grudgingly shared Lloyd with others and had difficulty accepting Lloyd as an autonomous being. She spent much time, like a distrustful spouse, wondering what her companion was up to when liberated from her control. One autumn when Cobbe was hard at work at their cottage in Wales, Mary absented herself and Cobbe complained to Mary Somerville that 'she came home to me like a truant husband'.[54] When Lloyd broached the subject of going to Rome alone for the winter, Cobbe soon put a stop to that: 'as if I were going to let my wife run about the world in that manner like an unprotected female and leave me behind!'[55] Cobbe manipulated the roles of passive wife and assertive husband as she negotiated her and Lloyd's 'marital' identities, and her complaints to Somerville about Lloyd's behaviour derived from her fear that she was not in control.[56]

Despite Cobbe's preference for female company and her assertion to Wister that she did not 'care a pin about what men think or feel',[57] she often found herself soliciting opinions from amongst the most revered English men whose selfless qualities differed so greatly from the arrogance and immorality Cobbe believed characterised the majority. John Stuart Mill was one whom she idolised. He was every woman's friend, an advocate of woman's suffrage and an opponent of wife abuse, and he had had what Cobbe would consider an ideal relationship based on equality and respect with his wife, Harriet. When he died in 1873 Cobbe wrote of his demise as 'a terrible loss to all women'.[58] She admired James Martineau and although never a Unitarian she attended his chapel in Little Portland Street on Sunday mornings and incorporated his evening sermons and ethical lectures at Manchester College into her own busy schedule. After services she would retire with Mary Lloyd, Sir Charles Lyell and his wife to the Lyells' house and partook of the religious refreshment Martineau had provided.

Cobbe enjoyed Lyell's company and admired him as a 'man of science as he was of old; devout, and yet entirely free thinking in the true sense; filled with admiring, almost adoring love for Nature, and also (all the more for that enthusiasm) simple and fresh-hearted as a child'.[59] Through Lyell Cobbe met and socialised with most of England's scientific luminaries. She enjoyed evenings with Mr and Mrs Francis Galton and Charles Darwin who, before his *Descent of Man* in 1871, impressed Cobbe as 'a most delightful person—full of fun and good nature'.[60] Cobbe was intrigued with scientific subjects. At a dinner attended by Dr Carpenter, Professor Tyndall and J. D. Morelli, she asked about gases, stellar clusters and planetoids, and she enjoyed Tyndall's Royal Institution lecture on why the sky was blue. But as she admitted to Mary Somerville, much of Tyndall's talk passed her by: of 'course I was stupid as usual and didn't half understand it'.[61]

At their house in Hereford Square, Kensington, Cobbe and Lloyd were never in need of company and during their twenty-year residence, Cobbe claimed that she and Lloyd attended at least 2,000 dinners and often entertained fifty visitors simultaneously, ranging from the Amberleys, Martineau and Mill to the Indian Brahmo Kesub Chunder Sen. Before she discovered how little they had in common, Gladstone too was welcomed with open arms. He was apparently a witty guest and entertained his companions with accurate and amusing impersonations of preachers; however, Cobbe was quite put out when he neglected to include Martineau in his after-dinner repertoire at Lady Louisa Egerton's in 1868.[62]

Cobbe made most of her social and political connections at the dinner parties she attended, and she proved herself to be a popular and entertaining guest. Her wit, conversation and personality drew people to her, and as she tottered around drawing rooms a devoted harem of admirers followed in her wake, hanging onto her every word. She made an intelligent rather than decorative table partner and people were continually struck by what they described as her contagious optimism, 'a great fountain of human sympathy...which bubbled up according to the need of her companions'.[63] Friends recalled her radiating abundant stores of sunshine and happiness, engulfing everyone with whom she came into contact. One suffrage colleague remembered 'the thrill of joy her entrance [to committee meetings] gave. It was as if a radiant sunbeam had lighted the office'.[64]

If Cobbe was a sunbeam, she was a rather large sunbeam. She once described her appearance as 'defective even to the point of grotesqueness from an aesthetic point of view'.[65] Arthur Munby wrote of her as a fat Turkish Sultana; Walburga, Lady Paget, noted that 'Miss Cobbe's bright blue eyes flamed when she spoke, but, to many, her huge size, her fine appetite, and rather mannish ways were repellent'[66] Constance Battersea was just as blunt about Cobbe's appearance: 'Her somewhat grotesque figure, surmounted by a fine intellectual head, made her a remarkable personality, one who could never have passed anywhere unnoticed'.[67] Cobbe did nothing to conceal her 'grotesqueness' and according to some she actually emphasised it: 'My dear,' one of her friends told her, 'it is not that you dress badly; you do not dress at all'.[68] She brushed off this remark with a chuckle and went on her merry way.

Cobbe cut an unorthodox figure with her short hair and free-flowing figure draped in a drab, functional dress. She believed that clothes should preserve 'liberty of action to all the organs of the body and freedom from pressure'.[69] She never wore corsets and detested tight-lacing, which she described as 'English suttee for a living husband'.[70] They contracted the lungs, pinched the heart and made the ribs cave in not out; they moulded women into an ideal shape, thereby destroying the individuality that

Cobbe valued so much. 'Brain-heating chignons' and tipped-back bonnets that did not shade the eyes, decolleté dresses that were indecent and exposed the skin to chills, thin-soled shoes that exposed the wearer to the cold pavement or damp grass, plus frills, flounces and furbelows also earned Cobbe's wrath. She did not even wear evening clothes to formal functions, and her rejection of conformity made her even more of a curiosity. Cobbe promoted the cause of women's dress reform by her own unconventional choice of fashion, although in print she adopted a more conservative doctrine: 'a reasonably fine, simply cut silk or cloth skirt, reaching to the ankles and no longer'.[71]

Cobbe was genuinely concerned with the harmful effects of nineteenth-century fashion. There is no doubt that the garments worn often had a detrimental effect on the health of Victorian women and constricted and controlled their lives. Resisting the dictates of female fashion was another way that Cobbe could defy conformity; her rejection was as much practical as rebellious. Corsets, stays and layers of garments could not have been comfortable for a woman of her girth to wear. She blamed her size on the injury she had sustained in 1862, but her incredibly large appetite that astonished and repulsed many a dinner companion undoubtedly played its part. Cobbe loved food. It provided fuel for the vital force which kept the body's physical, nervous and mental parts well oiled and allowed for a harmonic and genial existence. Her mental and physical well being depended upon a good appetite; ignore the vital force and illness would result: 'Here we want the food merely to keep up bodily warmth, and if we expend any of it in muscular, or in (far more exhausting) brain labour, the consequence is a sort of corporeal bankruptcy'.[72]

Cobbe required large quantities of fuel for brain labour, for as well as arguing vociferously for women's rights she wrote constantly, mostly about religion or philanthropy. The range and scope of her journalist activities made her representative of many of her working feminist colleagues,[73] and never a month went by when she was not posting an article to *Macmillan's*, *Fraser's*, the *Quarterly Review* or the *Contemporary Review* or planning her next missive. In 1863 she edited twelve volumes of Theodore Parker's writings for which she received £50 from the publishers, Messrs Trubner, and she contributed to America's slavery debate by writing two anti-slavery tracts, *The Red Flag in John Bull's Eyes* and *Rejoinder to Mrs Stowe's Reply to the Address of the Women of England*, at the time when she was active in the London Ladies' Emancipation Society founded in 1863. In 1864 she published the manuscript on religious duty that she had read to her father as he neared death, and brought out a collection of essays on her trips to Italy. There 'seem clever things in the book,' Robert Browing wrote to Isa Blagden after reading the work which Cobbe entitled *Italics*, 'for she is clever'.[74] 1864 also saw the appearance of Cobbe's *Broken Lights*, which was followed four years later by its sequel, *Dawning Lights*. Cobbe focused upon the imminent arrival of a new religious age, and her comments about the efficacy of prayer in *Dawning Lights* are significant for predating by four years the beginning of the Prayer Gauge Debate.[75]

In 1868 she began her long working relationship with the *Echo*. The proprietor of the paper, Arthur Arnold, had invited Cobbe to join his staff; from December 1868 until March 1875 Cobbe would go into the *Echo*'s offices on Catherine Street at 10 o'clock three mornings every week to write leading articles. According to one contemporary this made her the first woman to work day by day in the office of a newspaper.[76] When the paper was sold and Baron Grant replaced Arthur Arnold, Cobbe left for the *Standard*, albeit for a few short months until a pro-vivisection paragraph appeared on its pages. 'Sometimes it comes over me in the stately old rooms and beautiful gardens [of the home she shared with Lloyd] that I was born a gentlewoman and have rather made a downfall in becoming a hack scribbler to a halfpenny newspaper,' Cobbe wrote to Mary Somerville three years into the *Echo* job. 'But the scribbler is happier than ever the idle lady was (if indeed I ever was idle) and my regrets always end in a laugh'.[77] The scribbler was also earning a nice income; £300 per year with the *Echo* which, when coupled with her annual allowance and remuneration from her other literary pursuits, allowed her to lead a comfortable life. Over her lifetime, Cobbe estimated that she made £5,000 from journalism, far less than the amount her elder brother had inherited upon Charles Cobbe's death in 1857.

From the late 1860s onwards, books and articles about animals began to figure increasingly in Cobbe's journalistic output. Her first major work which focused on the life experiences of animals was a children's story, *The Confessions of a Lost Dog Reported by Her Mistress*, written in 1867. This piece was followed by 'The Consciousness of Dogs' for the *Quarterly*

Review in October 1872, 'Dogs Whom I Have Met' for the *Cornhill Magazine* two months later, and 'Animals in Fable and in Art' for the *New Quarterly Magazine* in April 1874. These works allowed Cobbe to articulate her beliefs about the capacity of domesticated animals, especially dogs, to think and to feel on a rudimentary level that approximated the human, and because they were emotionally so close to man and could express human qualities such as jealousy, disdain, fear and love, she argued that they deserved to be treated compassionately. Charles Darwin praised Cobbe's insight into the canine character; he told her about his own dog, Polly, in words that showed the dog to be a sagacious, loving companion rather than a pet over whom he exerted control.[78]

Cobbe continued to be concerned with the welfare of women, demanding their fair treatment on all social and political fronts. She was pleased with the progress that women were making in education, school and Poor Law administration, municipal government and marital relations, despite the ineffectiveness of the 1878 Matrimonial Causes Act. When the University of London agreed to allow women to take the same examinations as men in 1878 Cobbe chortled to Sarah Wister: 'the die is cast. We shall have women MAs and DDs too I daresay some of these days!'[79] She believed, however, that progress in any of these areas paled beside the main goal—parliamentary franchise, 'and till that point be reached,' she wrote in her introduction to Theodore Stanton's *The Woman Question in Europe* in 1884, 'there can be no final satisfaction in any thing which has been achieved'.[80]

Cobbe was a frequent correspondent of the feminist Lydia Becker throughout the 1880s, and advised her on some of the many suffrage memorials that poured into Parliament only to be rejected. Cobbe was particularly aware of the importance of socially and politically prominent names on petitions, and would canvas on Becker's behalf, using her social connections in London and, after 1884, Wales. While leaders of the Conservatives supported women's suffrage, their rank and file did not; leaders of the Liberal party refused to endorse female enfranchisement despite the support it received from its members.[81] Cobbe mentioned a number of times that it was not reason, but sentiment against which suffragists were contending, and sentiment was far more dangerous and difficult to assail than reason. She discovered the most sentimental and irrational opponent to women's suffrage in William

Ewart Gladstone, leader of the Liberal Party, and as Prime Minister in four Liberal governments between 1868 and 1894 the possibility that a woman's suffrage bill would pass was negligible. 'Gladstone has been the evil genius of our sex—& of our country,'[82] she told Lydia Becker after two Gladstonian ministries had refused female enfranchisement.

Cobbe's friend and editor of the *Spectator*, R. H. Hutton, believed that she was unfairly critical of Gladstone, yet her opinion of the statesman never improved. 'Gladstone has been our ruin & I wish all the women of England would join the Primrose League [as she herself did] to keep him & his party out of office for ever,' Cobbe told Lydia Becker in yet another letter complaining about the bleak future for women's suffrage.[83] Cobbe believed that only in Gladstone's absence would advances be made in women's rights: 'I am in great hopes of a final defeat for our arch-enemy Gladstone,' she informed Becker as a general election loomed in the 1880s. 'If the Tories were in I think that England—& Women are safe. If not—the deluge'.[84] But even with Tories in, women were not 'safe' and she correctly assumed that women's suffrage would not see success in her lifetime. Cobbe's opinion of Gladstone was further lowered by his commitment to pacifying Ireland and to Home Rule, which he publicly endorsed in 1886. The issue split not only the Liberal party, but also the woman's movement and Cobbe found herself siding with Millicent Fawcett and the Unionists in a reconstituted women's suffrage society in College Street, Westminster

In 1890 as she neared her seventieth birthday, Cobbe gave one of her final women's rights speeches to an audience still eager to hear her. It was almost thirty years since her first women's rights paper which she gave before the NAPSS in London, and although she was obviously depressed with the lack of progress that had been made since 1862, she remained firm in her belief that once women asserted themselves things would improve. The Conference of Women Workers in Birmingham heard Cobbe speak on 'Women's Duty to Women'. Her message was clear: 'the great Masculine Myth'[85]—that women were provided for from childhood to old age by men—had caused most men, and too many women, to turn a blind eye to the claims of the 'weaker' sex. When the wants of women were addressed, they were offered a paltry residue of the resources given to men; men got the best hospitals, the best education, the best care in old age. But Cobbe was not just demanding that the weak be protected by the strong; she wanted women to accept the fact that only they could protect themselves, and to do this they first had to empower themselves. Rise up! Cobbe demanded of her female audience, for only you will be able to claim the rights that are yours; to succeed you will find yourselves involved in work that is not pleasurable, but hard and heart rending. It was labour, however, which would advance the female sex and the nation. This was the unique role of women—to replace the corrupt world that men had created with a woman's loving and moral environment as God had intended.

Cobbe furthered God's kingdom through her efforts on behalf of Theism, workhouse reform and women's rights. There was, however, another issue that placed greater demands on her energy and emotions. In 1863 Cobbe discovered that man's inhumanity to animals was far worse than his inhumanity to man; it posed a greater threat to his moral self and to the emergence of a civilised society, and over the next forty years it drained Cobbe's mental and physical energies. Cobbe gave her time to Theists, to workhouse inmates and to women, but she gave herself to animals.

4

'THE RIGHTS OF MAN AND THE CLAIMS OF BRUTES'

Cobbe's physician had advised a trip to the baths as treatment for her injured ankle. Her decision to visit Aix-les-Bains in 1863 was fortuitous, not because it made her mobile, but because it introduced her to vivisection. One day while taking the waters, she read a disturbing article in an English newspaper detailing the teaching practices of the veterinary school at Alfort, France. Students were allowed to operate on aged, unanaesthetised horses in classes to teach and test surgical dexterity. Cobbe could not comprehend how the painful procedures, which included hoof removal, were necessary to a veterinary education; in England veterinary students practised their skills on the cadavers of animals, but in France a vivisectional approach to tuition had been part and parcel of the curriculum at Alfort, Lyon, Toulouse and Paris since the late 1700s. Up to sixty painful operations a day could be performed on a single unanaesthetised horse.[1]

Although most Britons were unaware of this veterinary practice in France there were some who protested against its content. In 1846 the Rev. David Davis, a dissenting minister, had petitioned Queen Victoria, a patron of the Royal Society for the Prevention of Cruelty to Animals since 1835; the Rev. Davies had also applied to the King of France, Louis Philippe, but both appeals fell on deaf regal ears.

The RSPCA, founded in 1824 as the Society for the Prevention of Cruelty to Animals, sent a deputation to Napoleon III in 1861 requesting him to put a halt to the atrocities. Napoleon was an expert horseman, and it was fully expected that the deputation would receive a favourable hearing. It did not. The operations at Alfort continued, and in 1863 it was the *Lancet* that criticised the French for these 'atrocities [which] we do not hesitate to stigmatize as unnecessary and horrible, and degrading

7. Frances Power Cobbe in a sedan chair at Aix-les-Bains, 1863 (unknown photographer). The Cobbe Archive.

to the men who practise them and the nation which permits them'.[2] 'How could an humane and civilised nation condone the atrocities at Alfort?' Britain's medical journals and newspapers asked their readers. It was this question Cobbe herself pondered as she took the baths at Aix-les-Bains.

Growing up as part of Ireland's landed gentry, Cobbe had been surrounded by animals. She rejected hunting but enjoyed angling, where her successes would have made even Izaac Walton proud. Newbridge was set in a natural oasis of green and blue that fed Cobbe's enthusiasm for fishing, and she personified Walton's 'compleat angler'—until, during her religious crisis, her understanding of her relationship with animals was changed. Cobbe realised that virtue, rather than happiness, was the aim of man's existence, whereas happiness, not virtue, was the only life for which an animal, irrational and incapable of being moral, had been created. Having gained this insight, she was able to bond with nature and question the assumption that man had an unchecked dominion over animals. Later in *Intuitive Morals* Cobbe developed this further, concluding:

> that the brutes in their present condition, and so far as we know of their destination, can only be considered as the complement of creation. To speak more accurately, their happiness is the end of their creation, our virtue not only of ours, but of the whole. Most absurd, however, is the old notion that the primary end of the existence of any sentient creature could be the benefit of another, and that the brutes are made expressly for the service of man.[3]

Cobbe did not deny that animals suffered in their lives, but it should not be at the hands of man; 'the brutes continually endure pain...for the obvious purpose of securing their lives and the integrity of their bodies. In other words, they suffer some Pain for the sake of their general Happiness, which, as we have seen, is the highest end of their existence'.[4] Because of Cobbe's ethical reawakening she was able to display an unusual level of sensitivity towards Newbridge's fishes. As characterless creatures, furthest removed from man and therefore conceived to be insensible to suffering of any kind, they were given little attention when it came to matters of pleasure and pain but no longer, Cobbe vowed, would she cause suffering to anything God had created in order to satiate her thirst for pleasure; she renounced fishing and was happier in spirit for watching the creatures live in water for the time God allotted to them.

It was easier for Cobbe to curtail her own associations with hunting and fishing than try to work out the bounds within which educated Frenchmen could operate on unanaesthetised horses. The article entitled 'The Rights of Man and the Claims of Brutes' that she penned in response to her discovery in France is indicative of her limited scientific knowledge but also of her limitless moral reservoir. She drew on her intuitive morality and her experiences with the poor to create her first anti-vivisection argument. Its humanitarianism had eighteenth-century foundations and it was structured around an anthropocentric understanding of man's relationship with animals. The pain of her injured ankle probably made her think more intensely about the suffering with which the Alfort horses lived daily, the alleviation of which she saw as important not only for the horse, but for the individual inflicting that pain, who suffered morally for it. Her emphasis on the cruel man's moral degeneration was typical of early arguments advocating animal welfare: man came first, animals second, and Cobbe only began to alter her views some twelve years later.

Cobbe wrote 'Rights of Man' at Aix-les-Bains and sent it to J. A. Froude, her brother's school-boy friend and now editor of *Fraser's Magazine*, who inserted it in the November 1863 issue. That this piece is first and foremost a didactic treatise is evident in the opening paragraph's story about an Eastern town which, because it was cruel to its non-human inhabitants, was punished first by drought, then by floods. All the inhabitants died except for one man, who had shown kindness to a camel. Cobbe compared her ancient story to a contemporary one, a supposedly civilised city with golden temples and refined people who congregated inside large public buildings where unheard of tortures to animals occurred. The implication that this society was France was obvious. 'We do not seem to have advanced much over the Moslem by our eighteen centuries of Christianity,'[5] a sombre Cobbe concluded. These refined and educated men who performed the outrageous acts at Alfort were no better than England's 'half-brutalized and sottish carter, or the the [sic] degraded and filthy dealer in 'marine store'' who mistreated animals because of beast-like impulses to hurt and maim.[6] In fact,

Cobbe considered the Alfort student to be worse than the lower-class man who, because of his ignorance, could be more easily excused for cruel behaviour. She expected educated men to know better. Veterinary atrocities could be halted if anaesthetics were used, and the student's depravity was evident to Cobbe because he omitted to use them. This caused pain to animals and adversely affected the relationship between man and God. 'If we break this trust [between man and animal], and torture them, what is our posture towards Him? Surely as sins of the flesh sink man below humanity, so sins of cruelty throw him into the very converse and antagonism of Deity; he becomes not a mere brute, but a fiend.'[7] Christianity and civilisation were synonymous, and the unanaesthetised operations at Alfort threatened both. Cobbe did not ask herself whether the curriculum was necessary for students to ascertain facts about equine physiology, because it was not required for her to do so. From her moral platform she was correct in asking herself only one question: was such behaviour compatible with a moral and civilised society?

It was a question that a minority of people had asked in the middle of the eighteenth century. At this time a new more humanitarian age began to dawn. There was a move away from René Descartes' mechanistic view of the world and a reaction to the overly rational explanations of nature offered by Enlightenment thinkers towards a more sentimental interpretation of man's place in the natural world. The cult of pet keeping, which developed at this time, encouraged the middle and upper classes to think of domestic creatures as proto-human, as 'idealized servants who never complained or model children who never grew up'.[8] Coupled with evangelicalism, which reinforced human pity and sympathy for other humans, both of the above developments made it ethically acceptable for a select literate, pet-keeping group to re-evaluate man's relationship with animals and apportion to them a degree of compassion hitherto absent. Yet although animals were being drawn into the realm of the human, they continued to be kept at a safe distance by the absence of moral awareness, which defined what it meant to be human and therefore crowning the hierarchy of creation.

A number of eighteenth-century ethicists pointed out that because man was at the apex of creation he had certain custodial responsibilities to fulfil towards those less well favoured. The philosopher David Hartley wrote in 1748: 'We seem to be in the place of God to them [animals], and we are obliged by the same tenure to be their guardians and benefactors'.[9] It was the acceptance of this type of thinking which separated civilised man from his uncivilised counterpart: awareness of the superiority of man and respect for all creation. It was commonly assumed that the working man resisted such humane thoughts: that he was routinely seen to mistreat animals in work and sport confirmed ideas about his base and callous nature. In an attempt to avert or subvert the spread of uncouth and uncivilised activities animal welfare laws were passed and animal welfare agencies were founded. By controlling human behaviour towards animals, early animal welfare advocates were not only protecting brutes; they were also forcing moral awareness upon the lower orders. They attempted to save the bodies of animals from suffering and human souls from damnation.[10]

Between 1800 and 1835 eleven bills dealing with animal cruelty were debated in parliament, though all were defeated except one introduced by the enthusiastic humanitarian, Richard Martin. Martin's Bill, passed in 1822 to Prevent the Cruel and Improper Treatment of Cattle, made individuals liable to prosecution for cruelty to both horses and cattle. In 1835 and 1849 these provisions were extended to include domestic pets, while bear-baiting and cock-fighting were also outlawed.[11] In the year of its founding the Society for the Prevention of Cruelty to Animals carried out 149 successful prosecutions under Martin's Act; the numbers increased dramatically with better policing by the Society so that between 1830–39, 1,357 prosecutions were carried out and by the 1890s the number had increased to 71,657.[12]

Despite the effectiveness of the 1822 Act, which legally punished animal cruelty, the old-world anthropocentric order had not collapsed. When Cobbe wrote her first anti-vivisection article in 1863, although animals were protected by law they still lacked rights. Of God's creatures only man could claim rights because he was a rational, morally autonomous individual, created in God's image and given the right to rule the world in God's stead; to include woman would be contentious. Man had social and moral responsibilities (whether he fulfilled them was another matter), and responsibility is itself a prerequisite for possessing rights and privileges. Animals were neither rational nor autonomous; they did not have any responsibilities, and therefore could not share common interests and mutual obligations that defined a community;

they were able to make claims on man but could not share his rights. The Bible was fundamental in reinforcing man's dominion over animals: 'Let us make man in our image,' Genesis proclaimed, 'after our likeness and let them have dominion over the fish of the sea, and over the fowl of the air, and over the cattle, and over all the earth, and over every creeping thing that creepeth upon the earth.'[13]

Cobbe had abandoned orthodoxy and angling, but not the concept that man was superior in his relations with animals. Her reading of Kant reinforced this idea, since 'relationships', concretely defined, could exist only between like, rational beings. Because animals were not rational, man obviously could not enjoy relationships with them, therefore animals were objects not requiring any special consideration. Kant did suggest that man refrain from intentionally causing beasts to suffer, but his reasons were, like those of his contemporaries, anthropocentric; cruelty towards animals would result in a hardening of the human heart and an inability to empathise with human suffering. He stressed that considerate treatment of animals by man was his duty towards himself. By adopting this attitude he reflected the limits and the utilitarian nature of animal welfare arguments that stretched from the late-eighteenth to the early-nineteenth century and defined what it was to be a civilised human.

Like Kant, Cobbe differentiated between animals and humans. It was clear in her mind that moral demands took precedence, and this defined for her the human–animal relationship: 'the being who is both moral and sentient, demands that his moral interests be primarily consulted, and his sentient interests secondarily; and the being who is only sentient and not moral is placed altogether subordinately, and can only claim that his interests be regarded after those of the moral being have been fulfilled'. Because of this moral–sentient dichotomy Cobbe accepted that the 'whole lower creation is for ever and utterly subordinated to the higher.'[14]

Although Cobbe understood man's relationship with animals to be hierarchical she agreed with Jeremy Bentham and Bishop Butler that animals had a claim to considerate treatment which was based upon their capacity for suffering. But Cobbe saw animals as 'un-moral' creatures (their needs could be fulfilled only after those of humans had been met), indicated by the title of her article, 'The *Rights* of Man and the

Claims of Brutes'. Cobbe was therefore able to sanction pain inflicted by man on animals when it was vital to human well-being. She was convinced that God had created certain animals to be slaughtered, and that man could actually be doing them a favour by killing them before a possibly painful demise in the course of their natural lives.[15] Nevertheless, slaughter had to be performed as quickly as possible, not only to save the animal from pain, but also to save the slaughterer from becoming brutalised by the act of killing and to save the individual who ate the meat from contracting disease from 'disturbed' or 'deranged' animal flesh.[16]

Cobbe believed, as did John Wesley before her, that as moral beings, men and women ruled 'the animal creation not as irresponsible sovereigns, but as the vicegerents of God.'[19] It was up to man as guardian of all God's creatures to ensure that an animal lived to be happy first and useful to man second. Animal life could be taken to satisfy man's wants but not his wantonness, and to knowingly inflict gratuitous pain and suffering upon a sentient creature was a moral crime. It violated man's relationship with animals and with God.

It was the issue of unjustified pain, rather than experimentation itself, which worried Cobbe in 1863. She believed that man, as a rational being, had the 'right to seek truth as he has a right to seek natural food, and may obtain it equally lawfully by the same measures. Thus we arrive at the conclusion that man has a right to take animal life for the purpose of science as he would take it for food, or security, or health'.[18] Man could *take* animal life, but not transform it into a 'curse', as Cobbe later called it, by inflicting unnecessary pain. Hence she could support the use of animals in science while condemning the tortures on horses at Alfort.

A number of scholars have discussed in detail the history of physiological research and the rise of animal rights.[19] By the time Cobbe wrote 'Rights of Man' continental physiologists considered vivisection to be a legitimate and efficient way to discover the mysteries of life, whereas their English counterparts preferred dissection. England's aversion to vivisection, however, did not mean that invasive and often painful exercises were totally shunned and as early as the eighteenth century there were exclamations of horror at these invasive practices. Joseph Addison ridiculed the Royal Society in two articles in 1710 in the *Tatler*; Alexander Pope criticised vivisection a number of times and often voiced his disgust that men were carving up living creatures which not only felt pain but also, in a radical suggestion, possessed souls. Samuel Johnson, unlike Pope, did not believe that animals had souls, but he did agree that their suffering made vivisection cruel and unnecessary, especially since no therapeutic benefits had as yet been derived from its practice. Despite such displays of compassion for the unfortunate animal, attention was focused clearly upon the individual who vivisected. Johnson suggested that, because experimentalists cut up animals and discovered similarities to humans, there was little to stop them moving on to helpless hospital patients.[20] Animal vivisection might lead to vivisection on man; the physician as care giver could be replaced by an evil harbinger of pain. This was the medical equivalent of William Hogarth's 1751 series of engravings, 'The Four Stages of Cruelty', which connected animal cruelty to homicide. Although Johnson and others agreed that vivisection brought with it new physiological discoveries, such as the circulation of the blood, they could not accept it as part of the civilising process, yet not until 1876 was any act passed to regulate it. The humane individual understood cruelty in sport and work, and it was these rather than the unfamiliar science that they sought to control by fusing Benthamite concern for animals with anthropocentric concern for humans.

The baths at Aix-les-Bains were doing Cobbe little good. She was becoming increasingly anxious and depressed, and she decided to abandon the water treatment in favour of a visit to her friend Isa Blagden at the Villa Brichieri on Bellosguardo, where the disturbing news of Alfort would be eased by soirées and lively conversation. However, in the same month that J.A. Froude published 'Rights of Man', Cobbe discovered that Italy was home to even more horrific animal treatment. During one of their evening receptions Cobbe and Blagden heard rumours from a number of their guests that Professor Moritz Schiff conducted vivisectional experiments on a variety of animals in his laboratory at the Speccola. The rumours were corroborated by Theodore Parker's physician, Dr Appleton from Harvard University, who had visited Schiff's laboratory and seen dogs, pigeons and other animals mangled and 'tortured' for no apparent purpose. The cries from these creatures had moved a number of people to complain, not about the experiments themselves, but about the noise which disturbed the neighbourhood.[21]

Cobbe had become the Italian correspondent for the *Daily News* in

1862, and she used her position on the paper to alert its readers to the atrocities in the supposedly civilised and refined Florence. On 18 December she wrote a column which began innocently enough, criticising Italy's inefficient postal system and praising ongoing improvements with the buildings and the roads. Then without warning Cobbe began an attack on Moritz Schiff. She was profoundly upset that this German professor was encouraging impressionable students to follow what was a morally repugnant example. After further investigation Cobbe discovered, to her horror, that vivisection in Italy was more widespread than the Schiff story suggested, and she wrote an additional letter to the *Daily News*. A Professor Moleschott was carrying out vivisections at Turin and similar 'atrocities' were occurring daily at Bologna. These men believed themselves to be engaged in worthwhile activities, but Cobbe believed otherwise. Their work was not scientific, it was cruel; God's craftsmanship in nature was not being brought to light, it was being desecrated by villains; Schiff and his students were violating the Moral Law, pure and simple. The Roman Catholic Church and what Cobbe considered its archaic and damaging anthropocentric doctrine, did nothing to stop these men, and because of the Church's apathy neither did anyone else: 'Sometimes in a quarrel between two men,' as Cobbe reminisced about her time in Italy during her Grand Tour of 1857–8, 'witnesses were willing to come forward, because, while making one their enemy, they ensured the friendship of another. But for a dog or a horse—who on earth would incur the animosity of a person who might torture the brute?'[22]

The answer to this rhetorical question was Cobbe herself. Secure in the belief that she was indeed vicegerent [sic] of God[23] she drafted a memorial demanding that Schiff stop his vivisections. It was translated into Italian and sent around Florence for signatures that represented, according to the historian Patrizia Guarnieri, 'the English and the other foreigners; extraneous to the life of the city, who frequented the Florentine villas.'[24] Cobbe's petition contained the names of a wide variety of socially prominent people from Italy and abroad. At the head of the document stood the name of 'the venerable' Mary Somerville who 'appeals at once with the authority of her learning and her years, and treats that the sacred name of science be not prostituted for the defence of cruelties, always brutalising to the performers, and generally useless to mankind.'[25] Fifty noblemen of 'the highest Tuscan houses,' 300 individuals from the middle class, ten physicians, all of the Protestant clergy, the American and English vice-consuls and prominent sculptors, painters and writers rounded out her petition.

Cobbe forwarded her memorial to Schiff. He was apparently not as impressed as Cobbe had hoped with the signatures of Italy's most prominent citizens and foreign visitors. He tossed it aside and wrote a letter to Florence's national paper, *La Nazione*, denying the assertions Cobbe had made in the *Daily News* letters and demanding that she prove them. Not one to miss a challenge, Cobbe immediately wrote back to *La Nazione* including a statement signed by Appleton of what he had witnessed at the Speccola. Cobbe, to date, had had little trouble making her views known in England, but now the editor of *La Nazione* refused to publish her letter and only after much persuasion did he agree to insert it as a paid advertisement. Appleton asked Schiff to use his influence with the editor to allow Cobbe's letter to be printed. According to Cobbe's melodramatic account, Schiff laughed in Appleton's face, and in that instant Cobbe's efforts to force Schiff to curtail his tortures dwindled into a meaningless attempt by an Englishwoman to interfere in the progress of Italian physiology. 'I was not in Italy the year of Fanny Cobbe's campaign against vivisection in Florence,' Cobbe's friend Fanny Kemble wrote in her published reminiscences, *Further Records*, 'but have often heard her refer to the violent opposition and personal enmity which her excursions in the cause of humanity drew upon her.'[26]

Cobbe probably exaggerated 'the violent opposition and personal enmity' from which she suffered in 1863; she was to endure much worse over a decade later in England. But she was roundly criticised in Florence for poking her unscientific nose in where it did not belong. Cobbe believed otherwise. As far as she was concerned Florence and the helpless animals, 'abandoned' by man and church, demanded her attention, and she poked her nose in where she knew it very rightly belonged.

Still in physical pain, and profoundly disturbed by the treatment animals received, Cobbe left the morally barren continent. She returned with Mary Lloyd to her beloved pet dog in 'civilised' England, where she believed no man was cruel enough to do what Schiff and his colleagues perpetrated on God's creatures and to caring women who tried to stop them.[27]

Vivisection in England

Cobbe's continental discoveries made a deep and disturbing impression upon her, and although they were pushed aside by other, more familiar issues such as women's suffrage, references to them began to crop up sporadically in writings that did not deal directly with scientific research. From 1864 until the end of the decade, Cobbe used vivisection, and especially the idea of pain and suffering, to bolster her arguments in other issues. She was not interested in discussing vivisection itself, nor was there, in 1864, a need for her to bring the issue forward. She drew on vivisection, 'the 'fiendish' vivisector and the pain he inflicted on the vulnerable, when she wanted to illustrate the destructiveness and inhumanity of all men. It did not take long, however, for Cobbe to be drawn into the physiologist's laboratory and once she was there, she could not and would not escape.

One of the first articles that Cobbe wrote for *Fraser's* after her return to Hereford Square was 'Hades', a paper in which she stressed the relationship between moral and social progress, and the importance of faith in immortality to bring about that progress. 'Hades' contributed nothing new about Cobbe's religious beliefs, but the topic provided her with the opportunity to offer an embryonic opinion of science's secular assault on the sacred (in this case Egyptian tombs). Since her grand tour Cobbe had been fascinated by Egyptology and she pursued it as an enthusiastic amateur. Hers was a non-invasive pastime confined to drawing up charts and tables of ruling pharaohs, and she condemned the professional Egyptologists' exploration and desecration of burial chambers in the name of progress. Their destructive research reminded her of the continental scientist and student who tore a living animal's body apart to learn about physiological processes and acquire surgical dexterity. Although she was disturbed by the destruction of sacred ground and ancient human remains, it was preferable to the destruction of life: 'Better let it [science] pull dead mummies to pieces, however, in Egypt,' she concluded, 'than dissect live horses and dogs in the schools of Paris.'[28]

Four months later, Cobbe made a similar, though more passionate, attack on vivisection in an article entitled 'The Morals of Literature'; the reader is not forewarned that her condemnation will come, and when it does it arrives with full moral force. In the initial paragraphs of her article, Cobbe sets out what she believed were appropriate literary guidelines for a writer to follow: truth, purity, simplicity and kindness. Those who deviated from this noble belletristic path and wrote for self advancement, notoriety or to spite others became vivisectors who wielded a pen, rather than a knife, and who destroyed the spiritual qualities of their God-given talent ensnaring readers in a world of lurid, sensational immorality. Why, Cobbe asked,

> are we to regard a great writer with adoring admiration, because he can with his pen tear open all the wounds, expose all the diseases of humanity—not only untouched by compassion, unmoved to any effort to heal or save, but glorying in his own mighty gifts, and busy only to 'build up the pyramid' of his own self-worshipped personality? Genius so employed is not human, far less is it Divine.[29]

Cobbe's sentiments about the literary vivisector were given a personal angle when her brother, Thomas, received a scathing review of his 1866 study on the *History of the Norman Kings of England*. Every throbbing nerve of Thomas's creative being had been laid bare by the reviewer who had rent Thomas's book and his talents as vivisectors 'tortured' living animals in order to discover the mysteries of life. Thomas was so deeply affected by the experience that he never wrote again, and Cobbe could not forgive the reviewer for the anguish he had caused.[30]

Vivisection also began to infiltrate Cobbe's arguments in support of women's rights. By the latter part of the century, once the vivisection debate was firmly established, anti-vivisectionists would make explicit the link between the sufferings of animals and those of women in order to underscore exploitation of the powerless by the powerful. But in the late 1860s, even though Cobbe had already explored the wrongs suffered by women and was beginning to discover those suffered by animals, the connection between the two was in its infancy. Once again, Cobbe used vivisection as a means of exposing inequitable power hierarchies; it was an approach which enabled her to demand that women become politically active. She used and manipulated vivisection to serve her purpose; she controlled it, it did not yet control her.

In demanding political, legal and social justice for women in her 1868 paper, 'Criminals, Idiots, Women and Minors', Cobbe asked her readers to sympathise with not only female suffering, but with that of God's other powerless creatures—animals. Men caused pain to both women and animals, neither of whom received just protection from abuse. 'Would any woman's devotion to science (does the reader think) lead her to practise vivisection?' Cobbe asked.

> Nay, but it is hard for a man to tell the misery and disgust, rising almost to revolt against the order of the world which fills many a woman's heart when she sees daily around her the instances of man's wanton and savage cruelty to the harmless creatures for whom she can only plead, and pleads usually in vain.[31]

The concept that only women could save what men destroyed was central to Cobbe's argument as it was to many pro-suffragists, and vivisection provided a novel and disturbing means to transmit this message to her readers. Her implied suggestion that vivisection, like other forms of animal cruelty, was an everyday occurrence was, however, inaccurate. In 1868 vivisection was not practised daily; it was practised occasionally by a relatively small number of experimentalists.

Within a couple of years, however, the situation began slowly to change, alongside developments in medical education. Thomas Neville Bonner notes in his book, *Becoming a Physician*, that by the middle of the nineteenth century, support for a liberal and classical medical education that trained doctors to be capable healers and gentlemen was being challenged by calls for a curriculum which addressed the aetiology of disease. This approach required 'practical' lessons in medicine and physiology, supported by direct 'hands on' training in laboratories and student participation in experimentation. The continent, and especially Germany, was more receptive to modifications to medical curricula than England where reform was promoted by what Neville Bonner refers to as 'independent and voluntary effort'.[32] John Burdon Sanderson, Michael Foster and E. A. Schäfer amongst others, who were already undertaking independent research, were the main advocates of change. If medical education was to be reformed then universities would have to hire staff trained specifically in vivisectional techniques of research.

In 1870 the Royal College revised its examinations: outside experts were brought in to examine students and candidates were required to have a greater knowledge of biological processes, not only derived from anatomical learning and the dissection of cadavers, but also from physiology. Teaching posts, therefore, had to be filled with competent physiologists who separated function from structure and stressed experimentation and the accumulation of facts rather than the natural theology and anatomical observation which had previously played a significant part in physiological investigation in England.[33] In 1870 John Burdon Sanderson, who had trained at the *College de France* in 1851 under the vivisector Claude Bernard, was appointed Professor of Practical Physiology and Histology at University College, London; Michael Foster, who had also studied in France in 1859, was selected as first Praelector of Physiology at Trinity College, Cambridge; and E. A. Schäfer, who had come under the influence of London's innovative Professor of Anatomy and Physiology, William Sharpey, became Assistant Professor of Physiology under Burdon Sanderson.

Also in 1870 the British Association for the Advancement of Science, meeting at Liverpool, appointed a committee to look into physiological experimentation. At the association's Edinburgh meeting in the following August, seven of the ten committee members, including Burdon Sanderson, signed a report containing guidelines for vivisection similar to those proposed by the English physiologist Marshall Hall forty years earlier. The use of anaesthesia was mandatory: experimentation for teaching purposes was to be painless or, if the possibility of pain existed, anaesthetics were to be utilised; painful experiments were to be carried out only by qualified persons and were not to be performed in veterinary colleges in order to teach manual dexterity. These recommendations were guidelines only, adopted by physiologists voluntarily and not enforced by the British Association, which had no intention of becoming a scientific watchdog.[34]

Cobbe had attended the 1870 British Association meeting and as she remembered, 'greatly rejoiced at this humane ukase of autocratic Science'.[35] She approved of the rules adopted by the British Association because they seemed to correspond to her understanding of vivisection—necessary but painless—and she was pleased that the medical community was taking responsibility for its actions and ensuring that unnecessary suffering would be avoided. Yet soon after these voluntary guidelines for vivisection were adopted, Cobbe discovered that they were regularly ignored. As 'time passed,' she recalled, 'we were surprised to find that nothing was done to enforce these rules in any way or at any place; and that the particular practice which they most distinctly condemn, namely, the use of vivisections as illustrations of recognized facts, was flourishing more than ever without let or hindrance'.[36]

Vivisection was not growing unchecked throughout universities and medical schools. Although the College of Surgeons required medical students to possess a knowledge of practical physiology, there continued to exist in many London teaching hospitals a reluctance to recognise physiology as distinct from anatomy; this was mainly due to the conservatism of senior clinicians (who gave lectures) and of the governing bodies.[37] Yet there is no doubt that, by the mid 1870s, medical curricula were changing. From the new generation of pro-vivisection clinicians and lecturers and from the appearance of texts, such as *The Handbook for the Physiological Laboratory* edited by John Burdon Sanderson in 1873, students were receiving encouragement to be active participants in discovering physiological processes in animals. At the same time steps were taken to build laboratories at Oxford, Cambridge, London and at regional universities.

Cobbe watched all of these developments from her London home with increasing alarm. She had eagerly welcomed science as she understood it in Paley's *Theory*, in the *Bridgewater Treatises*, at discourses at the Royal Institution and in conversations with Charles Lyell. She had even considered its merits when Darwin had published his theory of evolution in 1859, though she cringed in disgust at his 1871 suggestion that man inherited his moral sense.[38] She appreciated science in that it was celebratory of God's creation and the joys of life. By 1873, when *The Handbook* appeared and when the new approach to physiological investigation was beginning to gain ground in the universities, Cobbe saw that something had gone dangerously wrong. When, a few years later, she became even more disillusioned with science, she mournfully wrote: 'We turn to the books which in former years used to expound to us the marvellous and beneficent mechanism of the Almighty Anatomist, and we grow sick as we read of the worse than devilish cruelties whereby science has purchased her evermore unholy secrets'.[39]

Cobbe's worries increased in 1874, when the British Medical Association unintentionally encouraged a confrontation with animal welfare advocates at its annual meeting at Norwich. An interested and eager audience had arrived to listen to the French experimentalist Eugene Magnan lecture on the physiological effects of alcohol. After the lecture Magnan attempted to induce an epileptic fit in two dogs by injecting them with absinthe. He duly carried out the injection on the first dog at which a few members of the audience protested, concerned at the possible pain the creature was suffering. A vote was taken to determine if the experiment should continue; it did, but it was disrupted once more when one protester, T. Joliffe Tufnell, President of the Royal College of Surgeons of Ireland, cut the restraints of one of the animals and then left in search of magistrates to halt the proceedings. The gathering broke up in disarray. This event provided the opportunity for disparate anti-vivisection voices to coalesce, and once started 'the train of events toward a national agitation could not have been reversed'.[40]

John Colam, secretary of the Royal Society for the Prevention of Cruelty to Animals, decided to investigate the Norwich incident to determine whether Magnan and three other English physiologists who had condoned the experiment had been intentionally cruel. In October Colam used Martin's Act to prosecute the four doctors for cruelty to a dog. The case against Magnan and the three British doctors was heard at the Norwich Petty Sessions on 9 December 1874. Realising the legal bind into which he had fallen, Magnan had returned to France and was not present during the prosecution. The Magistrates agreed that Colam was justified in prosecuting the accused and during the trial they condemned vivisection as useless and demoralising. Colam was unable, however, to prove that the British physiologists were involved in performing the actual experiment, and the case was dismissed.[41]

Despite Colam's unsuccessful foray into court, the publicity given to the Norwich trial increased public awareness of vivisection. The press debated its merits and dangers, and medical publications, particularly the *Lancet*, pointed out that only those who possessed accurate physiological knowledge were qualified to deal with vivisection at a legal and scientific level. *Au contraire*, thought Cobbe. She judged vivisection ethically and believed that only intelligent, morally sound individuals were capable of determining vivisection's future. And while scientific men were proficient in one, she judged them to be deficient in the other.

After Colam's December defeat Cobbe began to realise that Martin's Act was apparently effective only in cases of cruelty to domestic animals in work and sport. It was clear to her that new legislation was needed, which would regulate the behaviour of the scientific community. In consultation with the wife of the senior surgeon of St Bartholomew's Hospital, Mrs Luther Holden, Cobbe decided that the RSPCA, as the most powerful and visible animal welfare organisation, was the best means to introduce such a measure into parliament. She drafted a memorial urging them to undertake the task and to accompany her plea she wrote the first two anti-vivisection pamphlets to appear in London, *Need of a Bill* and *Reasons for Interference*.

As both an animal lover and a supporter of state intervention, Cobbe asked politely and rationally (albeit with some hyperbole) for the RSPCA to check the unacceptable behaviour of vivisectionists before their activity had a chance to 'contaminate' society. Much mid-century legislation operated along similar lines, and attempted to regulate individual and group behaviour for public good. To convince the RSPCA to act Cobbe wrote of vivisection as an 'every-day exercise of hundreds of physiologists and young students of physiology throughout Europe and America,'[42] and suggested that, given the recent demonstration at Norwich, greater cruelties were perpetrated by ignorant students in private laboratories. She recognised the influential role that the RSPCA had played to date in animal welfare, but added that legislation had to be universal in its application; it had to target not only the 'brutal carters and ignorant costermongers' but also the 'learned and refined gentleman [who]...inflicted far more exquisite pain upon still more sensitive creatures'.[43] It was, she concluded, up to the RSPCA and not individuals to deal with animal cruelty in all of its forms, and in particular to stamp out the moral contagion of vivisection.

Cobbe's memorial demanded that the restriction of vivisection was to be promoted by the appointment of a sub-committee within the RSPCA to look into vivisection in England; by the prosecution of as many physiologists suspected of cruelty as possible; by the prosecution of publishers of vivisectional experiments if the guilt of the physiologist was difficult to prove; by the prohibition of all painful experiments except in authorised laboratories by authorised persons whose experiments should be registered; by the prohibition of painful experiments for instruction; and by the extension of the period for a prosecution from one month to six.

The memorial, like Cobbe herself, was not extreme. She did not call for the abolition of vivisection, but for the prohibition of painful experiments. She had tried to keep the memorial's content as conservative as possible for three reasons, all of which suggest she intended to pursue a moderate and solely restrictive policy. First, she understood the RSPCA to be a conservative group and realised that they would be most receptive to a moderate measure.[44] Second, although Cobbe objected to vivisection on ethical grounds, she recognised that scientific supporters were valuable to her memorial; therefore she avoided an indiscriminate attack on science, only targeting those individuals who advocated unrestricted and painful vivisection. It was important not to alienate the scientific community from whom she might be forced to call for support in the future. Third, she herself was not an abolitionist.[45]

Approximately 1,000 signatures appeared on Cobbe's request for restriction. Most 'were exclusively those of persons of some distinction social, political, artistic or literary,'[46] chief amongst whom were Thomas Carlyle, J. A. Froude, John Bright, John Ruskin, who was to resign his own chair at Oxford in 1884 in protest over a vivisection laboratory being established there, and James Martineau who echoed Cobbe's growing fears in his reply to her on 5 January 1875:

> My dear Miss Cobbe,
> I should have been very sorry not to join in the Protest against this hideous offence, and am truly obliged to you for furnishing me with the opportunity. The simultaneous loss from the morals of our 'advanced' Scientific men, of all reverent sentiment toward beings <u>above</u> them and towards beings <u>below</u> them, is a curious and instructive phenomenon, highly significant of the process which their nature is undergoing at both ends.[47]

The Archbishop of Canterbury and Henry Fawcett knew too little on the subject to sign her memorial, while William Gull criticised her for exaggerating the extent to which vivisection was practised in Britain. In Gull's letter one can detect a concern, which was to reverberate throughout the medical community once the vivisection debate developed, that laymen were not qualified to regulate the activities of his profession: 'I am not able to sign the Memorial you forward,' he informed Cobbe. 'The object against which the cry is raised is certainly not the monster you suppose, nor is it animated by the cruel spirit against which the signatees demand state interference'.[48] Cobbe's estimation of Charles Darwin plunged even further when she read his reply to her request for help.

> I would gladly sign the Report (1870) [sic] of the British Assoc. but I could not sign the paper [memorial] which you sent me before: as, judging from other sciences, I believe that Physiology will ultimately lead to incalculable benefits, and it can progress only by experiments on living animals. Any stringent law would stop all progress in this country which I should deeply regret.
>
> I admit in the fullest way that acquiescense [sic] in one form of cruelty is no reason for not earnestly trying to stop another form; but I cannot but be struck by the injustice with which physiologists are spoken of, considering that those who shoot birds for mere pleasure, cause by wounding them manifold more suffering than do the physiologists (besides the indirect suffering of traps); yet the sportsmen are not blamed, while physiologists are spoken of as 'demons let loose from hell'.[49]

Darwin was, perhaps, over sensitive to the invasiveness of Cobbe's petition. Nowhere in the memorial are physiologists referred to as 'demons let loose from hell'; although such phraseology was to be a future trademark of anti-vivisection rhetoric. In 1875 Cobbe was content to stress only the inhumanity, not the demonic character, of individuals who supported vivisection. Yet even at this early date physiologists undoubtedly considered Cobbe and her sympathisers to be hostile; animal-welfare advocates reached a similar conclusion about physiologists. Each faction believed that the other threatened the stability and welfare of society, and because each defined 'progress' differently, one along moral the other along scientific lines, they were beginning to antagonise each other. Battle lines were being drawn.

Cobbe's memorial was presented to the RSPCA with Lord Harrowby in the chair on 25 January 1875 by a deputation headed by her cousin's husband, John Locke, MP. The Committee thanked Cobbe and her supporters for their efforts, and the Baroness Burdett-Coutts, also present, made special mention of the efforts of the women memorialists because of the painfulness and repugnance of the question of vivisection to feminine sensibility. The RSPCA agreed to look into vivisection, and a sub-committee was duly appointed.

The medical community attacked Cobbe's initiative in organising a memorial against vivisection. They accused her, with some justification, of distorting and sensationalising the extent to which vivisection was practised in Britain and perceived her activities as unwelcome interference:

> It does not do to approach the consideration of this subject [vivisection] in a frame of mind excited by pictures of alleged cruelty. Statements are made in the memorial that cannot be justified, and the document is characterised by an exaggerated tone and an objectionable spirit.[50]

Cobbe's conduct was further challenged in *The Times* three days after her memorial was presented, by a 'blustering fellow',[51] Ernest Hart, the editor of the *British Medical Journal*. He questioned allegations she made regarding the extent to which vivisection was used in lectures in America, and by implication possibly in Britain, and he chastised the RSPCA for accepting:

> as fact that which is in part fiction and in part the distorted, swollen and almost unrecognizable shadow of the truth. They have lent their names to a very baseless and a very cruel calumny of the members of a profession whose history is more free from any stain of cruelty or selfishness than perhaps that of any class of men which can be named.[52]

Cobbe had consulted the physician Elizabeth Blackwell on the extent to which vivisection had been adopted by American experimentalists and had been assured that it was used for demonstrating physiological processes to students.[53] Given the reluctance of Americans and Englishmen to embrace a laboratory-based medical education, it was inaccurate for Cobbe to associate the former British colony with the continent. To lend greater credibility to her assertions, Cobbe asked Sarah Wister's physician husband, Owen, to send her some course syllabuses from medical schools in America. 'If Dr Blackwell was wrong I shall be only too glad to withdraw my assertion,' she wrote. 'But Dr Hart is so wretched a creature (he has cheated his creditors shamefully & he's under heavy suspicion of having poisoned his wife intentionally as well as actually) that his denial goes for nothing'.[54] Hart's character was questionable enough for Cobbe to maintain confidence in her convictions and disregard his criticisms of her memorial, despite their being echoed throughout the medical community.

Cobbe returned home to Hereford Square after the deputation optimistic that the RSPCA would confront vivisection with an enthusiasm comparable to that which it displayed towards cruelty in work and sport. A few days later, however, when she was requested to attend the first meeting of the appointed sub-committee, she realised that she had made a grave error in judgment. 'On entering the room my spirits sank,' she wrote,

> for I saw round the table a number of worthy gentlemen, mostly elderly, but not one of the more distinguished members of their committee or (I think) a single Peer or Member of Parliament. In short, they were not the men to take the lead in such a movement and make a bold stand against the claims of science. After a few minutes the chairman himself asked me: 'Whether I could not undertake to get a bill into Parliament for the object we desired?' As if all my labor with the memorial had not been spent to make them do this very thing! It was obviously felt by others present that this suggestion was out of place, and I soon retired, leaving the sub-committee to send Mr Colam round to make enquiries among the physiologists, a mission which might, perhaps, be represented as a friendly request to be told frankly 'whether they were really cruel'. I understood, later, that he was shown a painless vivisection on a cat and offered a glass of sherry; and there (so far as I know or ever heard) the labours of that sub-committee ended.[55]

Colam did more than Cobbe implied. He came under attack on requesting attendance at medical school lectures in February 1875 in order to gauge the prevalence of vivisection in Britain. The *British Medical Journal* took offence and interpreted his request as unwillingness to trust doctors and physiologists to follow the 1870 guidelines and to report, truthfully, to the RSPCA the content of vivisectional lectures.[56]

Cobbe's hope that the RSPCA would confront vivisection all but disappeared. She had tailored her memorial to the cautious nature of the Society and was disappointed to discover exactly how cautious they were. They were too moderate, too slow, too ineffectual, too unco-operative to save animals from man and man from himself.

It is unfair to suggest, as Andrew Ryan does, that at this time 'Miss Cobbe was clever, unscrupulous and in a hurry'[57] and could not wait for the RSPCA to act on the memorial. Nor is it entirely correct to conclude that the RSPCA's 'safety-first policy antagonized the zealots'.[58] Cobbe had yet to become zealous about anti-vivisection; in 1875 she was impatient rather than antagonised by the RSPCA's inactivity and she was not the only individual with anti-vivisectionist sympathies to feel this way. Others were also beginning to question the ability of the RSPCA to confront adequately the pace at which vivisection was progressing. The editor of the *Spectator*, R.H. Hutton, whom Darwin later referred to as 'a kind of female Miss Cobbe',[59] commented: 'we cannot help but foresee that if they [RSPCA] do not show a little more courage and a little more zeal, some other Society will grow up in their place which, by boldly doing the work from which they shrink, will succeed to their popularity and influence.'[60]

The RSPCA was not eclipsed by any other animal welfare society, although Hutton was correct to suggest that a new organisation would openly confront the issue from which the Society shrank. Little did he, or anyone else, realise how controversial and verbally violent the confrontation between science and morality would become through their 'boldly doing the work'. Little did Cobbe herself realise that in only a few months time she would be the rallying point for the cause which was to radically alter her life, occasionally for the better, more often for the worse.

5

FROM RESTRICTION TO ABOLITION AND BEYOND

Once Cobbe accepted that the RSPCA would not act on her memorial with the enthusiasm she had expected, she decided a society was needed specifically designed to confront vivisection; a society that would not be distracted by working-class cruelty and would not, as the RSPCA did, accept that science would voluntarily regulate its behaviour. Cobbe had identified a need but she hesitated to take the responsibility for meeting it, preferring instead to continue writing on behalf of animals. It took the rather frustrating experience of the 1875 Royal Commission on Vivisection, coupled with encouragement from friends, to convince her that if she did not act, then nobody would: animals would continue to suffer and science would continue to 'assault' the natural world.

A few days after her deputation to the RSPCA, Cobbe read a letter in the *Morning Post* from Dr George Hoggan, who joined the growing debate on vivisection with his own experience as an assistant in Claude Bernard's Parisian laboratory. Many of Hoggan's colleagues had worked on the continent, men such as John Burdon Sanderson; however, Hoggan shrank from physiology and the pain it so often produced. French physiologists, he recollected, had

> sacrificed daily from one to three dogs, besides rabbits and other animals, and after four months' experience I am of opinion that not one of those experiments on animals was justified or necessary. The idea of the good of humanity was simply out of the question, and would be laughed at, the great aim being to keep up with, or get ahead of, one's contemporaries in science, even at the price of an incalculable amount of torture needlessly and iniquitously inflicted on the poor animals.[1]

As for anaesthetic use Hoggan commented, 'I am inclined to look upon anaesthetics as the greatest curse to vivisectible animals. They alter too much the normal conditions of life to give accurate results, and they are therefore little depended on. They indeed prove far more efficacious in lulling public feeling towards the vivisector than pain in the vivisected'.[2] Curare, which served to immobilise the animal but left it sensitive to pain, was often the drug of choice. Hoggan described events in France but, given her negative view of *all* physiologists, Cobbe did not doubt that the same was happening to England's canine 'friend of man' in the dark recesses of laboratories operated by Burdon Sanderson and his colleagues.

It was the image of severe and unnecessary pain that motivated Cobbe to act, and she began to consult with Hoggan as to how anti-vivisection sentiment could be brought to bear on vivisection and vivisectors. Six days after Hoggan's testimony had been published, Cobbe told her Philadelphia friend Sarah Wister that, following her January memorial to the RSPCA: 'our feeble effort to combat that abominable crime of vivisection seems just to have fallen like a spark on a train of public indignation—& the response we have received has been quite wonderful,' but she added in light of Hoggan's testimony that 'the real battle is to come & God knows how long the war may last, but something will be done if we merely make these wretches feel the might of public opprobrium which their cruelties deserve'.[3]

One man had already taken the initiative. George Jesse of Cheshire, 'a retired civil engineer of prodigious idiosyncracy'[4] had founded in February 1875 the Society for the Abolition of Vivisection, an event that Cobbe acknowledged in her autobiography, but on which she did not dwell. It does not appear that either Hoggan or Cobbe sought to co-ordinate their efforts with the maverick Jesse in the months following the Society's foundation. Jesse wanted abolition, while Hoggan and Cobbe favoured restriction. Instead, Hoggan convinced Cobbe to abandon traditional methods of protesting in memorials, petitions and irate letters to newspapers in favour of direct legislative activity. With the help of some politically powerful acquaintances including Sir William Hart Dyke, the Conservative whip and Robert Lowe, MP for London University, Cobbe drew up a bill to regulate vivisection. It was presented by Lord Henniker in the House of Lords on 4 May 1875.[5]

Henniker's bill defined vivisection as 'the cutting or wounding or treating with galvanism or other appliances, any living vertebrate animal for purposes of physiological research or demonstration, also the artificial production in any living vertebrate animal of painful disease for purposes of physiological research or demonstration'.[6] It recommended that vivisection be confined to laboratories registered annually with the Home Secretary and liable to inspection. Anaesthetics were to be used, although experiments which required the animal to remain conscious were allowed provided that the physiologist obtained a licence granted by the Home Secretary at a cost of £10. Curare was deemed not to be an anaesthetic. Penalties under this measure were not to exceed £20.

Eight days after the anti-vivisectionists' bill had been introduced into parliament, the medical community drew up one of their own, encouraged by Charles Darwin and T. H. Huxley. Lyon Playfair, chemist and Liberal MP for the University of Edinburgh, introduced the physiologists' bill into the House of Commons, and convinced Lord Cardwell to do the same in the House of Lords.

The Playfair bill focused on the regulation of painful experiments, which were to be legalised and would not be subject to prosecution under Martin's Act. Physiologists could apply to the Home Secretary for a five-year licence to perform potentially painful experiments after obtaining the consent of one of the scientific bodies and of a professor of physiology, medicine or anatomy. Experiments which did not anaesthetise the animal were permissible for the purpose of new scientific discovery when anaesthetics would distort physiological observation and when suffering could be kept to a minimum. Physiologists were required to keep a record of all experiments performed. Penalties under the bill were not to exceed £50 or three months in jail.[7]

On 22 May the *Lancet* compared the two bills and its conclusion reflected the medical community's perception not only of its professional competence and clear headedness, but of the anti-vivisectionists' incompetence and narrow mindedness. Henniker's bill was criticised for being 'a very illogical and objectionable measure: illogical from whichever end it is regarded, and objectionable in every way'.[8] The Playfair bill was judged 'a much more carefully prepared bill than the other' and as 'far as can be gathered by a somewhat hurried perusal of this document, it appears to us to be a fair, just, and well-considered measure, and incomparably superior to another Bill [Henniker's] in the Lords'.[9] But not everyone in the medical community agreed with Playfair's recommendations. Huxley, who had initially encouraged Playfair to legislate in science's favour, disliked the invasive nature of the bill.[10]

Despite the more punitive measures in Playfair's bill, Cobbe dismissed it along with the 1871 British Association guidelines: it was 'a "pious opinion" or *Brutum fulmen*. Nothing more'.[11] Whereas Huxley found the measure too restrictive, Cobbe criticised it for its leniency. Painless investigation in licensed premises was not regulated nor were anaesthetics made mandatory. Control over the administration of chloroform or ether was in the hands of the individual physiologist, who was only required to give his word that he did not inflict unnecessary pain. How could a physiologist, Cobbe asked herself, be trusted to provide an accurate and truthful account of anaesthetic use when motivated by animal instinct to struggle and be competitive?

The simultaneous presentation of both bills in Parliament in May 1875 increased press coverage of experimental physiology, and a number of medical journals and editorials called for a government inquiry into vivisection. Members of the medical community had requested a Commission as early as the presentation of Cobbe's memorial in January, and in February the *Lancet* had demanded a reasonable investigation by reasonable people, 'to see whether these questions [of necessary and unnecessary vivisection] could not be determined after being quietly and calmly discussed by a commission, [rather] than to have them tossed about by a prejudiced passionate people after the present fashion.'[12] The Home Secretary, Richard Cross, announced a Royal Commission on 24 May, which pro-vivisectionists welcomed with relief: 'the Commission is to be issued,' Huxley wrote to Darwin on 5 June, 'and it is everything to gain time and let the present madness subside a little'.[13]

The Commission commenced on 5 July and consisted of four politicians from different sides, Viscount Cardwell (Chairman), W. E. Forster, Lord Winmarleigh and Sir John Burgess Karslake; two pro-vivisectionists, Huxley, who 'vowed I would never be a member of another Commission if I could help it, but I suppose I shall have to serve on this,'[14] and John Eric Erichsen; and one anti-vivisectionist, Cobbe's friend, R.H. Hutton. Cobbe was frustrated with the presence of

Erichsen and Huxley who 'acted,' she believed, 'not as judges on the bench examining evidence dispassionately, but as exceedingly vigorous and keen-eyed counsel for the physiologists'.[15] When the Commission had first been announced, Cobbe and Hoggan had been optimistic that it would recommend legislation favourable to anti-vivisection sentiments; as the months passed it became more and more unlikely that their hopes would translate into reality.

In their attempt to come to terms with an unfamiliar subject, the Royal Commission asked 6,551 questions of 53 witnesses who ranged from the RSPCA's John Colam to Cambridge's resident vivisector, Michael Foster, and included the distinguished physician William Gull, George Hoggan, Joseph Lister, Sir James Paget and John Simon, who was Medical Officer of the Privy Council and Local Government Board. Cobbe was not present nor did she offer any testimony, and as Richard French puts it, the 'connoisseur of antivivisectionist elan must always regret that history was deprived of a rotund, forceful, and articulate Frances Power Cobbe lecturing the eminent commissioners on the evils of scientific experimentation on living animals'.[16] It was hardly surprising, given the composition of the Commission, that there was some difficulty reaching a unanimous decision about vivisection in Britain. Journals that carried reports of the proceedings, such as the *Saturday Review*, the *Lancet* and *Nature*, stressed that attitudes towards pain and vivisection differed measurably at home and abroad. England was deemed to be a far more compassionate country than Germany or France when it came to the treatment animals received in scientific exploration; and the comparison between the civilised Briton and the uncivilised foreigner was voiced many times both within and without the proceedings.[17]

The inquiry was brought to a close with the submission of the Commission's report on 8 February 1876. Its findings were a combination of anthropocentrism and a recognition, by at least some of the participants, that domestic animals, with whom men and women shared a close, affectionate relationship, should not be vivisected. Due consideration was given by the Commission to the animals that were experimented upon, but mention was also made of the contributions that science had made to the quality of life. The discoveries of the circulation of the blood and of cow-pox vaccine were cited as two examples of scientific progress that had revolutionised medicine. It was agreed that painless vivisection in demonstration was highly beneficial to a medical education. Recommendations supported the regulation of vivisection, but not its prohibition because a complete curtailment of experimental freedom would only motivate physiologists to leave Britain and carry on their researches elsewhere where vivisection was not under legislative control. Live animals used in veterinary curricula were to be included in any future legislation defining the uses and abuses of vivisection. Anaesthetics should be used and pain avoided. Domestic creatures were offered added protection by R. H. Hutton's proposal that dogs and cats be exempt from the vivisector's knife. Lesser mammals and reptiles, which did not share so intense and quasi-human a relationship with man and were considered less sensitive to pain, were not so favoured, although it was suggested that the often-used frog be given some protection.

The purpose of the Royal Commission was not to aggravate either pro- or anti-vivisectionists, but to strike a balance between the two, which the *BMJ* correctly believed would not happen.[18] The Commission's report was somewhat of an anti-climax for both sides, neither of which spoke out passionately about the results.

It was during the Commission's proceedings that Hoggan began pressurising Cobbe to set up an anti-vivisection society. Cobbe was well aware of the need to neutralise the physiologists' influence and yet she resisted Hoggan's entreaties. Her experience with women's suffrage convinced her that she was suited neither to the role of leader nor follower in a formally constituted organisation, yet she also recognised that pro-vivisectionists were presenting a united front and could be successfully countered only by opposition similarly well organised.

By November 1875, after a great deal of vacillation, Cobbe agreed to assist in the founding of a restrictionist anti-vivisection society, named by Hoggan as the Society for the Protection of Animals Liable to Vivisection (SPALV), with herself and Hoggan as joint honorary secretaries. The two made ideal colleagues. Hoggan's amiable and flexible nature was the perfect foil for Cobbe's stubbornness which was the driving force of the Society.

Cobbe filled the SPALV with eminent men in the most prominent positions, not because she believed women to be incapable of running an organisation, but because they lacked the political clout upon which legislative success depended. She especially wanted to enlist Lord

Shaftesbury, 'the greatest social reformer of the Humanitarian century'.[19] Her initial plea for his presence on the Committee in mid-November was replied to with a wearied apology that he was 'already overlaid with business'.[20] Cobbe was not used to taking no for an answer and with a missionary zeal that equalled Shaftesbury's own, she eventually wore him down. On 18 February 1876 Shaftesbury took the chair at the SPALV's third meeting, and eventually became the Society's president. Until his death in 1885, Shaftesbury and Cobbe worked feverishly together on behalf of the suffering brutes.

The vice-presidents, like the president, were hand picked by Cobbe for their social and political prominence combined with their high moral standing. The Archbishop of York, the Marquis of Bute, Cardinal Manning, Lord Chief Justice Coleridge and the Lord Chief Baron, Sir Fitzroy Kelly, helped create the august quality Cobbe wanted to define her organisation. The executive was also a mixture of men and women which included Cobbe's companion Mary Lloyd.

The SPALV was soon joined by a number of anti-vivisection societies in England and Scotland, two of the most prominent being the abolitionist London Anti-Vivisection Society and the International Association for the Total Suppression of Vivisection. At this time the movement also started its own publication, the *Home Chronicler*, edited by A.P. Childs who ensured that both restrictionists and abolitionists would have equal representation in the journal's columns.

The SPALV moved into offices at 20 Victoria Street in the first week of March and remained there for twenty-three years. The office's location gave Cobbe the opportunity to rename SPALV the Victoria Street Society (VSS) by which name the organisation was known until 1898 when it was changed to the National Anti-Vivisection Society. The offices were situated on the first floor of a large house near the Broad Sanctuary and the Westminster Palace Hotel. Cobbe even made the Victoria Street's work more palatable to outsiders by her choice of interior design: 'bookshelves, pictures, curtains, and various little feminine relaxations...cover[ed], as far as might be, the frightful character of our work, so that friends should find our office no painful place to visit'.[21] Yet Cobbe did not want the anti-vivisection message to disappear behind lady-like adornments. Visitors were assaulted by publications and pictures that showed, in graphic detail, the evils of vivisection. Fanny

Kemble visited the VSS offices two years after their opening and remembered them as a place with a seemingly endless number of tables, 'strewed with pictorial appeals to the national humanity'.[22] Cobbe was to spend the next eight years here surrounded by energetic workers, producing a stream of 'appeals to humanity', in an office that looked out towards Westminster Abbey and the Houses of Parliament.

On 20 March 1876 Cobbe dispatched an all-male legation headed by Shaftesbury to the Home Office. Their mission was to convince the Home Secretary, Richard Cross, to bring in a bill based on the Commission's recommendations. Cross, a barrister and banker who, before the Conservative victory in 1874 had never held a government post, received the Victoria Street deputation. Aware of his Parliamentary inexperience and ignorance of vivisection, Cross handed responsibility for the proposed bill's contents back to the anti-vivisectionists. It did not take the VSS long to return to Cross the required material. The Society recommended that no experiment should be performed on any animal except when completely anaesthetised, and that no certificates should be granted for exemption from the rule.

However, Cobbe's hope that the government would act on the proposals submitted by the VSS and the Royal Commission was soon dashed. Disraeli only moved on the issue when prodded to do so by the Queen.[23] The country was preoccupied with revolts in the Balkans, 'The Bulgarian Horrors and the Question of the East,' as Gladstone phrased it in a pamphlet published in the autumn of 1876, and this concern overshadowed the Royal Commission's proposals. The only member of Disraeli's cabinet who showed any interest in experimental science was the Colonial Secretary, Lord Carnarvon, himself an anti-vivisectionist. It was to him that the task of drawing up a bill regulating vivisection was given, and even he was ambivalent about his responsibility:

> On the one hand there is the danger of going too far; on the other, the danger of not going far enough: on the one side there is the strong sentiment of humanity; on the other, there are the claims of modern science. It is a sea strewn with rocks, and it is not easy to steer safely through them.[24]

Carnarvon's bill, which he introduced in the House of Lords on 15

May, was drawn from careful study of both the Royal Commission's and the Victoria Street's recommendations. It allowed vivisection for new scientific discovery if the physiologist's specific aim was to benefit mankind. Painful experiments were acceptable only if they were certified by scientific or medical bodies and, following Hutton's advice, dogs and cats were exempt from vivisection.

The Victoria Street membership was divided on the bill. Shaftesbury did not believe it went far enough: 'the step was very narrow between the vivisection of the animal and the vivisection of the human being', he ominously warned.[25] He wanted total abolition, an option that he knew was as impractical to suggest as it would be to implement. Restrictionist anti-vivisectionists like Cobbe were optimistic about the bill's future, while abolitionists outside the VSS, like George Jesse, believed the measure favoured vivisectors. The RSPCA, whose interest in vivisection continued to be lukewarm, but who had been represented at the Royal Commission, were pleased with the results of Carnarvon's efforts to be fair and reasonable to both sentiment and science.

The medical community judged the bill differently and found it severely wanting. Parliament was dealing 'with a subject,' wrote *Nature*, 'of which almost all its members are profoundly ignorant'.[26] These unqualified individuals were drawing up legislation that appeased the demands of a minority and challenged the autonomy of experimentalists to regulate themselves. They were particularly opposed to clause 3 which allowed vivisection only if performed with the aim of prolonging human life, and clause 5 which exempted dogs and cats from experimentation. Physiological processes in canines and felines were similar to those in man, and without access to these creatures it would be extremely difficult for vivisectors to experiment to prolong human life, which was the main justification for vivisection as outlined by Carnarvon.

It was because dogs were so like man that Cobbe supported clause 5, and she did not hesitate to defend it in light of mounting criticism. In a letter to the *Daily Telegraph* on 24 June she emphasised that experimentalists were incapable of recognising the intrinsic quasi-human qualities that dogs possessed. Man, she noted, was not allowed to torture his fellow men because they were more than eating and digesting machines; they had intelligence and feeling and were capable of self sacrifice and generous and noble action. 'And can it be denied,' she pleaded, that in its humbler, narrower sphere the dog has such gifts also, and is capable of similar acts, and thereby is raised many steps above mere senseless matter? The clause in the new bill which exempts this—half-reasoning, wholly loving—animal from liability to torture is founded not only on the bare humanity which would give immunity from pain to the creatures which feel pain most acutely, but on a profound principle in the natural order of things.[27]

This was a principle that anti-vivisectionists believed their foes were unable to accept, and it had to be forced upon them by way of legislation that controlled their behaviour.

Physiologists did not want their autonomy taken away from them, and opposed scientifically 'ignorant' individuals setting guidelines for professional conduct. Although 'we would by all means subject him [the scientist] to control by those who have the requisite knowledge to exercise it,' the *Lancet* wrote, 'we would at the same time protect him as strongly as possible against meddlesome interference on the part of amateurs who might take action on foolish if not unworthy grounds'.[28] Letters began to appear in medical journals which urged all pro-vivisectionists to band together in defence of anti-vivisection assaults: 'I think it possible that medical men may feel reluctant in placing themselves in opposition to those who are raising the cry of humanity,' Samuel Wilks wrote in the *British Medical Journal*, 'but if one can judge from what one personally hears, the greatest indignation exists in our profession that a few physiologists...should be selected as a class for restrictive legislative measures. All feel with me that it is an insult to science and to our profession'.[29] Even *Punch* came out on the side of the physiologists satirically suggesting that they had been singled out for persecution by a society that freely sanctioned diverse forms of non-scientific animal cruelty ranging from angling to hunting, shooting and even lobster eating.[30]

Carnarvon's bill was brought from the Lords to the Commons on 27 June; it passed its first reading only to be deferred on numerous occasions throughout the summer. Deferrals were accompanied by a constant barrage of petitions from both pro- and anti-vivisectionists. By early August, the House of Commons had received 805 petitions with 146,889 signatures supporting the complete abolition of vivisection. On 10 July Ernest Hart, editor of the *British Medical Journal*, led a deputation to the

Whitehall chambers of Richard Cross with a 3,000-signature memorial from the British Medical Association requesting that the proposed measure be radically modified in favour of the physiologists. Influential newspapers such as *The Times* and the *Standard* that had previously been impartial began to express greater sympathy for science. On 9 August, Richard Cross introduced a revised bill with major concessions made to experimental science. Private places, not just laboratories, would be allowed to conduct experimental research; a special certificate would be necessary only when working without anaesthesia; prosecution of licensees could be undertaken only with the permission of the Home Secretary. The bill would apply to warm-blooded animals, and clauses 3 and 5, which had been the focus of much criticism, were removed. The medical community hailed their disappearance as a victory, while anti-vivisectionists shrieked that the government had turned its back on humanity by ensuring that 'man's best friend' would become the physiologist's victim.

In August as Carnarvon's altered bill was going through its final stages of debate Cobbe decided to leave London. Rather than watch an insipid bill become law, she sought refuge with Mary Lloyd by her side at Dolgelly on the west coast of Wales. On 13 August Cobbe wrote a depressed, but defiant, letter to the *Daily News* in which she made plain her impressions of Carnarvon's efforts and what she believed would be her future role in the anti-vivisection movement. 'Sir,' she began politely,

> I hope that none of your readers will imagine that the Cruelty to Animals Bill, read for a third time on Saturday, is either such a measure as the advocates of restriction of vivisection have proposed, or such as they will accept as a settlement of the question. We asked for an Act to protect animals from vivisection. The Home Secretary has given us an Act to protect vivisectors from prosecution...For myself and the many personal friends who feel with me, I can only say that we shall work for the future, not to obtain any legislative compromise (which the experience of this year has proved to be hopeless), but to arouse by every lawful means in our power the heart and conscience of the nation to revolt against the whole practice of vivisection, and to the condemnation of all concerned in its support.[31]

The Lords agreed to all amendments on 14 August and the next day the bill received royal assent and became An Act to Amend the Law Relating to Cruelty to Animals, commonly referred to as the Vivisection Act or the Cruelty to Animals Act.

The Act made it mandatory for any individual who wished to perform experiments to submit an application, endorsed by a president of one of the eleven leading scientific or medical bodies (for example, the Royal College of Surgeons) and a professor of medicine, to the Home Secretary. The location for the experiment had to be registered with the Home Secretary and licences were valid for one year, after which time they could be renewed. Experiments could be performed for the purpose of new scientific discovery or with the aim of prolonging human life and mitigating human suffering, but not for acquiring or practising manual dexterity. Experiments for demonstration or those without anaesthesia were possible only when certified by a medical body. Certificates were required for work on unanaesthetised animals, and would only be granted if it could be shown that the results of the experiment would be skewed by the use of an anaesthetic. The Act made it clear that curare was not acceptable as an anaesthetic. The Home Secretary was free to require written reports of all experiments performed, and periodically appoint inspectors to verify the information physiologists provided. Violations of the Act carried a £50 penalty for the initial offence, £100 or three months imprisonment for subsequent offences.

Neither anti- nor pro-vivisectionists were particularly impressed with the result of Cross's endeavours. In its altered form the measure was, according to the *Spectator*, a 'severely vivisected, and we might almost say, disembowelled, Vivisection Bill'.[32] Physiologists suggested that it was they who had been disembowelled and they were unimpressed with the restrictions placed on their profession while hunting escaped government control.[33] But at least clauses 3 and 5, which had been responsible for much of their anger, had been removed. *Nature* noted that the act went far beyond the Royal Commission, while the *British Medical Journal* expressed satisfaction that it would at least prevent another Norwich incident; it was also suggested that because the Act was now law, 'inconvenient as it may be, it yet behooves [sic] all physiologists and experimentalists implicitly to obey its enactments'.[34] The *Saturday Review* concurred, and advised the medical community to work with the Act else 'it is certain to have the effect of exasperating and inflaming the minds of an extreme party, whose hold on popular feeling is strong, and whose influence the doctors can scarcely desire to increase'.[35] Physiologists did not want to encourage anti-vivisection sentiment, but they were concerned that the Act would jeopardise their professional autonomy and scientific research and progress. To guard against such a possibility, the Physiological Society of Great Britain, formed in March 1876 by John Burdon Sanderson and Michael Foster, decided to closely monitor the administration of the Act.

The Move Towards Abolition

While physiologists presented themselves as a united front, their opponents began to quarrel. The Cruelty to Animals Act was a big disappointment for many, especially abolitionists, a large number of whom began to question the role that the VSS had played in the passage of legislation that sanctioned vivisection. George Jesse's society had never figured in the debate and the other two abolition societies —the London and the International—had been formed too late to take an active role. The Victoria Street Society had been the one organisation involved in the bill's passage and it was now the focus of RSPCA and abolitionist criticism. To offset this adverse publicity Cobbe began to consider the merits of prohibition.

It is unclear whether Cobbe had made a conscious decision at this time to switch her allegiance from restriction to abolition. She was dissatissfied with the 1876 Act, and yet was disinclined publicly to adopt a more extreme stance. In October 1876 she sent the VSS Committee an ultimatum: she would retain the office of honorary secretary only if the Society adopted the principle of total abolition. She had issued successful ultimatums before, during her religious struggle with her father, for example, and she expected that this one would force the VSS into accepting a more radical policy. A circular was sent out, a vote taken, and by 22 November it was agreed that 'the society would watch the existing act with a view to the enforcement of its restrictions and its extension to the total prohibition of painful experiments on animals'.[36] This fell short of Cobbe's original demand, but she accepted it nonetheless, which suggests that she had not yet sincerely committed herself to abolition. On 2 December she published her acceptance of the Committee's resolution in the *Home Chronicler* and wished the abolitionists well; one week later this was followed by her cordial undertaking that she would 'henceforth cheerfully work with my kind and judicious friends and associates on that platform [suppression of painful experiments]'.[37]

Wary of the VSS's policy, the International Association drew up legislation abolishing vivisection. J.M. Holt introduced the measure in January 1877 and in February the VSS endorsed the proposal. On 2 May the bill was debated in the House of Commons where it suffered an overwhelming defeat; 83 members voted in favour of the measure, 222 against. Disraeli's government had passed a vivisection bill in the previous session and had no intention of returning to debate on the subject.

The VSS was not distraught over the bill's defeat. Shaftesbury, who by merit of his reputation had a great deal of influence over the VSS and its members, wrote to Cobbe a few months later telling her that it would be injurious to the anti-vivisection cause to press abolition on an indifferent government. He advised that a cautious approach, namely restriction, was far more likely to yield results than radical demands that might alienate people. His views were shared by other VSS members including Dr Hoggan and the Archbishop of York, who ensured that the Society would respond to the political tenor of the country and not be derailed from its moderate course.

Cobbe was determined to expose as many people to vivisection as quickly as possible and in the spring of 1877 she launched a high-impact and visual anti-vivisection campaign, unlike anything seen before. The International Association followed a similar course of action, and although both it and the VSS were equally involved in distributing placards, the activity was associated with Cobbe.

In the spring of 1877, 1,700 handbills and 300 posters taken from illustrations in physiological handbooks were exhibited on the hoardings of London streets, and their impact on the everyday lives of Londoners had the desired effect. Almost immediately the *Home Chronicler* reprinted letters from people who both supported and opposed them. 'These horrible engravings are arousing public intelligence,' Caroline Giffard Phillipson wrote. 'Let us have more of them, and defy false delicacy'.[38] George Jesse, the honorary secretary of the Society for the Abolition of

Vivisection, wrote letters to the *Morning Post*, *The Times* and Charles Darwin disassociating himself from both Cobbe and her placards. 'And I suppose, therefore,' Darwin wrote to the pro-vivisectionist George J. Romanes, 'that these all originate with Miss Cobbe.'[39] The medical press considered exploitation of their material by anti-vivisectionists revolting: 'this Society [VSS] is at the present moment posting the streets of London with pictorial illustrations and with placards of a kind of which it is hard to suppose that any reasonable person can do other than regard them with the most extreme disapproval and disgust.'[40]

But criticism of Cobbe's decision to distribute the illustrations was particularly virulent in the lay press. On 12 May the *Home Chronicler*, while endorsing the pictures, reprinted a number of complaints that had appeared in the *Globe*. Cobbe defended her actions in a letter to the *Globe* the following day, yet on the whole, press reaction was mixed. Even the *Saturday Review*, often supportive of the anti-vivisectionists, was, in this instance, critical. A few years later the *Zoophilist* remembered Cobbe's campaign with admiration—'no step ever adopted by the Society had been more efficacious than this exhibition, or had caused more durable smart on the side of the physiologists.'[41]

For the remaining months of 1877 and up to the spring of 1878 Cobbe was occupied by her campaign to stop wife abuse, which she found similar to the scientific torture of animals: victimisation of the weak by the strong endorsed by law. But she found that anti-vivisection was beginning to place greater demands on her time. There was VSS business to attend to, information about vivisection to sift through, pamphlets to draft and meetings to address. Cobbe was a popular speaker and her presentations were usually opened and concluded by enthusiastic cheers from her audience. She also attended anti-vivisection bazaars and at one Brighton event in 1878 a 'painting on plaque, illustrating a well-known fable, sent by Miss Cobb [sic], excited much admiration'.[42] She also continued to attend lectures at the Royal Institution, an activity she had enjoyed for a number of years. Her absence from a lecture given by Huxley was noted by her friend James Martineau, who seemed disappointed that she was not present to disrupt Huxley's talk on William Harvey and his 'claptrap about Vivisection, and the persecution of scientific men in the present age.'[43]

Despite Cobbe's growing reputation as a passionate anti-vivisectionist, criticism of the VSS continued throughout 1877–8. In the view of the *Home Chronicler*'s editor, A. P. Childs, the VSS endorsed abolition in order to draw attention away from the London Society and the International Association not to save animals from experimentation. 'How much support, we should like to know, has the Victoria Street Society (PALV!) received, under a total misapprehension as to its 'objects', on the part of its supporters?' Childs boomed.[44] In the new year, Shaftesbury wrote to Cobbe telling her that he was receiving numerous sarcastic letters accusing the VSS of harming 'a great cause' because of its contradictory stance.[45] One letter the *Home Chronicler* printed on 19 January 1878 from a G. F. Goddard attacked the VSS as being more of a danger to the well-being of animals than to the practices of vivisectors.[46]

Widespread public criticism eventually convinced the Committee to clarify its position. At one meeting on 7 August, resolutions pledging the VSS to prohibition were proposed by Cobbe and Shaftesbury. They were seconded by General Mackenzie, and carried. The VSS formally accepted abolition. The decision, Cobbe later admitted, had been motivated by anthropocentrism and not by anxiety about animal welfare.[47] The *Home Chronicler* was pleased to note the VSS's decision to change its official title to the Society for the Protection of Animals *From* Vivisection. A number of new recruits soon arrived at Victoria Street, such as F. O. Morris who had refused Cobbe's request to join in the previous year because he believed her organisation had advocated only 'half measures'. However, because of the Society's more extreme stance some original restrictionist members withdrew including Dr Hoggan and his wife Frances, Mr de Fonblanque, the Archbishop of York and G. S. Bowyear.

In the summer of 1879 the introduction of an abolition bill by Lord Truro coincided with a proposal made by a group of leading physiologists, including James Paget, John Burdon Sanderson, George Yeo, Ernest Hart and Michael Foster, that a statue be erected honouring the pioneering work of the French vivisector, Claude Bernard who had conducted innovative research into the liver and pancreatic secretions. Truro's bill had its second reading on 15 July and it was supported by a number of petitions from anti-vivisection groups in England and Scotland. Cobbe was present in the Lords when Shaftesbury spoke for the measure and when the Bishop of Peterborough and Lord Aberdare, president of the RSPCA, spoke against it. The bill was defeated: 16 members voted for it, 97 (including Carnarvon) voted against it. On 16 March 1880, three years after its introduction, Holt's bill came down for a second reading in the House of Commons, but was stopped when an election was called, and Gladstone launched a successful campaign that saw the return of the Liberals the following month. The VSS drew up yet another anti-vivisection memorial in June and on 20 July dispatched it to parliament as Gladstone's second ministry began. It was signed by one hundred peers, bishops, MPs, authors, heads of colleges and officers of the army and navy. It rejected vivisection on utilitarian grounds and labelled the practice a moral crime.

The memorial received a lukewarm response and despite the best efforts of Shaftesbury, Gladstone refused to become involved in vivisection. Gladstone saw his mission was to pacify Ireland, not animal lovers. The VSS took the initiative and drew up their own prohibition bill with the help of Lord Chief Justice Coleridge and Sir J. E. Eardley Wilmot, MP, who had been appointed by Cobbe and committee members as parliamentary leader for the anti-vivisection movement. The bill was read in the Commons on 3 February 1881. R.T. Reid took charge of the bill in October but it never reached second reading.

Amidst the introduction and defeat of prohibition legislation the VSS decided to establish its own publication rather than relying on Childs's *Home Chronicler*. In May 1881 the *Zoophilist* was established with a £1350 bequest from Madame Van Manen-Thesingh. Charles Warren Adams, the Society's secretary, became editor of the weekly journal which provided its readers with information about the 1876 Act, vivisections at home and abroad and notice of VSS publications. Meanwhile the debate between physiologists and anti-vivisectionists intensified as leading physiologists, such as the surgeon James Paget, the paleontologist Richard Owen and the physician Samuel Wilks (whom Shaftesbury referred to as Butchers, Tartuffes and 'The Three Sons of Moloch')[48] denounced their opponents as meat-eating, hunting enthusiasts, 'well-meaning but ill-informed fanatics and paid agitators'.[49]

In October 1879 the VSS published a twenty-page pamphlet that Cobbe had been working on during the summer when she and Shaftesbury had been discussing Truro's abolition bill and the proposed statue of Claude Bernard. She agreed to support the bill, leaving responsibility for it in Shaftesbury's hands while she produced a condemnation of Bernard and those who proposed to honour his work. She called her treatise *Bernard's Martyrs*.

This pamphlet exposed in graphic detail the plight of animals confined to Bernard's 'torture chambers' and commented on his recent physiological treatise, *Leçons de Physiologie Opératoire*. Cobbe began by condemning her countrymen's decision to honour their French colleague and held him up as a model for a 'New Vice', a vice bred from a disregard for pain and suffering. It was not like other vices that were 'hot and thoughtless'. The man who succumbed to the vivisecting spirit was:

> calm, cool, deliberate, perfectly cognizant of what he is doing; understanding, as indeed no other man understands, the full meaning and extent of the waves and spasms of agony he deliberately inflicts. [The vice] does not possess the ignorant or hunger-driven or brutalized classes; but the cultivated, the well fed, the well dressed, the civilized, and (it is said) the otherwise kindly disposed and genial men of science forming part of the most intellectual circles in Europe. Sometimes it would appear, as we read of these horrors—the bakings alive of dogs, the slow dissections out of quivering nerves, and so on, that it would be a relief to picture the doer of such deeds as some unhappy half-witted wretch, hideous and filthy in mien or brutalized by drink, so that the full responsibility of a rational and educated human being should not belong to him, and that we might say of him, 'He scarcely understands what he does'. But, alas! this New Vice has no such palliations and possesses not such unhappy outcasts, but some of the very foremost men of our time; men who would think scornfully of being asked to share the butcher's honest trade; men addicted to high speculation on all the mysteries of the universe; men who hope to found the Religion of the Future, and to leave the impress of their minds upon their age, and upon generations yet to be born.[50]

Cobbe used as illustrations of the 'New Vice' examples of Bernard's work. Domestic creatures, she emphasised, were chosen because of their heightened sensitivity, but were treated with unnecessary roughness; many were manually half-asphyxiated in order to facilitate their preparation for experimentation that was often endured without anaesthesia.

In order for her readers to understand fully the pain Bernard caused Cobbe included copies of woodcuts taken from Bernard's book, 'inserted even at the risk of making this paper too horrible for lay readers'.[51] But that horror had to be communicated to those outside the scientific clique. Catheterisation of the blood-vessels and experiments upon the pancreatic secretions, the latter which required the animal to be unanaesthetised, were reprinted by Cobbe from *Leçons* in detail; she described muscles being drawn apart by forceps, incisions made and tubes inserted. She made special reference to Bernard's comment that the pancreatic secretions differed in man and beast, which allowed her to question the purpose of his experiments. Obviously, she concluded, they were performed out of curiosity because the pancreatic secretions of canines added nothing to Bernard's knowledge of those of humans. If he seriously intended to contribute to the understanding of human physiology Cobbe believed that he would use anatomical dissection and clinical observation and not needlessly torture and destroy dogs, those creatures which anti-vivisectionists considered to be the most sensitive and trusting of all animals.

Cobbe found relief from Claude Bernard in the new year when she gave a series of lectures on women's rights in London, which she repeated at Clifton in December and were published as *The Duties of Women* in 1881. But this was a brief respite, and she soon found herself attacking Louis Pasteur for his research into the treatment of anthrax. On 19 August 1881 she read a letter in the *Church Times* that praised Pasteur's work, suggesting that his success was 'a practical answer to the anti-vivisection craze; for if M. Pasteur had been forbidden to subject animals to the contagion of disease, he would never have made a discovery from which the lower animals will be the first gainers'.[52] In response on 9 September Cobbe expressed outrage that a religious paper whose Christian readers were supposed to believe in a Divine law of right and wrong, would print letters that referred to anti-vivisection as a 'craze' and praise the work of a scientific torturer who violated the Moral Law. Indeed, perhaps the *Church Times* and its readership were not really Christian, for destruction of life was incompatible with a belief in God: 'If "craze" there be on this subject, I venture to think it is on the side of those who believe in God and also believe in Vivisection. The latter article of faith essentially belongs to the Atheistic confession'.[53]

8. Experiment for testing the time required for injected poisons to traverse the circulation, from Bernard's *Physiologie Opératoire*, reprinted in Cobbe's *The Modern Rack*

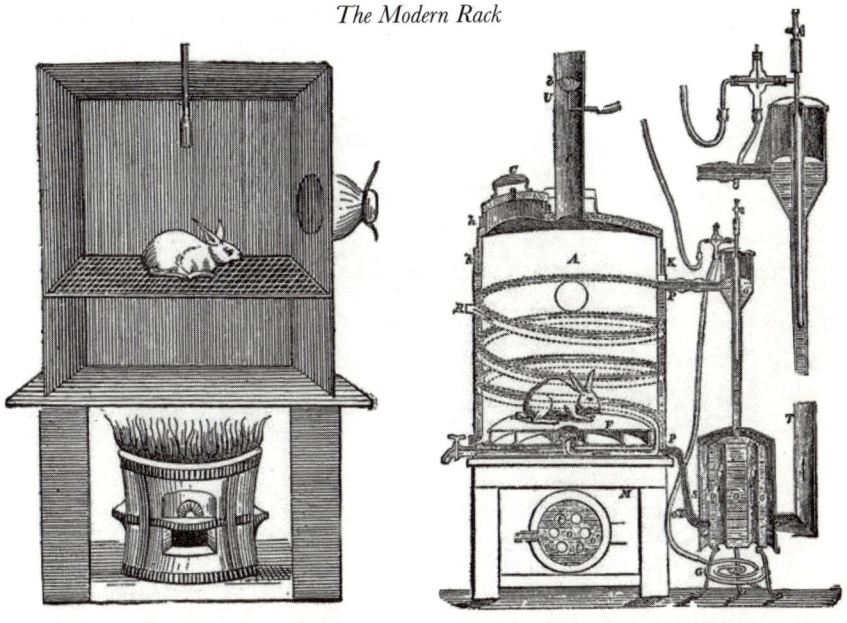

9. and 10. Claude Bernard's 'apparatus for the study of the Mechanism of Death by Heat', from his *Leçons sur la Chaleur Animale*, reprinted in Cobbe's *The Modern Rack*

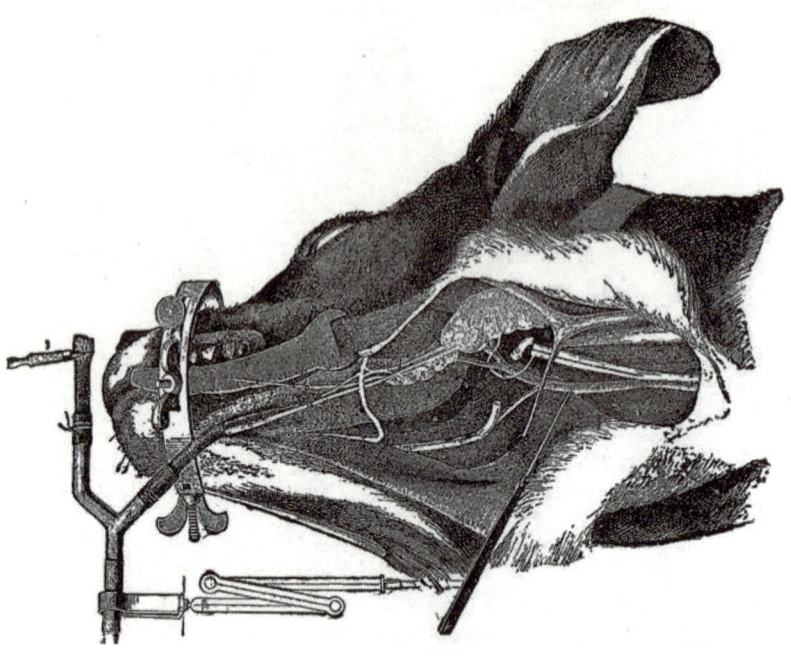

11. Method for exposing the salivary glands of a dog, from Cyon's *Atlas*, reprinted in Cobbe's *The Modern Rack*.

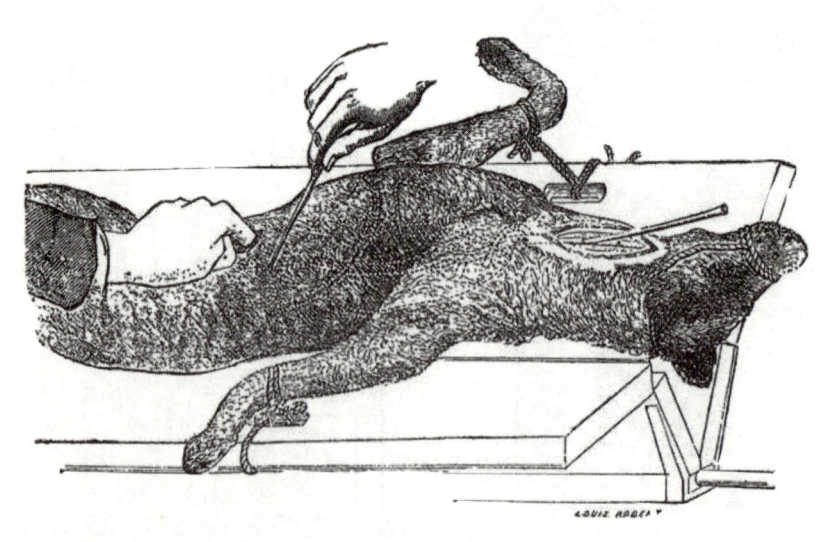

12. Claude Bernard's method for catheterism of the blood vessels, to obtain blood samples and temperature recordings, from his *Physiologie Opératoire*, reprinted in Cobbe's *The Modern Rack*.

Cobbe continued to scour scientific and medical journals and match the contents against Home Office Returns in the hope that she would discover a violation of the 1876 Act. There had been one prosecution soon after the bill was passed when a medical lecturer, Dr Gustav Adolph Arbrath, had been given a nominal fine for advertising experimentation on a living animal.[54] No more prosecutions had been forthcoming. Cobbe was adamant that if she only looked hard enough she would discover a violation of the Act and by bringing the perpetrator before the public expose the 1876 Act as a farce.

While reading proceedings of the International Medical Congress held in London in August 1881 Cobbe made a startling discovery regarding the discussions between the physiologists David Ferrier and Friedrich Goltz. The *British Medical Journal* and the *Lancet* reported that Ferrier's talk on cerebral localization had included a display of cerebral lesions in monkeys that the experimentalist had induced over the course of his researches. Cobbe compared the report with the most recent Home Office return which gave no indication that Ferrier had received the necessary certification. Convinced that she had discovered a violation of the the 1876 Act, Cobbe decided to prosecute the Scotsman.

Shaftesbury encouraged Cobbe's ambition to force the doctor to admit publicly his crime although he warned her to be very careful. 'I should rejoice in a conviction of Ferrier the Butcher,' he told her, but would be equally pleased if she could successfully expose the man as a cruel torturer. Prosecution, he suggested, was risky, and could 'have no middle result'.

> If you fail, you are lost—if you win, the gain, no doubt, will be great. But while I see many ways towards less loss, I do not see many towards gain.
>
> Let us think, however before we finally decide, what means we have on our side.
>
> ...who is to plead that truth, & set it before the Public? They, who undertake the cause for us must be men of real knowledge, forensic ability, and high reputation.
>
> Have we men of that stamp on our side?...
>
> They must be men, equally skilled in attack and defence— Unfortunately, it often happens that those who are wise, cannot

speak; & those who can speak, are not wise—And this is a subject on which bold assertion, backed by scientific character, would overpower both Judges, & the Public, who have nothing, at their command, but ordinary experience.

Here is my fear—and, surely, it is not altogether unreasonable.[55]

Cobbe ignored Shaftesbury. She was working for sacred ends and was deaf to 'secular' warnings. Determined to launch a successful prosecution she mounted her chariot of moral righteousness and drove it with characteristic flair into the fray, blind to the potential consequences. On 3 November Mr Waddy, QC, applied for a summons under the Vivisection Act against Ferrier. On 8 November, Shaftesbury wrote to Cobbe expressing cautious optimism, generated more by his faith in God than in the capabilities of the prosecution. Two days later, the VSS represented by Waddy, Mr Besley and the Lord Chief Justice's son, Bernard Coleridge, launched their case in Bow Street Police Court. Cobbe was present, confident in a successful outcome.

Cobbe rejected scientific evidence defending vivisection, but she and those representing her accepted without question the accuracy of the reports in the *BMJ* and the *Lancet*. It appeared that Ferrier had violated the Act and there was little doubt that it would be a relatively straightforward case. Counsel for the defence, who was the solicitor for the British Medical Association, revealed that it was Gerald Yeo and not Ferrier who had performed the experiments, and while Ferrier was not licensed, Yeo was. Once this was brought before the court the foundations upon which the prosecution rested crumbled. Cobbe and her legal advisers foundered and resorted to the far-fetched accusation that even as an observer, Ferrier required a licence. Sir James Ingham weighed the evidence carefully, although very quickly. Ferrier was not guilty of a violation. The case was dismissed. The honorary secretary of the VSS emerged disheartened by the outcome, but was determined that she would not be humiliated again.

1881 was not a good year for Frances Cobbe. She found herself being attacked on all sides by her adversaries and also came into conflict with several of her colleagues. Like many nineteenth-century organisations, the group was anything but a cohesive entity. There were endless squabbles about everything from policy to personal rivalry, and Cobbe contributed to internal discord through a combination of stubbornness over policy, insensitivity to the feelings of others, and insecurity about her position within the movement.

In the late 1860s Cobbe had become friendly with the proprietor of *The Lady's Own Paper*, the mystic and vegetarian Anna Kingsford who shared many of Cobbe's feminist ideas together with her hatred of vivisection. By 1873 Kingsford had begun to study medicine in France in the company of her friend Edward Maitland, but without husband and daughter, in order to better understand and protest against animal experimentation. Kingsford had returned to London early in 1881 and asked Cobbe for assistance in promoting both herself and her anti-vivisection message. Cobbe refused her help on the grounds that as a wife and mother, Kingsford should not have a public career. Despite Cobbe's insistence in her feminist treatises on women's independence, she felt that a woman who had chosen to marry and have children should remain within her home and care for her dependents. Independence and public activity were meant for single women like herself; one could not be a good public figure and a good mother. Kingsford was flouting all the social, marital and maternal propriety that Cobbe held dear. Cobbe was also probably uneasy with Kingsford's vegetarianism, which contrasted sharply with her own way of living. On a personal level, Cobbe may have felt threatened by Kingsford, a highly educated individual, challenging Cobbe's position within, and her control of, the antivivisection movement.

It did not take Cobbe long to cast aspersions on Kingsford's character in private conversation, suggesting that she was an immoral and irresponsible mother to her child and a shame to the female race. Kingsford's suitability for a leading role in a moral crusade was thrown into doubt as Cobbe succeeded, through gossip and innuendo, in making her a social outcast. This behaviour was indicative of the jealousy, personal ambition and drive for leadership status that plagued many a social reform movement.[56] Kingsford's biographer and fellow anti-vivisectionist, Edward Maitland, noted that he had 'sufficient insight into the character of the persecutrix [Cobbe] to recognise her as capable of indulging any amount of jealousy of one whose endowments bid fain to make her a formidable rival in the cause with which Miss Cobbe had identified herself'.[57]

As with all the less flattering incidents in her life, Cobbe's brush with Kingsford never made it to the pages of her autobiography, nor does her surviving correspondence provide us with any insight, although Maitland's biography does. Kingsford's husband, Algernon, came to his wife's rescue and threatened Cobbe with legal action if she did not stop her malicious gossip. The rumours continued to circulate, but Cobbe managed to escape Algernon's threat, her assassination of Kingsford's character successful. Anna Kingsford worked briefly with the International Association and then independently crusaded against vivisection and for spiritualism and vegetarianism until her premature death in 1888. By banishing Kingsford, Cobbe not only lost an important colleague; she also alienated many vegetarians and mystics. Yet her actions were not atypical, and would be repeated by others, such as Stephen Coleridge, years later. Cobbe believed that she, not Kingsford, was the 'chosen one' who would lead animals to the promised land. It was all a question of God's will being done, and Cobbe knew that He wanted her to do it. Cobbe also believed that vegetarianism and spiritualism, both fringe activities, had no place in a moral crusade that sought to eradicate scientific cruelty to animals. Nor did Kingsford.

Anti-vivisectionists may have had antagonistic relationships with one another, but what they all agreed on was that vivisection was increasing out of all proportion to need. From 1876 to 1890 the number of licensed vivisectors and registered laboratories rose. In 1878, for example, 27 vivisectors were licensed and performed 481 experiments; in 1883 there were 44 persons licensed, 32 of whom experimented. By 1890, the figures had increased to 110 and 77 respectively. By 1892, 180 persons were licensed, of whom 125 performed a recorded 3,960 experiments, 2,239 were exempt from using anaesthetics. In 1883 the number of certificates dispensing with anaesthetics had been only 55. Eight years later 2,661 experiments were recorded, 1,363 of which did not utilise anaesthetics.[58] Not only were the numbers of vivisections and vivisectors increasing at an alarming rate, so were the numbers of certificates granted to vivisectors allowing them to dispense with anaesthetics; a matter of particular concern to the anti-vivisectionists

The trials and tribulations of 1881 may have drained Cobbe emotionally, but they did not deplete her stamina, and in January 1882 she offered a blinding rebuttal to a series of pro-vivisection articles in the

December issue of *Nineteenth Century* penned by James Paget, Richard Owen and Samuel Wilks. 'May every New Year open to you with as effective an appeal in the cause of God's humbler Creatures as that with which you inaugurated 1882,' Shaftesbury wrote to her when her article, 'Vivisection—Four Replies' appeared in the *Fortnightly Review*. 'Paget, Owen, Wilks are reduced to their just proportions. They may be always, as they affirm seeking the truth, but undoubtedly, they are never telling it', he continued.[59]

Cobbe denounced all three men as villainous, unfeeling, inhuman creatures 'behind the age in moral perception,'[60] fired by that *ésprit de corps* that was destroying science and society. She agreed with Paget that savages felt pain less than civilised man and wild animals less than domesticated ones, yet she argued that this did not mean that certain classes of animals were any less sensitive to suffering than man. Paget had compared unanaesthetised vivisections performed in 1881 to human surgery performed before chloroform. Cobbe retorted that surgeons did not tear open a man's backbone and irritate the spinal marrow as Auguste Chauveau, Charles-Édouard Brown-Séquard and others had done to numerous dogs and horses. Cobbe also had a ready response to Paget's assertion that vivisection was far less cruel than field sports. The two were completely different and borne by two different breeds of animal:

> in comparing the agonies of vivisected animals with the pangs of creatures killed in the chase or the arena, we must remember that the former are endured in cold blood by animals fasting, thirsting, tied down on the torture trough, and possibly curarized. The latter are borne by creatures so excited that, like soldiers in battle, they are comparatively unconscious of them till they are ended by death.[61]

Cobbe concluded her critique of Paget by commenting that his article offered an erroneous account of vivisection because he omitted callous incriminating information. She then moved from Paget's suppression of facts to Owen's mis-statement that all VSS workers were 'hired scribes' and Wilks's claim that anti-vivisectionists based their arguments on the inutility of vivisection. Cobbe reminded Wilks that anti-vivisectionists approached vivisection principally as a moral problem, and therefore employed moral arguments.

Cobbe's article encouraged others to express their pro- and anti-vivisection sympathies and insults were freely bandied about in the *Nineteenth Century* and the *Fortnightly Review*. A reviewer for *Nature* subjectively noted after perusing the offerings that as

> regards the general tone or manner of pleading, there can be no doubt that the advantage inclines largely to the side of the physiologists; for while—with perhaps a slight exception in the case of some of the passages in the essays by Prof. Owen and Dr Wilks— the physiologists state their arguments in a calm and tolerant spirit, the essays on the other side—with the exception of one by Mr Hutton—present, in a painfully marked degree, the features of bitterness and ill-temper.[62]

Even Anna Kingsford, whom Edward Maitland believed could make the anti-vivisection movement scientifically credible, did not emerge unscathed for her contribution to the debate entitled 'The Uselessness of Vivisection' which appeared in the *Nineteenth Century*. *Nature*'s reviewer lumped Kingsford in with Cobbe: 'the writings of these ladies upon the subject are so extravagant and ill advised that even an ignorant reader must feel their judgment upon this head to be valueless'.[63] Cobbe's article followed a set pattern of attacking vivisection and vivisectors with a moral fervour that rendered scientific discussion null and void. Cobbe's weaknesses were that she relied too heavily on foreign experiments to make conclusions about English vivisectors and that she generalised about all physiologists. Gerald Yeo noticed these flaws in her argument and criticised Cobbe in the *Fortnightly Review*: 'I am surprised that one who aspires to logical acumen, and speaks so glibly of syllogisms, should put forward an argument which bears so plainly stamped on the face of it the character of a deduction from the particular to the universal'.[64] He also accused Cobbe of ignoring statistics on pain and argued that out of one hundred experiments performed, seventy-five were painless; twenty were as painful as vaccination; four were as painful as the healing of a wound; and only one as painful as a surgical operation. Cobbe was also caught out for suggesting that movement during operations was proof of pain. Yeo pointed out that any movement the animal made during procedures was reflex action, a result of anaesthetic use. 'Miss Cobbe's information is inaccurate, and her ideas of pain are as distorted as her views about cruelty,' he concluded.[65] She came in for particularly harsh criticism for suggesting that physiologists used horses for research into the nervous system, a practice that according to Yeo had ceased in England some seventy years before. Cobbe's information may have been distorted, but that distortion had an important role to play in anti-vivisection propaganda, which revolved around the issues of pain, suffering and exploitation of the powerless, and which alienated as many people as it attracted.

The most important weapon for anti-vivisectionists lay in the power of the printed word, the placard and the magic lantern, all of which could, Cobbe believed, encourage Britons to embrace anti-vivisection and accept her millenarian vision for the future; this entailed controlling scientific behaviour, realigning man with nature and reassessing power hierarchies, objectives still sought by anti-vivisectionists today. Cobbe's propaganda campaign assaulted people's senses and shocked them into accepting that a re-evaluation of man's relationship with God's creation was vital if animals were to be saved from scientific torture and if man was to be saved from moral degeneration.

On 7 January 1882 Cobbe wrote to Shaftesbury asking him his opinion about using sandwich men and graphic placards at churches on Sundays to greet parishioners and shame the clergy who were in general apathetic and non-committal on the subject of vivisection. Cobbe was full of enthusiasm; it took the Earl three weeks to convince her that her plan lacked diplomacy. 'You will stir up the anger of many who would think that they ought not to be so employed on the day of rest.'[66] This initial plea for restraint was followed by others which tempered criticism of Cobbe with praise: 'My terror was lest you in your burning, & most noble, zeal should have organized an onslaught of such a kind as to give an appearance of mobbing a Clergyman; & that too, when in his Church, & during service'.[67] Twelve days later Shaftesbury was still trying to dissuade Cobbe from the sandwich men idea and there was a flurry of letters between the two with Shaftesbury expressing alarm and Cobbe's eventual acquiescence.

Shaftesbury's New Year's struggles with Cobbe's crusading methods did not end there. He arranged with Cobbe to hold an educational magic lantern show. Cobbe was hesitant at first, asking him if it was safe and desirable: 'To be sure it is very desirable, & very safe,' was his reply. 'We can have all sorts of slides; appalling ones for the Adults; gentler ones to breed the love of Animals, for the Children.'[68] Both agreed that it would be wise to begin the presentation with slides that encouraged the audience to think of animals as lovable and affectionate, but they disagreed on how best to proceed with the show. Cobbe believed that the next series of slides should show vivisections in all of their gory detail. Shaftesbury did not want to risk alienating those present with graphic images, and he urged Cobbe to be more sensitive: 'respecting those Slides for the Magic Lantern,' he wrote.

> I am very anxious that we should withhold, for the present, the slides of terror and disgust—the slides to touch the hearts of Children & adults, & beget tenderness & compassion towards Animals we may exhibit immediately; but the others reserve, I pray you, for a better opportunity, & a more serious blow.[69]

Two days later, Cobbe replied to Shaftesbury's letter:

> I am very much puzzled about the magic lantern. You see the terrible slides (4 or 5) are the _raison d'etre_ of the lecture. We (our Society & its Branches) cannot undertake to give lectures on kindness to animals generally. That is the business of Jermyn St [RSPCA] & our Lecturer & the Lecture rooms let us are all for the anti-Vivisection work alone. My idea, which I must have badly explained to you, was that instead of all the lecture being on our painful subject, the beginning of it should be of a kind to interest the audience tenderly in animals, which would introduce the latter part with greater force. Your reply made me fancy you quite approved this plan, & so I have ordered the 5 slides (taken exactly of course from the physiologists [sic] own books) & they are in process of painting. We had arranged also with a regular exhibitor to lend and exhibit a large magic lanthorn [sic] for 25s. a night.
>
> Of course if you think this will be unwise dear Lord Shaftesbury, I will simply drop the scheme & let the lecturer give his lectures as before without any exhibition—reserving the whole affair for another time if it ever seem desirable.[70]

No further references are made to the show. It may have been cancelled or perhaps Cobbe accepted Shaftesbury's advice and mounted a tamer version of the original. But generally Cobbe did not approve of half measures and it must have taken a great deal of effort on her part to bow to more cautious elements in her Society; she would not have done so to anyone other than Shaftesbury whom she revered as a great humanitarian, friend and adviser.

In March 1882 the Association for the Advancement of Medical Research (AAMR) was founded and staffed by a well-known coterie of vivisection sympathisers—Sir William Jenner, Sir William Gull, Sir James Paget, Dr Farquharson, Samuel Wilks, Joseph Lister, Burdon Sanderson, Michael Foster, Dr Pye Smith and Gerald Yeo. The Association might not have come about so soon had Cobbe not launched her prosecution of Ferrier the previous year, antagonising the scientific community and encouraging them to replace the Physiological Association, formed in the mid-1870s, with a stronger organisation. Physiologists were concerned that more prosecutions might follow, and to prevent this from happening the AAMR approached the Home Secretary William Harcourt, who had replaced Richard Cross after the 1880 election, in May and offered their assistance with scrutinising applications from physiologists and dispensing licences to successful candidates. Harcourt agreed to their suggestion. Science now had control of the decision-making process and, it was perceived, control of the government, and as Shaftesbury told Cobbe just about anyone could vivisect.[71]

Cobbe was outraged and she told readers of the *Daily News* the following spring that she could not believe that a responsible government would grant vivisectors, whose activities were supposed to be circumscribed by the 1876 Act, the liberty to circumvent its provisions and contribute to deciding who could and could not acquire a licence. 'To apply to the Land League to keep the Fenians in order would in comparison be an ordinary proceeding on the part of the Executive,' she sarcastically commented.[72]

In 1883 Cobbe was drawn into Oxford's vivisection debate when Oxford Convocation elected J.S. Burdon Sanderson as Professor of Physiology by a vote of 88–85. His victory was close, due in part to the virulent campaign launched by the anti-vivisectionists. For over ten years Burdon Sanderson had promoted laboratory work among University

College students and the anti-vivisectionists made sure that he knew that his presence would not be welcome at Oxford. Convocation thought otherwise, and Cobbe wrote of their decision as a 'deplorable defeat'.[73] The *Spectator* considered it to be 'one of the greatest calamities, in the interests of true civilization and true Science, that has happened in our time'.[74] John Ruskin resigned his Slade Professorship, and anti-vivisectionists protested.

Two years later a contributor to the *Pall Mall Gazette* wryly noted, using an apt comparison between anti-vivisectionists and fox-hunters, that the 'Anti-vivisectionists at Oxford are still hard at work worrying Professor Burdon Sanderson, and endeavouring to run him to earth as if he were a common fox' over a proposed grant to his laboratory.[75] Cobbe wrote back, defending her colleagues: 'It is the contagion of the new passion for scientific cruelties, through the professor's mind, on the minds of his pupils which is the thing to be dreaded'.[76] Henry Acland and an anonymous FRS responded accordingly: Cobbe was misled, she knew nothing of Burdon Sanderson who exerted only the most elevating influence over his students. 'The ill-natured and ill-mannered attack upon the personal character of Professor Burdon Sanderson which Miss Cobbe has published in your columns will doubtless carry its own refutation in the opinion of every one who is able to distinguish between good breeding and the reverse.'[77] On 11 March the results of what was a noisy Convocation were published: 412 voted to give Burdon Sanderson a £500 grant per year for his laboratory, 244 were opposed. Science carried the day again.

Vivisection, Education and Women

Perhaps because of the two defeats at Oxford, one of the highest and supposedly most civilised seats of learning, Cobbe became preoccupied with the impact that vivisection would have on education, the purpose of which as she understood it was to inspire the development of mind and soul, not destroy the latter for the benefit of the former. In 1886 she sent a circular to 700 schoolmasters entitled *Physiology as a Branch of Education* as a protest against the presence of physiology in universities where it would, she wrote, 'excite in the minds of the young witnesses a curiosity unmingled with pity, such as may subsequently prompt them to become the most merciless experimenters; or, at least, advocates and apologists of scientific cruelty.'[78] The following year she sent a number of letters to the educational journal, *School*, to impress upon its readers that science teachers would not only instruct minds in the principles of physiology but would encourage curiosity and materialism and destroy spirituality. She emphasised that educational corruption of the student could only be countered by a moral home influence, which was the prime responsibility of the mother. By implication, she blamed negligent mothers for the ease by which vivisection was spreading. 'It is because hitherto men have not been so prepared, have had actually no ideas at all about any moral obligation towards animals,' Cobbe wrote in 'The Long Pull', 'that the vivisecting crew have been able to persuade them to condone their doings'.[79]

To counteract the influence of the 'vivisecting crew' Cobbe launched a shock propaganda campaign. She complained about the extent of explicit medical reporting in journals and newspapers, and did not like being exposed to 'sickening surgical details', 'deathbed details' and 'nauseating accounts' of symptoms of illustrious patients'.[80] Nor did she approve of the ease by which young men and women could read the *Lancet* and the *British Medical Journal* (hardly daily fare) with their 'hideous diagrams and revolting details of disease and monstrosity'.[81] Such gruesome literature, Cobbe believed, did not elevate the mind, but led to a decline of decency. Her own 'nauseating accounts' and 'sickening surgical details' of vivisections were, however, both necessary and different from the human cases published in medical journals. The privacy of the physiologist's torture chamber was in no way comparable with that of the sickroom: the sickroom, by merit of its relationship to death and immortality, had to remain private; the physiological laboratory, because it embodied torture reminiscent of that practised by barbarians of another age, could not be shrouded in secrecy. It had to be made public through propaganda that forced readers and listeners to identify their pains with those suffered by the vivisected animal and that characterised the physiologist as a pariah whose lifestyle no truly humane person would be tempted to emulate.

In some instances, people thought that Cobbe went to unnecessary extremes to convert the unconverted: Eleanor Sidgwick told Millicent Fawcett that Cobbe's 'anti-vivisection literature is hardening and demoralizing and tending to create a morbid interest in pain for pain's sake'.[82] The combination of disturbing verbal and visual evidence was too much for others to bear: 'Dear Miss Cobbe forgive my weakness,' Eleanor Vere Boyle pleaded. 'I cannot, dare not, read what you enclose. Nor will I grieve my son with the fiendish details.'[83] But Cobbe persisted in her efforts, for as in her other reforming endeavours with workhouse inmates and abused wives, she felt compelled to educate the public about suffering and exploitation and to convert them to a moral (her moral) understanding of the relationship between men, women, animals and society.

Although a number of Cobbe's female friends were sickened by vivisection, she insisted that they read her literature and pledge themselves to her crusade. Female participation was important to many a nineteenth-century moral reform movement. Women were the moral guardians of society and Cobbe called on them to labour on behalf of animals in the same way as she had called on them to save unprotected humans during her early reforming years. Social activism also dovetailed with Cobbe's definition of feminism: it required women to act autonomously and with conviction in the public sphere, while vivisection itself was one of those masculine evils that only women could assail as they brought God's kingdom to earth. Reflecting on her own involvement in the movement after years of labour, Cobbe believed herself 'to have the better right to be heard in such a crusade than a man, or even than a priest...[and] I...think that on questions of mercy a woman is likely to have a truer, sounder judgement, *qua* woman, than a man'.[84] Women should be heard defending animals, yet she cautioned them, as she had done when writing in support of women's suffrage, to be very careful with their public show of support—'*Don't* be sentimental! Don't, above all things, be hysterical and tearful. There is reason enough for our womanly tears, God knows! but don't shed them in public, my sisters! Don't let our opponents say that our party is composed of excitable people, and our object a sentimental *fad*.'[85]

But that was just what many people thought of the anti-vivisection movement, dominated by 'hypocritical humbugs and hysterical old maids'.[86] Even Cobbe had occasion to complain that 'we are tormented by silly hysterical women who can do nothing only make our movement appear foolish'.[87] Yet still she appealed to them for assistance. Because women were politically powerless, Cobbe knew that their influence would be limited, but theirs was a social power that was no less important in eradicating the evil in question than political pressure. If the churches, the Quakers, and 'all the women in England', Cobbe told her Bristol anti-vivisection audience at Redland Park Hall in January 1890,

> insignificant as we are politically, would exert their social power, would turn their backs on every vivisector and student of vivisection and refuse to touch their bloodied hands, or permit their sons and daughters to associate with them anymore than with swindlers and adulterers—then, even then, the thing [vivisection] would be stopped.[88]

She exhorted women not to send their children to schools where physiology was taught; not to invite known vivisectors to their dinner parties; not to have doctors who professed vivisecting sympathies attend them during illness. Eleanor Vere Boyle exercised her autonomy and proudly wrote to Cobbe that she refused doctors 'whose hands are stained with that crime [vivisection]'.[89]

While Cobbe was encouraging women to channel their natural sympathies towards anti-vivisection, she discovered that her scientific enemies were beginning to exert more and more influence over the lives of female students. In 1890 Cobbe heard that Mrs Burdon Sanderson, wife of the infamous *Handbook* editor, was being considered as a member of the Council of Somerville Hall, that bastion of female education named after Mary Somerville who had been a signatory to Cobbe's first anti-vivisection memorial in Italy in 1863. Cobbe admitted that she knew nothing of Mrs Burdon Sanderson, but was shocked to think that Somerville Hall would consider associating itself in any way with John Burdon Sanderson. She dashed off a letter to Mrs Vernon Harcourt, honorary secretary to Somerville Hall, in protest of the election which would, as far as Cobbe was concerned, tarnish the school's reputation, disgrace the memory of Mary Somerville, and inevitably lead to the young Somerville women practising vivisection, thereby destroying their souls and the moral future of England.

Cobbe's letter was read before the Council of Somerville Hall on 4 December and she received a diplomatic reply from Henry Pelham, the Chairman of the General Meeting. He reassured Cobbe that Mrs

Burdon Sanderson's election would not change the opinion of the college towards vivisection: students who took up physiology would continue, as they had done for a number of years, to attend Professor Burdon Sanderson's lectures; vivisection demonstrations were prohibited by the university's regulations; and Mrs Burdon Sanderson would not have any share in decisions made regarding the curriculum. Cobbe did not believe Pelham. She asked if she could publish his reply to her protest in a pamphlet she was writing about the incident. Two days later Pelham replied that Cobbe was over reacting, and he lodged his own protest, 'very respectfully against any attempt to prejudice the Hall by inferences which have no other basis than a wholly mistaken, and, as I venture to think, an exceedingly strained interpretation of a very simple and innocent act.'[90] Cobbe published a series of letters between herself, Harcourt and Pelham in 1891 entitled *Somerville Hall. A Misnomer*, reiterating the contamination of female students by the vivisecting spirit.

In the same year as the Somerville Hall incident, Cobbe heard disturbing rumours about Girton girls vivisecting in the privacy of their rooms after attending vivisectional lectures given by Michael Foster. Since arriving at Cambridge twenty years earlier, Foster had transformed the institution into a place of advanced physiological research and teaching, and female students studying for Physiology in the Natural Science Tripos were required, by Emily Davies and the Girton Committee, to attend lectures, some of which were illustrated by experiment at the University laboratory.[91] It was suggested to Cobbe by an unnamed source that the female students did more than just listen to Foster's words. 'I would gain enlist your powerful influence,' Cobbe wrote to Millicent Fawcett,

> & that of your daughter in opposing this dreadful (but unquestionably growing & contagious) passion for vivisection; the new vice (as it really seems to be) of scientific cruelty. It is quite horrible enough among the young men—who some of my men friends at Cambridge tell me can quite be marked for their hardness on all subjects. But to have those women-colleges whose growth we watched with such sympathy—& which you must regard with such righteous pride, [illegible] with training schools for girl vivisectors, wd be too miserable a catastrophe![92]

Eleanor Sidgwick informed Fawcett that Cobbe was mistaken; female students at Cambridge did not vivisect. They attended lectures where experiments took place, but the animal was always anaesthetised and was killed before the anaesthetic wore off; vivisecting without a licence was illegal under the 1876 Act; students were not licensed and the college would never sanction the practice. 'These are the facts,' Sidgwick told Fawcett, 'but I hardly know whether you will think them worth communicating to Miss Cobbe. They might irritate rather than soothe!'[93] Fawcett did set the record straight with Cobbe who let the matter drop. But she was disturbed by science's wanton destruction of women's higher education that she herself had nurtured in the 1860s.

Five years later Cobbe learned that fifteen-year-old girls at the Waverly Road Higher Grade School in Birmingham, run by the School Board, were required to dissect rabbits in their advanced science course. By some means the issue was brought up in the House of Commons at which time the clerk to the Birmingham School Board commented that the exercise was a necessary part of the curriculum and 'the actual dissection was nothing more than any girl would necessarily perform in preparing a rabbit for stewing...and has probably been done without remark in most cookery kitchens.'[94] Laughter resonated throughout the House. Cobbe was not amused. 'Permit me, Sir,' she wrote to the *Daily News*,

> as a woman who for the last half century has pleaded for the 'Higher Education of Women,' to express my alarm at finding that the present Minister of Education in England thus deliberately sanctions a system which ought to be described as emphatically the Lower Education of Women, namely, that which is best suited to deprive them of womanliness.[95]

While school girls were dissecting rabbits at Waverly Road, Cobbe made more exaggerated and near hysterical claims about education in American schools: 'Mistresses of girls' schools, we are assured, have dissected their household cat alive for the instruction of their young-lady pupils; and the professors in several universities eagerly avail themselves of this method to give dramatic interest to their otherwise dull lectures.'[96] This was difficult for Cobbe to substantiate, but it reflected the extent to which her anti-vivisection argument was becoming increasingly unreasonable. Yet on another level it reflected her awareness of differences between masculine and feminine characteristics and her fear that the latter were being crushed by an aggressively masculine curriculum. Women were supposed to save the world from destruction, not contribute to it by participating in vivisection.[97]

Cobbe was more interested in the moral message within her treatise than its accuracy. It did not matter to her if she occasionally blurred the line between fact and fiction. Many of her contemporaries would agree for as Josef Althoz writes, it 'is characteristic of the Victorians that they were more interested in truthfulness than in truth; they were more concerned with the moral character of the speaker than with the factual correctness of his statement.'[98] In her efforts to reshape and recreate her society, Cobbe showed herself to be very much a product of it, and while she did not think it important to be accurate in her defence of animals, others did.

6

'Health and Holiness'

In the spring of 1881 Cobbe turned her attention from physiologists to doctors. Her relationship with the medical profession was based on a mistrust that had its roots in her girlhood when she watched her mother become an invalid, a fate that she had escaped by refusing to continue the damaging treatment her doctors offered for her injured ankle. In the 1860s she had criticised the care provided by physicians for workhouse inmates, although she recognised that much of the fault lay with those who had formed the Poor Law and administered relief. Cobbe was stunned at the support that physicians offered physiologists on 10 July 1876 and from this time onward she believed that they shared some very disturbing characteristics with vivisectors. They were 'scientific' and 'clinical' in their approach to patient care, and spent a great deal of time observing symptoms. Cobbe was convinced that they did so to advance their knowledge, not to heal the patient. She labelled them materialistic, and believed that they exerted far too much control over the public and the government.

Cobbe first publicly censured physicians in her 1878 article, 'The Little Health of Ladies' in which she attacked the idea that women needed continual medical assistance to function to their biologically and culturally determined optimum.

> That the Creator should have planned a whole sex of Patients—that the normal condition of the female of the human species should be to have legs which walk not, and brains which can only work on pain of disturbing the rest of the ill-adjusted machine—this is to me simply incredible.[1]

Three years later came a vitriolic condemnation of the entire medical profession for oppressing everyone, everywhere—'The Medical Profession and its Morality' (to which Cobbe did not append her name) and which appeared in the *Modern Review* in April 1881. The *Zoophilist* noted in its review of the article:

> The *Modern Review* is chiefly noteworthy for a remarkable and unusually outspoken paper on 'The Medical Profession and its Morality'. We have not space for more than a very passing notice of an article which should be carefully read and studied, more especially by the doctors themselves. For it must be owned that the Modern Reviewer is not a believer in the medical profession.[2]

Cobbe disliked the arrogance which she believed characterised the profession as a whole. The 'united profession of the Healing Art have lifted themselves as a body altogether to a higher plane than they ever before occupied,' Cobbe began in language that sounded very much like that used by critics of mid-century state intervention.

> By dint of cohesion and generalship they form a complex phalanx, and have obviously suddenly arrived at the consciousness of corporate power. The Medical Council, already far ahead of Convocation, has become a little Parliament, destined soon to dictate to the larger Senate of the kingdom, not only concerning its own interior affairs, but also concerning everything which can by possibility be represented as affecting the interests of public health…Even the Government of the country appears unequal to the task of contending with the profession since Sir Richard Cross succumbed to the deputation which invaded the Home Office many hundreds strong, and reduced him to the humilitating [sic] concession of turning his own Vivisection Bill from a measure to protect animals into one to protect physiologists…In all newspaper correspondence, indeed, wherein medical men express their views…a new tone of dominance, not to say arrogance, is perceptible; nor do many lay writers on the press or speakers in public meetings venture to allude to the profession without a sort of rhetorical genuflexion, such as a Roman Catholic pays *en passant* in referring to the Pope or the saints.[3]

Their social origins certainly did not fit them for such treatment. Most doctors, Cobbe suspected, came from the 'secondary professional classes' or from the ranks of tradesmen and artisans.[4] These men, she surmised, entered medicine not to heal, but to make money, to become famous by some scientific discovery, or to rise socially. Historians of medicine have discovered that medical entrepreneurs used evolving specialist hospitals to advance their careers; their selfish efforts earned them criticism from many general practitioners who felt that specialisation threatened their livelihood.[5] Cobbe criticised the motivation for entrepreneurial activity because it transformed medicine from a healing art into competition. Competitiveness was predicated upon the individual and individual gain; it dulled the ability to respond to distress, and if physicians practised selfish rather than selfless medicine then they could not possibly be sympathetic nor provide adequate, let alone compassionate, care.

Given the resentment expressed by some general practitioners towards their entrepreneurial colleagues, Cobbe's comments were not without support. She did not, however, differentiate between general practitioners and specialists but condemned inaccurately all physicians as lower class 'Tartuffes' whose displays of sympathy were merely part of their stock in trade. A few years later George Bernard Shaw, who was to defend Cobbe in 1892 against assaults lobbied by vivisectors, made similar sweeping statements about doctors in the preface to his play 'The Doctor's Dilemma'. On the whole doctors were 'just like other Englishmen: most of them have no honor [sic] and no conscience'.[6]

Cobbe envisaged the ideal doctor as compassionate and sympathetic beyond all else; she also believed that this was virtually impossible in a profession that was messy and smelly and distasteful. 'To begin with,' she wrote,

> no man of a poetic temperament is likely to become a doctor, for very obvious reasons. To make the weaknesses and maladies of our poor human frames the subject of a whole life's study and attention, so that a man should, as it were, live evermore in a world of disease; to pass from one sick room to another, and from a distressing sight to a fetid odour, in endless succession; to acquire knowledge by the dissection of corpses, and employ it, when gained, in amputating limbs, delivering women in childbirth, dressing sores,

and inspecting everything ugly and loathsome to the natural senses,—this is surely a vocation which calls for either great enthusiasm or great callousness.[7]

Both enthusiasm and callousness opposed Cobbe's conviction that medicine was a healing *art*. It was absurd for Cobbe to condemn an entire profession because doctors were engaged in labour that she found repugnant and to label them abnormal. Twenty years earlier she had defended Elizabeth Garrett's right to a medical education and career. Garrett would have been educated in dissection and anatomy and as a qualified practitioner she would have dealt with pain and fetid odour and women in childbirth. Cobbe had thought nothing of the labours of a doctor when defending a woman's right to a career, and she had argued that the medical arts were infinitely more suited to the female temperament than to the male.

Despite her intense distaste for medicine Cobbe still wanted to see more women enter the profession. In 'The Medical Profession and its Morality' she criticised the gender divide and the 'clique-ishness' and working-class trades unionism that she believed defined medicine and which excluded women from scaling the economic heights of the profession. 'Never, indeed, has there been a more absurd public manifestation of trades unionism [within medicine] than this effort to keep ladies out of the lucrative profession of physicians, and crowd them into the ill-paid one of nurses'.[8] Cobbe must have forgotten her earlier position that medicine was *not* supposed to be about remuneration.

According to Cobbe, the degeneration of the doctor began with the education of the fledgling healer. Like an earlier generation of physicians, Cobbe believed that a doctor's character deserved extremely careful tuition. As early as 1875 she had noted that 'men at the age of ordinary medical students are…filled with curiosity and exceedingly empty of sympathy and pity'[9] and were more likely to display those dreaded characteristics of the vivisector, enthusiasm and callousness. Because she believed that medical students came from the lower classes, they entered medical school as ruffians:

> The medical student…undergoes a transformation like that of a larva, when it becomes a moth. One day we notice Bob Sawyer, as

a rowdy and dissipated youth, with linen of questionable purity, and a pipe and foul language alternately in his mouth; the *bête noire* of every modest girl, and the unfailing nuisance of every public meeting, where he may stamp and crow and misbehave himself. Anon, Robert Sawyer, Esq., MD, or MRCS, emerges the pink of cleanliness and decorum, to flit evermore softly through shaded boudoirs, murmuring soothing suggestions to ladies suffering from headaches, and recommending mild syrups to teething infants. His old celebrated canticle—

Hurrah for the Cholera Morbus,
Which brings us a guinea a-day,

has unaccountably been changed for such burning zeal to save humanity from disease, that he is ready to persecute anti-vaccinators to the death, or cut up any number of living dogs and cats in the most horrible manner merely on the chance of discovering some remedy for human suffering.[10]

Although Cobbe wrote of physicians as a unified, materialistic enclave, there were a number of 'dissenters' who broke rank to criticise changes in medical education: the replacement of the old 'gentlemanly' style of teaching with new laboratory instruction. Cobbe's preoccupation lay not so much with the mode of training as with the near soul-destroying effects it would have on character and moral fibre. Some, such as the Reverend Edward Thring, Headmaster of Uppingham School, to whom Cobbe had sent her pamphlet, *Physiology as a Branch of Education* in 1886, concurred, as did this Edinburgh medical student who admitted in the *Scottish Leader* in January 1890 that by 'seeing these frequent experiments of one kind or another on living animals, we tend to become brutalized and degraded, callous, and indifferent to death or pain in others, and unfitted for our present work in the infirmary and for future private practice'.[11]

The vivisection of animals took place in laboratories in medical schools attached to hospitals which, by association, made the latter centres of learning not just of care-giving. Physicians who attended patients in hospital also often lectured at the medical school and the students went from one building to another. Dr Edward Berdoe commented, 'the wall which divides the vivisector's laboratory from the hospital ward is but a paper one'.[12] It did not take Cobbe long to conjure up hellish images of doctors and students wending their way with scientific rather humanitarian zeal from the medical school laboratory to the vulnerable hospital patient or private patient. Once again Cobbe exaggerated the support that physicians gave to physiology and she exaggerated too the 'demonic' character of the teaching hospital in an anonymous letter she wrote to the *Daily News* in January 1882, hoping, she told Shaftesbury, that doctors would 'not find out the witch who has raised this little storm about their ears!'[13] 'Sir,' Cobbe began,

> It was an old complaint that 'wretches hang that jurymen may dine'. Is it possible that in these days of humanity other 'wretches' are left to groan in agonies of disease that medical students may learn?...Next to prolonging the illness of a patient for the instruction of medical students would naturally follow the step of inducing some interesting disease for the same object. Are we to expect this kind of devotion to science in our hospitals? Your obedient servant,
>
> NIHIL HUMANI[14]

Jonathan Hutchinson, surgeon and defender of vivisection and teaching hospitals, responded the following day arguing that teaching hospitals were necessary for proper medical training.[15] Cobbe and her supporters could not agree. It had been common practice for medical students to pay a fee and walk the wards of London's hospitals, so patients had always been 'observed'. Now, however, anti-vivisectionists believed that afflictions were maintained so that students could learn about the effects of disease; hospitals were places where little curative care was given, and where unnecessary operations, aided by the advent of anaesthetics, were performed.[16] Patients, Cobbe wrote in 'The Medical Profession and its Morality', in terminology which echoed her anti-vivisection arguments, 'are sacrificed not merely at the shrine of knowledge, but on the anvil of manipulative skill. That operations are performed for the sake either of acquiring such skill, or keeping the surgeon's hand well "in"—as well as of earning enormous fees—we have the best evidence'.[17] And, according to Cobbe and the anti-vivisectionist physician Elizabeth Blackwell, vivisection was to blame. Vivisection, Blackwell wrote in *Essays in Medical*

Sociology, 'tends to make us less scrupulous in our treatment of the sick and helpless poor. It increases that disposition to regard the poor as so much "clinical material", which has become, alas! not without reason a widespread reproach to many of the young members of our most honourable and merciful profession'.[18]

As invasive medicine became increasingly prevalent in hospitals the *Home Chronicler* and the *Zoophilist* began to report scores of what they understood were experiments on patients. The *Home Chronicler* had made tentative steps in this direction in 1876 when they published one experiment performed on a twelve-year-old girl at St Mary's Hospital suffering from 'chorea', or nervous movements. She was put through a course of hemlock, faradization (electrical treatment), arsenic and 2 drachms ($^1/_8$ oz.) of steel wine three times daily. After she worsened, the treatment was altered to ten grains of bromide of potassium and five grains of chloral hydrate at night; then chloroform was administered and she was injected with morphia. If 'this was not "experimentation on a living animal" with a vengeance', the journal wrote, 'what was it?'[19] Three years later, the same publication alerted its readers to 'Questionable Experiments on Men' that traced the effects of pituri, (a narcotic drug derived from a shrub), on respiration and pulse as reported in the *Lancet*.[20]

Throughout the 1880s and 1890s the horrific spectre of human vivisection became an increasingly popular way of denouncing physiological experimentation and anti-vivisection poets and novelists, such as Alfred, Lord Tennyson and Wilkie Collins, made it a theme in some of their works.[21] Stories of human vivisection were given added currency by the Jack the Ripper murders; Cobbe was not the only person to entertain the idea that the mutilated corpses were the work of a physiologist gone mad. Many of the experiments cited were, like the bulk of evidence presented by anti-vivisectionists, of foreign origin and perhaps not widely adopted in England; this did not stop the crusaders from suggesting that similar atrocities occurred at home, especially given the fact that some hospitals, including King's College and St Barts, held vivisection licences.[22]

Anti-vivisectionists used developments in human vivisection to re-emphasise the vulnerability of specimens of research. In his 1890 publication, *Kochism: Experiment, Not Discovery* which detailed research and surgery on consumptive patients by the German bacteriologist Robert

Koch, the VSS's Benjamin Bryan noted that the objects of study were the poor, who were plentiful in number but wanting in power to protect themselves from exploitation.[23]

Cobbe echoed Bryan's concern in her pamphlet, *Cancer Experiments on Human Beings*, which appeared in the same year as Bryan's anti-Koch treatise: she stressed the patients' social and economic vulnerability as doctors grafted cancer 'on the breasts of poor patients who were unconscious from chloroform and helpless in their hands'.[24] A seemingly endless plethora of similar cases appeared in the pages of the *Zoophilist*, all highlighting the exploitative and potentially abusive nature of hospital care. Cases were documented in Paris and Berlin whereby doctors inoculated patients with cancer to trace its progress through the human body instead of trying to cure the disease. The journal also disclosed that conjunctivitis was being induced in young patients at a children's hospital in Moscow and a Glasgow surgeon, researching immunity against cholera, was experimenting on children with a serum derived from the blisters of measles sufferers. In 1893 the *Zoophilist* reported that Koch continued his researches into tuberculosis and inoculation on the numerous inmates of the Valduna Asylum in Austria. At home, the Chelsea Hospital was accused of performing surgical experiments on its female patients in 1894.[25]

Anti-vivisectionists had warned that the day would come when doctors would no longer be satisfied with vivisecting animals; they now hunted for their human prey in the city hospitals, and like animals in physiological laboratories, the human victims were unable to protest and were placed under the complete control of the medical community. 'In other words,' the *Zoophilist* noted, 'the poor working man or woman who seeks the shelter of one of our public hospitals, will henceforth be—if the doctors can have their way—actually a prisoner'.[26]

Germs, Sanitation and Health

The discovery of bacteria by Louis Pasteur in 1856 and the advent of microbiology throughout the 1880s and 1890s simultaneously revolutionised understanding about contagious disease and created anxiety about medicine and medical progress. For example, Koch's discovery of the tuberculosis bacillus in 1882 created 'an immediate sensation throughout Europe',[27] yet rather than judging such discoveries as evidence of progress the *Zoophilist* chose instead to refer derisively to them as evidence of 'Microbomania'.[28]

It is somewhat difficult to conclude what Cobbe thought about the origins of disease. Her work in the slums of London and Bristol during the 1860s must have impressed upon her the close connection between dirt, overcrowding and illness. She frequented the Royal Institution, conversed with London's scientific community and was reading medical journals at least by the mid-1870s, if not before, so she was not ignorant of change. Initially she seems to have been receptive to the germ theory, although her understanding of it was flawed. In an article to the *Echo*, penned sometime in either the late 1860s or early 1870s, Cobbe used bacteriological terminology to suggest that humans could contract disease by eating the meat of animals mistreated during slaughter. Her comment was not in opposition to her holistic understanding of well being; it resonated with vegetarian claims that slaughtering inflicted pain and that meat-eating was bad for health; it was also characteristic of contemporary thought which suggested that germs could arise spontaneously:

> if the ox or sheep, or still more if the young and tender calf or lamb, be tired, heated, frightened, or tortured, 'ere it die, there can be no manner of doubt that the juices of its body are in a condition which, when taken into our own, become the source of most grievous disorders. How many of the diseases which waste our frames have their origin in such meat, no one can yet decide; but the researches of microscopists are yearly enabling us better to judge how, among the infinitesimally small germs in which so often lie the seeds of death, may easily be included the ferment of a tortured animal's blood.[29]

By the 1880s Cobbe rejected the germ theory because it had become too closely connected with modern medicine and research, and because she believed that it encouraged men and women to sacrifice what she discerned as the spiritual aspect of health in favour of its physical counterpart. Because doctors told their patients that germs and not their individual conduct was responsible for their state of health there was little incentive for people to lead a morally and physically clean life. The preference for health over holiness Cobbe termed hygeiolatry, one 'of the two disaster-laden moral heresies which concern these relations of Health and Holiness,'[30] the other being the gratuitous sacrifice of health for holiness in such exercises as fasting. She deplored what she referred to as the 'Scientific Spirit of the Age' that made 'Disease…the most important of facts and the greatest of evils. Sin, on the other hand, is a thing on which neither microscope nor telescope nor spectroscope, nor even stethescope [sic], can afford instruction'.[31]

It would have been ethically inconsistent of Cobbe to suggest that God would punish sinners by making them sick. Instead she seems to have subscribed to a relatively common attitude towards well being which suggested that when healthy, the body and mind worked in unison; spiritual bankruptcy could easily upset the balance and provide an ideal breeding ground for disease.[32] A close correlation existed between conduct and health, and Cobbe was acutely aware of the individual's responsibility to self, to God and to the Moral Law to lead a pure and virtuous life in order to be both physically and morally strong. Body and soul had to be considered as one in tracing the cause of illness and treatment had to harmonise the two. Men and women were responsible for their state of health and could not become dependent on the new priests of science, doctors, to build up physical strength while destroying moral integrity.

Sanitation complemented Cobbe's understanding of the causes and consequences of and cures for illness, and like many an early sanitarian (Florence Nightingale and the Poor Law Commissioner Edwin Chadwick, for example) it was a concept that she associated with dirt not germs. The germ theory supported sanitation as an effective approach to controlling contagion, yet it did so in a way that Cobbe found antagonistic to her understanding of disease and medical treatment. It created what she called a new 'Doctor's Doctrine' that placed 'the interests of Health in the van, and those of Duty in the rear,'[33] and ignored 'not the Body, but the soul'.[34]

In theory, Cobbe should have continued to support sanitation throughout the latter part of the century because as a preventive health measure it rendered vivisection obsolete; one did not have to experiment on animals in order to conclude that clean surroundings and virtuous living promoted good health.[35] Most anti-vivisectionists continued to have faith in sanitation. As late as 1894 the Reverend J. Baird told his audience at a Bristol anti-vivisection meeting that 'were moral and physical sanitation more freely studied and applied vivisection would soon become a thing of the past'.[36] And although Cobbe was committed to 'moral and physical sanitation' she was critical of the extremes to which both were being taken. 'Of course in many directions this new caution [sanitation] is good and rational', she wrote in the *Contemporary Review* in 1887,

> More temperate diet, more airy bedrooms, better drained houses and more effectual ablutions, are real improvements on the habits of our ancestors. But the excess to which hygienic precautions are carried, the proportion which such cares now occupy amid the serious interests of life, is becoming absurd, and conducting us rapidly to the state of things wherein, if we are not 'killed' by Fear, we are paralyzed by it for all natural enjoyment. The old healthful, buoyant spirit seems already fled from the majority of English homes.[37]

The influence that the medical community was beginning to wield over people was derived from the body of medical knowledge and discourse they held. The learned 'professional' gave advice that the uninformed 'consumer' was to accept as the 'gospel truth'. To Cobbe, sanitation was becoming very much like a religion, not Christian, but pagan, and doctors were building themselves up to be worshipped in their capacity as health givers. Cobbe saw multitudes of patients cowering before the scientific deity who convinced the populace to believe in and fear the invisible microbe, and it was this fear, not God, which Cobbe believed now influenced behaviour. This in turn could mean only one thing—the decline of England. What Cobbe called 'hygieolatry' would, she believed, 'at the best create a generation of hypochondriacs and valetudinarians, not of robust and stalwart Englishmen'.[38] People would be compelled to think of themselves primarily as patients rather than morally autonomous beings, and women would become particularly susceptible to doctors:

> we, women, above all are born to be their Patients. We are ushered

into the world by them. We are vaccinated as Patients, become mothers as Patients, are perpetually being 'treated' and coddled as Patients, and, of course, at last we die as Patients. [39]

Concentrating on the body and ignoring the soul was not the way to good health, and only once the mind was lifted above the merely corporeal would soul healing, Cobbe's equivalent of faith-healing, be able to establish physical and moral longevity. 'If Faith and Piety and Hope so elevate the Soul as to enable it to dispel disease, like Gabriel in Guido's pictures striking down Lucifer, then, beyond all doubt, Mistrust and Pessimism and Fear must correspondingly depress the Soul, and leave Lucifer master of the situation'.[40] Cobbe had rejected the existence of the Devil in her theological treatises. She now reinvented him in her anti-medical literature. He was the doctor.

Good health was something that Cobbe believed came naturally from virtuous living and respect for the vital force, it was something that a vibrant person could transmit to a sickly one[41] and it was something natural that science was destroying:

> It is at best only a negative sort of Health which is gained by all the fussing now in vogue. Real Health, like Happiness, and the Kingdom of Heaven, 'Cometh not with observation'. If it had been good for us to know exactly how our lungs are breathing, our pulses beating and our stomachs and livers doing their work inside of us, I suppose that (on old-fashioned principles) we should have been created to see it all; and (on those of Darwin) we should by this time have developed, not merely eyelids, but also chestlids, to open at pleasure and peep in upon our most private affairs. Dear old Dame Nature, however, has supplied us with nothing of the sort, but has tucked us in nicely and tidily with white skin like little children in their cots, and bid us go to sleep, and she will sit by us and take care that all goes well.[42]

Cobbe's aversion to sanitation, bred from her fear and distrust of science and her sentimentalisation of medicine, was turning her away from the reforms that she had advocated over twenty years earlier in Bristol and London. Then she had argued that it was useless to force morality to grow in a dunghill, and she did not consider the sanitary efforts of the state complete until the slums were infiltrated, by force if necessary, run-down property appropriated and the filth which bred disease and immorality eradicated. As she saw science extend its iron grip to all Britons, Cobbe revised her opinion of public health measures, believing that for the most part they destroyed moral responsibility and condoned vice rather than cured disease; they replaced what was natural with something that was artificial; they violated the rights of individuals in the name of public good and destroyed the structure upon which her very Christian society, rooted as it was in the idea of the individual, was built. She bitterly complained that in 'public life it is notorious that whenever a Bill comes before Parliament concerning itself with sanitary matters there is exhibited by many of the speakers, and by the journalists who discuss it, a readiness to trample on personal and parental rights in a way forming a new feature in English legislation'.[43] Trampling on rights was not as new as Cobbe suggested; it was also something that she herself had done to the poor in London and Bristol.

Cobbe fought against the idea that the preservation of health was the standard by which the morality of actions was to be judged. This 'is what is tacitly assumed by the majority of the medical profession, and by not a few of the clergy; and that the whole House of Commons, for years back, habitually assumes it whenever any measure concerning Public Health is under debate,' she told her audience at the Cambridge Ladies' Discussion Society on 6 November 1891. 'Many of such measures involve gross violations of principles heretofore deemed sacred regarding personal and family rights and the moral interests of the community,' she continued with exaggeration bred from anxiety.

> But scarcely ever do we find a solitary MP stand up and vindicate the claim of those higher rights and interests to be, at least, weighed in the balance, against the newest fad of the Sanitarians. The only question ever asked is: 'Will the proposed measure be advantageous to the Public Health?' Never: 'Will it violate the rights of parents and children? Will it degrade still further fallen women? Will it teach the whole class to shift from themselves the care of their nearest ones in sickness, and thereby lose all the sweet influences which come to rich men from the fulfilment of that sacred charge?' It is impossible to foresee where this doctrine will land us if it be not

shortly exposed and discredited.[44]

Cobbe had had little difficulty justifying her infiltration of families and her work boarding out children as a 'moral mother' in the 1860s, and had persuasively convinced others that in 'all civilized countries the existence of some state rights over the children of citizens are admitted'.[45] But once she concluded that the state was being adversely influenced by science, she brought down her wrath on those who dared to do as she had done twenty years earlier. Where she had intervened to force the individual to exercise moral responsibility, science now intervened to prevent that God-given right and duty.

Cobbe was particularly hostile to notification and isolation in cases of contagion. Separation of family members afflicted with a contagious disease was, she believed, a 'horrible proposal'[46] and a 'modern tyranny'[47] because it was born of germ theory and allowed physicians to exercise complete control over the sick individual. Equally reprehensible was the degree to which the state intervened in the private domestic sphere, threatening the close ties and obligations that bound its members together. Cobbe was adamant that caring for sick individuals was a family, not state, responsibility yet notification and isolation encouraged parents and siblings to renounce their duty. The disintegration of the family, the cornerstone of nineteenth-century stability was, she believed, well under way. It could be rebuilt only if Britons rejected medical advice and accepted their God-given responsibilities towards those in need.

> [The] cruelty of this proposal to tear asunder the holiest ties in the hour when they ought to be closest drawn, is a surprising revelation of the poltroonery to which we are advancing in our abject terror of disease. Better would it be that pestilence should rage through the land, and we should die of 'the visitation of God,' than that we should seek safety by the abandonment of our nearest and dearest in the hour of mortal trial.[48]

Isolating sick individuals smacked of incarceration and suggested that the innocent patient was to blame for the transmission of disease and not the attending physician who moved from one case to another without hindrance. 'It appears to be not a little inconsistent on our part to pass an Act of Parliament invading the liberty of the subject and the sacred rights of parents and wives,' Cobbe wrote to the editor of *The Times* on 15 November 1889, the year in which the Notification of Infectious Diseases Act was passed, 'all for the sake of securing safety from infection from a peaceful patient in his bed, and at the same time allow the doctors who have been hanging over and touching him to carry everywhere and spread broadcast without let or hindrance, the germs of his disease'.[49] What is interesting about Cobbe's comment here is her reference to 'germs' being spread by doctors. By the time her letter appeared in *The Times* she was anti-germ theory; she could tolerate it, however, when it provided her with the opportunity to criticise the medical community.

Not surprisingly her opinion about vaccination also underwent a metamorphosis during this time, and this brought her into line with a contemporaneous agitation that shared a spiritual affinity with anti-vivisection: anti-vaccination. In 1840 a Vaccination Act had been passed that provided free vaccination for the poor and in 1853 vaccination was made compulsory for all infants within the first three months of life. The 1867 Act made it mandatory for all children under the age of fourteen to be vaccinated and doctors were encouraged to report negligent parents.[50]

Resistance to the Act arose almost immediately amongst individuals who considered the legislation an attack on parental rights and individual liberties. In 1867 the Anti-Compulsory Vaccination League was founded, followed by the National Anti-Compulsory Vaccination League in 1874, William Tebb's London Society for the Abolition of Compulsory Vaccination in 1879, and the amalgamation of this Society and provincial branches into the National Anti-Vaccination League in 1896.[51] Cobbe did not support the principle of individuals being free to spread disease. She did, however, denounce medical tyranny and compulsion, which made her representative of the general outcry that arose during the slow and piecemeal transition from permissive to compulsory public health legislation.

Cobbe did not involve herself in resistance to the 1867 Act; she approved of it and its predecessor and believed that such legislation were legitimate tools of state intervention for public health. In her 1868 publication *Dawning Lights* and in articles to the *Theological Review* throughout the 1860s, Cobbe had commended the work of men like Edward Jenner for showing parents that medicine rather than prayer would save their children from smallpox: 'Science has shown how immunity from that disease may be secured'.[52] By the 1880s these same people were no longer doing the right thing if they submitted to the law, and she defended, as did the radical Peter Taylor and others concerned with individual dignity, 'the heretic victims of these modern Inquisitors, the parents who refuse to allow their children to be vaccinated'.[53] Her criticism also reflected a common assumption that vaccination was unnatural and that it injected impurities into humans; it also, she lamented, did away with the need for 'clean living'. Is it 'really to be believed,' Cobbe wrote in 'The Janus of Science', 'that the order of things has been so perversely constituted as that the health of men and beasts is to be sought, not as we fondly believed by pure and sober living and cleanliness, but by the pollution of the very fountains of life with the confluent streams of a dozen filthy diseases?'[54] In 1890 she made the unscientific claim that the increase in cancer deaths, from 5,000 in 1860 to over 17,000 thirty years later, was 'directly due to vaccination, forced on the nation by the men of science'.[55] One month before her death in 1904 she wrote in despair to the Chairman of the Anti-Vaccination League that vaccination propagated that dreaded false principle of public health, 'the exaltation of Bodily above Moral Health; and of freedom from Disease above freedom from Sin'.[56]

Cobbe's anti-vivisection literature continually demanded that men and women build up their moral characters to withstand suffering. She sincerely believed that people would far rather endure pain than obtain relief from treatment that had been arrived at through animal experimentation, and as she told readers of the *Liverpool Daily Post* in 1892, 'it would be better for mankind to suffer from epidemics, small and great, for ages to come rather than learn to approve of such sinful cruelty to the brutes, such fatal petrifying of human hearts and consciences'.[57] 'For after all,' Cobbe told her many readers,

> our bodies are destined to perish sooner or later, and the relief or help which science at its best can ever afford them is a very small matter. There is a greater interest even than the sanitary interest of which we make so much these days—it is the interest of the hearts and souls of men. It is of more importance that tender and just and

compassionate feelings should grow and abound than that a cure should be found for corporeal disease.[58]

R. H. Hutton, editor of the *Spectator*, shared Cobbe's sympathies and admitted that he would rather watch his wife suffer from pain than relieve her sufferings by using treatment developed on animals.[59] It is difficult to gauge the influence of Cobbe's and Hutton's arguments on public opinion. In the context of the vivisection/vaccination debate, their effect seems to have been not so much to convince people to suffer pain and to do so gladly and morally, but to give weight to suggestions made in the press that anti-vivisectionists were man-hating, animal-loving fanatics.

Shaftesbury had warned Cobbe soon after she founded the VSS not to create the impression that she cared for animals more than humans,[60] but from 1881 onwards her continual tirades against medicine, hospitals and doctors and her outbursts demanding that those in pain suffer virtuously put her under suspicion. In 1884, when Cobbe launched her rhetorical arsenal at Louis Pasteur's researches into rabies and its human equivalent, hydrophobia, the *Daily News*, while acknowledging the kindness of Shaftesbury, Manning and Cobbe, also noted that sentiments towards animals could run to extremes, allowing the individual to feel,

> more excruciatingly for the crushed beetle than for the human sufferer whose agonies the knowledge acquired by the infliction of scarcely appreciable pain upon an inferior organization might tend to relieve. The generous aims of the society [VSS] are beyond question. But its members, like many enthusiasts, seem to lack balance and judgment and a sense of moral proportion.[61]

Cobbe denied the connection between perceived misanthropy and excessive love for animals.[62] Others were less diplomatic than the *Daily News* in their criticism and emphasised that the anti-vivisection movement was dominated by ignorant, pet-loving, unmarried women who displaced their frustrations at not fulfilling their 'natural' maternal and wifely duties by hurling emotionally charged verbal abuse at learned men: 'Why does our silly contemporary the [sic] *Times* publish letters of the stupid old maid, Cobbe?...It is enough to make one's gorge rise to hear these fools of dog fanciers speak as if hydrophobia were a trifle, and the life of a human being of less value even than the life of a nasty, rabid brute of dog.' 'Really this old maid, Cobbe, ought to be deprived of pen and ink. Her last in the *Standard* (a stupid paper) is enough to make one sick.'[63] wrote another. Cobbe received many missives in response to her articles, and rather than being worried by them, she dismissed them all. 'They are always somewhat smudged, unpaid and unfastened, and are generally ill-spelt,'[64] she explained.

But they were not all of questionable quality. In 1885 Annie Besant launched a personal attack on Cobbe's blind faith in God and her irrational hatred of science, asking her to remember that 'if her God had not devised frightful diseases for the torture of men and of brutes, scientists would not need to inflict passing pain to win permanent cure for pain'.[65] Professor Virchow, vivisector and discoverer of the single cell and thrombosis, criticised anti-vivisectionists in 1893, when research was being conducted into tetanus, as nothing more than a bunch of 'ladies, who are so fond of their cats and dogs that they are unwilling to see them used for the advancement of medicine'.[66] A Father John Vaughan suggested in the *Echo* that many anti-vivisectionists were 'silly old women of both sexes [who] bestow considerably more thought and care and money upon dogs and cab-horses than upon the suffering poor'.[67] The French author Émile Zola questioned anti-vivisectionists' priorities as did Lord Justice Lindley in his address to the students of St Thomas's Hospital. Individuals who dealt with human suffering saw vivisection as a blessing and implied that those who tried to stop it were ignorant fools. 'If some of these "anti-vivisectionists," as they term themselves, will devote themselves to nursing in the ward of a London hospital for a time,' one nurse explained,

> and see the recovered and lessened suffering (the result of knowledge gained by experiments), and then compare the treatment and comparative ignorance of the alleviation eighty years ago, they may perhaps then feel inclined to direct their energies to a more profitable theme than the discussion of a subject on which they think they know a great deal, but in fact know nothing, showing that 'a little knowledge is a dangerous thing'.[68]

By the time of this letter to *The Times* in the autumn of 1892, Cobbe's lopsided attacks on science were becoming increasingly ludicrous, whereas the claims of medicine were beginning to receive respect. In 1891 London hosted the International Congress of Hygiene and Demography, by which time a significantly large number of people accepted that the germ theory was the basis upon which preventive medicine could be built. The Congress was opened by the Prince of Wales and at its close Queen Victoria received some of the participants who had been recommended by the honorary secretary General, Dr G.V. Poore, who had just been appointed by the Home Office as an Inspector of laboratories. Cobbe scrutinised the list of men presented to her humanitarian majesty and discovered that Dr Auguste Chauveau was a known vivisector whose article on the 'Excitability of the Spinal Marrow and especially of the Convulsions and Pain produced by working on that Excitability' Cobbe located in Brown-Séquard's *Journal de Physiologie*. Cobbe felt that it was 'a matter of public concern'[69] that foreign vivisectors were welcomed by the Queen, and she attacked Chauveau in a pamphlet published by the VSS, *Guest for Queen Victoria*. The public *should* be concerned that the Queen received vivisectors, Cobbe maintained, but *was* it?

Yet another attempt to discredit the medical profession and to reassert her moral authority followed close on the heels of the 1891 Congress. On 6 November Cobbe read an address entitled *Health and Holiness* to the Cambridge Ladies' Discussion Society. In it she concluded:

> The supreme good of the Body is Health.
> The supreme good of the Mind is Knowledge.
> The supreme good of the Heart is Love.
> The supreme good of the Soul is Holiness.
> As the Soul is above the Body, as the Life
> Immortal is above our perishing existence here, so is
> Holiness above Health, and above Knowledge; and
> above all Love, which is not Holy.[70]

Despite the emphasis that Cobbe placed on love, health and holiness medical progress continued to move in the direction of applied research. In 1894 the British Institute for Preventive Medicine (founded in 1891, much to Cobbe's horror) was manufacturing diphtheria anti-toxin and the Wellcome Physiological Research Laboratories (established by two American pharmacists in 1880) were starting their own production of the serum. Government grants and private endowments enabled research to progress. In 1897 the Prince of Wales suggested that his mother's Jubilee be celebrated by the creation of a fund to support teaching hospitals, institutions of which he heartily approved (his endorsement, coupled with his questionable moral character, did not endear him to Cobbe in the least); the London School of Tropical Medicine was founded in 1899 by the Colonial Office under Joseph Chamberlain; and the Imperial Research Fund for the Study of Cancer was inaugurated in 1901. In 1914 the government-financed Medical Research Committee (later the Medical Research Council) was founded. A strong, publicly supported infrastructure of highly respected individuals and institutions rose to carry British science and pharmacological research into the twentieth century.

In 1897 Joseph Lister was elevated to the peerage. Cobbe could not compete with that. Her influence as a moral and cultural guide to human conduct waned as science's standard flew higher. But it had not always been like this for the dedicated Irishwoman. When she ran the anti-vivisection flag up the mast in Victoria Street in the spring of 1876, Frances Power Cobbe was the woman to whom others went for advice and information on the immorality of vivisection. Within a few years the tide had begun to turn; in the face of scientific and medical progress Cobbe became a crank and a fanatic.

7

CONTROVERSY AND RETIREMENT TO WALES

On 16 March 1882 a letter from an H. H. Johnston appeared in *Nature*, a journal sympathetic to experimentalists and often openly hostile to anti-vivisectionists. Johnston was both a critic of animal cruelty and an advocate of vivisection. He reported that when Cobbe had called on 'a distinguished man of science' to solicit his support for her crusade she was dressed in a manner unbefitting a woman working to end animal abuse. Her hat was adorned with an ostrich feather; her muff was decorated with a bird of paradise; and the umbrella that she carried was set off with an ivory handle.[1]

Anti-vivisectionists were constantly criticised for their meat-eating, sporting, and fur and leather-wearing proclivities. Yet anyone who knew Cobbe would be suspicious of Johnston's story. She was not known for her fashion sense and would not have adorned herself in the manner described by Johnston. Cobbe replied to the story in the press with her usual buoyant humour:

> these 'facts' [which Johnston related] may possibly be 'accurate enough for scientific purposes'…but they have given much merriment to those who happen to be acquainted with my real 'outward presentments'. Suffice it to say, that I never paid such a visit as Mr Johnston describes;…never used an ivory-handled umbrella; never wore a bird of paradise, or any other bird, either in or near my muff, or any other portion of my attire; and finally, having never possessed such an object in my whole life, am driven to think that the only Muff connected with the ridiculous story, must be the person who assures us he 'knows' it to be true.[2]

Johnston provided Cobbe with a public apology a few days later: '"A fellow feeling makes us wondrous kind", and I am sure Miss Cobbe, having been so often victimised herself, and led to believe ridiculous tales of hideous and impossible torture inflicted by high-minded, scientific gentlemen, will sympathise with me in my chagrin at finding myself a victim to my own gullibility'.[3]

Johnson's accusation was tame compared with what followed. On 21 November 1882 Shaftesbury wrote to Cobbe that he was 'much grieved by the state of things in the Society' and was taken aback by the 'astounding, and novel, statements by yourself about Miss Coleridge'.[4]

By the autumn of 1882 a close friendship had developed between two hard-working VSS colleagues: the Society's secretary and editor of the *Zoophilist*, fifty-year-old Charles Warren Adams, and thirty-six year-old Mildred Coleridge, daughter of the Lord Chief Justice. At a committee meeting, Cobbe accused Coleridge of 'undue familiarity' with Adams and soon convinced the Lord Chief Justice that his daughter had been ruined in one of the VSS's 'darkened rooms'. What prompted the accusation remains unclear, however, Cobbe's remarks initiated a crisis between the Coleridges and Adams which lasted for a number of years.[5]

While Adams was making overtures to Mildred Coleridge he was also remonstrating with Cobbe for not paying him for contributions he had made over the years to the *Zoophilist*, and informed her that she also owed him profits from the sale of his recent anti-vivisection book, *Coward Science*. The president of the VSS, Lord Shaftesbury, was blissfully unaware that anything untoward was happening in Victoria Street. 'I have been kept in complete ignorance of these things,'[6] he fumed in a November 1882 letter to Cobbe. Relations between various VSS members rapidly deteriorated and Shaftesbury advised Cobbe to disentangle herself. The 'Separation between the Committee & Mr Adams had better be effected without a moment's delay, but in as peaceable, and as friendly, a manner as possible. You cannot hope for the continuance of Miss Coleridge on the Committee; nor can you, I think, persist in the publication of the Zoophilist'.[7] Shaftesbury's diary entry for the 21 November is less reserved than were his comments to Cobbe:

> Much, & serious, vexation I heard on the subject of the Anti-vivisection Soc. in Victoria Street. 'The Cobbe' has not been judicious,

& sufficiently careful. The Sec. has been self seeking, ambitious, deceptive, & wicked. I complain of both of them, as having kept, from my knowledge, things that I ought to have known. But he is by far the greater Sinner; for my ignorance of Miss Cobbe's facts could only have led me to some misjudgement in speech & action—but ignorance of the secretary's facts might have involved me; and it may yet involve me, in a very deep, harassing, & painful responsibility.[8]

Cobbe too was upset by Adams' demands and her rendition of events makes it abundantly clear where she believed the blame for dissension within her Society lay: 'I am just demented with worry', she told Sarah Wister one day after she received Shaftesbury's letter: 'Secretary & clerk both going—& giving me quite incredible trouble by their wickedness.'[9] Nor were her spirits raised, she added, by the impending arrival on 4 December of 'the very awful anniversary' of her sixtieth birthday.[10]

Throughout November, Shaftesbury urged Cobbe to be judicious in her dealings with Adams: 'We must go on as cautiously as we can—We are not as yet safe. That man has, instead, many modes of annoyance—and it is said that he has some weapon, which, if brought to act on the public mind might, by dexterous misrepresentation, produce much temporary mischief'.[11] On 1 December Adams informed Shaftesbury that he was planning to sue for the money owed to him.

Cobbe's worry of being brought before public scrutiny made itself felt. 'You must not think too much of any dispairful thing I write this winter,' she told Sarah Wister.

> The perfidy (I can call it no less) of one of my ablest fellow workers who I thought loved me sincerely has been a miserable experience & my fears for the society were really killing while they lasted. My one thoroughly capable supporter & adviser Ld. Shaftesbury being out of town & everything having to go through endless telegrams & letters, made it so bad. But we seem to be emerging into calmer seas & my dear blessed Mary who has laboured & borne everything with & for me is beginning to be hopeful.[12]

The seas did not become any more calm; in fact, they became rougher and choppier. Cobbe took over the editorship of the *Zoophilist* in the new year, and Adams' endeavours to receive what he believed to be rightfully his continued well into the spring, summer and autumn. In December, Cobbe found herself in court and in the papers.

Adams, as determined to receive his due as was Cobbe not to admit defeat, was not represented by counsel but pleaded his own case. He brought action to recover £158 11s. for his literary work and submitted as evidence receipts that had been given to him from time to time for his efforts. Cobbe and her co-defendants were represented by a Mr Finlay who argued that writing articles for the *Zoophilist* was included in the plaintiff's £250 a year salary. But the Court learned that soon after receiving Adams's initial demand the VSS Committee had given him £103 for his literary efforts, although Adams had returned the sum. In response the VSS committee gave him a 100 guineas honorarium for *Coward Science*, the money being drawn from a fund containing earnings from published material. Finlay knew then that his clients did not have a chance of winning their case; after consulting with them he rose in court and told Mr Justice Lopes that he would not persevere in his defence. 'You have adopted the course, Mr Finlay, which I should have expected you to take,' Lopes replied. 'It is perfectly clear from the terms of the resolutions that the 100 guineas was in the nature of an honorarium, and nothing else. How the committee failed to realize that the plaintiff was entitled to be paid for his literary work it is difficult to understand'.[13] The judge found in favour of Adams for the amount claimed.

Cobbe came out of the proceedings as a woman in control neither of her organisation's funds nor its members. 'It cannot be helped,' Shaftesbury informed a despondent and defeated Cobbe:

> There it is. It has not pleased God to give us the victory. Of all the accursed things on the face of the earth, there is nothing like an unjust Judge! I suppose that he is a Vivisectionist and sought to do you an injury…
>
> We must have patience & trust that God will, in His own time, make all things straight.
>
> Do not vex yourself about the matter, nor talk 'Stuff' about paying, yourself, the [£]100.[14]

The following spring *Le Zoophile*, a French version of the *Zoophilist* that Cobbe had started only a few months earlier, failed. She decided to resign her position as honorary secretary of the VSS and retire to Mary Lloyd's house at Hengwrt in Wales. London now offered her little happiness. 'The quantity of work which was thrown on me was beyond my power to bear,' she explained to Sarah Wister. 'Plus all the worry those wretched people [Adams and the Coleridges] gave me—& I felt that the time had come at an Annual Meeting to hand over my official work to [Benjamin] Bryan (our good Secretary) & the Sub. Committee of excellent workers who now meet every week'.[15] On 25 June 1884 the Committee of the VSS accepted Cobbe's resignation 'with many expressions of regret'.[16] Shaftesbury's diary entry for 27 June read: 'the loss is irreparable'.[17] 'I am extremely grieved to hear you are going to leave your work,'[18] R. H. Hutton wrote to Cobbe after learning of her decision. At the annual meeting of the VSS on 1 July, Bryan waxed sentimental about Cobbe's departure: 'you must recollect that Miss Cobbe is no ordinary person. She is not only a person who labours, but a person who feels, and the combination of work with anxiety is too much for the human frame, and almost too much for the human mind'.[19] Cobbe was leaving London, not the crusade to which she had devoted the last ten years, as she made clear in her farewell speech.

> I must, with great sorrow, leave the vanguard of the battle and fall or retire into the rear—and leave others younger and stronger in my place. You know that I am long past the age when officers of the British Army are now required, whether they will or no, to retire—so you must think of me as an officer *en entraite*, or rather, I should say, on the Reserve List, for I am not by any means thinking of taking my name off the rolls of your army. On the contrary, I hope, after a little rest, to strike some good sound blows yet on the brazen skull caps of the vivisectors.[20]

Following Cobbe's resignation a collection from Cobbe's admirers in Britain and overseas, organised by Mildred Coleridge's brother, Stephen, raised £1,000 from which Cobbe was to receive annual instalments of £100, the first of which arrived on 26 February 1885.

Mary Lloyd's Welsh house was a large residence that undoubtedly reminded Cobbe of Newbridge, although it was not built to such a grand scale. Lloyd and her two sisters had inherited the property upon the death of Robert Vaughan who had been married to a Lloyd.[21] Set in the rugged countryside of north Wales, every window of the dwelling provided a panoramic view of the mountains, covered in purple heather and green fern in summer and russet foliage in autumn. For the next twelve years Lloyd and Cobbe embodied the spirit and lifestyle of latter-day Ladies of Llangollen.

The peace of Wales restored Cobbe's energy and allowed her to continue to exert as much influence as she could over the anti-vivisection crusade. She harassed the Queen's private secretary, Henry Ponsonby, throughout the 1880s, sending him copies of the *Zoophilist* and graphic woodcuts, urging him to present them before the Queen's humanitarian eyes.[22] Because Cobbe suffered both rheumatism and gout, she usually chose not to make the long journeys from Hengwrt into Bristol and London for meetings, but she rarely missed the opportunity of sending in papers that others could read on her behalf and she tried to send in at least one article a month to the *Zoophilist*. Her letters regularly appeared in the London and provincial newspapers.

Despite her literary presence at Victoria Street doubts about support for abolition surfaced soon after her departure. Reid's Cruelty to Animals Amendment Bill had been introduced in the summer that Cobbe moved to Wales; its failure signalled to the Coleridge brothers, Stephen and Bernard, that perhaps it would be wise to return the VSS to restriction. In the following summer, 1885, Cobbe received a letter from a colleague, M.G.P. Martyn, advising her to temper her dependence upon Stephen Coleridge, for although he was 'earnest about the Society, and all that,' he was not to be trusted. Do 'not lean upon him,' Martyn exhorted. 'I heard one of his close relations lament your being as she called it "taken in" by him, and thought I might caution you....Do use him, make him employ his talents for good, do not give him up, but be cautious'.[23] With the death of Lord Shaftesbury, one of her most stalwart supporters, Cobbe's position within the VSS became even more tenuous. She managed to silence the Coleridges, unbeknownst to her only temporarily, with *The Fallacy of Restriction*, a pamphlet published in 1886 and reprinted in 1895. After this incident, while business at Victoria Street carried on as usual, Cobbe's personal life was clouded by the death of her eldest brother, Charles, in the summer of 1886.

The impact of professional and personal problems on Cobbe was offset somewhat by a resurgence of public interest in many of her previously published works, which were published in new editions. These reissues were not confined solely to her non-scientific literature, which suggests that even though Cobbe's anti-vivisection rhetoric was extreme and personal, by the mid-1880s her message about human morality and 'rights' (broadly and arbitrarily defined), exploitation and inequality continued to appeal to many.

Alone to the Alone, a collection of Theistic prayers first published in 1871 went into a third edition in 1881 and an author's edition in 1894. 'The Moral Aspects of Vivisection', one of Cobbe's early anti-vivisection treatises that appeared in the *New Quarterly Magazine* in 1875, was published as a pamphlet and went into a sixth edition in 1884. *Science in Excelsis*, also brought out in 1875, went into a fifth edition in 1885. The following year she lambasted education with her *Physiology as a Branch of Education* and in 1888 she changed direction by writing a suffrage paper entitled *Our Policy* that was printed by the London National Society for Women's Suffrage. She returned to science and in the same year that she enlightened society about suffrage, Smith, Elder and Co. brought out a series of previously published papers in a collection entitled *The Scientific Spirit of the Age and Other Pleas and Discussions*. 1888 also saw Williams and Norgate bring out the eighth American edition of the popular *Duties of Women*, originally published in 1881; it was reissued in London in 1894 and 1905. *The Friend of Man; and His Friends,—the Poets*, published in 1889, was a thoughtful if somewhat emotional work in which Cobbe proved to her satisfaction that the only friend canines possessed was the poet, or at least the individual who possessed an artistic temperament. This work provided a contrast to a collection entitled *The Modern Rack* that Cobbe compiled the same year. This work was a condemnation of vivisection and vivisectors, individuals who, like the physicians about whom she had written in 1881, did not possess an artistic temperament and were materialistic, greedy and destructive of God's world.

As the 1880s came to a close, Cobbe collaborated with Benjamin Bryan on *Vivisection in America* and she was overjoyed to find herself an ally in America, a Mr Peabody, who would eventually found the New England Anti-Vivisection Society in 1895 and who printed 10,000 copies of Cobbe's pamphlet for distribution in the United States. She continued to write and speak on religion and woman's suffrage, welcomed respites from vivisection, although as she informed Sarah Wister she was drawn to that 'horrid business' writing non-stop 'till I go to bed tired to death'.[24]

In the early months of 1890 a heated conflict broke out between Cobbe and Lloyd and the occupant of Hereford Square, the eighty-year-old former actress Fanny Kemble. Cobbe had originally met Kemble in the 1850s through their mutual friend, Cobbe's neighbour Harriet St Leger. Kemble and Cobbe had stayed in touch over the years, and when the opportunity to rent Cobbe's and Lloyd's London home offered itself, Kemble agreed to move in. Yet there were problems from the start. The combination of poor drainage and damaged roof tiles, made it a most distasteful abode for the elderly resident. Cobbe had called in the repairman, Hancock, to improve things before Kemble's arrival, all to no avail. For five years Kemble withstood the conditions at Hereford Square. By 1890 she could stand it no longer and she issued Lloyd and Cobbe 'a very curt *ultimatum*':[25] if Hancock did not install a completely new drainage system then she would leave.

Kemble's demand required that the basement be demolished in order for new pipes to be fitted, the possibility of which made Cobbe reel. She did not have much faith in builders. The two women refused to entertain their tenant's dictatorial request. 'So the thing had to be done,' Cobbe informed Kemble's daughter Sarah Wister in February, '& is now practically a fait accompli. We are very sorry for ourselves for the loss of a good tenant is very serious to Mary....but we are more mortified that all our hopes & efforts to make yr mother comfortable have failed, & sorry to think she will scarcely anchor herself again'.[26] Cobbe could not believe that the house was the cause of Kemble's departure and accused Kemble's servants of causing trouble for both landlord and tenant: 'there was some influence at work to make Mrs Kemble continually dissatisfied and restless;—that the servants were in league with Hancock—or else tired of the house and wishing to go elsewhere'.[27] Cobbe and Lloyd were profoundly sorry for all the conflict and trouble and not least for losing a tenant whose rent was a welcome addition to what Cobbe considered to be the rather paltry income they jointly earned. Without it there would be difficulties in maintaining Hengwrt and the two women decided to alleviate their financial demands by letting the property and moving to a small cottage.

In a financial arrangement that mirrored the hierarchy of their relationship, it was Cobbe who was the main wage earner. Cobbe's patrimony and testimonial brought in at least £300 per annum and, in addition, she received remuneration from her writings. Cobbe's was an adequate middle-class income but, without the rent, not one that would maintain a large country house. However she believed the onus was on her to support the household and, in spite of the money that was coming in, she moaned that she 'was... a poor woman, and not in a position to help my friend to live (as we both earnestly desired to do) in her larger house in Hengwrt....I reflected painfully that if I had been only a little better off, she [Lloyd] might not have been obliged to relinquish her proper home'.[28] Within twelve months of Kemble's departure from Hereford Square, the women arranged for a tenant to rent Hengwrt; he was to arrive on a Monday morning in October to make them an offer.

Four days before the new tenant's visit Cobbe received a letter from a Liverpool solicitor informing her that she had been bequeathed some money from an animal-loving Theist, Mrs Richard Vaughan Yates. Cobbe assumed that the bequest would be a small amount and would go to the Victoria Street Society but when she discovered that £25,000 had been left to her personally she was ecstatic *and* annoyed that had she not had to pay 'horrible taxes' on it, the amount would have been £30,000.[29] Cobbe's financial worries were over: she and Lloyd could remain at Hengwrt; she could work for the VSS without having to ask for payment for writings; and she could donate to the organisation the testimonial that had been established upon her retirement as honorary secretary. Financial security, however, did not quell problems with other, more public aspects of Cobbe's life.

Controversy

A few months before the arrival of the solicitor's letter Cobbe had decided to widen her appeal for anti-vivisection support and canvass those whom she called the 'humane Jews of England'. This started a controversy that dragged on for four years, damaging further her reputation and that of the anti-vivisectionists. Almost ten years earlier Cobbe had written an article entitled 'Progressive Judaism' for the *Contemporary Review* in which she exhorted Jews to follow the example set by Benjamin Disraeli whose father had converted the family to Christianity. She advised them to adopt an evangelical idea of God's personal relationship with each soul, and she made a point of stressing the necessity for them to be more fully aware of loving God's creatures, human and non-human. With the right kind of encouragement Cobbe did not doubt that the Jews of England would support the cause that she held so dear, and in 1891 she wrote and printed at her own expense a pamphlet entitled *An Appeal to the Humane Jews of England*, and sent it out to 200 members of the faith. She reinforced her message with letters in February and March to the *Jewish Chronicle* that graphically described the pain endured by helpless animals in procedures such as baking, burning, severing and scooping out brains.

She tactlessly initiated her appeal with the observation that the Jewish race was in general cruel and corrupt, and in proportion to Christians were over represented in vivisection. She singled out German Jews as 'the worst vivisectors in Europe',[30] and to her February letter she added a list of known vivisectors including Goltz and Schiff and claimed that these men and their colleagues were supported in their endeavours by the press, 'so largely under Jewish influence'.[31] Cobbe did not seem aware that her dogmatic statements would alienate more people than they would attract, and she continued her sermon to the Jews with aggressive and offensive rhetoric. It 'remains a deplorable fact', she thundered in the *Jewish Chronicle*, 'that so extraordinary a number of men of Jewish race should stand before the world self-charged with deeds which must cause every reader, who has not been initiated in the dread mysteries of the laboratory, to shudder'.[32]

The 'humane Jews of England' were taken aback by Cobbe's remarks and the editor of the *Jewish Chronicle* answered Cobbe's initial letter with restraint:

> That a disproportionate number of continental vivisectors are Jews is an accident due to the restrictions hitherto placed upon Jewish industry. Medicine has been one of the few professions in which Jews were able freely to engage, and progress in medicine—or, to be more exact, in physiological science—is regarded on the continent especially, as having the practice of vivisection for one of its essential conditions'. Indeed, the connection with Judaism of the men whose names Miss Cobbe enumerates is of the slightest....Only the

smallest proportion still adhere to their ancestral religion, the rest have abjured it. To treat vivisection then as a Jewish practice would involve a sturdy defiance of fact.[33]

A Dr M. Cohn contributed to the discussion, suggesting that Cobbe had 'been misled by German anti-Semites' while B. Louis Abrahams, writing from the physiological laboratory at University College, called Cobbe the 'archpriestess' of anti-vivisectionists.[34]

Cobbe received monetary assistance from four Jewesses whom she knew personally, but no further response was forthcoming from the rest of the community. 'My appeal' Cobbe mournfully informed the editor of the *Jewish Chronicle*

> which came truly from my heart, and was prompted by honest faith in the humanity of Jews, fell as dead as if addressed to so many stones....I started on this laborious and futile undertaking confident that I should disprove the remark...'*the Jews are a cruel people*', and vindicate the compassionateness of a race over whom Christianity has not exercised its boasted influence. I now sorrowfully own myself mistaken.[35]

Cobbe turned her back on all Jews because she believed that by rejecting her they embraced vivisection.

However, the letters that appeared in the *Jewish Chronicle* in response to Cobbe suggested that perhaps she was anti-Semitic. Morris Rubens, used material provided by one of Cobbe's adversaries, the brain surgeon Victor Horsley, two English Rabbis and George Jesse of the Society for the Abolition of Vivisection to conclude that Cobbe was more interested in spreading anti-Semitism than she was in drawing Jews to her cause. Historians have indicated that anti-Semitism existed within the anti-vivisection movement,[36] yet apart from this one incident there is little evidence to show Cobbe disliked Jews simply because they were Jewish: she was tactless rather than anti-Semitic. In 1894 the Bombay Education Society's Steam Press brought out Rubens's *Anti-vivisection Exposed, including a disclosure of the recent attempt to introduce Anti-Semitism into England*. The *Zoophilist* jumped to Cobbe's defence, backed up her claims, and asked its readers to look over her, by now dated, 'Progressive Judaism' to see how wrong Rubens was in his accusation.[37] The damage was nonetheless done and more was to come the following year when Cobbe assaulted yet another religious creed for not yielding to her animal-loving will.

In October 1895 Cobbe joined another organisation, the Animal Psychology Bureau, with the hope, as she told Sarah Wister, that it would publish information denouncing the 'Thing' theory of animals held by the Jesuits;[38] a proposition that Cobbe could not accept. She did her bit for the cause by denouncing Jesuits with the moral force of a Theist and the dogmatic righteousness of a 73-year-old vicegerent of God in an article for the *Contemporary Review* entitled 'The Ethics of Zoophily', a vitriolic condemnation of the anthropocentrism of Catholicism that allowed the 'vile practice' of vivisection to flourish. The Rev. George Tyrell responded to Cobbe in the *Contemporary Review* the following month and, like Rubens, Tyrell stressed Cobbe's intolerance:

> Miss Cobbe is so engrossed in the defence of the rights of animals that she has not time to consider the rights of her opponents to fair play and immunity from careless and calumnious handling....In the discussion of a question which is purely philosophical, she has industriously gone out of her way on every available opportunity to vilify my religion and to say everything that could be most offensive to me as a Catholic, a priest, and a Jesuit. It is a poor cause that must have recourse to such weapons.[39]

The Nine Circles

These incidents impacted negatively upon Cobbe's reputation as a humanitarian and defender of the downtrodden. More profound and more damaging, not only for herself but for the VSS, was the controversy that she generated in 1892 when she set out to compile a series of experiments, both domestic and foreign, that would impress upon the British reading public once and for all the utter immorality and shameful brutality of vivisectors. She preferred not to journey into London to carry out her research; repeated bouts of rheumatism and sciatica had made travelling uncomfortable. Instead, she relied on a trusted co-worker, Georgine M. Rhodes, to gather information in London and help her sift through an endless selection of physiological experiments and publish them in a suitably disturbing style. Cobbe entitled her work *The Nine Circles of the Hell of the Innocent* which she hoped would take her readers on as terrifying a journey as did Dante's *L'Inferno*. The first circle consisted of experiments that mangled the animal; the second circle addressed artificial diseases; the third circle, poisoning; the fourth circle, suffocation; the fifth circle, burning and freezing; the sixth circle, starvation; the seventh circle, flaying and varnishing; the eighth circle, miscellaneous torments such as clamping natural orifices, spinning living animals, destroying brains until the animal behaved like a 'Jack Pudding'; the ninth and final circle, moral experiments, for example, amputating the breasts of mothers nursing their young.

The *Zoophilist* advertised the book's publication, priced at one shilling, in May, and it was enthusiastically endorsed by Cobbe's colleagues including Edward Berdoe who had proofread it. At the annual meeting of the VSS at the Westminster Palace Hotel on Wednesday afternoon, 22 June, the Rev. Canon Wilberforce stood before the audience 'Now I am holding in my hand a book,' he began,

> and it is a book that I want to impress upon you, that it is your duty very strongly to circulate in every direction....This is a book called *The Nine Circles*, which has just been produced by the prolific pen and the tender loving heart of that great woman Frances Power Cobbe. (Cheers.)[40]

Readers did not question the veracity of its contents. 'The facts given are all taken from the reports of physiologists themselves,' one aged and blind woman wrote to the *Evening Dispatch*, 'and cannot, therefore, be charged with exaggeration'.[41]

The medical community did not see it in the same way and three months later they launched their critique. On 6 October 1892 a Church Congress met at Folkestone to discuss vivisection, something towards which anti-vivisectionists had been working almost since the movement had begun. But Victor Horsley, a brain surgeon, vivisector and Cobbe-hater, was present and he took advantage of the opportunity to offer a rebuttal to her latest attack. Horsley accused Cobbe of deliberately falsifying twenty out of twenty-six experiments, including those performed by a Dr Shore, by omitting references to anaesthetics and deliberately implying that not only were vivisectors heartless creatures insensitive to pain, but that they knowingly refused to obey the law. Cobbe, the pillar of the anti-vivisection community, he claimed, was nothing less than a liar.

Cobbe, in physical discomfort from sciatica relieved only by morphine, replied to Horsley's accusations on the 8th and 13th in *The Times*, the *Standard*, the *Pall Mall Gazette*, the *Echo* and the *Manchester Guardian*. She admitted that references to anaesthetics were indeed missing from *The Nine Circles*, but distanced herself from the errors.

> [The] book was compiled for me—not by me—and, as it happened, in London while I was at home here in Wales...I am bound to admit that the words 'Morphia' and 'Chloroform' are to be found as he [Horsley] states at the head of Dr Shore's experiments. The fact that their use is *Alleged* ought certainly, in my judgment, to have been stated in the excerpt, and would have been so, had I (as Professor Horsley imagines) had the original under my eye...
>
> The question cannot be narrowed to a dispute about the details of one or of twenty experiments, [nothing]...can prevent the English public from coming to the point: 'Has vivisection led—and is it leading—to excessive cruelty; and if so, ought it to be tolerated and legalized?'[42]

Horsley replied immediately, emphasising Cobbe's responsibility for the book and her substitution of fiction for fact; 'and I therefore confidently await from all those who care for truth and honesty the withdrawal of their names and support from the society of which she is the moving spirit'.[43]

But few VSS members withdrew their names. Over the years Cobbe had lost many friends, but she had also retained a coterie of loyal supporters who now pledged their support of their leader. Edward Berdoe jumped to Cobbe's defence on 10 October, placing the blame for any omissions squarely on his own shoulders because he had been responsible for proof-reading the work. Georgine M. Rhodes's letter to the *Spectator* on 12 November admitted that the responsibility for the omissions rested with her. George Bernard Shaw, a fellow Irishman and antivivisectionist, demanded that Horsley recognise that what was at issue was not whether Cobbe was a liar, but whether he, Horsley, was a scoundrel.[44]

The controversy, initially caused by the serious omission in *The Nine Circles*, escalated into a debate about the treatment female anti-vivisectionists received in public. Despite Cobbe's forceful personality she was portrayed in various newspapers and journals as a hapless victim to whom others had to spring to the defence. *The Sunday Times* wrote that 'it may be time to remind this most indignant scientist [Horsley], that in polite society, gentlemen do not call ladies "liars"!'[45] Although vivisection was never a feminist issue, Cobbe's confrontation with Horsley brought to the public's attention the issue of what constituted 'womanly' behaviour at the time when the 'New Woman' of the 1890s appeared on the scene. Ernest Hart wondered whether Cobbe's behaviour that he wrote of as 'unlimited abuse, unchecked fabrication, boundless insult, reckless vilification, and the ascription to the most eminent leaders of one of the noblest of professions of ferocity worthy of a Nero, and the falsehood of an Ananias' was the new 'privilege of womanhood'.[46]

Other papers addressed the rough treatment Cobbe received:

This distinguished gentleman [Horsley] is a brain specialist and an enthusiastic vivisector...but that is no reason why the superior creature, even in these days of freedom for both sexes, should in the calm and serene atmosphere of a Church Congress assail an old lady of seventy with bitter vituperation and senseless rage. I admit that some of the Anti-vivisection literature is somewhat ferocious in style; but this does not justify the unmanly attack on Miss Cobbe in a neutral assembly when she was not present to defend herself.[47]

Cobbe was present at a large meeting at St James's Hall on 27 October that had been organised to defend her against Horsley's verbal blitz. Her status as 'victim' and the support given from her colleagues and the various press made it easier for her to admit responsibility for *The Nine Circles*:

Amongst those [publications] which I issued 'on my own hook', I am happy to say, was this book called *The Nine Circles*. Therefore, our dear and honoured Society is not responsible for that book. I am alone responsible...The book came out; and it appears now that there are some mistakes in it. Mrs Rhodes had not attended to all the details as I had desired; and she left out certain things which ought to have been stated. I took it for granted—I was quite wrong to do so—that all my directions had been carried out, and I made myself responsible for this book. Therefore, whatever error there is in the matter is mine, and I beg that that will be quite understood.[48]

Cobbe's words were responded to by loud cheering. George Russell, Undersecretary of State for India, passed a resolution sympathising with Cobbe and asserted the gathering's 'unbounded confidence in her integrity'.[49] After sympathetic words from Herbert Philips, Dr Haughton, the Rev. J. H. Baird and Surgeon-General Gordon, Cobbe rose, moved by the show of support: 'My friends,' she said,

I can only say this, that you will send me back to my Welsh home very happy. I confess I left it rather depressed, because such attacks as have been made upon me are somewhat startling. But your excessive kindness, and the cordiality with which you have met me, have made me exceedingly happy; and I shall go on, please God, with the fight in the confidence that I have with me the hearts of noble men, and kindly, good women. God bless you.[50]

Cobbe received enthusiastic applause, 'and one of the most successful meetings in the history of the movement, was brought to a close'.[51]

At Hengwrt there soon arrived other pledges of support. One week short of her seventieth birthday she received a letter from her old friend James Martineau who told her 'how deeply affected [we have been] by the abominable treatment which you have received at the hands of the Doctors who have certainly given abundant evidence of their skill in vivisection'.[52] The writer Mrs Humphrey Ward, who had never been able to muster up the same degree of anti-vivisection energy that Cobbe possessed, nonetheless wrote to her friend ensuring her that Horsley's words had done more damage to his side than to Cobbe's.[53] Other societies then rallied around the tired woman in an unusual display of anti-vivisection solidarity. In December, the Scottish Anti-Vivisection Society and the Torquay branch of the VSS passed a resolution sympathising with Cobbe; in February 1893 the French Anti-Vivisection Society presented Cobbe with an address, expressing their '*juste indignation àpropos d'attaque [sic] dont vous avez été victime de la part d'un homme vulgaire et grossier, incapable du reste d'apprécier votre valeur'*.[54]

In July 1893, *The Nine Circles* was republished under careful scrutiny. It included an effusive apology from Cobbe and it was no coincidence that she portrayed herself as the most trusting and trustworthy of animals, sensitive above all others to the vivisector's cruelty. 'I throw myself upon your mercy,' she pleaded, 'and I hope you will all consider me in the light of an old watch dog who has barked very conscientiously at the tramps for a long time, but once he has given a growl when there was no proper cause for it, and is much ashamed of it—as every good dog would be'.[55]

In the following year Cobbe began work on her autobiography which covered her seventy-one years in 662 pages. Published in 1894, under the title *Life of Frances Power Cobbe. By Herself*, it garnered favourable reviews and redeemed some of the reputation tarnished by *The Nine Circles* incident. Cobbe wrote *Life* throughout the winter of 1893-4 in between suffering from debilitating bouts of bronchitis and writing various anti-vivisection articles. 'I really believe it will prove an interesting book,' she informed Wister. 'I have tried to write not merely a book of sketches & souvenirs but a real Life seen from inside—& though it cost me something to make the effort, I have told my real story of my old religious struggles & of the various joys & sorrows of a varied life'.[56]

Cobbe initially planned to bring her book out in London privately and allow it to be published only after her death so that others could deal with the tiresome task of securing permission to reprint correspondence, but she later decided otherwise. She was interested in having it printed in America and asked Wister if she could sound out publishers who would be interested in her story. Wister approached Houghton and Mifflin who agreed to bring the book out in United States.

Cobbe experienced only minor difficulties in placing the autobiography with a British publisher. She had originally intended that Fisher Unwin take responsibility for her autobiography; however, once she learned that they were arranging the printing and distribution of Annie Besant's autobiography, 'a woman I specially dread—& with whom it wd be too good fire for my enemies to bracket me in the reviews,'[57] she changed her mind. George Bentley agreed to publish *Life* in the autumn 'at 21/ [twenty-one shillings] to the Public, on 10% Commission, and we take the risk of Bad Debts'.[58] Two months after the book came out,

Cobbe received £400 from Bentley on account. 'How much that would have been to me a few years ago,' she told Wister.[59]

Praise of Cobbe's autobiography poured in from admirers in both Britain and overseas. These 'proofs of the place she held in many hearts was a true solace to a woman of tender affections,' Cobbe's anti-vivisection colleague, Blanche Atkinson, wrote in her introduction to the posthumous edition of *Life*, 'who had to bear more than the usual share of the abuse and misrepresentation which always fall to those who engage in public work and enter into public controversies'.[60] In November the *Zoophilist* inserted a full page of press excerpts praising both Cobbe and her autobiography, and even publications that were often critical of anti-vivisection and anti-vivisectionists could not ignore the immense contribution that Cobbe had made to the philanthropic world during the latter half of the closing century: 'Her reminiscences of life, men and events, are full of interest and variety,' *The Times* wrote on 28 September. 'All this will attract many readers who do not greatly concern themselves with Miss Cobbe's labours, many of them of high value, and all of them inspired by a genuine if sometimes too indiscriminating benevolence'.[61] In March of the following year a further £600 arrived at Hengwrt from the sales of *Life*.

Cobbe's version of her life is overly optimistic and events are smoothly and harmoniously presented by the writer who was highly selective. There were controversial and embarrassing moments in her life that she decided to ignore, for example, her conflicts with Childs, Adams, Shaftesbury and Kingsford. Cobbe brought her autobiography up-to-date a few months before her death in 1904, but the revisions are woefully inadequate.

In two years following the appearance of *Life* Cobbe and Lloyd both suffered from rheumatism and sciatica and it grieved Cobbe to see Mary's gradual and painful decline. 'Poor Mary has not derived any benefit at all from Buxton. Indeed the baths weakened her & so far made her less able to contend with her wretched rheumatism,' Cobbe told Wister as winter approached the year the two moved to Wales in 1884. 'It makes me very unhappy as you will well understand,' she continued.

> We are likely now I hope to be left in peace in this dear place for the winter & it is the one thing she really enjoys. As to 'climbing her

hills' which you talk of alas I fear she will never do so again. She walks a mile or two sometimes on the flat road but always suffers for it... I suppose there is no new cure for rheumatism discovered in America? I am sure Dr Wister wd. gladly let us know at any time if he hears of one really effective.[62]

Cobbe was distraught watching Lloyd's decline in health. In earlier anti-vivisection treatises she had dispassionately advised that men and women bear their pains virtuously. Now she sought relief for herself and the woman she loved. She was thankful of the medical advances in the harsh winter of 1894–5 when she and Lloyd both found themselves close to death: 'Mary & I were both very ill with bronchitis & only pulled through with a new medicine called "Codeia" [an alkaloid derived from morphine] which magically stops paroxysms of coughing'.[63] Both women became virtual shut-ins during the colder months. Lloyd remarked to Wister that Cobbe's restricted mobility was 'a great annoyance to her energetic temperament'.[64] Cobbe admitted to Wister in the autumn of 1895, 'I dread the long cold winter, when she [Mary] cannot get out & wears out her eyes reading. We old women ought to visit & play cards only we hate both occupations'.[65]

The following year Mary Lloyd died and Cobbe wrote poignant letters to Sarah Wister and Millicent Fawcett. She reflected on her three-decade long arrangement with Lloyd as the happiest and most fulfilling years since her mother's death:

> Thirty-four years of a friendship as nearly perfect as any earthly love may be—a friendship in which there never was a doubt or a break or even a rough word—& which grew more kinder [sic] as the evening closed—is assuredly one of God's greatest benedictions in any human life. She died with my arms round her interchanging words of love to the last, in her own beloved home, which had been my very happy lot to restore to her.[66]

Four weeks after Lloyd's death Cobbe wrote another letter to Wister, who had recently lost both husband and her Philadelphia home, pleading with her to take Mary's place:

Who is taking care of you, my dear, dear Sarah? What can you think of without the care & peace of your home? Will you not come to me? Do so, I entreat to spend as many months as you will in this utter quiet & without any cares—only with me to care for you....

I will not trouble you with more—but unless you have somebody who loves you still better than I (which is saying a good deal!) or who will better care for you there—than I can here—come to your old friend & rest your dear heart & brain at Hengwrt.[67]

But Wister declined Cobbe's offer. She had children and grandchildren in Philadelphia who had greater claims on her company than did Cobbe. Cobbe's nieces dutifully visited the following spring, but their presence did not alleviate the depression into which she was falling: 'I am glad to see them & thankful for their affection, but I feel perhaps even more alone than when alone,'[68] a state in which her mourning was made easier, but which she was soon to find extremely depressing.

Lloyd was buried at Llanelltyd cemetery. Cobbe had erected a grey granite tombstone, with Lloyd's name and date of death carved into it and accompanied by a bronze plaque with an inscription from Longfellow. A portion of the tombstone was left blank for Cobbe's own name. Lloyd's final resting place was, for Cobbe, perfect: it overlooked a woods and an estuary that ran down to the sea. Cobbe planted a number of rose bushes around the grave, and had a seat built on which she could rest after making the tiring trek to the natural oasis.[69]

Not long after Lloyd died one of Lloyd's two ponies also died, the other, Cobbe told Wister, whinnied for her departed mistress, 'till I go out & pet her as well as I can'.[70] Cobbe comforted the distraught animal which in turn comforted the distraught woman. She told Millicent Fawcett that she had suffered 'almost a mortal blow, and I have yet to learn how I am to live without the one who has shared all my thoughts and feelings so long. But I am very thankful that the pain of loneliness is mine—not hers as it would have been had I gone first and she been left alone.'[71]

When Mary Lloyd died, a part of Cobbe died too. Her zest for life vanished, and her letters no longer reveal a forceful, dynamic woman who both commanded and received attention. What energies remained, Cobbe would sorely need as yet another major public confrontation loomed on the horizon.

8

Fin de Siècle

Cracks in Victoria Street solidarity had begun to appear in the mid 1880s when Stephen and Bernard Coleridge had suggested a return to restriction. The VSS sought Parliamentary support for one more abolition bill in 1892, but their search ended in failure. The country was even less sympathetic to abolition in the 1890s than it had been in 1877 when J. M. Holt's abolition bill was defeated in the House of Commons. Perhaps, the VSS Committee thought, Coleridge was right; abolition might no longer be expedient; legislative success might possibly lie in the restriction of experiments rather than their eradication. One lone, still resonant, voice from Wales thought otherwise.

Cobbe's control over Victoria Street was waning and her elevation to Vice President in 1895 was a titular honour in recognition of her years of devotion to the cause rather than an endorsement to lead the movement into the coming century. Stephen Coleridge had, by this time, been appointed honorary secretary, and had set about restructuring the Society. On 21 July at a general meeting at Westminster Hall the VSS voted to change its official title to the National Anti-Vivisection Society (NAVS). The Society's first meeting under its new name was held on 6 October 1897 at Coleridge's home where resolutions condemning the 1876 Act were passed and a new executive committee elected, which two years later included Ernest Bell, Colonel J. Mount-Batten, J. G. Swift McNeill, MP and Ellen Elcum Rees.[1]

Cobbe's developing conflict with Coleridge not only reflected a shift in opinion about vivisection; it also brought to the surface an undercurrent of personal mistrust and antagonism, which for a number of years had been bubbling beneath an anaemic sense of solidarity and commitment to a single ideological stance. The confrontation also serves to reinforce

Richard French's suggestion that participation in the anti-vivisection movement was as much about career mobility and professional hierarchy as it was about conviction in a principle.[2] Cobbe not only opposed Coleridge's stance on restriction: she was also shocked by his attempt, as she saw it, to secure complete control of the VSS; it is, however, incorrect to lay blame for their breakup solely on Cobbe's shoulders.

Upon reflection Cobbe believed that the Coleridge brothers had not been quelled by *The Fallacy of Restriction* in 1886. Instead they spent the following 12 years biding their time and waiting for an opportunity to reintroduce restriction and eliminate her influence over policy. On the afternoon of 9 February 1898 a National Council meeting was held at the Westminster Palace Hotel and a resolution was presented asking 'that, while the demand for the total abolition of vivisection will ever remain the ultimate object of the National Anti-vivisection Society, the Society is not thereby precluded from making efforts in Parliament for Lesser Measures, having for their object the saving of animals from scientific torture'.[3] A vote was duly taken with those for and against the resolution moving to opposite sides of the hall. They were counted by two men, one from each group. Twenty-nine members of council accepted the proposal, 21 rejected it.[4] The National Anti-Vivisection Society abandoned the course that Cobbe propounded 20 years earlier and returned to restriction.

Cobbe had not been present at the council meeting, but she soon learnt of the events in her absence and she was both hurt and angered. People had warned her about Coleridge as early as the mid-1880s. Cobbe was usually a good judge of character, and had she suspected that Coleridge harboured any self-serving plans for himself and the VSS she would have confronted him without hesitation as she had with Anna Kingsford. 'I am in very great troubles about my work,' she dismally told Sarah Wister in April.[5] Fired by anger Cobbe gathered her little remaining physical strength and swooped down on 20 Victoria Street. She rallied her few loyal supporters and led them to Bristol where, after a couple of months of intense organisational planning, she formed the British Union for the Abolition of Vivisection (BUAV) with £10,000 that she had intended to bequeath first to the National Society, then to the London Society. She also withdrew her annual £100 donation to the NAVS and contributed it to the British Union.

Those who joined Cobbe numbered only 5 per cent of the National's members and included Mark Thornhill, Mr and Mrs Adlam, who had originally been involved with the International Society, and Lady Mount Temple. The sparse membership meant that the BUAV would need the support of other abolitionist groups in order to match the strength of the NAVS. Several branch societies—the Bristol and West of England Anti-Vivisection Society, the Electoral Anti-Vivisection League (London), the York Anti-Vivisection Society, the Macclesfield Anti-Vivisection Society, the Liverpool and District Anti-Vivisection Society—immediately affiliated themselves with the BUAV which Cobbe nicknamed the 'Golden Candlestick'.[6] The most important organisation to ally itself with the BUAV was the London Anti-Vivisection Society, although they emphatically refused to relinquish their autonomy and merge with the Union.

The BUAV was not able to replicate the social influence of the NAVS. In 1899 the vice-presidents of the NAVS included the Duke and Duchess of Portland and the Duchess of Somerset; honorary members included Lord Abercromby, Jacob Bright, Lewis Morris, Comtesse de Noailles, Anna Swanwick and Lawson Tait. In comparison, the BUAV's roll lists relatively obscure individuals. The honorary secretary was Muriel Roscoe of Bristol, a Miss Baker was secretary and John Norris Esq. KC of London was honorary treasurer. Cobbe bestowed upon herself the presidency and appointed Blanche Atkinson as honorary secretary of the North Wales branch, formed simultaneously with the Bristol branch.

Cobbe was both enthusiastic and disheartened at having to start yet another anti-vivisection society at the age of seventy-five. She was forced to launch the Union without socially and politically powerful individuals such as Shaftesbury and Cardinal Manning who had been vital to the formation of the VSS. At the same time she had faith in the loyalty of her allies, and was confident that she would not again have to worry about a trusted co-worker appropriating her authority and re-routing her society's policy towards something in which she did not believe. 'I am working now to build up another AV society on sound principles,' she told Sarah Wister one month before the society's official founding in June 1898,

> never to be departed from—& I am getting a good deal of support, but it is a very different thing combining with a few good hearted but unimportant men & women from fighting as I did at first, with

such helpers as those dear friends—all now dead—who used to sit round our Committee table in Victoria St. The very success of my work with the great array of numbers I gathered for that Society is crushing to my new poor effort. But I shall work yet while I live a little while & then I can have the wealth which has fallen so strangely to me [the 1891 bequest] in safe hands.[7]

On 1 June a pamphlet written by Cobbe explaining her departure from the NAVS appeared, provoking a defensive reply from Coleridge; epistolary bullets soon ricocheted between the two camps. In *Why We Have Founded the British Union for the Abolition of Vivisection* Cobbe reiterated her commitment to abolition and her rejection of what she referred to as 'half measures'. She stressed that the 'responsibility for the schism rests entirely with those who have changed the policy of the *National Society*', and that by accepting 'lesser measures' the Society was no longer opposing vivisection, but was tolerating it 'under a slightly amended form'.[8] Coleridge considered her treatise to be a personal attack, and he vindicated his decision to return the NAVS to restriction in his rebuttal *Step By Step*. Cobbe delivered the first blow of the 'attack' by suggesting that perhaps the February vote had not been taken fairly. She also thought that Coleridge was being unfairly secretive about the proceedings because he had not published the names of the voters from each side. Cobbe's suspicions stemmed from her distrust of Coleridge, but they were unfounded. There was nothing furtive about the February meeting; those who were present knew how their colleagues had voted. Coleridge then accused Cobbe of altering the results of the Council vote, claiming her figures as twenty-nine in favour of the National's resolution, twenty-three against. 'She therefore begins her attack upon us with an inaccuracy,'[9] Coleridge charged, playing on Cobbe's reputation for altering facts and figures to serve her ends. He belaboured the point, writing to the Union's honorary secretary, Muriel Roscoe, in 1901 when another Union publication, *Chronology of the Anti-Vivisection Movement*, reprinted the incorrect figures. By this time, however, a new edition of *Why We Have Founded the British Union for the Abolition of Vivisection* had been published with corrections inserted.

Step by Step interwove the perceived wisdom of restriction with the futility of abolition by praising the National and criticising Cobbe as an irrational old woman, doomed to fail. Cobbe, Coleridge wrote, was cocooned in North Wales, too isolated from parliament and public opinion, unable to gauge the best future for, and hold credible command of, the anti-vivisection crusade. She was illogical, too, if she refused to concede to lesser measures as stepping stones for more radical ones. But for Cobbe, principles and convictions were not bargaining tools. She feared that 'lesser measures' would compromise the movement, allow physiologists to have even greater freedom to vivisect than they presently enjoyed, place animals in greater jeopardy, and completely anaesthetise 'the public conscience'.[10] She was becoming increasingly desperate with what she perceived as the government's waning support for anti-vivisection, and her words were tinged with paranoia. She claimed that in the early years of the vivisection controversy parliamentary support had been on her side: 'now,' she dismally wrote, '[it is] understood to be against us; and certainly neither Lord Salisbury, nor Mr Balfour (whose brother was a Vivisector), nor the Home Secretary show any disposition to befriend us; while the Premier loads the most notorious Vivisectors with baronetcies and knighthoods'.[11] And according to Cobbe, the Liberals were no better than the Conservatives: 'the leaders even of that party are against us'.[12] Cobbe asked the readers of her pamphlet to respect her decision to stand by her convictions and to support her in 'this last effort of my old age to help to deliver the brutes...from their tormentors' by supporting the BUAV.[13]

Although Coleridge was inflamatory in his criticisms, he correctly recognised that Cobbe's decision to leave Victoria Street was motivated not only by her faith in abolition and her principles, but also by self-preservation.

> I believe our subscribers will recognise in the whole spirit of Miss Cobbe's pamphlet that impatience of any interference with her autocracy in the ranks of the anti-vivisection army which a long enjoyment of supreme command may very naturally have engendered; but I think they will also understand the impossibility of an arrangement by which those in London and in daily touch with public affairs should resign their authority to Miss Cobbe, a permanent absentee in Wales, and retain nothing but the responsibility for the failures and mortifications that such abdication would necessarily entail....

> It is not enough for Miss Cobbe to differ from us, and to leave us; she thinks fit to go further and to use all her strength to tear down, if she can, the National Anti-vivisection Society.
>
> It seems to many of us a pitiful task for those reverend hands, nor is it the less pitiful for being wholly unsuccessful.[14]

Coleridge accused Cobbe unfairly of destroying the unity of the anti-vivisection movement, but it is questionable whether much unity had ever existed. Internecine warfare had been part and parcel of the crusade since its inception; Cobbe and Coleridge had participated in many quarrels with VSS colleagues before the 1898 split, a fissure for which Coleridge was as much to blame as Cobbe. Both were inflexible and stubborn and, given the dynamics of human interaction, especially over questions of ideology and personal judgment and authority, compromise was impossible.

On 15 April 1899 the BUAV issued the first number of the *Abolitionist*. The journal was published with funds made available by Muriel Roscoe and was edited by John Verschoyle, Vicar of Huish Champflower near Wiveliscombe. The choice of the journal's name conjures up associations with that other great, nineteenth-century abolition movement, anti-slavery, and its mouthpiece, also called the *Abolitionist*. Cobbe had been involved in anti-slavery in the early 1860s: she had sat on the executive of the Ladies' London Emancipation Society in 1863, had written two anti-slavery tracts, *The Red Flag in John Bull's Eyes* and *Rejoinder to Mrs Stowe's Reply to the Address of the Women of England,* and had corresponded with Theodore Parker and Sarah Wister on the subject. She despised slavery in much the same way as she despised vivisection: both slave owner and vivisector exploited powerless members of society for their benefit; both violated the Moral Law and victimised the weak while they, the strong, demoralised themselves.[15] The journal's name was chosen not because of any connection to anti-slavery, but because it explained clearly, concisely and in one word, the BUAV's policy. A zoophilist could embrace either restriction or abolition; an abolitionist could espouse only one policy.

The *Zoophilist* favourably reviewed the appearance of the new anti-vivisection publication in May, but combined praise with subtle criticism: 'We very readily recognize that our friends of the British Union are actuated by the purest motives and inspired by the liveliest enthusiasm in confining their demands exclusively to what cannot be got, but we hope and believe that they will concede to us the credit of as pure a motive and as lively an enthusiasm in the prosecution of efforts for what can be got'.[16] Two years later the restrictionist journal protested against the graphic rhetoric employed by its rival. BUAV supporters, however, preferred to think of their publication as a 'thoughtful, moderate, and well-balanced periodical,'[17] and for the most part its format followed that of the *Zoophilist*, although to more radical ends.

Cobbe's ideological rigidity, which contributed to her ousting from the Society she had co-founded in 1875, was not unexpected in one so deeply committed to her beliefs. She had assumed that only she had the wisdom to lead the anti-vivisection charge, whether it was from London or from Wales. Only a few years earlier many of her former colleagues, who now welcomed her departure, had defended her against attack by Victor Horsley. But rather than being revered as the foundress of a great cause she was considered a burden best shed. At a meeting of Council and affiliated societies on Tuesday 9 May 1899 at the French Saloon, St James Restaurant, Ernest Bell commented on the increase in subscriptions the National was receiving now that Cobbe had removed herself from its ranks:

> The result of the new policy which the Society has adopted has been that I think we have more than doubled our subscription list and have obtained support in very influential quarters. We have reason to believe that there are far more members of Parliament who will now support our cause than there were under the old regime. For this we must thank our honorary secretary Mr Coleridge. (Applause.) I suppose I may now say it without offence, before he came the Society had got into a rather somnolent bent, humdrum sort of condition— the sort of condition when rather extreme measures are necessary, and when the right moment came the right man came with it....At any rate the Society since Mr Coleridge has been its honorary secretary has advanced by leaps and bounds. (Applause.)[18]

The remainder of the meeting continued to celebrate the NAVS's vision for the future with Coleridge at the helm and lament the past under Cobbe's tenure.

Cobbe realised that in light of her failing health it would be wise to find a successor. On the surface her choice was perhaps not a particularly wise one considering that the anti-vivisectionists were accused from all sides of being archaic and fanatically opposed to medical progress. But it made sense for Cobbe to select someone who could confront Coleridge on his own ground; someone who was as firmly bound to abolitionist principles as was she; someone whom she could trust to take the BUAV where she wanted. Cobbe set her sights on Dr Walter Hadwen of Gloucester.

Hadwen was a contemporary of Coleridge; they were both born in 1854 and were to die four years apart, Hadwen in 1932 and Coleridge in 1936. During the 1870s and 1880s, Hadwen worked as a chemist in Highbridge where he was prosecuted under the 1867 Vaccination Act for refusing to have his children vaccinated. Within a few years he became a qualified doctor and moved to Gloucester where he wrote numerous anti-vaccination articles for the movement's publication, the *Inquirer*. During the height of the Gloucester smallpox epidemic in 1895–6, Hadwen blamed the insanitary conditions in the town and in hospitals for the speed at which the disease spread. Cobbe liked the man she met at Gloucester. He was a sanitarian and an anti-vaccinationist; he considered germ theory to be 'another phase of witchcraft fetish';[19] he stuck to his guns in the face of widespread criticism; he was medically qualified. Hadwen was, according to Cobbe's requirements, the perfect individual to lead the BUAV into the coming century.

The relationship between the NAVS and the BUAV went from bad to worse over the next few years. Early in 1902 Coleridge accused BUAV member Edith Carrington of infringement of copyright because she had included passages in a pamphlet, *Legal and Illegal Cruelty*, previously published in National Society literature, without permission or acknowledgement.[20] Dr Hadwen commented to the London Society's honorary secretary, Sidney Trist, 'that Coleridge is very contemptuous about the British Union, and says that the London Society is the only one with any real fight in it, or which does anything'.[21] Trist told Hadwen in March that a number of anti-vivisectionists were 'losing heart at the distressing internecine warfare which has been the daily bread of the movement almost since Mr Coleridge came into it'.[22]

Cobbe avoided any direct confrontation with Coleridge. She had neither the energy nor the desire to resort to verbal fisticuffs with a former colleague. She told him as much in an undated letter, which may have been sent as early as the founding of the British Union, in which her exhaustion is apparent. 'Dear Stephen,' she began,

> I asked you six or more weeks ago, to allow our correspondence to fall into abeyance, lest it might became acrimonious. You have since sent me several more-or-less unpleasant letters, and as I find that my silence does not secure me immunity from your arrows, and that I know no reason why I should allow myself to be your target after your last pamphlet, I am today returning unopened the letter from you which I found in my bag this morning.
>
> As this will in all probability be the last letter you will ever receive from me, I will close it by the assurance that, though you have well nigh ruined the work of my life—& of a life dearer to me than my own: I am still yr. old friend.[23]

Cobbe felt that Coleridge had betrayed her and their friendship. Uncharacteristically, she withdrew from confrontation and concentrated her energies on herself. As 1902 drew to a close Cobbe would need to call on all her resources to defend herself in yet another publicly humiliating encounter.

The nearly two decades that Cobbe had spent at Hengwrt had turned it into, what the *Abolitionist* called, a 'paradise for domestic animals' and 'a refuge for the wild life of the surrounding country'.[24] Cobbe took in strays and unwanted pets and the comfort she received from her menagerie was immense, especially after Lloyd's death. However, it was an old cart horse, destined for the knacker's, but saved by Cobbe, that was the object of the final physically and emotionally damaging public vilification that she suffered.

In old age Cobbe had come to deplore hunting of any kind. When she met up with a couple of otter hunters on Hengwrt property in the summer of 1902 she denounced their sport and refused them access to the otters on her land. The hunters decided to retaliate, causing Cobbe 'a horrible worry'.[25] A few days after the confrontation Cobbe harnessed her carthorse, a grey gelding named Beverly, to her carriage and was driven by her coachman into Barmouth where she was met by the men whom she had thrown off Hengwrt property. One of them commented how 'groggy' the horse looked; it might, he suggested, have been mistreated during the journey into town. The police were called. They could find nothing untoward with Cobbe's treatment of the animal, but they were sent by the Chief Constable (whom Cobbe called 'my special enemy'[26]) to intercept her on her return journey. Judging by the illegibility of her handwriting in a letter written to Sarah Wister soon after the event, one can gather that she was immensely upset and humiliated by the publicity that surrounded the incident:

> Then they sent 9 days later a Vet whom I had dismissed years ago for cruelty to my dog—& he swore all sorts of lies.
> My counsel & the most eminent Vet in this part of the world, did all they could & I was acquitted, but all the papers are ringing with false reports & satirical remarks & I am truly crazed with rage.[27]

The accusations were as unbelievable to her friends as the 'muff' incident had been 20 years earlier. 'You say that the charge against me of cruelty (to my poor pet old horse) is like accusing one of yr temperance leaders of drinking,' she wrote to Wister. 'One friend here said it was like charging Josephine Butler with misconduct! Lord Hobhouse said it was like suggesting that the Archbishop of Canterbury was drunk!'[28] The *Abolitionist* carried an address in October from the Union's branch societies defending Cobbe's reputation as a humane, principled animal lover who at nearly 80-years old did not need the vexation of public embarrassment, but who did need help defending herself.[29] Gone were the days when Cobbe vociferously responded to attacks with unbridled passion. The charges against her were quickly dismissed, but the experience left her shattered. She was able to distance herself from the incident by travelling with her niece Helen, her brother Thomas's daughter, and an invalid carriage for the winter to Clifton where she gave a speech on women's suffrage and presided over British Union Committee and other drawing-room meetings.

The strains of the past year exacerbated Cobbe's poor health; in addition to rheumatism and gout she suffered from heart trouble, which worsened after the confrontation with the otter hunters and the local authorities. She attended as many local anti-vivisection meetings in Wales as possible mainly because, as she told Wister, she needed to feel useful.[30] She continued to attend and preside over BUAV meetings but, as she lamented to Wister many times, she was nothing but a poor, lonely woman who tired of conversation with outsiders and relied on her few servants to provide the companionship that she needed. Physical frailty was accompanied by its emotional counterpart. Able to stay at Hengwrt after Lloyd's death she wrote in her letters as if it was the one last thing close to Mary Lloyd that she could hold onto. Like Newbridge before it, Hengwrt evoked memories for Cobbe of happier times. Meals and bedtime were the highlights of her day; she believed that she was fit only to sit in her chair and stare at the world around her with tired eyes that had witnessed much injustice and now wished to close forever. She complained that her writing powers were rapidly ebbing, and noted that the days seemed so long—'there are so many hours in the 24'.[31] At one time there were not enough hours for Cobbe to do all that she wanted; now she willed time to pass as she laboured under the 'sad, sad cloud of age & helplessness'.[32]

The dawning of a new century contributed to her sense of despair. The death of Queen Victoria in 1901 had been a great blow to Cobbe; she detested the new King, Edward VII, 'only the bad, fast lot hail his reign'.[33] Added to his 'loose-living', which Cobbe found morally reprehensible, was his participation in the Conference on Demography and Hygiene in 1891 and his open support of teaching hospitals in 1897, all of which were clear indications to Cobbe of how immoral and inappropriate a role model he was: 'the whole country seems to have deteriorated in the direction of Amusement seeking in place of fidelity to Duty,'[34] she lamented. Equally reprehensible to Cobbe were events in South Africa. She considered the government's conduct during the Boer War to be outrageous, although she did not elaborate in either published sources or her correspondence; the concentration camps may have upset her, or it may have been the carnage and death in war that she found incomprehensible. She was so ashamed and angry with the Conservatives that she withdrew on principle from the Primrose League, founded in 1883 to promote conservative ideals, and became a Dame of the Women's Liberal Federation in the winter of 1901–2, although in her heart she could never be anything but conservative.[35]

Her public writings were as pessimistic as her private correspondence. 'Schadenfreude' was the penultimate contribution that she made to the

Contemporary Review in 1902, and it is difficult to discern in it the optimism that the *Abolitionist* commented upon.[36] In 'Schadenfreude' Cobbe restated her belief that because God was good and loved everyone equally, He would never create a place of eternal suffering. The sooner the world accepted this, the sooner Christianity could progress. However, Cobbe also recognised that 'Schadenfreude', pleasure in the pain of others, was as strong as, if not stronger, in 1902 as it had been 40 years earlier. Not only men but children and women, who were supposed to save society from atrocity, were encouraged to be cruel to animals; hunting and shooting continued to amuse many people; the Boer War hardened human hearts and encouraged Britons to respond to their animal passions for conflict, revenge and punishment creating, Cobbe wrote, 'a new undercurrent of ferocity dimly discernible through the whole spirit of the nation'.[37]

Cobbe's despair over Schadenfreude encouraged her to address once again the issue of women's suffrage, for it was in female enfranchisement and women's greater participation in public that she believed the key to the future stability and improvement of society lay. Cobbe wrote *Justice for the Gander—Justice for the Goose* while she was in Bristol in the winter of 1902, and she made time to read it as an address to the Ladies' Club at Clifton on 2 January. The address was published in the *Contemporary Review* in May and was her final literary contribution to the periodical. Cobbe said nothing new in this piece. It once again combined the radical demand for women's suffrage with the conservative argument that women were different from men and deserved the vote in order to fulfil their manifest destiny and save England from moral destruction. She equated opposition to her argument with support for the damaging idea that the weak should be subject to the strong, and everyone knew how disastrous such subjection had been not only for women, but for the poor and animals as well. Had Cobbe lived long enough, she would have been bitterly disappointed to discover war used as justification for women's suffrage in 1918, and doubtless she would not have found society much improved once women did have political power.

There were some bright moments in Cobbe's life that lifted her spirits, if only momentarily. On 4 December 1902 she celebrated her eightieth birthday and to her delight received a congratulatory address signed by many of her British and American admirers. Whatever the opinion may have been of those whom Cobbe had antagonised, there were still many people who found a place for her in their hearts. The Bishops of Hereford, Exeter, Manchester, and Ossory, the Deans of Canterbury, Ely, Durham, Ripon, Hereford, Winchester, St Davids and Norwich, Archdeacons Wilberforce and Wilson, Henry James, Frederic Harrison, Millicent Fawcett, Josephine Butler, Florence Nightingale, Anne Thackeray Ritchie, Lady de Rothschild, the Rev. Estlin Carpenter and Mark Twain, Julia Ward Howe, Thomas B. Aldrich and Horace H. Furness were among the 346 who signed the address.[38] Cobbe also received congratulations from the Ragged School Union, London, continental anti-vivisection societies and the Central Committee for Women's Suffrage, London. Cobbe thanked them all. She found comfort in the knowledge that she had not been forgotten. She proudly watched the expansion of the BUAV, which by 1903 had fifteen branch societies including a London office in Parliament Mansions, Victoria Street, near to that of the VSS.[39] But most times she was very difficult to cheer. She begged Wister to visit her in the summer of 1903 and there was a sense of immediacy in her plea: it 'must naturally be—,if not my last summer, but almost so. I have no reason to regret that it should be so. My 80 years have been very rich and full. Now they are poor & of no value to anybody'.[40]

The summer of 1903 was Cobbe's last. She was kept busy that year with correspondence surrounding the Coleridge libel case,[41] but in general lacked interest and energy. Her spirits sank further as she reflected on her life, now empty without Mary Lloyd, throughout the autumn and into yet another seemingly endless Welsh winter. Her depression and despair about life in general came out strongly in an unpublished essay that she penned early in the new year:

> In youth we can hate our enemies. In age we either despise or dread them. Youth has anger. Age scarcely churns up anything stronger than annoyance. In youth our joys are sunshine. In age such joys as are left us are moonlight, reflected from the joys of those dear to us. The griefs of youth bring despair, for all life lies before us in which we shall suffer from them. The griefs of age bring desolation; but we know there is only a little time in which we shall feel them.[42]

One morning in the first week of April of the following year, Cobbe rose from bed on which her dog Browny, named after Elizabeth Barrett Browning, had kept her company the night before and walked to the window. The previous days had not gone well; she had been unable to sleep and had worked feverishly at her writing desk until the early morning hours; she suffered from dizzy spells and palpitations, but she believed that God would give her the strength to launch yet another attack against science. As she turned towards her writing table, the *Abolitionist* sentimentally recorded, 'the gateway of the unseen world opened and she passed through. To die in harness was her wish, and to pass swiftly and suddenly, and she had her wish'.[43] All the major newspapers reported her death from heart failure, and even the *British Medical Journal* paid tribute to her as 'the Boadicea of the war versus experimental research'.[44] Sandwiched between a New York court case about who owned East Beach and a story about a runaway horse, The *New York Times* pronounced 'FRANCES POWER COBBE IS DEAD'.[45] The *Athenaeum* wrote that she 'showed what an able woman with no great advantages or interests behind her could do by sincerity, enthusiasm, and hard work'.[46] The *Spectator*, to which Cobbe had contributed frequently, devoted just one small paragraph to her on 16 April, noting that during 'the conflict [with science] she contracted a wild distrust of the men of science, which once and again made both her action and her language exceedingly rash; but she was a good woman and a capable one, as free from self-interestedness as from fear. She dreaded nothing, in fact, except premature interment, against which she made elaborate provision in her will'.[47]

Cobbe, like many Victorians, had a fear of premature burial and she turned to her trusted medical advisers to allay her fears. In her will dated September 1902, Cobbe ordered that her friend Frances Hoggan MD, or in her absence Dr Evan Williams of Bala or Dr Arthur Hughes of Barmouth be paid twenty guineas 'to perform on my body the operation of completely and thoroughly severing the arteries of the neck & windpipe (nearly severing the head altogether) so as to render my revival in the grave absolutely impossible'.[48] If her wishes were not carried out, the will would be null and void. It was Dr Walter Hadwen who was summoned by telephone after Cobbe's death to perform the grisly task.

Cobbe's generous will showed that she had wisely invested the money that she had received in 1891 in LNR shares which offered a good, although by 1903 somewhat diminished, return. She had had a codicil drawn up in June providing for a reduction in the monetary bequests to friends and family, which ranged from £50–£2,000, should the value of her estate not provide the BUAV with at least £5,000. Ultimately her bequests were adjusted accordingly, and the BUAV received £500 less than Cobbe had originally anticipated. Blanche Atkinson received the copyright of all of Cobbe's books and Cobbe bequeathed her entire literary collection to the Barmouth Library.[49]

Cobbe's funeral was a sober, sparse affair. Although at one time she had supported cremation[50] she had instructed that she be placed in a simple coffin, not made of any durable material but only 'sufficient to carry my body decently to the grave & without any ornament or inscription whatever.'[51] She wanted to be conveyed to Llanelltyd Cemetery in her own carriage by her own coachman, and not in a funeral hearse, nor on men's shoulders. Her wishes were duly carried out. Her favourite hymn, 'Nearer, my God, to Thee', was sung and a simple service was conducted by the Rev. J. Estlin Carpenter. No mourning was worn, 'and the flowers that draped the coffin and the whole open carriage were lit up with a warm glow of colour by a magnificent mass of red roses'.[52] Cobbe's nieces, Mr and Mrs Lloyd Price, representatives from the British Union, a deputation from the Barmouth Library and Dr Hadwen were among those present. Wreathes were sent from all sections of the British Union, from several surviving members of Cobbe's family, Lady Battersea, the Lloyd Prices, from her American friend, Louisa Lee Schuyler, the Women's Liberal Federation and from the National Canine Defence League. The *Abolitionist* does not mention any representation from the National Anti-Vivisection Society. Cobbe was buried next to her beloved companion Mary Charlotte Lloyd.

In October 1892, as Cobbe's confrontation with Victor Horsley erupted, Charles Warren Adams had written in the anti-vivisection publication, *Verulam Review*, that the anti-vivisection movement was not Frances Power Cobbe and Frances Power Cobbe was not the anti-vivisection movement.[53] Nonetheless throughout the nineteenth century her name was synonymous with the crusade to end animal research and it was for this work, above all others, that she was best known. She had been responsible for the first anti-vivisection petition to appear in Italy in 1863 and had played a large part in the 1876 Act which, despite faults for which she cannot be blamed, was a vast improvement over Martin's

Act that did not protect animals in research. In 1875 she had co-founded one of the first anti-vivisection societies, the Victoria Street Society; this was followed 23 years later by the British Union for the Abolition of Vivisection. In the year of her death there were 20 societies affiliated with the British Union. True, she did not achieve her goal of abolishing animal experiments, but it was her unrelenting effort that was morally powerful (although sometimes verging on the unscientific, the sentimental and the hypocritical) and which brought her success, and with it many problems. But these problems paled beside her contribution and dedication to reform. Her literary outpourings had been phenomenal, especially those concerning animal welfare. She exposed the inherent inequality and potential for exploitation in hierarchically constructed relationships between men and women and animals. Through skilful and often disturbing discourse, she succeeded in making public the private world of the vivisector's laboratory and forced her audiences to question the concept of progress. As a politically powerless woman, she was immensely successful in making sure that her principles infiltrated parliament and she succeeded in forcing the government and society at large to become aware of, and debate, animal welfare.

In the 1904 edition of her autobiography, Cobbe wrote:

> It is my supreme hope that when, with God's help, our Anti-vivisection controversy ends in years to come, long after I have passed away, mankind will have attained *through it* a recognition of our duties towards the lower animals far in advance of that which we now commonly hold…The long-oppressed and suffering brutes will then be spared many a pang and their innocent lives made far happier; while the hearts of men will grow more tender to their own kind by cultivating pity and tenderness to the beasts and birds. The earth will at last cease to be 'full of violence and cruel habitation'.[54]

Cobbe would be disappointed to discover that the vivisection controversy has not been resolved; that the hearts of men have not grown any more tender either towards 'their own kind' or towards animals; and that the world continues 'to be full of violence and cruel habitation'.

9

A MATTER OF CONSCIENCE

As with many female biographies this work may be seen as an effort to 'rescue' a woman from the historical wilderness, yet an attempt has been made to go beyond a narrow mandate. Its main purpose has been to examine the thoughts and activities of a Victorian woman who moved from being a highly respected religious writer and reformer to one who was criticised and ridiculed. The book also tries to reassess contemporary and historical opinion of Cobbe, and to place Cobbe the individual within a wider ethical, cultural and political debate. Historians have routinely focused upon Cobbe's feminism and have assessed her life in terms of the male oppressor/female victim dialectic. But it is inaccurate to recreate Cobbe's life story using traditional feminist models of the female life experience. The challenges that Cobbe faced as she forged a public life for herself as an unmarried woman in Victorian England are readily acknowledged, but are not used as an excuse for any shortcomings. Cobbe was a strong woman, confident in her abilities; she was headstrong and stubborn; insensitive and intolerant; she plunged into numerous confrontations with colleagues and adversaries, and had both a positive and negative effect on the causes that she championed. Yet despite her flaws, Cobbe proved herself to be an important figure on the nineteenth-century social and political scene.

Frances Power Cobbe had dominated the anti-vivisection movement for 30 years, yet the crusade did not suffer any cataclysmic upheaval after its mentor died. The number of vivisections increased, from 11,645 in 1901, to 32,562 in the year of her death, and then to 88,634 just four years later.[1] The BUAV continued to consolidate its position, despite Sidney Trist's assertion a few years earlier that it would collapse upon Cobbe's death;[2] two of Cobbe's nieces, Frances Conway and Helen

13. Frances Power Cobbe, age 20
(*The Strand Magazine*, 1893)

14. Frances Power Cobbe, age 55
(*The Strand Magazine*, 1893)

15. Frances Power Cobbe, age 72

Louisa, daughters of Cobbe's late brother Thomas, were members of committee. In June, John Norris died and Walter Hadwen became treasurer; he replaced Muriel Roscoe as honorary secretary in 1905, and the Hon. Ernest Pomeroy was appointed treasurer in his place.[3] In the following year the second Royal Commission on Vivisection was appointed. No new act was forthcoming, but in 1913 it was decided that the Association for the Advancement of Medical Research would relinquish its role in determining who was to receive a licence to perform physiological research. In 1906 a statue was erected in Battersea commemorating a brown dog, whose sufferings had been the focus of a 1903 publication, *The Shambles of Science*, written by Liesa von Schartau and Louisa Lind-af-Hageby. In 1907 a group of medical students intent on destroying the statue clashed with trades unionists, feminists and the police. The riots prompted heated discussions within Battersea Council, and in 1910 the statue was removed. It was not replaced until 1985.

In 1909 two large international congresses were held in England. The first congress was organised by the Animal Defence and Anti-Vivisection Society, and the second by the World League Against Vivisection. The former advocated a gradualist approach while the latter, under the influence of Walter Hadwen, demanded abolition. The ideological rift in the movement continued in the rivalry between the National Anti-Vivisection Society and the British Union.[4] For example, as the second Royal Commission got underway in 1906, the BUAV's secretary, Beatrice Kidd, noticed correspondence in the *Torquay Directory and South Devon Journal* that named Stephen Coleridge as the founder of the anti-vivisection movement. Kidd and another correspondent to the *Abolitionist* were incensed that Coleridge should receive credit for something that he had not done, and letters appeared in the paper denouncing the claim that Coleridge was the guiding light of so great a crusade. The one true leader, it was argued, was Frances Power Cobbe because the policy of the movement was abolition for which Cobbe, not Coleridge, stood.[5]

Despite their differences, the Union and the National continue today the work that Cobbe began in 1875. They have since been joined by numerous other societies world wide, and have been absorbed into an animal rights movement that is often characterised by non-activists as extreme, illogical and fanatical, one which sentimentalises animals and which wields enough political power to threaten the *status quo*.[6] Cobbe and her colleagues were seen by many of their contemporaries in a similar light. Criticism of animal rights supporters has been relatively consistent over time, as has the moral message which these activists promote: animals have rights, and these rights are violated because of speciesism and the selfish demands of humans. Anti-vivisectionists today would criticise Cobbe's views on meat eating and hunting, but they would in all likelihood concur with the substance of her theorising on the potentially exploitative nature of the human/animal relationship.

A need for autonomy and control dominated Cobbe's life. As a child she had resisted the intellectual limits placed on her by her education, and as a young adult she challenged paternal and religious authority; this resulted in her enduring a tense relationship with her father who died in 1857. She fought to have her voice heard in debate, and clashed with several of her contemporaries because of her dogmatic approach to activism and her intolerance towards those who resisted her proselytising. She struggled unsuccessfully to maintain cultural authority in late-Victorian society and waged a similar battle within the Victoria Street Society from which she and her abolitionist sentiments were ousted in 1898.

Although Cobbe rebelled against social convention she was also a product of it. She condemned inequitable power structures, yet supported them when she felt threatened by various permutations of democracy, for instance working-class enfranchisement and social mobility. Theism may have told Cobbe that each man and woman, no matter what his or her social origins, had been created as a rational, morally autonomous individual; she was adamant, however, that 'religious democracy' not be extended to the secular areas of life. She showed herself to be anti-libertarian by supporting state intervention, a dominant feature of mid-century Britain. Her religious background had impressed upon her the importance of the concept of the individual in relation to God, yet she recognised that behaviour had to be controlled for both personal and public good, and individual and state intervention was the principle means by which this could be achieved. However, she altered her views in later years and became especially critical of compulsory vaccination.

Cobbe spent a great deal of time as a surrogate mother infiltrating working-class families in Bristol and London in the 1860s, spouting pearls of self-help wisdom alongside a firm conviction in her abilities to bring about spiritual and material improvement. Often Cobbe adopted the philanthropic spirit of aggressive superiority and condescension. Her recommendations for social improvement lacked imagination, yet they were not superfluous even if they often corresponded to contemporary wisdom and reinforced the *status quo*.

The family was the cornerstone of Victorian stability and Cobbe was convinced that she had a right to make dysfunctional families conform to her moral norm. Adults needed to have their animal impulses curtailed and children needed to be removed from homes deleterious to their moral health and be boarded out to spiritually and physically stable environments. The result, she and others like her hoped, would be morally responsible men and women and stable working-class families all of which would provide a secure base for England's social pyramid. Cobbe never expected that improvement would provide the opportunity for the lower classes to move up the social ladder and few of her contemporaries would have suggested otherwise.

Cobbe applied her theorising on power hierarchies to women's rights and created a model of female emancipation based upon women's difference from men. She believed in equal rights, but not equality between the sexes. She also felt strongly about the duties of wives, mothers and daughters towards spouses, children and parents, and demanded that these private responsibilities be met before public activities were undertaken. Using Cobbe's rationale, the only women who could be liberated from exploitation were the single and the childless, and realistically this would only be possible if these women had the financial resources to avoid remunerative employment. Cobbe was a feminist and demanded female education, employment and enfranchisement; her approach to and arguments in favour of women's rights reflects the plurality that characterised nineteenth century feminism.[7] Women, Cobbe believed, should be allowed to take their domestic, nurturing qualities, which were more God like than the competitive aggression of men, out of the private sphere and apply them to the public realm. God had endowed women with characteristics so like His own for one purpose: to make society a better, more just and loving place. It was, therefore, a sin to deny women their rightful role, but it was also irresponsible of women to abandon their private duties in favour of public activity. This restriction compromised somewhat Cobbe's feminist commitment to female self improvement, and suggests that her recommendations were exclusionary rather that all encompassing.

As the only daughter of a landed Anglo-Irish family, Cobbe found that she had what could be considered typically female responsibilities; these increased once her mother's infirmity worsened. Cobbe willingly accepted her daughterly duties, yet she was able to avoid those associated with being a wife and mother, and early in her life made a decision not to marry. She successfully resisted her parents' attempts to find her a suitable suitor and negotiated a socially secluded life. Cobbe rejected a heterosexual union for fear that it would force her to compromise her autonomy; however, she had to balance this strong independent spirit with an equally strong need for companionship, and she felt driven, especially after her mother's death, to find someone to care for. She was fiercely self reliant and she did not fear her own company, but she was anxious that she not be left alone. She ultimately enjoyed a 32-year long relationship with Mary Lloyd.

As the nineteenth century drew to a close, Cobbe found herself excluded in Wales without Lloyd who had died in 1896. Solitude was now no longer a life choice. Cobbe found trying the days, weeks and months that dragged on. She had to live without comfort or companionship; she was deprived of the social contact she had enjoyed when she had lived in London and the personal contact provided by her beloved companion.

It was not only the relationship between men and women that interested Cobbe. That between man and animal was of great concern to her also, as it was to a number of Victorians. Not only was the treatment of animals an indication of the way in which humans would treat each other, but according to Cobbe it was also an indication of the extent to which humans lived by a Moral Law based on love, benevolence and virtue. Cruelty to animals did not bode well for the formation of a compassionate society: it encouraged man's beast-like tendencies to surface and thereby threaten his morality; it taught that might was right; and it subjected the weak to the strong. Unlike some of her contemporaries, such as Anna Kingsford and Edward Maitland, Cobbe did not adopt a vegetarian diet, nor did she advocate the use of 'vegetable leather' in place of its animal counterpart; to do so was artificial, for God had intended that man make use of animals in as painless a way as possible. For example, slaughtering was acceptable because meat eating was a natural part of God's planned relationship between man and animals and was necessary for the vital force; vegetarianism was not natural because it upset that force. Cobbe was even able to excuse some forms of hunting because she believed that certain animals had been designed for pursuit.

Cutting up living animals to learn about physiological processes or introducing disease into them as a way to discover cures for human afflictions was, for Cobbe, the most unnatural and horrific violation of the human/animal relationship. Science was natural when it brought man closer to an understanding of God's work; it was destructive when it tortured sentient creatures, and to the horror of many an anti-vivisectionist domestic animals, with whom pet-loving Britons formed close, quasi-human relationships, were most often used.

Cobbe's anxiety about scientific and medical materialism increased once human vivisection entered the debate. Her understanding of medicine was one that harked back to a time when the patient controlled the treatment he or she received, and treatment was based upon an holistic understanding of a 'total body system'[8] that took into account the spiritual and corporeal elements of health. From the late-eighteenth century onwards, this bedside medicine was replaced by the more 'sinister' hospital medicine and laboratory medicine. Developments in histology, pathology and physiology encouraged physicians to look on illness and treatment with a clinical eye; the patient no longer narrated his symptoms to his physician in the privacy of his home; his body was submitted to physical examination and investigation. The patient's identity was eroded; he moved from a human individual to a cluster of cells and tissues. The patient suffered a loss of control, was threatened by medical exploitation and was deemed in need of protection. A 'patient', Cobbe wrote in 'The Medical Profession and its Morality', 'is to a doctor…the much-coveted *subject of his studies*.'[9] Her ominous warnings have resurfaced in press coverage of hospital scandals, and reports of xenotransplantations in which humans contract animal illness.[10] They encourage the reading public—patients or potential patients—to think critically of the medical community and to question the wisdom of medical progress and the faith placed in heroic medicine. Cobbe thought critically about science and medicine with enthusiasm.

Cobbe began her philanthropic career as a highly respected reformer. Through hyperbole and her fear of scientific materialism she descended into fanaticism and was branded a sentimental and hysterical crank. She was not an irrational extremist: her protest, however unrestrained, was rooted in a rational critique of power relations; many of her sentiments were shared by respected contemporaries and actually reflected general anxiety about the fragile relationship between the sacred and the secular in nineteenth-century society. Cobbe's anti-vivisection rhetoric was a logical extension of her broader ethico-religious and reforming stance that focused on the natural and rejected the artificial, and it was intricately tied in with her understanding of the Moral Law, the existence of a loving God and her loathing of the exploitation of the vulnerable. Her comments on human vivisection, while extreme, are not far removed from concerns being expressed today about medical tyranny. The anti-vivisectionists' goal is one that seeks not only to reform but to reinterpret and redefine man's place in the natural world, and reapportion to the powerless a just measure of respect and consideration that befits their vulnerable, albeit subordinate, position in an anthropocentric world. Cobbe sought a moral order that embraced and nurtured, and did not destroy. Many anti-vivisectionists share her beliefs today, and they realise, as did she, that their aims will be difficult to implement.

In 1792 Mary Wollstonecraft wrote that 'the women who have distinguished themselves have neither been the most beautiful nor the most gentle of their sex'.[11] Cobbe may have been more arrogant, offensive and acerbic and masculine than many of her contemporaries, both male and female, yet these qualities, combined with her belief in God and His world and in her abilities as a morally autonomous woman to civilise society, gave her the power to be heard by her contemporaries for over half a century. Frances Power Cobbe was one of the most respected, revered and controversial figures that the nineteenth-century British Isles produced. 'We may learn from her life,' Cobbe's colleague and adversary Stephen Coleridge, honorary secretary of the National Anti-Vivisection Society, noted in one eulogy:

> that there are still to be found in our country women as well as men who are ready to endure much for a cause they hold sacred; ready to give their brains and hearts to a movement they believe to have its foundations in the well-springs of Divine love, ready to jeopardise worldly prosperity, the affections of old friends, and all things that make this life precious or even endurable, for what their consciences bid them hold even more priceless.[12]

NOTES

Introduction

1. Louisa May Alcott, 'Glimpses of Eminent Persons', the *Independent*, 1 November 1866. See also Joel Myerson and Daniel Shealy, eds., *The Journals of Louisa May Alcott*, Boston and Toronto: Little Brown and Company, 1989, p.151 for Alcott's meeting with Cobbe. See p.153 for the article that she wrote for the *Independent*.
2. I am grateful to Andrew Linzey of Mansfield College, Oxford, for this information.
3. The Revd. Professor Andrew Linzey, 'Making Peace with Creation', a paper given at Harris Manchester College, 15 June 1997, p.1.
4. See, for example, Frances Power Cobbe, 'The Medical Profession and its Morality', *Modern Review*, 2, 1881, p.309.
5. See Barbara Caine, *Victorian Feminists*, Oxford: Oxford University Press, 1992, p.104.
6. The Historical Society of Pennsylvania (HSP), Wister Family Papers, Box 4, Frances Power Cobbe to Sarah Wister, 6 January n.y.
7. Elizabeth Eastlake to Frances Power Cobbe, 18 April 1889. Frances Power Cobbe Collection, Huntington Library, CB 401.
8. Ellice Hopkins, 'The Industrial Training of Pauper and Neglected Girls', *Contemporary Review*, 42, 1882, p.141.
9. Frances Power Cobbe, 'The Morals of Literature', *Fraser's Magazine*, 70, 1864, p.129.
10. On female autobiography see Valerie Sanders, *The Private Lives of Victorian Women: Autobiography in Nineteenth Century England*, Hertfordshire: Harvester Wheatsheaf, 1989; Sidonie Smith, *A Poetics of Women's Autobiography: Marginality and the Fictions of Self-Representation*, Bloomington: Indiana University Press, 1987; Mary Jean Corbett, *Representing Femininit: Middle-Class Subjectivity in Victorian and Edwardian Women's Autobiographies*, Oxford: Oxford University Press, 1992; Judith Johnson, *Anna Jameson: Victorian, Feminist, Woman of Letters*, Hants: Scolar Press, 1997: 'The reader perhaps expects "truth", but it will always be a truth that is rendered, constructed, filtered, arbitrated, and finally authorised, so that the version of the subject which emerges is, as Smith expresses it, "a cultural and linguistic fiction constituted through historical ideologies of selfhood and the processes of our storytelling"' (p.21).

1 Early Years

1. For background information on the Cobbe family see Bernard Burke, *A Genealogical and Heraldic History of the Landed Gentry of Ireland*, London: Harrison and Sons, 1912; Gilbert, *A History of the City of Dublin*, Shannon: Irish University Press, 1972, first published 1854–9; John D'Alton, *The History of County Dublin*, Cork: Tower Books of Cork, 1976, first published Dublin: Hodges and Smith, 1838; Frances Power Cobbe, *Life of Frances Power Cobbe by Herself*, 2 vols., Boston and New York: Houghton, Mifflin and Company, 1894, I, pp.1–25.
2. Frances Power Cobbe to Millicent Fawcett, 1 May n.y., c. 1893. Fawcett Autograph Collection, v. VIII. The Women's Library.
3. Cobbe, *Life*, I, pp.41–2..
4. See Sanders, *The Private Lives of Victorian Women*, pp.69–70.
5. Cobbe, *Life*, I, p.27.
6. Ibid., p.30.
7. Ibid., p.33.
8. Ibid., pp.35–6.
9. It was unfortunate that Cobbe's entry into education coincided with the height of pretentious female schooling. See Josephine Kamm, *Hope Deferred: Girls' Education in English History*, London: Methuen and Co Ltd, 1965; Mary Cathcart Borer, *Willingly to School: A History of Women's Education*, London: Lutterworth Press, 1975; Sheila Fletcher, *Feminists and Bureaucrats: A Study in the Development of Girls' Education in the Nineteenth Century*, Cambridge: Cambridge University Press, 1980. Brunswick Terrace formed part of a development which had been built in 1825 called Brunswick Town. For its history see Antony Dale, *Fashionable Brighton, 1820–1860*, London: Ariel Press Ltd, 1967
10. Cobbe, *Life*, I, p.47.
11. Ibid., pp.53–4.
12. Ibid., pp.55–6
13. For example, see Martha Somerville, ed., *Personal Recollections from Early Life to Old Age of Mary Somerville*, Boston: Robert Brothers, 1874; Janet Horowitz Murray, *Strong Minded Women and Other Lost Voices from Nineteenth Century England*, New York: Pantheon Books, 1982; Dale Spender, *Women of Ideas and What Men Have Done to Them*, London: Ark Paperbacks, 1983, p.231. Other, less dissatisfied young women also advanced their learning by self-study and intense reading, see for example Gordon A. Haight, *George Eliot: A Biography*, pp.23–7; R.K. Webb, *Harriet Martineau: A Radical Victorian*, London: William Heinemann Ltd, 1960, p.47, whose education at the hands of her dissenting father had, unlike Cobbe's, allowed for 'an extraordinary education'.
14. Cobbe, *Life*, I, p.62.
15. Ibid., p.65.
16. For a reproduction of the photograph see 'Portraits of Celebrities at Different Times of Their Lives', *Strand Magazine*, 6, 1893, p.52.
17. Derek Hudson, *Munby Man of Two Worlds: The Life and Diaries of Arthur J. Munby 1828–1910*, London: John Murray, 1972, p.226.
18. Cobbe, *Life*, I, p.149.
19. Ibid., p.64.

20. See D'Alton, *History of County Dublin*, p.164. For religion in Ireland see Sean Connolly, *Religion and Society in Nineteenth-Century Ireland*, the Economic and Social History History of Ireland, 1985; D.H. Akenson, *The Church of Ireland: Ecclesiastical Reform and Revolution, 1800–85*, New Haven and London: Yale University Press, 1971.
21. D'Alton, *History of County Dublin*, p.164
22. Cobbe, *Life*, I, pp.72–3.
23. Ibid., p.75.
24. See, for example, Frank Turner, 'The Victorian Crisis of Faith and the Faith that was Lost', in R. Helmstadter and B. Lightman, eds., *Victorian Faith in Crisis: Essays on Continuity and Change in Nineteenth-Century Religious Belief*, London: Macmillan, 1990. Reprinted in Frank Turner, *Contesting Cultural Authority: Essays in Victorian Intellectual Life*, Cambridge: Cambridge University Press, 1993, pp.73–100. All quotations taken from Helmstadter and Lightman. See also D.W. Bebbington, *Evangelicalism in Modern Britain: A History from the 1730s to the 1980s*, London: Unwin, Hyman Ltd, 1989, p.129.
25. Cobbe, *Life*, I, p.76.
26. Quoted in Haight, *George Eliot*, p.39.
27. Frances Power Cobbe, 'Hereditary Piety', 1870, in Frances Power Cobbe, *Darwinism in Morals, and Other Essays*, London: Williams and Norgate, 1872, pp.57–8.
28. Cobbe understood that she was questioning both biblical and paternal authority. See Susan Budd, *Varieties of Unbelief: Atheists and Agnostics in English Society 1850–1960*, London: Heinemann, 1977, p.120, wherein she suggests that because the spiritual God and the secular father were two interconnected authoritarian figures, children who rejected the one felt they were also rejecting the other. See also Turner, 'Victorian Crisis of Faith', p.31.
29. Cobbe, *Life*, I, p.80.
30. Frances Power Cobbe, 'Agnostic Morality', *Contemporary Review*, 43, 1883, p.783.
31. Cobbe, *Life*, I, pp.81–2.
32. Ibid., p.85.
33. Frances Power Cobbe, 'Recollections of James Martineau: The Sage of the Nineteenth Century', *Contemporary Review*, 77, 1900, p.175.
34. Robert C. Albrecht, *Theodore Parker*, New York: Twayne Publishers Inc, 1971, p.56.
35. Cobbe, *Life*, I, p.87.
36. Ibid., pp.88–9.
37. Ibid., pp.99–100.
38. Theodore Parker to Frances Power Cobbe, 5 May 1848, Frances Power Cobbe Collection, CB 657.
39. Ibid.
40. Quoted in Cobbe, *Life*, I, p.92.
41. Frances Power Cobbe, *The Duties of Women*, Boston: Geo. H. Ellis, 1881.
42. See, for example, Frances Power Cobbe, *Broken Lights: An Inquiry into the Present Condition and Future Prospects of Religious Faith*, London: Trubner and Co, 1864, p.67. Cobbe expanded on this further during a meeting of the Kensington Discussion Society soon after publishing the above: the parent 'has no right to

demand of him any sacrifice encroaching on Personal or Religous Duty' and 'The solemn charge of moral freedom once received in adult life must be relinquished to no human master or guide, even if everytie of blood & reverent love unite us to them'. See 'What is the True Basis, and What are the Limits of Parental Authority?' Emily Davies Papers, Box IX, the London Association of Schoolmistresses and the Kensington Society, Girton College, Cambridge, ED IX KEN 5, pp.5, 7. In her examination of Cobbe as feminist, the historian Barbara Caine argues that Cobbe was the repressed victim of her father, 'an imperious and arrogant man'. Caine, *Victorian Feminists*, p.116. This is not so. Cobbe set the conditions of her return, not her father.

43. Cobbe, *Life*, I, pp.94–5. Caine does not believe that Cobbe was as happy as she made out in her autobiography. She suggests that Cobbe disliked being her father's companion and did not treat him as well as she had treated her mother, preferring instead to antagonise him as a means of testing her autonomy. See Caine, *Victorian Feminists*, p.115.
44. Cobbe, *Life*, I, p.97.
45. Frances Power Cobbe, *Essay of Intuitive Morals, Being an attempt to Popularise Ethical Science*, part 1, 'Theory of Morals', London: Longman, Brown, Green, and Longmans, 1855, pp.94–5.
46. Ibid., pp.95–6, 100, 208–9.
47. Ibid., pp.162–3.
48. Frances Power Cobbe, 'Doomed To Be Saved' in Frances Power Cobbe, *Hopes of the Human Race, Hereafter and Here: Essays on the Life after Death*, London: Williams and Norgate, second edition, 1880, pp.159–60.
49. Cobbe, *Intuitive Morals*, p.124.
50. Ibid., p.159.
51. Cobbe, *Life*, I, p.76.
52. The publisher A. James of Dublin had brought out Richard Chaloner Cobbe's *The Duty and Manner of Rejoicing for National Deliverance* over 100 years before Cobbe's ethical treatise made it to Longmans. For Cobbe's view of herself as a 'heretic' see Cobbe, *Life*, I, p.70.
53. Cobbe, *Life*, I, p.100.
54. Theodore Parker to Frances Power Cobbe, 4 December 1857. Frances Power Cobbe Collection, CB 661.
55. Quoted in Cobbe, *Life*, I, p.101.
56. F.B. Sanborn, 'Frances Power Cobbe: A Life Devoted to the Promotion of Social Science', *Journal of the American Social Science Association*, 42, 1904, p.66; the *Abolitionist*, V, 1904–5, p.3.
57. Mary Ward to Frances Power Cobbe, 28 May 1888. Frances Power Cobbe Collection, CB 806.
58. Annie Besant, *A World Without God: A Reply to Miss Frances Power Cobbe*, London: Freethought Publishing Company, 1885, p.3.
59. Cobbe, *Life*, I, p.188.
60. Quoted in ibid., p.194.

2 The Grand Tour and Work in Bristol

1. Cobbe, *Life*, I, p.195.
2. Ibid.
3. Ibid.
4. Ibid., p.196. See also Frances Power Cobbe, 'A Day at Athens', *Fraser's Magazine*, 67, 1863, p.601.
5. Cobbe, 'Day at Athens', pp.602–3.
6. Cobbe, *Life*, I, p.202.
7. Frances Power Cobbe, 'The Eternal City', *Fraser's Magazine*, 65, 1862, p.573.
8. Frances Power Cobbe, 'The City of Victory', *Fraser's Magazine*, 65, 1862, p.317. The woman is not named.
9. Ibid.
10. Ibid.
11. Ibid., p.320.
12. Frances Power Cobbe, *Hours of Work and Play*, London: N. Trubner and Co, 1867, p.149.
13. Ibid., p.154.
14. For a discussion of imperialism see Claire Midgley, ed., *Gender and Imperialism*, Manchester: Manchester University Press, 1998; Antoinette Burton, *Burdens of History: British Feminists, Indian Women and Imperial Culture, 1865–1915*, Chapel Hill, London: University of North Carolina Press, 1994. Heloise Brown, 'An Alternative Imperialism: Isabella Todd, Internationalist and "Good Liberal Unionist"', *Gender & History*, 10, 3, November 1998; Catherine Hall, *White, Male and iddle Class: Explorations in Feminism and History*, Oxford: Polity Press, 1992
15. Frances Power Cobbe, 'The City of Peace', *Fraser's Magazine*, 67, 1863, p.732.
16. Cobbe, 'City of Victory', p.329.
17. Frances Power Cobbe, 'The City of the Sun', *Fraser's Magazine*, 63, 1861, p.671.
18. Cobbe, 'The City of Peace', p.733. It was the cult of the picturesque that made Elizabeth Simcoe love Canadian scenery and that reconciled her to living in 'primitive dwellings and tents'. Marian Fowler, 'Portrait of Elizabeth Simcoe', *Ontario History*, 69, 1977, p.96.
19. Cobbe, 'City of Sun', p.673.
20. Cobbe, 'Day at Athens', p.608.
21. Cobbe, *Life*, I, p.247.
22. Cobbe, 'City of Sun', p.671.
23. Frances Power Cobbe, 'The Final Cause of Woman', in Josephine Butler, ed., *Woman's Work and Woman's Culture*, London: Macmillan and Co, 1869, p.20.
24. Frances Power Cobbe, 'What Shall We Do With Our Old Maids?', *Fraser's Magazine*, 66, 1862, p.597.
25. See William Rathbone Greg, 'Why are Women Redundant?', *National Review*, 14, 1862. See also Murray, *Strong Minded Women*, pp.48–61.
26. Cobbe, *Life*, I, pp.184–5.
27. Frances Power Cobbe, 'The Evolution of the Social Sentiment', in Cobbe, *Hopes of the Human Race*, p.210.
28. Cobbe, 'Old Maids', p.601.
29. Frances Power Cobbe, 'Female Charity—Lay and Monastic', *Fraser's Magazine*,

66, 1862, p.774.
30. Ibid., p.775.
31. Frances Power Cobbe, 'Celibacy v. Marriage', *Fraser's Magazine*, 65, 1862, p.233.
32. Cobbe, *Life*, I, p.251.
33. Journal of Red Lodge and Girls' Reformatory, 12693 (2), 12 November 1858, p.64, Bristol Record Office.
34. For a discussion of pauper children, criminality, reform and education see Ivy Pinchbeck and Margaret Hewitt, *Children in English Society*, 2 vols., London: Routledge and Kegan Paul, 1969, II; Eric Hopkins, *Childhood Transformed: Working Class Children in Nineteenth Century England*, Manchester: Manchester University Press, 1994.
35. Jo Manton, *Mary Carpenter and the Children of the Streets*, London: Heinmann Educational Books Ltd, 1975, p.148.
36. Mary Carpenter, *Reformatory Schools for the Children of the Perishing and Dangerous Classes for Juvenile Offenders*, New Jersey: Patterson Smith, 1970, originally printed 1851, p.73.
37. Journal of Red Lodge and Girls' Reformatory, March 1859, p.77.
38. For the symbolic implications of cutting girls' hair in Board Schools in the nineteenth century (necessitated by health rather than as punishment) see Anna Davin, *Growing Up Poor: Home, School and Street in London, 1870–1914*, London: Rivers Oram Press, 1996, p.139.
39. See, for example, Journal of Red Lodge and Girls' Reformatory, May 1859, p.89. For punishment and schooling amongst the working classes see Davin, *Growing Up Poor*, pp. 133–42; J.S. Hurt, *Elementary Schooling and the Working Classes, 1860–1918*, London: Routledge and Kegan Paul, 1979; Carpenter, *Reformatory Schools*, pp.78, 89–91.
40. See, for example, Frances Power Cobbe, 'The Indigent Class—Their Schools and Dwellings', *Fraser's Magazine*, 73, 1866, p.149; Cobbe, *Life*, I, pp.269–70. Cobbe visited Red Lodge many years later in 1892 and was pleased to note 'the improved physical aspect of the poor girls in the charge of our [Carpenter's and Cobbe's] successors'. The flattened form of head, which Cobbe associated with hereditary crime, was no longer visible. See Cobbe, *Life*, I, p. 266.
41. Cobbe, *Hopes of the Human Race*, p. 182.
42. Cobbe's understanding of education for the working classes, especially working-class girls, (respectable appearance and civilised behaviour) was typical of her time. Anna Davin has noted that such an ethos was commonplace amongst London's Board Schools in the late-nineteenth century. See Davin, *Growing Up Poor*, pp.133–42.
43. Cobbe, *Life*, I, p.257.
44. Minor Deposits, 1311A, National Library of Wales. By permission of Llyfrgell Genedlaethol Cymru/The National Library of Wales.
45. Cobbe, *Life*, I, p.281.
46. Ibid., p.253.
47. Journal of Red Lodge and Girls' Reformatory, May and July 1859, pp.86, 99.
48. Theodore Parker to Frances Power Cobbe, 5 July 1859. Frances Power Cobbe Collection, CB 666.
49. Mary Carpenter to Frances Power Cobbe, 17 March 1859. Frances Power

Cobbe Collection, CB 70.
50. Ibid., 23 July 1859, CB 75.
51. Ibid., 28 November 1859, CB 79.
52. The emphasis Cobbe placed on her suffering in these later letters to Carpenter is not unusual. Webb notes the same in correspondence between Harriet Martineau and Florence Nightingale: 'Like so many Victorians, she [Martineau] revelled in illnesses which were painful and distracting, though not usually quite so bad as she made them out. One need only turn over the correspondence between Miss Martineau and Miss Nightingale to become aware of the distinction presumably mortal illness conferred'. Webb, *Harriet Martineau*, p.7.
53. Mary Carpenter to Frances Power Cobbe, 1 December 1859. Frances Power Cobbe Collection, CB 80. Manton interprets this letter as a censure for Cobbe's irrational behaviour and exaggeration of fact. Carpenter's comment, 'I do hope you will come back at once unless you are getting really better', is, however, suggestive of sympathy not indifference.
54. Mary Carpenter to Frances Power Cobbe, 2 December 1859, Frances Power Cobbe Collection, CB 81.
55. See Frank Prochaska, *Women and Philanthropy in Nineteenth-Century England*, Oxford: Oxford University Press,1980, pp.147–8; Martha Vicinus, *Independent Women: Work and Community for Single Women, 1850–1920*, London: Virago Press Ltd, 1985, p.43.
56. Mary Carpenter to Frances Power Cobbe, 6 December 1859. Frances Power Cobbe Collection, CB 83.
57. Ibid., 9 December 1859, CB 85.
58. Theodore Parker to Frances Power Cobbe, 1 January 1860. Frances Power Cobbe Collection, CB 670.
59. Cobbe, *Life*, I, p.278.
60. Ibid.
61. For comments about the condition of the workhouses see Louisa Twining, *Recollections of Life and Work: Being the Autobiography of Louisa Twining*, London: Edward Arnold, 1893, pp.115–6; Louisa Twining, *Workhouses and Pauperism and Women's Work in the Administration of the Poor Law*, London: Methuen and Co, 1898. See also M.A. Crowther, *The Workhouse System, 1834–1929*, London: Batsford Academic and Educational Ltd, 1981, pp.37–43 for the general mixed workhouse; Anne Digby, *Pauper Palaces*, London: Routledge and Kegan Paul, 1978; Anne Digby, *The Poor Law in Nineteenth-Century England and Wales*, London: Historical Association, 1982; Cobbe, *Life*, I, pp.278–80; Frances Power Cobbe, 'Workhouse Sketches', *Macmillan's Magazine*, 3, 1861.
62. In voluntary hospitals consultants were unpaid but took work therein for prestigious contact with wealthy patrons and to receive fees for teaching. The workhouse doctor, on the other hand, had to accept his post because private practice did not support him adequately or because he needed to secure his territory: 'A workhouse doctor did not expect his work to increase his prestige, rather the reverse', Crowther, *The Workhouse System*, p.156. See pp.156–190 for medical care in the workhouses. See also Twining, *Workhouses and Pauperism*, pp.200–05; M.W. Flinn, 'Medical Services Under the New Poor Law', in Derek Fraser, ed.,

The New Poor Law in the Nineteenth Century, London: Macmillan, 1976, pp.45–66.
63. Twining, *Workhouses and Pauperism*, p.125; see also Twining, *Recollections*, pp.113–14, 136, 117 for the problems Louisa Twining met as she attempted to organise a workhouse visiting society. Her request to admit visitors to workhouses was denied a number of times before guardians finally allowed women access to workhouse inmates after Twining spoke at the 1858 Social Science Congress at Liverpool. See also Crowther, *The Workhouse System*, pp.68–9.
64. See Cobbe, *Intuitive Morals*, pp.33, 167; Cobbe, 'Workhouse Sketches', pp.455–6; Frances Power Cobbe, 'The Fitness of Women for the Ministry of Religion' in Frances Power Cobbe, *The Peak in Darien with Some Other Inquiries Touching Concerns of Soul and the Body*, Boston: Geo. H. Ellis, 1882, p.253; Frances Power Cobbe, 'Social Science Congresses and Women's Part in Them', *Macmillan's Magazine*, 5, 1861, p.91.
65. Cobbe, *Intuitive Morals*, pp.158–9.
66. Cobbe, 'Philosophy of the Poor Laws', p.379.
67. Ibid.
68. Cobbe, *Life*, I, p.286.
69. See Cobbe, 'Philosophy of the Poor Laws', p.379. See also Margaret Elliot and Frances Power Cobbe, *Destitute Incurables in Workhouses*, a paper read at the Social Science Meeting, Glasgow, September 1860, published 1861, p.14.
70. Poor rates were levied according to relief expenditure and the amount of poverty within the parish, which often hit the small man hardest; wealthy individuals often resided in more lightly-rated suburban parishes. Only in 1861 was the basis for assessing parochial contributions to the union common fund changed from relief expenditure to rateable value, from the concept of poverty to that of property. See Michael Rose, ed., *The Poor and the City*, Leicester: Leicester University Press, 1985, p.10.
71. Elliot and Cobbe, *Destitute Incurables*, p.11.
72. Frances Power Cobbe, 'The American Sanitary Commission and its Lessons', *Fraser's Magazine*, 75, 1867, p.411. See also Prochaska, *Women and Philanthropy*, p.15: 'If there was a conviction peculiar to nineteenth-century philanthropic women it was their belief, inspired by Christ, that love could transform society'. See also Eileen Janes Yeo, 'Social Motherhood and the Sexual Communion of Labour in British Social Science, 1850–1950', *Women's History Review*, 1, 1992, p.66. Only with the arrival of the NAPSS did women's intuitive sense of morality complement economic and political theory upon which much relief was based.
73. See Twining, *Recollections*, p.170. Twining's hands-on support for Cobbe did not go any further; she was more concerned with the Home for Girls that she had helped set up on New Ormond Street in 1861.
74. See Flinn, 'Medical Services Under the New Poor Law', pp.45–66 for improvements in medical care for workhouse inmates. Only in 1885 did the Medical Relief (Disqualification Removal) Act allow individuals who received state medical care to retain the vote.
75. Twining, *Workhouses and Pauperism*, p.188; see also pp.156–7, 164.
76. Frances Power Cobbe, *The Workhouse as an Hospital*, London: Emily Faithfull and Co, 1861, pp.9–10.

77. See, Cobbe, 'Evolution of the Social Sentiment'. Sidney Webb adopted a similar argument. See Sidney Webb, 'Reform of the Poor Law', *Contemporary Review*, 58, 1890, pp.106–7.
78. Cobbe, 'Philosophy of the Poor Laws', p.390.
79. It was only in 1870 that every Poor Law authority in London maintained some kind of school away from the main workhouse; outside London there were 49 detached schools. See Francis Duke, 'Pauper Education', in Fraser, ed., *The New Poor Law*, pp.67–86 for workhouse schools.
80. See, for example, Frances Power Cobbe, *Friendless Girls, and How To Help Them: Being an Account of the Preventive Mission at Bristol*, a paper read at the Social Science Congress in Dublin, 1861, published by Emily Faithfull and Co, n.d., c. 1862, pp.8–9; Cobbe, 'Workhouse Sketches', pp.452–5; Cobbe, 'Philosophy of the Poor Laws', p.383; Twining, 'Women as Public Servants', p.957.
81. Cobbe, *Friendless Girls*, p.8.
82. Ibid., pp.8–9. See also Duke, 'Pauper Education', p.86 who argues that advances in workhouse education throughout the nineteenth century in the area of recreation and physical activity – i.e. balls, hoops, cricket, football – and relaxation of corporeal punishment provided a substitute for parental affection. Anna Davin has noted a similar 'softening' towards discipline in London's Board Schools by the closing years of the nineteenth century. See Davin, *Growing Up Poor*, p.127.
83. Cobbe, *Friendless Girls*, p.4. See also Ellice Hopkins, 'The Industrial Training of Pauper and Neglected Girls', *Contemporary Review*, 42, 1882, pp.145, 150. Louisa Twining writes of Cobbe and the Elliots as being the pioneers 'of all subsequent efforts on their [workhouse girls'] behalf' (Twining, *Workhouses and Pauperism*, p.5). Cobbe has not received much historical credit for her achievements in this area; most attention is drawn to Mrs Nassau Senior's and Angela Burdett Coutts's exertions on behalf of workhouse servants. See, for example, Crowther, *The Workhouse System*, p.68. Twining in her *Recollections* also emphasises the role of Mrs Nassau Senior, but gives credit to 'a still earlier beginning [that] was made by Miss Tucker, at Marylebone, in her 'Preventive Mission for Girls', and by Miss Cobbe and Miss Elliot, at Bristol', p.213.
84. HSP, Wister Family Papers, Box 4, Frances Power Cobbe to Sarah Wister, 6 January n.y.
85. Ibid., 29 May 1898.
86. See Lionel Rose, *Massacre of the Innocents: Infanticide in Great Britain, 1800–1939*, London: Routledge and Kegan Paul, 1986, p.48. Crowther cites the same numbers, although claims that workhouse children without parents or close relatives made up approximately half of all indoor children throughout the nineteenth century. See Crowther, *The Workhouse System*, p.203. In the period 1837–8 children between the ages of 0–15 years made up 50.7% of Bridge's workhouse population; by 1887–8 this had dropped to 23.8%, see pp.233, 234.
87. Cobbe, *Life*, I, p.279.
88. Frances Power Cobbe, 'Religion of Childhood', in Cobbe, *Darwinism in Morals*, p.78.
89. Hopkins, 'Industrial Training', p.144.
90. Cobbe, 'Indigent Class', p.146.

91. See, for example, Carpenter, *Reformatory Schools*, pp.56–7; Maude Althea Stanley, *Work About the Five Dials*, London: Macmillan & Co, 1878, p.30.
92. Cobbe, 'Philosophy of the Poor Laws', pp.381–5.
93. See Prochaska, *Women and Philanthropy*, footnote, p.150. For Stuart-Wortley's comments see Jane Stuart-Wortley, 'Emigration', in Baroness Burdett-Coutts, ed., *Woman's Mission: A Series of Congress Papers on the Philanthropic Work of Women*, London: Sampson Low, Marston & Co, 1893, p.90.
94. Cobbe, *Life*, I, p.311.
95. Anna Jameson, *The Communion of Labour*, quoted in Prochaska, *Women and Philanthropy*, p.177.

3 The Claims of Women and Life in London

1. Frances Power Cobbe, 'The Little Health of Ladies', *Contemporary Review*, 31, 1878, pp.294–5.
2. Frances Power Cobbe, 'The Education of Women, and How it would be Affected by University Examinations', a paper read at the Social Science Congress, London 1862, reprinted in Frances Power Cobbe, *Essays on the Pursuits of Women*, London: Emily Faithfull, 1863, pp.219–20.
3. Ibid., pp.224–5. For the feminist struggle for education see Philippa Levine, *Feminist Lives in Victorian England: Private Roles and Public Commitment*, Oxford: Blackwell, 1990, chapter 7.
4. HSP, Wister Family Papers, Box 4, Frances Power Cobbe to Sarah Wister, 21 March 1874.
5. Frances Power Cobbe, 'Woman Suffrage: Justice for the Gander—Justice for the Goose', *Contemporary Review*, 83, 1903, p.658, a paper read to the Ladies' Club, Royal York Crescent, Clifton, 2 January 1903.
6. Cobbe, 'Final Cause of Woman', pp.5–6.
7. Frances Power Cobbe, 'The Defects of Women and How to Remedy Them', *Putnam's Magazine*, August 1869, p.230. Minor Deposits 1314A, National Library of Wales.
8. See Cobbe, 'Old Maids', p.596, 609. Levine points out that the issue of control was prominent in the feminist campaigns. See Levine, *Feminist Lives*, for example, pp.148–9.
9. Emily Davies Papers, Box IX, The London Associaton of Schoolmistresses and the Kensington Society, ED IX KEN 5, Girton College, Cambridge. For the Society's importance in drawing feminists together from all over England see, for example, Levine, *Feminist Lives*, pp.60–1.
10. Emily Davies to Barbara Bodichon, 14 January 1863, Barbara Bodichon Papers, Girton College, B309.
11. Ibid., 21 August 1866, Barbara Bodichon Papers, Girton College, B316.
12. See Levine, *Feminist Lives*, pp.62–3.
13. Emily Davies to Barbara Bodichon, 14 January 1863, Barbara Bodichon Papers, Girton College, B309.
14. Bessie Rayner Parkes to Barbara Bodichon, nd., Bessie Rayner Parkes Papers, Girton College, BRP V, 95–119, #133.
15. Frances Power Cobbe to Helen Taylor, 4 December 1867. Mill-Taylor

Correspondence, British Library of Political and Economic Science, v. 12.
16. HSP, The Wister Family Papers, Box 4. Frances Power Cobbe to Sarah Wister, 10 December 1873.
17. Frances Power Cobbe to Mary Somerville, n.d., headed Glenasmoil Co Dublin. Somerville Papers, Dep. c.358 (MSFP 18–19), Bodleian Library.
18. Cobbe, *Life*, II, p.527. Cobbe's argument fits in with the feminist goal to feminise politics and prevent the masculinisation of political women. See Levine, *Feminist Lives*, p.106.
19. See Cobbe, 'Old Maids', p.595; Cobbe, 'Celibacy v. Marriage', p.234; Frances Power Cobbe, 'The Subjection of Women', *Theological Review*, 6, 1869, p.364. Cobbe was not the only feminist to think thus. See Barbara Caine, 'Feminism, Suffrage and the Nineteenth-Century English Women's Movement', *Women's Studies International Forum*, 5, number 6, 1982, p.544. Cobbe's attempts to recreate marriage in its ideal form, and also defend the decisions of women who remained single, reflected the general mid-nineteenth-century view of feminists who, according to Philippa Levine, attempted 'to remould rather than reject marital practice whilst at the same time not annul the worth of the single woman'. See Levine, *Feminist Lives*, p.42.
20. Cobbe, 'Subjection of Women', p.364.
21. Frances Power Cobbe, 'Criminals, Idiots, Women and Minors', *Fraser's Magazine*, 18, 1868, pp.777–8.
22. Ibid., p.783.
23. Cobbe, 'Subjugation of Women', p.367.
24. A. James Hammerton, *Cruelty and Companionship: Conflict in Nineteenth-Century Married Life*, London and New York: Routledge, 1992, p.103.
25. Cobbe, 'Wife Torture', *Contemporary Review*, 32, 1878; Frances Power Cobbe to Helen Taylor, 6 February n.y. Mill-Taylor Correspondence, v. 12. James Hammerton has noted that while this view was typical, it was also incorrect. See Hammerton, *Cruelty and Companionship*. See also George Robb, '"I will kill you by inches": Wife Beating and Wife Murder in Victorian England', unpublished paper presented at the Midwest Conference on British Studies, Lawrence, Kansas, October 1997.
26. Cobbe, *Life*, II, pp.394–5.
27. See Cobbe, 'Wife Torture', p.63. Cobbe's choice of words is appropriate; until 1828 a charge of petit treason could be brought against a wife for murdering her husband. See Maeve Doggett, *Marriage, Wife-Beating and the Law in Victorian England*, South Carolina: University of South Carolina Press, 1993, pp.49–50.
28. Courtney Stanhope Kenny, *The History of Marriage on Property and on the Wife's Legal Capacity*, London: Reeves, 1879, p.153. For comments on beating and confining wives see pp.152–4.
29. Reprinted in the *Spectator*, 50, 1877, p.1617
30. In her article on feminists and wife beating, Jan Lambertz considers Cobbe's article an 'anomaly', standing out against the 'episodic and fragmentary' material that appeared. See Jan Lambertz, 'Feminists and the Politics of Wife-Beating', in Harold L. Smith, ed., *British Feminism in the Twentieth Century*, Aldershot, Hants: Edward Elgar, 1990.
31. Jessie Boucherett, 'Frances Power Cobbe', *Englishwoman's Review*, 35, 1904,

p.133.
32. Frances Power Cobbe to Helen Taylor, 6 February n.y. Mill-Taylor Correspondence, v. 12. See also Kenny, *History of the Law of England*, p.154.
33. Hammerton, *Cruelty and Companionship*, p.39.
34. Cobbe, 'Wife Torture', p.85. For the effect of children on adults, see Lawrence Bauer and Carol Ritt, 'Wife Abuse, Late Victorian English Feminists and the Legacy of Frances Power Cobbe', *International Journal of Women's Studies*, 6, 3, 1983, p.201.
35. HSP, The Wister Family Papers, Box 4. Frances Power Cobbe to Sarah Wister, 17 May 1878. Henry James had created a similar relationship between three of his characters in *The Bostonians*: Olive, Verena and Basil. Verena realises her potential when she is in the company of Olive rather than Basil. See Lillian Faderman, *Surpassing the Love of Men: Romantic Friendship and Love Between Women from the Renaissance to the Present*, London: The Women's Press, 1981, p.194.
36. See Emily Davies to Barbara Bodichon, 3 December 1862, Barbara Bodichon Papers, Girton College, B302; Frances Power Cobbe to Helen Taylor, 4 December 1867, Mill-Taylor Correspondence, v. 12.
37. See Faderman, *Surpassing the Love of Men*, p.161. Faderman, Carroll Smith Rosenberg and Martha Vicinus note in their respective works that relationships between women, what Vicinus terms homoerotic friendships, were a common feature in Victorian England and America, and were accepted as natural 'because women saw themselves, and were seen as kindred spirits who inhabited a world of interests and sensibilities alien to men' (p.160). Women's communities, such as the one Cobbe discovered in Italy in the late 1850s, and the suffrage movement, fostered a sense of same-sex solidarity and companionship. Women involved in such arrangements could write of them as foremost spiritual because theirs was a world understood to be untainted by the corrupt baseness—including sex—that characterised the male public realm. Some participants, Vicinus argues, were sexually aware, others were not, but most 'consistently spoke of their love in terms that replicated heterosexual love'. See Vicinus, *Independent Women*, p.158; Levine, *Feminist Lives*, pp.64–75; Caine, 'Feminism, Suffrage and the Nineteenth-Century English Women's Movement', p.545. Regarding Cobbe's relationship with Lloyd, Caine writes that there 'is no way of knowing what, if any, sexual relationship existed between the two women. But it is evident that this relationship provided a more than adequate alternative to marriage'.
38. Liz Stanley, 'Romantic Friendship? Some Issues in Researching Lesbian History and Biography', *Women's History Review*, 1, 2, 1992, p.210. For a discussion on lesbianism in history see Carroll Smith-Rosenberg, 'The Female World of Love and Ritual: Relation between Women in Nineteenth-Century America', *Signs*, 1, 1, 1975, pp.1–29; Martha Vicinus, 'Distance and Desire: English Boarding School Friendships, 1870–1920' in Martin Baume Duberman, Martha Vicinus and George Chauncey Jr., eds., *Hidden From History: Reclaiming the Gay and Lesbian Past*, New York: New American Library, 1989, pp.212–229; Martha Vicinus, '"They Wonder to Which Sex I Belong": The Historical Roots of the Modern Lesbian Identity' in Denis Altman et al., eds. *Homosexuality: Which Homosexuality?*,

London: Gay Men's Press, 1989.
39. See Smith-Rosenberg, 'Female World of Love and Ritual', p.9; Stanley, 'Romantic Friendship?', p.195. Martha Vicinus notes such relationships often developed in boarding schools, Vicinus, *Independent Women*, p.34; Vicinus, 'Distance and Desire'.
40. Faderman, *Surpassing the Love*, p.142.
41. Emily Hamer, *Britannia's Glory: A History of Twentieth-Century Lesbians*, London: Cassell, 1996, p.28.
42. Vicinus, '"They Wonder to Which Sex I Belong"', pp.187–8.
43. HSP, Wister Family Papers, Box 4. Frances Power Cobbe to Sarah Wister, 17 May, n.y., c. 1878.
44. Minor Deposits, 1310A, National Library of Wales. By permission of Llyfrgell Genedlaethol Cymru/The National Library of Wales.
45. Quoted in Faderman, *Surpassing the Love of Men*, p.160.
46. HSP, Wister Family Papers, Box 4. Frances Power Cobbe to Sarah Wister, May 1873.
47. Frances Power Cobbe to Mary Somerville, 6 September 1871. Somerville Papers, Dep. c. 358 (MSFP 18–19).
48. HSP, Wister Family Papers, Box 4. Frances Power Cobbe to Sarah Wister, 13 July, n.y., pre-1884.
49. Frances Power Cobbe to Mary Somerville, 27 December n.y. Somerville Papers, Dep. c. 358 (MSFP 18–19).
50. Frances Power Cobbe, *Life of Frances Power Cobbe as Told by Herself*, with additions by the author and an introduction by Blanche Atkinson, London: Swan Sonnenschein and Co, Lim., 1904, pp.709–10.
51. Ibid., p.710.
52. Frances Power Cobbe to Mrs Glover, 13 July 1892. Fawcett Autograph Collection, v. VIII.
53. Cobbe, *Life*, II, p.359.
54. Frances Power Cobbe to Mary Somerville, October 25. Somerville Papers, Dep. c. 358 (MSFP 18–19).
55. Ibid., 7 August.
56. Cobbe had written of the ideal mother/daughter relationship in similar terms with herself in control. See Cobbe, *Life*, I, pp.88–9.
57. HSP, Wister Family Papers, Box 4. Frances Power Cobbe to Sarah Wister, 17 May 1878.
58. Frances Power Cobbe to Mary Somerville, headed 13th, n.y. Somerville Papers, Dep. c. 358 (MSFP 18–19).
59. Cobbe, *Life*, II, p.404.
60. Frances Power Cobbe to Mary Somerville, 8 August. Somerville Papers, Dep. c. 358 (MSFP 18–19). See also Adrian Desmond and James Moore, *Darwin: The Life of a Tormented Evolutionist*, London: Michael Joseph, 1991, pp.554, 572.
61. Frances Power Cobbe to Mary Somerville, 7 May n.y., c.1871. Somerville Papers, Dep. c. 358 (MSFP 18–19); also an undated letter about Tyndall's lecture.
62. See J. Estlin Carpenter, *James Martineau, Theologian and Teacher: A Study of His Life and Thought*, London: Philip Green, 1905, p.413. For Cobbe's relationship with

Gladstone before they split on women's suffrage and vivisection, see Frances Power Cobbe to William Ewart Gladstone, 2 March n.y., British Library Manuscripts, 44785, f.92; 21 April n.y., c. 1876, British Library Manuscripts, 44449, f. 276.

63. The *Abolitionist*, V, 1904–5, p.41. See also Walburga Lady Paget, *In My Tower*, London: Hutchinson & Co, second edition, 1924, I, pp.133, 187; Constance Battersea, *Reminiscences*, London: Macmillan & Co, pp.222–3.
64. Review of *Life*, *Englishwoman's Review*, 26, 1895, p.59.
65. Quoted in the *Abolitionist*, V, 1904–5, p.41.
66. Paget, *In My Tower*, p.187. Cobbe's 'mannish' ways, coupled with her cropped hair and disinclination to follow the dictates of feminine fashion would qualify her as the sexologist Krafft-Ebing's 'mannish lesbian'. For a discussion of the sexologists and their impact on defining 'lesbian' and the connection between male appearance and lesbianism see, for example, Carroll Smith-Rosenberg, 'Discourses of Sexuality and Subjectivity: The New Woman, 1870–1936', in Duberman, Vicinus, Chauncey, eds., *Hidden From History*, pp.264–80; Faderman, *Surpassing the Love of Men*, Hamer, *Britannia's Glory*, Vicinus, '"They Wonder to Which Sex I Belong"', pp.184–6.
67. Battersea, *Reminiscences*, p.222.
68. The *Abolitionist*, V, 1904–5, p.41.
69. Cobbe, 'Little Health of Ladies', p.283. See also Cobbe, 'The Defects of Women', p.230.
70. Cobbe, 'Little Health of Ladies', p.285.
71. Ibid., pp.286–7.
72. Frances Power Cobbe, 'Catching Cold', in Cobbe, *Re-Echoes*, p.256. See also Frances Power Cobbe, 'Fat People', ibid., p.20.
73. See Levine, *Feminist Lives*, p.151. Levine's survey of nineteenth-century feminists revealed that with the exception of teaching, writing provided the most employment opportunities for women; 32% of Levine's sample had books published.
74. Edward C. McAleer, ed., *Dearest Isa. Robert Browning's Letters to Isabella Blagden*, Austin: University of Texas Press, 1951, p.199. Patrizia Guarnieri does not hold *Italics* in as high esteem as did Browning. See Guarnieri, 'Moritz Schiff (1823–1904): Experimental Physiology and Noble Sentiment in Florence', in Nicolaas Rupke, ed., *Vivisection in Historical Perspective*, London: Croom Helm, 1987, p.113.
75. In *Dawning Lights*, pp.173–4, Cobbe exposes the errors in praying for physical changes, such as victory in battle or cures during sickness, and argues that prayers can only be the basis for spiritual support and strength during times of trouble. She does not seem to have engaged in the Prayer Gauge Debate once it got underway in 1872, but a number of her contemporaries, such as John Tyndall (to whom she sent *Dawning Lights*), William A. Knight and F.W. Newman, kept the debate going throughout the 1870s. For a further discussion of the Prayer Gauge Debate see Turner, *Contesting Cultural Authority*, pp.151–2.
76. See Review of *Life*, *Englishwoman's Review*, p.61.
77. Frances Power Cobbe to Mary Somerville, 6 September n.y., c. 1871. Somerville Papers, Dep. c. 358 (MSFP 18–19).
78. See Charles Darwin to Frances Power Cobbe, 28 November 1872. Frances

Power Cobbe Collection, CB 386.
79. HSP, Wister Family Papers, Box 4. Frances Power Cobbe to Sarah Wister, 17 May 1878.
80. Frances Power Cobbe, introduction to Theodore Stanton, ed., *The Woman Question in Europe: A Series of Original Essays Edited by Theodore Stanton*, London: Sampson Low, Marston, Searle, and Rivington, 1884, p.xiv.
81. For political parties' attitudes towards women's suffrage see Constance Rover, *Women's Suffrage and Party Politics in Britain, 1866–1914*, London: Routledge and Kegan Paul, 1967.
82. Frances Power Cobbe to Lydia Becker, 14, n.m., n.y. NUWSS Collection, M50/12/50.
83. Ibid., 5 August n.y., c. 1886. NUWSS Collection, M50/12/51. For Hutton's comment see R.H. Hutton to Frances Power Cobbe, 16 March 1885. Frances Power Cobbe Collection, CB 513.
84. Frances Power Cobbe to Lydia Becker, 26 November n.y., post 1884, NUWSS Collection, M50/12/53.
85. Frances Power Cobbe, 'Women's Duty to Women', a paper read at the conference of Women Workers, held in Birmingham, November 1890. NUWSS Collection, M50/65, p.2.

4 'The Rights of Man and the Claims of Brutes'

1. See Paul Elliot, 'Vivisection and the Emergence of Experimental Physiology in Nineteenth-Century France', in Rupke, ed., *Vivisection in Historical Perspective*, pp.50–4; Richard French, *Antivivisection and Medical Science in Victorian Society*, New Jersey: Princeton University Press, 1975, pp.30–1; *British Medical Journal*, ii, 1863, p.226; *The Times*, 11 August 1863.
2. The *Lancet*, 1863, ii, p.317.
3. Cobbe, *Intuitive Morals*, p.35.
4. Ibid., pp.39–40.
5. Frances Power Cobbe, 'The Rights of Man and the Claims of Brutes', *Fraser's Magazine*, 68, 1863, p.589. Cobbe referred to the camel story again in her 1889 publication *The Friend of Man*. See Frances Power Cobbe, *The Friend of Man; and His Friends,—the Poets*, London: George Bell & Sons, 1889, p.63.
6. Cobbe, 'The Rights of Man', p.598. Comparisons between vivisectors and the working class became the norm in later anti-vivisection literature; see Nicolaas Rupke, 'Pro-vivisection in England in the Early 1880s: Arguments and Motives', in Rupke, ed., *Vivisection in Historical Perspective*, p.203: See also Harriet Ritvo, *The Animal Estate: The English and Other Creatures in the Victorian Age*, Cambridge, Massachusetts: Harvard University Press, 1987, p.163.
7. Cobbe, 'The Rights of Man', p.601.
8. Keith Thomas, *Man and the Natural World: A History of Modern Sensibility*, New York: Pantheon Books, 1983, p.118.
9. Quoted in Thomas, ibid., p.155.
10. Owen, *English Philanthropy*, p.179; Ritvo, *The Animal Estate*, p.132.
11. An Act to Consolidate and Amend the Several Laws Relating to the Cruel and Improper Treatment of Animals, and the Mischiefs Arising from the Driving of

Cattle, and to Make Other Provisions in Regard Thereto, *Public General Statutes*, 5 & 6 Wm. IV, c. 59; An Act for the More Effectual Prevention of Cruelty to Animals, *Public General Statutes*, 12 & 13 Vict., c. 92.

12. See Owen, *English Philanthropy*, p.179; Keith Tester, *Animals and Society: The Humanity of Animal Rights*, London: Routledge, 1991, p.115; Ritvo, *The Animal Estate*, p.145. Although the RSPCA was successfully using its powers of policing, defiance of anti-cruelty laws was widespread and it, like cruelty itself, was blamed on the inability of the lower classes to control their passions. See Ritvo, ibid., pp.148–150.
13. *Genesis*, 1:26.
14. Cobbe, 'Rights of Man', p.590.
15. See Frances Power Cobbe, 'The Moral Aspects of Vivisection', *New Quarterly Magazine*, 4, 1875, p.229.
16. See Chapter 6, endnote no. 29.
17. Cobbe, 'Rights of Man', p.600. For Wesley see John Wesley, 'The General Deliverance', I, sec. 3 in John Emory, ed., *The Works of the Rev. John Wesley, A.M.*, 7 vols., 3rd American complete and standard edition, New York: Carlton and Porter, 1856, II, p.51.
18. Cobbe, 'Rights of Man', p.593.
19. There is an ever-increasing selection of work on the topics of vivisection and animal rights. See, for example, the collection edited by Nicolaas Rupke, *Vivisection in Historical Perspective*; French, *Antivivisection and Medical Science in Victorian Society* (this continues to be the seminal work on vivisection and antivivisection); Brian Harrison, 'Animals and the State in Nineteenth-Century England" *English Historical Review*, 88, 1973; James Turner, *Reckoning with the Beast. Animals, Pain, and Humanity in the Victorian Mind*, Baltimore: The Johns Hopkins University Press, 1980; Ritvo, *The Animal Estate*; Richard Ryder, *Victims of Science: The Use of Animals in Research*, London: Davis Poynter, 1975.
20. See Andreas-Holger Maehle and Ulrich Tröhler, 'Animal Experiment-ation from Antiquity to the End of the Eighteenth Century: Attitudes and Arguments' in Rupke, *Vivisection in Historical Perspective*, p.31; Wallace Shugg, 'The Cartesian Beast-Machine in English Literature, (1663–1750)', *Journal of the History of Ideas*, 29, 1968, pp.279–92.
21. Similar complaints had been made in France about the cacophony emanating from laboratories and disturbing the patients at the Hospital des Cliniques. The *BMJ* reported from *Opinion Nationale* one such letter: 'Will you, whose solicitude for the sick is so great, join your complaints to ours in order to obtain from the competent authorities that henceforward no more dogs shall be taken to the Practical School, and that the repose, the sleep, the moral tranquillity of our poor lying-women shall be respected?' *British Medical Journal*, ii, 1863, p.251.
22. Cobbe, *Italics*, p.103. For a discussion of the perceived cruelty of Roman Catholic countries see, for example, Harriet Ritvo, 'Animals in Nineteenth Century Britain: Complicated Attitudes and Compelling Categories' in Aubrey Manning and James Serpell, eds., *Animals and Human Society: Changing Perspectives*, London and New York: Routledge, 1994, pp.106–7.
23. Cobbe often referred to society's, and, by implication, her own, role as

vicegerent of God when dealing with unfortunates. See, for example, Frances Power Cobbe, 'Zoophily', in Cobbe, *The Peak in Darien*, p.155: 'To be kind to them [animals], and rejoice in their happiness, seems just one of the few ways in which we can act a godlike part in our little sphere, and display the mercy for which we hope in our turn'. See also Cobbe, *Life*, II, p.559; Frances Power Cobbe, *The Theory of Intuitive Morals, being a corrected reprint of the third edition of An Essay on Intuitive Morals*, London: Swan Sonnenschein & Co, Ltd, 1902, fourth edition, p.262.

24. Patrizia Guarnieri, 'Moritz Schiff', in Rupke, ed., *Vivisection in Historical Perspective*, p.112.
25. *Daily News*, 29 December 1863.
26. Frances Ann Kemble, *Further Records, 1848–1883: A Series of Letters by Frances Anne Kemble Forming a Sequel to Record of a Girlhood and Records of Later Life*, London: Richard Bentley and Son, 1890, I, pp.212–3.
27. Little did Cobbe realise, or perhaps want to accept, just how cruel Englishmen were. See Ritvo, 'Animals in Nineteenth Century Britain', pp.106–7.
28. Frances Power Cobbe, 'Hades', *Fraser's Magazine*, 69, 1864, p.301.
29. Cobbe, 'Morals of Literature', p.130.
30. See Cobbe, *Life*, II, pp.523.
31. Cobbe, 'Criminals, Idiots', p.793.
32. Thomas Neville Bonner, *Becoming a Physician: Medical Education in Britain, France, Germany, and the United States, 1750–1945*, Oxford: Oxford University Press, 1995, p.259.
33. The Court of Examiners of the Royal College of Surgeons 'bowed to the inevitable and recognised their inability to examine candidates in anatomy and physiology, recommending that a separate board of experts on these subjects be appointed to do so.' Richard French, 'Some Problems and Sources in the Foundations of Modern Physiology, 184–1870,' *History of Science*, 10, 1971, p.34. It took until 1892, however, for the Council of the College to bring in examiners who were neither members nor fellows. For changes in attitudes towards physiology, see Roy M. MacLeod, 'Resources of Science in Victorian England: The Endowment of Science Movement, 1868–1900', in Peter Mathias, ed., *Science and Society, 1600–1900*, Cambridge: Cambridge University Press, 1972; W.H. Brock, 'Medicine and the Victorian Scientific Press', in W.F. Bynum, Stephen Lock and Roy Porter, eds., *Medical Journals and Medical Knowledge*, London: Routledge, 1992, p.74. See also John M. Robson, "The Fiat and Finger of God: The Bridgewater Treatises," in Helmstadter and Lightman, eds., *Victorian Faith in Crisis*.
34. *Report of the British Association for the Advancement of Science*, 41st Meeting, London, 1872, p.144. For Marshall Hall see Diana Manuel, 'Marshall Hall (1790–1857): Vivisection and the Development of Experimental Physiology', in Rupke, *Vivisection in Historical Perspective*, pp.48–77
35. Cobbe, *Life*, II, p.566.
36. Ibid., pp.566–7.
37. See W.J. O'Connor, *Founders of Physiology. A Biographical Dictionary, 1820–1885*, Manchester: Manchester University Press, 1988, p.208. See also Christopher Lawrence, 'Incommunicable Knowledge. Science, Technology and the Clinical

Art in Britain, 1850–1914', *Journal of Contemporary History*, 20, 1985, pp.503–520; Lindsay Cranshaw, '"Fame and Fortune by Means of Bricks and Mortar": The Medical Profession and the Specialist Hospital, 1800–1948', in Lindsay Cranshaw and Roy Porter, eds., *The Hospital in History*, London: Routledge, 1989, who makes similar comments with regards to specialist disciplines. For medical education see M. Jeanne Peterson, *The Medical Profession in Mid-Victorian London*, Berkeley and Los Angeles: University of California Press, 1978, especially Chapter 2.

38. See Frances Power Cobbe, 'Darwinism in Morals', in Cobbe, *Darwinism in Morals*.
39. Cobbe, Introduction, *Hopes of the Human Race*.
40. French, *Antivivisection and Medical Science*, p.55.
41. See ibid., pp.55–7; *Spectator*, 47, 1874, p.1551; *The Times*, 10 December 1874; *British Medical Journal*, i, 1875, p.158 for discussions about the trial.
42. *Animal World*, VI, 1875, p.38. The Memorial also appeared in *The Times*, 26 January 1875.
43. *Animal World*, VI, 1875, p.38.
44. For the conservative nature of the RSPCA which influenced the stand the organisation took on vivisection see Brian Harrison, 'Animals and the State', pp.786–820; Richard Ryder, *Animal Revolution: Changing Attitudes Towards Speciesism*, Oxford: Basil Blackwell, 1989, p.91; French, *Antivivisection and Medical Science*, p.33, suggests that because vivisection was carried out by highly educated members of a prestigious profession and not by working-class offenders with whom the Society was concerned they were undecided as to how it should be approached. See also Turner, *Reckoning With the Beast*, pp.56–7, who suggests that because the RSPCA was made up mostly of the genteel and conservative, its policy was also quite conservative to maintain their membership. The RSPCA received much of their information on vivisection from scientists and for the most part believed that technology would actually improve scientific experimentation and ease the suffering of animals. They equated scientific progress with social progress and therefore they did not oppose vivisection as strongly as they did working-class cruelty which they understood threatened the whole of society. See French, *Antivivisection and Medical Science*, and Ritvo, *The Animal Estate*, pp.157, 165.
45. For an example of Cobbe's conservatism see Frances Power Cobbe to Helen Taylor, 22 December 1874. Mill-Taylor Correspondence, v. 12.
46. Introduction to bound volume. 'Anti Vivisection Letters' 1874–1877, British Union for the Abolition of Vivisection Archives, Brynmor Jones Library, University of Hull, Publications: Pamphlets: 1873–1994, DBV 25/1. The replies which Cobbe received to her pleas for support in December 1874 are contained in this volume. See also, HSP, Wister Family Papers, Box 4. Frances Power Cobbe to Sarah Wister, 8 February 1875, for comments about the memorial.
47. James Martineau to Frances Power Cobbe, 5 January 1875. 'Anti Vivisection Letters', BUAV Archives, DBV 25/1.
48. William Gull to Frances Power Cobbe, portion of undated letter. 'Anti Vivisection Letters', BUAV Archives, DBV 25/1.

49. Charles Darwin to Frances Power Cobbe, n.d., c. January 1875. 'Anti Vivisection Letters', BUAV Archives, DBV 25/1. See also Emma Darwin to Frances Power Cobbe, 14 January n.y. in ibid.; Charles Darwin to his daughter, Henrietta, 4 January 1875, in Henrietta Litchfield, ed., *Emma Darwin. A Century of Family Letters, 1792–1896*, London: John Murray, 1915, II, pp.219–20 for Darwin's views on vivisection.
50. The *Lancet*, i, 1875, p.173. See also *The Times*, 4 February 1875.
51. HSP, Wister Family Papers, Box 4. Frances Power Cobbe to Sarah Wister, 8 February 1875.
52. *The Times*, 28 January 1875.
53. HSP, Wister Family Papers, Box 4. Frances Power Cobbe to Sarah Wister, 8 February 1875.
54. Ibid.
55. Cobbe, *Life*, II, pp.577–8.
56. See *British Medical Journal*, i, 1875, p.215.
57. Andrew Ryan, 'History of the British Act of 1876: An Act to Amend the Law Relating to Cruelty to Animals', *Journal of Medical Education*, 38 (1), 1963, p.216.
58. Harrison, 'Animals and the State', p.808.
59. *British Medical Journal*, I, 1904, p.1266.
60. *Spectator*, 48, 1875, p.369.

5 From Restriction to Abolition and Beyond

1. *Morning Post*, 2 February 1875.
2. Ibid.
3. HSP, Wister Family Papers, Box 4. Frances Power Cobbe to Sarah Wister, 8 February 1875.
4. French, *Antivivisection and Medical Science*, p.89.
5. See Cobbe, *Life*, II, pp.580–2 for events leading up to the bill. See also *Hansard*, 3rd series, 224, p.17 for reading of the bill. For the text of the bill see 'Report of the Royal Commission', Appendix iii, Section 6, pp.637–8.
6. 'Report of the Royal Commission', Appendix iii, Section 6, p.638.
7. The *Lancet*, i, 1875, p.704 for a description of the bill. See also 'Report of the Royal Commission', Appendix iii, Section 7, pp.638–9; *Hansard*, 3rd series, 224, p.542; *Spectator*, 48, 1875, pp.623–4; French, *Antivivisection and Medical Science*, p.70.
8. The *Lancet*, i, 1875, pp.732–3.
9. Ibid., pp.697, 733.
10. For Huxley's response to the bill see, for example, his letters to Darwin in Leonard Huxley, ed., *Life and Letters of Thomas Henry Huxley*, London: Macmillan & Co Ltd, 1913, II, pp.168–70.
11. Cobbe, *Life*, II, p.584.
12. The *Lancet*, i, 1875, p.280; see also p.173; *British Medical Journal*, I, 1875, p.158.
13. Huxley, ed., *Life and Letters*, p.170. See also *Hansard*, 3rd series, 224, pp.794, 993. The *Spectator*, led by the anti-vivisectionist R.H. Hutton, believed that a Commission would not get at the truth of vivisection and that 'without compulsory powers, the Commission will be a total failure'. *Spectator*, 48, 1875, p.679.

14. Huxley, ed., *Life and Letters*, p.170.
15. Cobbe, *Life*, II, p.584.
16. French, *Antivivisection and Medical Science*, p.101.
17. See, for example, *Saturday Review*, 41, 1876, p.295, 296, 773; The *Lancet*, i, 1876, p.784; *Nature*, 25, 1882, p.432. The Royal Commission on Vivisection, VSS, pp.11, 12, 21, 27, 47.
18. See *British Medical Journal*, ii, 1875, pp.25–6.
19. See the *Zoophilist*, XII, 1892–3, pp.110.
20. Lord Shaftesbury to Frances Power Cobbe, 17 November 1875. 'Anti Vivisection Letters', BUAV Archives, DBV 25/1.
21. See Cobbe, *Life*, II, p.592.
22. Kemble, *Further Records*, II, p.49.
23. See Elizabeth Longford, *Victoria RI*, London: Weidenfeld and Nicolson, 1964, p.406; W.F. Moneypenny and G.E. Buckle, *The Life of Benjamin Disraeli, Earl of Beaconsfield*, New York: The Macmillan Company, 1910, V, p.483; Ryder, *Victims of Science*, p.194; French, *Antivivisection and Medical Science*, p.112; Mark Ozer, 'The British Vivisection Controversy', *Bulletin of the History of Medicine*, 40, 1966, pp.166–7 for the Queen's influence on passage of the 1876 Act.
24. *Hansard*, 3rd series, 229, p.1002. For Shaftesbury's views, see E. Hopper, *Life and Work of the Seventh Earl of Shaftesbury*, London: Cassell & Co Ltd, 1896, III, p.373
25. *Hansard*, 3rd series, 229, p.1016.
26. *Nature*, 14, 1876, p.172.
27. *Daily Telegraph*, 24 June 1876, reprinted in the *Home Chronicler*, I, 1876, p.6. See also France Power Cobbe, *Bernard's Martyrs: A Comment on Bernard's Leçons de Physiologie Opératoire*, London: Society for the Protection of Animals from Vivisection, 1879, p.4.
28. The *Lancet*, I, 1876, p.830.
29. *British Medical Journal*, i, 1876, p.742.
30. See *Punch*, 70, 1876, p.249. See also p.105. The accusation had more than a ring of truth in it.
31. The *Daily News*, 15 August 1876. See also *Home Chronicler*, I, 1876, p.140.
32. *Spectator*, 49, 1876, p.1001.
33. See *British Medical Journal*, ii, 1876, p.231, 265; the *Lancet*, ii, 1876, p.245; *Saturday Review*, 41, 1876, p.672.
34. *British Medical Journal*, ii, 1876, pp.371, 245. See also *Nature*, 14, 1876, pp.65, 248.
35. *Saturday Review*, 41, 1876, p.804.
36. Cobbe, *Life*, II, p.599.
37. *Home Chronicler*, I, 1876, pp.378–9.
38. Ibid., II, 1877, pp.749–50.
39. Quoted in the *Zoophilist*, VII, 1887–8, p.138. For Jesse, see the *Lancet*, i, 1881, p.525.
40. *British Medical Journal*, i, 1877, p.555.
41. The *Zoophilist*, VII, 1887–8, p.138.
42. Ibid., V, 1878, p.234.
43. James Martineau to Frances Power Cobbe, 29 January 1878, Frances Power Cobbe Collection, CB 601.

44. *Home Chronicler*, III, 1877, p.1258.
45. Lord Shaftesbury to Frances Power Cobbe, 23 January 1878, Frances Power Cobbe Collection, CB 144.
46. *Home Chronicler*, IV, 1878, p.45.
47. Cobbe, *Life*, II, p.607. Such rationale is not inconsistent with Cobbe's understanding that vivisection was immoral first, useless second, and that the interests of man always came before those of animals.
48. Lord Shaftesbury to Frances Power Cobbe, 17 December 1881, Frances Power Cobbe Collection, CB 240. See also 3 December 1881, CB 236; 5 December 1881, CB 237; 6 December 1881, CB 238.
49. Samuel Wilks, 'Vivisection: Its Pains and Uses', *Nineteenth Century*, 10, 1881, p.944. This article was part of a trio that appeared in the month of December. See also Richard Owen and James Paget.
50. Cobbe, *Bernard's Martyrs*, p.xvi.
51. Ibid., p.13.
52. *Church Times*, 19 August, 1881. See also 12 August 1881.
53. Ibid., 6 September 1881.
54. See French, *Antivivisection and Medical Science*, p.201.
55. Lord Shaftesbury to Frances Power Cobbe, 26 October 1881. Frances Power Cobbe Collection, CB 227.
56. See French, *Antivivisection and Medical Science*, pp.224–5. Brian Harrison notes such behaviour was evident in many nineteenth-century charities: 'Philanthropic sectarianism ensured that charities were as inefficient in relieving human misery as the religious bodies in spreading Christianity. They were often more energetic in denouncing alternative remedies for the problems they attacked than in tackling them. Considerations of personal ambition, class prejudice, and denominational proselytism no doubt lie behind such virulent enmities'. Brian Harrison, 'Philanthropy and the Victorians', *Victorian Studies*, 9, 4, 1966, p.365. For other examples of philanthropic sectarianism see Brian Harrison, *Drink and the Victorians*, London, Faber and Faber, 1971; George K. Behlmer, *Child Abuse and Moral Reform in England, 1870–1908*, Stanford: Stanford University Press, 1982, especially Chapter 5; Judith Walkowitz, *Prostitution and Victorian Society: Women, Class and the State*, Cambridge: Cambridge University Press, 1980. Cobbe's clash with Kingsford was not just the result of conflicting personalities; see John Vyvyan, *In Pity and In Anger*, London: Michael Joseph, 1969, p.102.
57. Edward Maitland, *Anna Kingsford: Her Life, Letters, Diary and Work*, London: George Redway, 1896, 2 vols, II, p.444. Unlike Maitland, the historian Coral Lansbury writes of Cobbe at the start of her vendetta with Kingsford as '[p]ractical, genial, and diplomatic'. Coral Lansbury, *The Old Brown Dog: Women, Workers and Vivisection in Edwardian England*, Wisconsin: The University of Wisconsin Press, 1985, p.93.
58. See The *Zoophilist*, XIII, 1893–4, pp.52–3 for the returns over a ten year period. See also the annual returns at the BUAV archive, DBV 25/46–25/50.
59. Lord Shaftesbury to Frances Power Cobbe, 4 January 1882. Frances Power Cobbe Collection, CB 246.
60. Frances Power Cobbe, 'Vivisection—Four Replies', *Fortnightly Review*, 37 o.s., 31 n.s., 1882, p.91.

61. Ibid., p.93.
62. *Nature*, 25, 1881–2, p.429.
63. Ibid., p.430.
64. Gerald Yeo, 'The Practice of Vivisection in England', *Fortnightly Review*, 31, n.s., 1882, p.360.
65. Ibid., p.363.
66. Lord Shaftesbury to Frances Power Cobbe, 7 January 1882. Frances Power Cobbe Collection, CB 248. The anti-CD agitation had also used sandwichmen during a demonstration at Colchester; see Walkowitz, *Prostitution and Victorian Society*, p.106.
67. Lord Shaftesbury to Frances Power Cobbe, 9 January 1882. Frances Power Cobbe Collection, CB 249. A Church Anti-vivisection Society was not founded until 1890.
68. Ibid., 11 January 1882, CB 251.
69. Ibid., 21 January 1882, CB 257.
70. Frances Power Cobbe to Lord Shaftesbury, 23, n.m., c. January 1882. Shaftesbury Estates, SE/NY 158(14).
71. See Lord Shaftesbury to Frances Power Cobbe, 6 September 1882. Frances Power Cobbe Collection, CB 280. Very few applicants were refused a vivisection licence once the process was handed over to the AAMR and the number of practising vivisectors and experiments performed rose steadily over the next few years; the number of licences increased from 42 in 1882 to 638 in 1913. Between 1876–1882 Cross and Harcourt between them had refused 26 applicants. Between 1882–1890 there were only three refusals and none of the rejected applicants were affiliated with a medical or research institution. See French, *Antivivisection and Medical Science*, pp.186–7, 207–8.
72. The *Daily News*, 11 April 1883.
73. *Spectator*, 57, 1884, p.517. Supporters of Burdon Sanderson included Sir Henry Acland, Regius Professor of Medicine and the very Reverend Henry George Liddell, Dean of Christ Church. Opponents included Charles Dodgson, John Ruskin and H.P.Liddon, Bishop of Oxford.
74. Ibid., p.180.
75. *Pall Mall Gazette*, 80, 5 March 1885. In words typical of those spoken by the medical profession about anti-vivisectionists, W.J. O'Connor refers to this incident as the 'childish last course' of the anti-vivisection fight at Oxford. See O'Connor, *Founders of British Physiology*, p.144.
76. *Pall Mall Gazette*, 80, 7 March 1885.
77. Ibid., 10 March 1885.
78. Cobbe, *Life*, II, p.619.
79. Frances Power Cobbe, 'The Long Pull I', in the *Zoophilist*, IV, 1884–5, p.82.
80. The *Globe*, 6 February 1888, reprinted in the *Zoophilist*, IV, 1884–5, p.183. See also Frances Power Cobbe, 'The Scientific Spirit of the Age', in Cobbe, *The Scientific Spirit of the Age and Other Pleas and Discussions*, Boston: Geo. H. Ellis, 1888, p.30.
81. Cobbe, 'Scientific Spirit', p.29.
82. Mrs E. Sidgwick to Millicent Fawcett, Spring, 1891. Fawcett Autograph Collection, v. IV, part B.

83. Eleanor Vere Boyle to Frances Power Cobbe, 20 January n.y. Frances Power Cobbe Collection, CB 33.
84. Frances Power Cobbe, 'The Ethics of Zoophily', *Contemporary Review*, 68, 1895, pp.497–8.
85. The *Zoophilist*, IX, 1889–90, p.80. For her thoughts of feminist activity, see Cobbe, 'Criminals, Idiots, Women and Minors', p.794.
86. E. de Cyon, 'The Anti-vivisection Agitation', *Contemporary Review*, 43, 1883, p.500.
87. HSP, Wister Family Papers, Box 4. Frances Power Cobbe to Sarah Wister, 13 July, n.y.
88. The *Zoophilist*, IX, 1889–90, p.230.
89. Eleanor Vere Boyle to Frances Power Cobbe, 15 January n.y. Frances Power Cobbe Collection, CB 32. Women flocked to save animals, but whether this was due to Cobbe's convincing rhetoric is difficult to determine. Women had figured prominently in the RSPCA since its founding and anti-vivisection would have been attractive to many. By the latter part of the century, women comprised anywhere from 40% – 60% of the anti-vivisection leadership and rank and file members of animal welfare societies were overwhelmingly female, 70% in the VSS. In 1894 the *Verulam Review* noted that the 'enormous majority of the women of England are unquestionably on our side. Were it not for them in truth, the movement could hardly be carried on at all'. Quoted in French, *Antivivisection and Medical Science*, p.240. See also Prochaska, *Women and Philanthropy*, for women's part in animal welfare societies; Mary Ann Elston, 'Women and Anti-vivisection in Victorian England, 1870–1900' in Rupke, ed., *Vivisection in Hitorical Perspective*, pp.259–94. Regarding Henrietta Darwin's early support of Cobbe's activities in 1875, and to female participation in anti-vivisection in general, Desmond and Moore write: 'Henrietta, a confirmed hypochondriac, had jumped on the bandwagon. Like so many closeted Victorian matriarchs, she identified with suffering life. Victoria's maidens formed the anti-vivisection core and read their own misery into the vivisector's victims'. Desmond and Moore, *Darwin: Life of a Tormented Evolutionist*, p.615.
90. Frances Power Cobbe, *Somerville Hall: A Misnomer, A Correspondence with Notes*, London: VSS, 1891, p.9.
91. See Caine, *Victorian Feminists*, pp.138–9. See also Hilda Kean, 'The "Smooth Cool Men of Science": The Feminist Response to Vivisection', *History Workshop Journal*, 40, 1995, p.27. Even though Emily Davies wanted men and women to have equal access to an education she did not want to see women 'become' men; this is just what anti-vivisectionists feared would happen if women were given an education that included vivisections.
92. Frances Power Cobbe to Millicent Fawcett, 16 January 1891. Fawcett Autograph Collection, v. IV, part B. See also 28 February 1891.
93. Eleanor Sidgwick to Millicent Fawcett, 25 February 1891. Fawcett Autograph Collection, v. IV, part B.
94. The *Zoophilist*, XVI, 1896–7, p.5.
95. Ibid.
96. Frances Power Cobbe, 'Our Cause in America', the *Zoophilist*, XV, 1895–6, p.295.

97. Despite Cobbe's fears about the effects of vivisection and dissection on a woman's character, no woman held a vivisector's licence from the Home Office until 1898 and the London School of Medicine for Women did not register with the Home Office for live animal experimentation until the second Royal Commission on Vivisection issued its Report endorsing the legal control of vivisection in 1912. The Physiological Society did not admit women until 1915 and they were rarely teachers in Universities and Medical Schools. See Elston, 'Women and Anti-vivisection', p.281; W.J. O'Connor, *British Physiologists, 1885–1914: A Biographical Dictionary*, Manchester: Manchester University Press, 1991, p.1.
98. Joseph Althoz, 'The Warfare of Conscience with Theology', in Gerald Parson, ed., *Religion in Victorian Britain*, Manchester: Manchester University Press, 1988, IV, 'Interpretations', p.154.

6 'Health and Holiness'

1. Cobbe, 'Little Health of Ladies', p.278.
2. The *Zoophilist*, I, 1881–2, pp.5–6.
3. Frances Power Cobbe, 'The Medical Profession and its Morality', *Modern Review*, 2, 1881, pp.296–8.
4. Cobbe was not the only person to generalise about doctors. Josephine Butler and many who protested against the Contagious Diseases Acts in the 1870s and 1880s regularly attacked regulationists 'as licentious aristocrats who conspired to control women through state sanction and monopoly...Butler, for instance, repeatedly condemned those 'terrible aristocratic doctors', when in fact medical spokesmen for regulation were ambitious members of her own social class', Walkowitz, *Prostitution and Victorian Society*, p.108. Cobbe aligned physicians with the lower, not upper, classes and found them as reprehensible as did Butler.
5. See Cranshaw, 'Fame and Fortune by Means of Bricks and Mortar', p.202. See also Peterson, *The Medical Profession in Mid-Victorian London*, especially Chapter 6, 'Medical Entrepreneurship and Professional Order'.
6. George Bernard Shaw, 'Preface on Doctors' in *The Doctor's Dilemma: A Tragedy*, originally published 1911; all quotations taken from *The Bodley Head Bernard Shaw: Collected Plays with their Prefaces*, v. III, London: The Bodley Head, 1971, pp.229–30.
7. Cobbe, 'Medical Profession and its Morality', pp.303–4. O'Connor also points out that a number of physiologists were of, what Cobbe would consider, a 'poetic' temperament, creating and tending elaborate gardens. See, for example, Michael Foster, in O'Connor, *Founders of Physiology*, p.171.
8. Cobbe, 'Medical Profession and its Morality', p.322.
9. Cobbe, 'Moral Aspects of Vivisection', p.228.
10. Cobbe, 'Medical Profession and its Morality', p.305.
11. The *Scottish Leader*, 27 January 1890, reprinted in the *Zoophilist*, IX, 1889–90, pp.248–9. For Thring, see the *Zoophilist*, VII, 1887–8, p.127.
12. Ibid., XIV, 1894–5, p.76.
13. Frances Power Cobbe to Lord Shaftesbury, n.d., c. January 1882. Shaftesbury

Estates, SE/NY 158(13).
14. *Daily News*, 12 January 1882. 'Nihil humani est mihi alienum' – 'May nothing human be alien to me'. Signing her letter Nihil Humani allowed Cobbe to stress her humanitarianism.
15. Ibid., 13 January 1882.
16. See, for example, letter from Eleanor M. Beeby in *Light*, 26 May 1900, reprinted in the *Zoophilist*, XX, 1900–01, pp.86–7; letter from E. Berdoe to the *Pall Mall Gazette*, 10 July 1891, reprinted in the *Zoophilist*, XI, 1891–2, p.63; article in the *Echo*, 20 July 1892, reprinted in the *Zoophilist*, XII, 1892–3, p.110; '"Research" in Hospital Wards', the *Zoophilist*, XX, 1900–01, p.158; 'Scientific Research versus the Cure of Disease', letter written by J.H. Thornton, Deputy Surgeon General (retired) to the *Zoophilist*, XV, 1895–6, pp.232–3.
17. Cobbe, 'Medical Profession and its Morality', pp.311–2.
18. Quoted in Coral Lansbury, 'Gynaecology, Pornography and the Anti-Vivisection Movement', *Victorian Studies*, 28, 1985, p.419. For more extensive comments made by Blackwell about vivisection see Elizabeth Blackwell, *Essays in Medical Sociology*, London: Ernest Bell, 1902, 2 volumes. See especially her 'Erroneous Method in Medical Education' and 'Scientific Method in Biology'. Shaw also wrote about vivisection and doctors. See his preface to *The Doctor's Dilemma*, pp.259–285.
19. *Home Chronicler*, I, 1876, pp.185–6.
20. See *Anti-Vivisectionist*, VI, 1879, pp.163–4.
21. See, for example, Tennyson's 'The Children's Hospital' and Collins's *Heart and Science*.
22. See the *Zoophilist*, IV, 1884–5, p.61.
23. Benjamin Bryan, *Kochism: Experiment, not Discovery*, London: VSS, 1890, p.11. See also the *Zoophilist*, XIX, 1899–1900, p.208. The 'antivivisectionist case against the hospitals was predicated upon the belief that medical enthusiasm for knowledge and notoriety left no room for the humane and merciful treatment of the diseased and injured', French, *Antivivisection and Medical Science*, p.325. Such a view was not confined solely to anti-vivisectionists. Jeanne Peterson has pointed out that lay governors of hospitals came into direct conflict with physicians and surgeons over the issue of students learning from patients' illnesses. See Peterson, *The Medical Profession in Mid-Victorian London*, p.174.
24. Frances Power Cobbe, *Cancer Experiments on Human Beings*, London: VSS, 1890, p.1. In *Prostitution and Victorian Society*, Judith Walkowitz discusses class prejudice regarding experimentation in venereal disease. 'Cruel medical experiments', she writes, 'were performed on poor hospital patients of either sex who were inoculated with syphilitic and gonorrheal pus, so that doctors could observe the progress of the two diseases', Walkowitz, *Prostitution and Victorian Society*, p.55. In light of Walkowitz's statement, Cobbe's claims are certainly not exaggerated rantings.
25. See the *Zoophilist*, XI, 1891–2, p.60; XII, 1892–3, p.31; XIII, 1893–4, p.2, 81, 101; XIV, 1894–5, pp.49–50, 64, 76–7, 81.
26. Ibid., XIII, 1893–4, p.300.
27. K. Codell Carter, 'The Koch-Pasteur Dispute on Establishing the Cause of Anthrax', *Bulletin of the History of Medicine*, 62, 1, 1988, p.52.

28. See the *Zoophilist*, XV, 1895–6, pp.240–1. See also Michael Worboys, 'Germ Theories of Disease and British Veterinary Medicine', *Medical History*, 35, number 3, 1991, pp.308–27 for the impact of germ theory on veterinary medicine; M. Weatherall, *In Search of a Cure: A History of Pharmaceutical Discovery*, Oxford: Oxford University Press, 1990, p.42.
29. Cobbe, 'London's Hecatombs', p.102. For vegetarians see Thomas, *Man and the Natural World*, Chapter 6; Colin Spencer, *The Heretic's Feast: A History of Vegetarianism*, Hanover, New Hampshire: University Press of New England, 1995.
30. Frances Power Cobbe, *Health and Holiness: An address read to the Cambridge Ladies' Discussion Society, November 6th, 1891*, London: George Bell and Sons, 1891, p.4.
31. Cobbe, 'Scientific Spirit of the Age', pp.12–13.
32. See Walkowitz, *Prostitution and Victorian Society*, p.56; Frank Prochaska, 'Body and Soul: Bible Nurses and the Poor in Victorian London', *Historical Research*, 60, 1987, 337–48; Lori Williamson, 'Soul Sisters: The St John and Ranyard Nurses in Nineteenth Century London', *International History of Nursing Journal*, 2, 2, winter 1996, pp.33–49 for connections made between spritual and bodily health and well-being.
33. Cobbe, 'Medical Profession and its Morality', p.16.
34. Frances Power Cobbe, 'Faith Healing, Fear Killing', *Contemporary Review*, 51, 1887, p.796.
35. See French, *Antivivisection and Medical Science*, p.331. See also Turner, *Reckoning With the Beast*, pp.103–4.
36. The *Zoophilist*, XIV, 1894–5, p.54.
37. Cobbe, 'Faith Healing, Fear Killing', p.805.
38. Ibid., p.806. See also the *Zoophilist*, VII, 1887–8, pp.126–7.
39. Cobbe, *Health and Holiness*, pp.7–8. In the early 1860s the *BMJ* had voiced similar concerns over the advent of the specialist. See Cranshaw, 'By Means of Bricks and Mortar'. Many general practitioners felt threatened by specialists because the latter changed the nature of disease from 'widespread underlying state' to that of localism. See Peterson, *The Medical Profession in Mid-Victorian London*, pp.272–4.
40. Cobbe, 'Faith Healing, Fear Killing', p.804.
41. HSP, Wister Family Papers, Box 4. Frances Power Cobbe to Sarah Wister, 4 August.
42. Cobbe, *Health and Holiness*, pp.5–6.
43. Cobbe, 'Faithless World', p.803.
44. Cobbe, *Health and Holiness*, pp.26–9.
45. Cobbe, 'Philosophy of the Poor Laws', p.382.
46. Cobbe, 'Medical Profession and its Morality', p.324.
47. Cobbe's letter to the Chairman of the Anti-Vaccination League, March 1904, reprinted in the *Animal's Defender*, VII, 1904, p.20.
48. Cobbe, 'Medical Profession and its Morality', p.324.
49. *The Times*, 15 November 1889. See also Cobbe, 'Medical Profession and its Morality', footnote, pp.324–5.
50. For provisions of the 1867 Act see 'An Act to Consolidate and Amend the Laws Relating to Vaccination', *Public General Statutes*, 30 & 31 Vict., c. 84. For progress

in vaccination see Weatherall, *In Search of a Cure*.
51. See Dorothy Porter and Roy Porter, 'The Politics of Prevention: Anti-Vaccinationism and Public Health in Nineteenth-Century England'. *Medical History*. 32, number 3, 1988, pp.231–52.
52. Cobbe, *Dawning Lights*, p.174. See also Cobbe, 'The New Creed and the Old – III', p.43.
53. Cobbe, 'Medical Profession and its Morality', p.297. For Taylor see Harrison, 'State Intervention and Moral Reform', pp.291–2. Taylor's criticism is similar to Cobbe's: compulsory vaccination was 'the most absolute invasion of the sacred right of the parent, of the right of individual liberty, at the bidding of medical supervision, that his country knows'. See also Shaw, preface to *The Doctor's Dilemma*, pp.249–57.
54. Frances Power Cobbe, 'The Janus of Science', in Cobbe, *The Modern Rack*, p.121.
55. *Macclesfield Courier and Herald*, 21 December 1889, reprinted in the *Zoophilist*, IX, 1889–90, p.201.
56. Cobbe's letter to the Chairman of the Anti-Vaccination League, p.20.
57. *Liverpool Daily Post*, 27 February 1892, reprinted in the *Zoophilist*, XI, 1891–2, p.278.
58. Frances Power Cobbe, *Controversy in a Nutshell*, London: VSS, n.d., c. 1895, p.5. Edward Maitland's anti-vivisection message also stressed man's selfishness: 'It is the essential doctrine of Christianity that man attains salvation by the sacrifice of the lower nature in himself to the higher, and of himself for others, in love. Vivisection exactly reverses this rule by involving the sacrifice of the higher nature in oneself to the lower – the sentiments of the soul to the promptings of the body – and of others form oneself, in selfishness.' Maitland to the *Pall Mall Gazette*, 14 July 1893.
59. The *Zoophilist*, XV, 1894, p.8.
60. See Lord Shaftesbury to Frances Power Cobbe, 6 September 1878. Frances Power Cobbe Collection, CB 151.
61. *Daily News*, 27 June 1884
62. Frances Power Cobbe, *The Friend of Man; and His Friends,–the Poets*, London: George Bells & Sons, 1889, p.88.
63. The *Zoophilist*, IX, 1889–90, pp.166, 262.
64. Ibid., p.166.
65. See Besant, *A World Without God*, p.19.
66. Virchow in the *Westminster Gazette*, 28 March 1893, quoted in the *Zoophilist*, XIII, 1893–4, p.14.
67. Father Vaughan's letter in the *Echo*, 10 February 1894, quoted in the *Zoophilist*, XIII, 1893–4, p.285.
68. E.M. Warner in *The Times*, 12 October 1892. For Zola, see the *Zoophilist*, XVI, 1896–7, p.7.
69. Frances Power Cobbe, *A Guest for Queen Victoria*, London: VSS, 1891, p.1.
70. Cobbe, *Health and Holiness*, p.29.

7 Controversy and Retirement to Wales

1. *Nature*, 25, 1881–2, p.459.

2. Ibid., p.483.
3. Ibid., p.506. Cobbe returned to the incident four years later when she was again charged with wearing feathers. See the *Zoophilist*, VI, 1886–7, p.63.
4. Lord Shaftesbury to Frances Power Cobbe, 21 November 1882. Frances Power Cobbe Collection, CB 291.
5. *The Times*, 24 November 1886. For the entire incident see *The Times*, 19 & 24 November 1886; *Spectator*, 57, 1884, pp.1567, 1574–5; *Daily Telegraph*, 24–26 November 1884. Adams brought a charge of libel against Bernard Coleridge, Mildred's brother, in November 1884 after Coleridge wrote a letter to his sister in which he claimed Adams had run away with his first wife, a minor, had ill-treated her and was a money-seeker. The jury found in favour of Adams and awarded him £3,000. The judge overruled their decision and in June 1885 Adams launched an appeal. He lost. See *The Times*, 5 & 10 June 1885.
6. Lord Shaftesbury to Frances Power Cobbe, 21 November 1882. Frances Power Cobbe Collection, CB 291.
7. Ibid.
8. Broadlands Papers, Shaftesbury Diaries, v. 12, SHA/PD/12, 1881–85. University of Southampton Library. See also 25 November 1882.
9. HSP, Wister Family Papers, Box 4. Frances Power Cobbe to Sarah Wister, 22 November 1882.
10. Ibid.
11. Lord Shaftesbury to Frances Power Cobbe, 24 November 1882. Frances Power Cobbe Collection, CB 292.
12. HSP, Wister Family Papers, Box 4. Frances Power Cobbe to Sarah Wister, 13, n.m., n.y., c. 13 December 1882.
13. *The Times*, 10 December 1883.
14. Lord Shaftesbury to Frances Power Cobbe, 10 December 1883. Frances Power Cobbe Collection, CB 347. Mildred Coleridge married Charles Adams on 24 June 1885 a couple of weeks after Adams's failed appeal (see n.5) and one year before he appeared in court again, this time bringing a charge of malicious and fraudulent publication against the Coleridges. During the November 1886 trial the Lord Chief Justice Coleridge admitted to the court that 'Miss Cobb [sic] told me a great deal at that time, but I have since thought she exaggerated, and from my long acquaintance with you [presumably Adams] I thought I was wrong in making that particular statement against you and withdrew it'. *The Times*, 24 November 1886. The court found in favour of the defendants.
15. HSP, Wister Family Papers, Box 4. Frances Power Cobbe to Sarah Wister, 4 August n.y., c. 1884.
16. The *Zoophilist*, IV, 1884–85, p.45.
17. Broadlands Papers, Shaftesbury Diaries, v. 12, SHA/PD/12, 1881–5, 27 June 1884.
18. R.H. Hutton to Frances Power Cobbe, 24 June 1884. Frances Power Cobbe Collection, CB 512.
19. The *Zoophilist*, IV, 1884–5, p.71.
20. Ibid., p.73.
21. See Thomas Nicholas, *Annals and Antiquities of the Counties and County Families of*

Wales, London: Longmans, Green, Reader & Co, 1872.
22. Henry Ponsonby to Frances Power Cobbe, 13 August 1884, CB 696; 17 September 1884, CB 697; 29 January 1887, CB 698; 4 February 1887, CB 699. All Frances Power Cobbe Collection.
23. M.P.G. Martyn to Frances Power Cobbe, 27 June 1885, in envelope marked 'Warnings to Miss Cobbe against Mr Coleridge'. BUAV Archives, Miscellaneous: 1885–1992, DBV 35/2.
24. HSP, Wister Family Papers, Box 4. Frances Power Cobbe to Sarah Wister, 30 July, n.y., probably c. 1889/90.
25. Ibid., 19 February 1890. See this letter for the entire incident.
26. Ibid.
27. Ibid.
28. Cobbe, *Life*, II, p.639.
29. HSP, Wister Family Papers, Box 4. Frances Power Cobbe to Sarah Wister, 30 July, n.y., c. 1889/90.
30. Cobbe, *Life*, II, p.618. In her 1889 publication *The Friend of Man; and His Friends, – the Poets* Cobbe noted that although Jews had historically been able to express tenderness to animals in general, they had been notorious for their hatred of dogs (see p.35). Dogs were one of the most popular animals to vivisect.
31. *Jewish Chronicle*, 13 February 1891, reprinted in the *Zoophilist*, X, 1890–1, p.211.
32. Ibid.
33. *Jewish Chronicle*, 27 February 1891.
34. Both quotations from the *Jewish Chronicle*, 20 February 1891.
35. *Jewish Chronicle*, 7 August 1891, reprinted in the *Zoophilist*, XI, 1891–1, p.92.
36. See French, *Antivivisection and Medical Science*, p.347; Peter Bartrip, 'The *British Medical Journal*: A Retrospect', in Bynum, Lock, Porter, eds, *Medical Journals and Medical Knowledge*, p.134. The incident both cite is one in which Charles Adams criticised Ernest Hart as being from 'that pushing race'. Bartrip also notes that Hart often earned that designation.
37. See the *Zoophilist*, XV, 1895–6, p.275.
38. HSP, Wister Family Papers, Box 4. Frances Power Cobbe to Sarah Wister, 7 October 1895.
39. The Rev. George Tyrell, 'Jesuit Zoophily', *Contemporary Review*, 68, 1895, pp.713–14.
40. The *Zoophilist*, XII, 1892–3, p.77.
41. Letter from E.P. Nichol, *Evening Dispatch*, Edinburgh, 12 August 1892, reprinted in the *Zoophilist*, XII, 1892–3, p.137.
42. The *Zoophilist*, XII, 1892–3, pp.184–5.
43. Ibid., pp.186–7.
44. See G.H. Bowker, ed., *Shaw on Vivisection*, London: George Allen and Unwin, 1949, pp.63–4.
45. Quoted in the *Zoophilist*, XII, 1892–3, p.213. See also p.214.
46. See Ernest Hart, 'Women, Clergymen, and Doctors', *New Review*, 7, 1892, p.711.
47. From the *Hastings and St Leonard's News*, 21 October 1892, reprinted in the *Zoophilist*, XII, 1892–3, p.214.
48. *The Nine Circles, or the Torture of the Innocent: Being Records of Vivisection, English and*

Foreign, compiled by Georgine M. Rhodes, second and revised edition, London: Society for the Protection of Animals from Vivisection, 1893, Appendix C, pp.142–3. See also the *Zoophilist*, XII, 1892–3, pp.194–5.
49. The *Zoophilist*, XII, 1892–3, p.201.
50. Ibid., p.203. Hart believed that if the audience knew the truth, namely that Cobbe was a liar, she would have retired to Wales less happy and instead of being protected and praised for her work, she would have been punished. See Hart, 'Women, Clergymen, and Doctors', p.711.
51. The *Zoophilist*, XII, 1892–3, p.203.
52. James Martineau to Frances Power Cobbe, 15 December 1892. Frances Power Cobbe Collection, CB 610.
53. Mary Ward to Frances Power Cobbe, 18 December 1892. Frances Power Cobbe Collection, CB 812.
54. Quoted in the the *Zoophilist*, XII, 1892–3, p.273.
55. Rhodes, *The Nine Circles*, p.143.
56. HSP, Wister Family Papers, Box 4. Frances Power Cobbe to Sarah Wister, 1 March 1894. See also Frances Power Cobbe to Lydia Becker, 12 June, n.y. NUWSS Collection, M50/12/49.
57. HSP, Wister Family Papers, Box 4. Frances Power Cobbe to Sarah Wister, 7 June 1894.
58. To Mr Bentley verbally from P.B., 30/8/94. British Library Manuscripts, 46625, f. 187.
59. HSP, Wister Family Papers, Box 4. Frances Power Cobbe to Sarah Wister, 20 November 1894.
60. Blanche Atkinson, Introduction, in Cobbe, *Life*, 1904, p.vi.
61. Quoted in ibid.
62. HSP, Wister Family Papers, Box 4. Frances Power Cobbe to Sarah Wister, 31 October c. 1884.
63. Ibid., 24 March 1895.
64. HSP, Wister Family Papers, Box 4. Mary Lloyd to Sarah Wister, 4 October 1896.
65. HSP, Wister Family Papers, Box 4. Frances Power Cobbe to Sarah Wister, 7 October 1895.
66. Ibid., 21 November 1896. See also Frances Power Cobbe to Millicent Fawcett, 11 November 1896. Fawcett Autograph Collection, v. VIII.
67. Frances Power Cobbe to Sarah Wister, 17 December 1896. The Wister Family Papers, Box 4.
68. Ibid., 14 March 1897.
69. See, for example, 'The Funeral of Frances Power Cobbe', the *Abolitionist*, V, 1904–5, p.1.
70. Frances Power Cobbe to Sarah Wister, 14 March 1897. The Wister Family Papers, Box 4.
71. Frances Power Cobbe to Millicent Fawcett, 11 November 1896. Fawcett Autograph Collection, v. VIII.

8 Fin de Siècle

1. See the *Zoophilist*, XIX, 1899–1900, p 20. See also typewritten sheet headed

1. 'The Society was originally called "The Society for the Protection of Animals Liable to Vivisection" in folder marked 'Coleridge Case'. BUAV Archive, Miscellaneous: 1885–1992, DBV 35/2.
2. See French, *Antivivisection and Medical Science*, p.224.
3. The *Zoophilist*, XX, 1900–01, p.154. See also Special Council Meeting of the National Anti-vivisection Society, 9 Feb., Westminster Palace Hotel. The Honble. Stephen Coleridge's Resolution. BUAV Archives, Coleridge Case Folder, DBV 35/2.
4. Cobbe increases the number of dissenters to twenty-three. See Cobbe, *Life*, 1904, p.690.
5. HSP, Wister Family Papers, Box 4. Frances Power Cobbe to Sarah Wister, 27 April 1898.
6. Ibid., 29 May 1898.
7. Ibid.
8. Frances Power Cobbe, *Why We Have Founded the British Union for Abolition of Vivisection*, first published 1898, BUAV Archives, DBV/25/3, p.5.
9. The Hon. Stephen Coleridge, *Step By Step.Being a Reply to a Pamphlet by Miss Frances Power Cobbe, entitled—'Why We Have Founded the British Union for Abolition of Vivisection'*, London: The National Anti-Vivisection Society, 1898, p.3.
10. Cobbe, *Why We Have Founded*, p.9.
11. Ibid., p.8.
12. Ibid., p.9.
13. Ibid., pp.12–13.
14. Coleridge, *Step By Step*, p.8.
15. For Cobbe on slavery see, for example, Frances Power Cobbe, *Rejoinder to Mrs Stowe's Reply to the Address of the Women of England*, London: Emily Faithfull, 1863; Frances Power Cobbe, *The Red Flag in John Bull's Eyes*, London: Emily Faithful, 1863.
16. The *Zoophilist*, XIX, 1899–1900, p.9.
17. John Cowper Powys, *Anti-Vivisection*, London: BUAV, n.d., p.1.
18. The *Zoophilist*, XIX, 1899–1900, p.41. See also pp.42–3. See also Stephen Coleridge, 'The Aim and Policy of the National Anti-Vivisection Society', the *Zoophilist*, XX, 1900–01, p.139.
19. Beatrice E. Kidd and M. Edith Richards, *Hadwen of Gloucester: Man, Medico, Martyr*, London: John Murray, 1933, pp.160–1.
20. See the collection of correspondence in the BUAV archives, DBV/35/2.
21. Sidney Trist to Walter Hadwen, 11 January 1902. Coleridge Case folder, BUAV Archives, DBV 35/2.
22. Ibid., 22 March 1902.
23. Frances Power Cobbe to Stephen Coleridge, 22 June n.y., in envelope marked 'Miss Cobbe's last letter to Coleridge', Colderidge Case folder, DBV 35/2.
24. The *Abolitionist*, V, 1904–5, p.42.
25. HSP, Wister Family Papers, Box 4. Frances Power Cobbe to Sarah Wister, 26 August n.y., probably 1902.
26. Ibid.
27. Ibid. See also 3 August n.y. for additional remarks and the Vet's report that exonerated Cobbe.

28. HSP, Wister Family Papers, Box 4. Frances Power Cobbe to Sarah Wister, 23 November n.y., c. 1902.
29. See the *Abolitionist*, III, 1902–3, p.78.
30. See HSP, Wister Family Papers, Box 4. Frances Power Cobbe to Sarah Wister, 29 August n.y., c. 1901.
31. Ibid., 26 June n.y., post 1900.
32. Ibid., 5 February 1901.
33. Ibid.
34. Ibid., 9 May, c. 1903. See also 16 April, n.y.
35. Ibid., 5 February 1901.
36. See the *Abolitionist*, III, 1902–3, pp.13–14.
37. Frances Power Cobbe, 'Schadenfreude', *Contemporary Review*, 81, 1902, p.659.
38. The *Abolitionist*, III, 1902–3, p.100. See also *The Times*, 6 December 1902.
39. By this time the BUAV had moved from 20 Triangle to 14 St James Barton, Bristol. See the *Abolitionist*, IV, 1903–4, p.67.
40. HSP, Wister Family Papers, Box 4. Frances Power Cobbe to Sarah Wister, 9 May c. 1903.
41. The Coleridge libel case originated with the publication in 1903 of *The Shambles of Science*, written by two medical students, Liesa von Schartau and Louisa Lind-af-Hageby. The publication purported to be an eyewitness account of a series of vivisections performed on a terrier by W.M. Bayliss at the University of London. Stephen Coleridge publicised the women's claims and for his efforts was successfully sued by Bayliss for libel. Coral Lansbury deals with the event and subsequent developments in her book *The Old Brown Dog*.
42. Frances Power Cobbe, 'Youth and Age', published posthumously by Constance Battersea in *Spectator*, 92, 1904, p.771.
43. The *Abolitionist*, V, 1904–5, p.7.
44. *British Medical Journal*, i, 1904, p.854.
45. The *New York Times*, 6 Apr. 1904.
46. *Athenaeum*, 1904, (1), p.466.
47. *Spectator*, 92, 1904, p.591.
48. Cobbe's will, Somerset House. Codicil to this will dated 2 June 1903. Punctuation has not been inserted.
49. All information in Cobbe's will. Cobbe had decided to leave her entire literary collection to Barmouth in 1899 if a site and building could be found for a library. See the *Zoophilist*, XIX, 1899–1900, p.99; HSP, Wister Family Papers, Box 4, Frances Power Cobbe to Sarah Wister 14 Mar. n.y.; E. Rosalie Jones, *A History of Barmouth and Its Vicinity*, Barmouth: John Evans and Nephew, 1909, p.83. The Cambrian Railway Company gave land in town on a long lease without payment of ground rent. £400 was subscribed by a Mrs Talbot on the condition that the building be of native stone and not be started until the cost of construction had been secured.
50. I am indebted to Stephen White for informing me of Cobbe's participation in the cremation movement.
51. Cobbe's will, Somerset House.
52. See 'The Funeral of Frances Power Cobbe', p.2.
53. See Charles Warren Adams, 'The Anti-vivisection Movement and Miss Cobbe',

Verulam Review, III, 1892, pp.197–208.
54. Cobbe, *Life*, 1904, pp.688–9.

9 A Matter of Conscience

1. See Annual Returns, Home Office, 1894–1904, BUAV Archives, DBV 25/47; 1905–1915, Ibid., DBV 25/48. E.M. Tansey, 'The Wellcome Physiological Research Laboratories, 1894–1904: The Home Office, Pharmaceutical Firms, and Animal Experiments', *Medical History*, 33, 1 1989, pp.40–1 for the increase in experimentation.
2. See Sidney Trist to Walter Hadwen, 21 December 1901. Coleridge Case folder, BUAV Archives, DBV 35/2.
3. See Executive Committee Minutes, p.72, BUAV Archives, DVB 2/1.
4. This is a rivalry that continues today. See *Annual Report & Accounts*, BUAV, 1992, p.7. The National did not respond to my enquiry regarding their relationship with the Union. See also accounts of various incidents in the Coleridge Case folder, BUAV Archives, DBV 35/2.
5. 'The leadership of the anti-vivisection cause: Replies to the Hon. Stephen Coleridge's claim'. Reprinted from the *Torquay Directory*, April 11th 1906. Coleridge Case folder, BUAV Archives, DBV 35/2.
6. Think of what has happened to the veal industry in England and the support given by animal rights activists to the Parliamentary Labour Party's continuing efforts to outlaw hunting.
7. See Caine,. *Victorian Feminists* and her *English Feminism, 1780–1980*, Oxford: Oxford University Press, 1997.
8. See N.D. Jewson, 'The Disappearance of the Sick-Man from Medical Cosmology, 1770–1870', *Sociology*, 10,1976, pp.225–44.
9. Cobbe, 'Medical Profession and its Morality', p.302.
10. One such case that has come to light occurred in the United States when a man was infected with a baboon virus after receiving the creature's liver in a 1992 xenotransplantation. See the *Daily Mail*, 1 October 1999.
11. Mary Wollstonecraft, 'A Vindication of the Rights of Woman', in *The Norton Anthology of English Literature*, New York, W.W. Norton & Co, 4th edition, II, p.124.
12. Stephen Coleridge, *Animal's Defender*, VII, 1904, p.22.

BIBLIOGRAPHY

Archives

Barbara Bodichon Papers, Girton College, Cambridge
Bessie Rayner Parkes Papers, Girton College, Cambridge
Bristol Record Office
British Library Manuscripts
British Union for the Abolition of Vivisection. Brynmor Jones Library, University of Hull
Broadlands Papers, SHA. University of Southampton Library
Cobbe MS. Autograph Collection. Bodleian Library
Emily Davies Papers, Girton College, Cambridge
The Fawcett Autograph Collection. The Women's Library
The Frances Power Cobbe Collection. Huntington Library
The Frederic Harrison Collection. British Library of Political and Economic Science
Mill-Taylor Correspondence. British Library of Political and Economic Science
MS Acland. Bodleian Library
National Union of Women's Suffrage Societies Collection. Manchester Public Library
New Minor Deposits, 1309–1315A, National Library of Wales
Shaftesbury Estates, Dorset
Somerset House
Somerville Papers, owned by Somerville College, deposited and administered by the Bodleian Library (catalogue compiled by Mrs Elizabeth Patterson)
The Wister Family Papers. The Historical Society of Pennsylvania

Journals, Newspapers, Parliamentary Books, etc.

The *Abolitionist*
Animal World
Reports of the British Association for the Advancement of Science British Medical Journal
Church Times
Daily News
Daily Telegraph

Englishwoman's Review
Hansard
Home Chronicler. From 1879 onwards, *Antivivisectionist*
Jewish Chronicle
The *Lancet*
Manchester Guardian
Nature
Pall Mall Gazette
Parliamentary Papers
Public General Statutes
Punch
Saturday Review
Spectator
The Times
The *Zoophilist*

Primary Sources—Books

Battersea, Constance. *Reminiscences*. London: Macmillan and Co., 1922.
Burdett Coutts, Baronness (ed.). *Woman's Mission. A Series of Congress Papers on the Philanthropic Work of Women by Eminent Writers*. London: Sampson Low, Marston & Company, 1893.
Burdon Sanderson, John (ed.). *Handbook for the Physiological Laboratory*. Philadelphia: Lindsay and Blakiston, 1873.
Butler, Josephine. *Woman's Work and Woman's Culture*. London: Macmillan and Co., 1869.
Carpenter, Mary. *Reformatory Schools for the Children of the Perishing and Dangerous Classes for Juvenile Offenders*. New Jersey: Patterson Smith, 1970. Originally published in 1851.
Cobbe, Frances Power (ed.). *Alone to the Alone: Prayers for Theists, by Several Contributors*. London: Williams and Norgate, 1872. Second edition.
—*Broken Lights: An Inquiry into the Present Condition and Future Prospects of Religious Faith*. London: Trubner and Co., 1864.
—*Darwinism in Morals, and Other Essays*. London: Williams and Norgate, 1872.
—*Dawning Lights: An Inquiry Concerning the Secular Results of the New Reformation*. London: Edward T. Whitfield, 1868
—*The Duties of Women*. Boston: Geo. H. Ellis, 1881.
—*Essay on Intuitive Morals, Being an Attempt to Popularise Ethical Science. Part I, Theory of Morals*. London: Longman, Brown, Green, and Longmans, 1855.
—*Essays on the Pursuits of Women*. London: Emily Faithfull, 1863.
—*The Friend of Man; and His Friends,—the Poets*. London: George Bell & Sons, 1889.
—*Hopes of the Human Race, Hereafter and Here. Essays on the Life after Death*. London: Williams and Norgate, 1880. Second edition.
—*Hours of Work and Play*. London: Trubner and Co., 1867.
—*Italics. Brief Notes on Politics, People, and Places in Italy in 1864*. London: Trubner and Co., 1864.
—*Life of Frances Power Cobbe. By Herself.* Boston and New York: Houghton, Mifflin

and Company, 1894. 2 volumes.
—*Life of Frances Power Cobbe as Told by Herself.* With additions by the author and an introduction by Blanche Atkinson. London: Swan Sonnenshein and Co., Lim., 1904.
—*The Modern Rack. Papers on Vivisection.* London: Swan Sonnenshein and Co., 1889.
—*The Peak in Darien, With Some Other Inquiries Touching Concerns of the Soul and the Body.* Boston: Geo. H. Ellis, 1882.
—*Re-Echoes.* London and Edinburgh: Williams and Norgate, 1876.
—*Religious Duty.* London: Trubner and Co., 1864.
—*The Scientific Spirit of the Age and Other Pleas and Discussions.* Boston: Geo. H. Ellis, 1888.
—*Studies New and Old of Ethical and Social Subjects.* Boston: William and Spencer, 1866.
Kemble, Frances Anne. *Further Records. 1848–1883. A Series of Letters by Frances Anne Kemble Forming a Sequel to Record of a Girlhood and Records of Later Life.* London: Richard Bentley and Son, 1890. 2 volumes.
Parker, Theodore. *Views of Religion.* Boston: American Unitarian Association, 1890. Third edition.
The Nine Circles, or the Torture of the Innocent. Being Records of Vivisection, English and Foreign. Compiled by Georgine M. Rhodes. London: Society for the Protection of Animals from Vivisection, 1893. Second and revised edition.
Stanton, Theodore (ed.). *The Woman Question in Europe. A Series of Original Essays Edited by Theodore Stanton.* London: Sampson Low, Marston, Searle, and Rivington, 1884.
Twining, Louisa. *Recollection of Life and Work. Being the Autobiography of Louisa Twining.* London: Edward Arnold, 1893.
Workhouses and Pauperism and Women's Work in the Administration of the Poor Law. London: Methuen and Co., 1898.
Walburga, Lady Paget. *In My Tower.* London: Hutchinson and Co., 1924. Second edition. 2 volumes.

Primary Sources—Articles

Adams, Charles Warren. 'The Anti-vivisection Movement and Miss Cobbe'. *Verulam Review.* III, 1892, pp.197–209.
Alcott, Louisa May. 'Glimpses of Eminent Persons'. The *Independent.* 1 November 1866.
Cobbe, Frances Power. 'Mr Lowe and the Vivisection Act'. *Contemporary Review.* 29, 11 o.s., 1877, pp.335–47.
—'The Little Health of Ladies'. *Contemporary Review.* 31, 1878, pp.276–96.
—'Wife Torture in England'. *Contemporary Review.* 32, 1878, pp.55–87.
—'Vivisection and Two-Faced Advocates'. *Contemporary Review.* 41, 1882, pp.610–26.
—'The Last Revival'. *Contemporary Review.* 42, 1882, pp.182–9.
—'Progressive Judaism'. *Contemporary Review.* 42, 1882, pp.747–63.
—'Agnostic Morality'. *Contemporary Review.* 43, 1883, pp.783–94.
—'A Faithless World'. *Contemporary Review.* 46, 1884, pp.795–810.
—'Faith Healing, Fear Killing'. *Contemporary Review.* 51, 1887, pp.794–813.
—'The Lord was not in the Earthquake'. *Contemporary Review.* 53, 1888, pp.70–83.

—'The Two Religions'. *Contemporary Review.* 58, 1890, pp.839–48.
—'The Ethics of Zoophily'. *Contemporary Review.* 68, 1895, pp.497–508.
—'Schadenfreude'. *Contemporary Review.* 81, 1902, pp.655–6.
—'Woman Suffrage. Justice for the Gander—Justice for the Goose'. *Contemporary Review.* 83, 1903, pp.653–60. An address originally delivered to the Ladies' Club, Royal York Crescent, Clifton, 2 January 1903.
—'Dogs Whom I Have Met'. *Cornhill Magazine.* 26, 1872, pp.662–78.
—'Modern Sorcery'. *Cornhill Magazine.* 30, 1874, pp.36–43.
—'Sacrificial Medicine'. *Cornhill Magazine.* 32, 1875, pp.427–38.
—'The Celt of Wales and the Celt of Ireland'. *Cornhill Magazine.* 36, 1877, pp.661–78.
—'What is Progress, and Are We Progressing?' *Fortnightly Review*, 7 o.s., 1 n.s., 1867, pp.357–70.
—'The Devil'. *Fortnightly Review.* 16 o.s., 10 n.s., 1871, p.180–91.
—'Vivisection—Four Replies'. *Fortnightly Review.* 37 o.s., 31 n.s., 1882, pp.88–104.
—'The City of the Sun'. *Fraser's Magazine.* 63, 1861, pp.670–84.
—'Celibacy v. Marriage'. *Fraser's Magazine.* 65, 1862, pp.228–35.
—'The City of Victory'. *Fraser's Magazine.* 65, 1862, pp.317–31.
—'The Eternal City'. *Fraser's Magazine.* 65, 1862, pp.565–79.
—'What Shall We do with Our Old Maids?' *Fraser's Magazine.* 66, 1862, pp.594–610.
—'Female Charity—Lay and Monastic'. *Fraser's Magazine.* 66, 1862, pp.774–88.
—'A Day at the Dead Sea'. *Fraser's Magazine.* 67, 1863, pp.226–38.
—'A Day at Athens'. *Fraser's Magazine.* 67, 1863, pp.601–12.
—'The City of Peace'. *Fraser's Magazine.* 67, 1863, pp.719–38.
—'The Rights of Man and the Claims of Brutes'. *Fraser's Magazine.* 68, 1863, pp.586–602.
—'Hades'. *Fraser's Magazine.* 69, April 1864, pp.293–311.
—'The Nineteenth Century'. *Fraser's Magazine.* 69, 1864, pp.481–94.
—'The Morals of Literature'. *Fraser's Magazine.* 70, 1864, pp.124–33.
—'The Philosophy of the Poor Laws and the Report of the Committee on Poor Relief'. *Fraser's Magazine.* 70, 1864, pp.373–94.
—'Ireland and Her Exhibition in 1865'. *Fraser's Magazine.* 72, 1865, pp.403–22.
—'The Indigent Class—their Schools and Dwellings'. *Fraser's Magazine.* 73, 1866, pp.143–60.
—'The Conventional Laws of Society'. *Fraser's Magazine.* 74, 1866, pp.667–73.
—'The American Sanitary Commission and its Lessons'. *Fraser's Magazine.* 75, 1867, pp.401–44.
—'Household Service'. *Fraser's Magazine.* 77, 1868, pp.121–34.
—'Criminals, Idiots, Women, and Minors'. *Fraser's Magazine.* 78, 1868, pp.777–94.
—'To Know, or Not to Know?' *Fraser's Magazine.* 80, 1869, pp.776–87.
—'Workhouses Sketches'. *Macmillan's Magazine.* 3, 1861, pp.448–61.
—'Social Sciences Congresses and Women's Part in Them'. *Macmillan's Magazine.* 5, 1861, pp.81–94.
—'The Medical Profession and its Morality'. *Modern Review.* 2, 1881, pp.296–328.
—'Animals in Fable and in Art'. *New Quarterly Magazine.* 2, 1874, pp.563–94.
—'The Moral Aspects of Vivisection'. *New Quarterly Magazine.* 4, 1875, pp.222–37.

—'The Consciousness of Dogs'. *Quarterly Review*. 133, 1872, pp.226–42.
—'Personal Recollections of Mrs Somerville'. *Quarterly Review*. 136–7, 1874, pp.39–54.
—'Youth and Age'. Published posthumously by Constance Battersea in the *Spectator*. 92, 1904, p.771.
—'The New Creed and the Old, in Their Secular Results—I'. *Theological Review*, 4, 1867, pp.1–21.
—'The New Creed and the Old, in Their Secular Results—II'. *Theological Review*. 4, 1867, pp.241–58.
—'The Organization of Charity'. *Theological Review*. 4, 1867, pp.553–72.
—'The New Creed and the Old, in Their Secular Results—III', *Theological Review*. 5, 1868, pp.26–51.
—'The Subjection of Women'. *Theological Review*. 6, 1869, pp.355–75.
—'Evangelical Character'. *Theological Review*. 11, 1874, pp.449–69.
Coleridge, Lord. 'The Nineteenth Century Defenders of Vivisection'. *Fortnightly Review*. 37 o.s., 31 n.s., 1882, pp.225–36.
de Cyon, E. 'The Anti-vivisection Agitation'. *Contemporary Review*. 43, 1883, pp.498–510.
Foster, Michael. 'Vivisection'. *Macmillan's Magazine*. 29, 1874, pp.367–76.
Greg, William Rathbone. 'Why Are Women Redundant?' *National Review*. 14, 1862, pp.434–60.
Gull, William. 'The Ethics of Vivisection'. *Nineteenth Century*. 11, 1882, pp.456–67.
Hart, Ernest. 'Women, Clergymen, and Doctors'. *New Review*. 7, 1892, pp.708–18.
Hoggan, George. 'Vivisection'. *Fraser's Magazine*. 11 n.s., 1875, pp.521–8.
Hopkins, Ellice. 'The Industrial Training of Pauper and Neglected Girls'. *Contemporary Review*. 42, 1882, pp.140–54.
Kingsford, Anna. 'The Uselessness of Vivisection'. *Nineteenth Century*. 11, 1882, pp.171–83.
Lowe, Robert. 'The Vivisection Act'. *Contemporary Review*. 28, 1876, pp.713–24.
Ouida. 'The Future of Vivisection'. *The Gentleman's Magazine*. 252, 1882, pp.412–23.
Paget, Stephen, Owen, Robert and Samuel Wilks, 'Vivisection. Its Pains and Uses'. *Nineteenth Century*. 10, 1881, pp.920–48.
—'Portraits of Celebrities at Different Times of Their Lives'. *Strand Magazine*. 6, 1893, pp.51–6.
Sanborn, F.B. 'Frances Power Cobbe: A Life Devoted to the Promotion of Social Science'. *Journal of the American Social Science Association*. 42, 1904.
Twining, Louisa. 'Workhouse Cruelties'. *Nineteenth Century*. 20, 1886, pp.709–14.
—'Women as Public Servants'. *Nineteenth Century*. 28, 1890, pp.950–958.
Tyrell, the Rev. George. 'Jesuit Zoophily'. *Contemporary Review*. 68, 1895, pp.708–15.
Wilks, Samuel. 'The Ethics of Vivisection'. *Contemporary Review*. 41, 1882, pp.812–18.
Wollstonecraft, Mary. 'A Vindication of the Rights of Woman'. *The Norton Anthology of English Literature*. New York: W.W. Norton and Company, 1979. Volume II, fourth edition, pp.112–37.
Yeo, Gerald. 'The Practice of Vivisection in England'. *Fortnightly Review*. 37 o.s., 31 n.s., 1882, pp.352–68.

Primary Sources—Pamphlets

Besant, Annie. *A World Without God. A Reply to Miss Frances Power Cobbe*. London: Freethought Publishing Company, 1885.
Bryan, Benjamin. *Kochism: Experiment, not Discovery*. London: VSS, 1890.
Cobbe, Frances Power. *Bernard's Martyrs. A Comment on Claude Bernard's Leçons de Physiologie Opératoire*. London: Society for the Protection of Animals from Vivisection, 1879. Hereafter referred to as the VSS.
—*Cancer Experiments on Human Beings*. London: VSS, 1890.
—*A Charity and a Controversy. Address by Frances Power Cobbe at the Annual Meeting of the VSS*, 20 June 1889. London: VSS, 1889.
—*The Churches and Moral Questions*. London: VSS, 1889.
—*Comments on the Debate in the House of Commons, April 4, 1883, on Mr Reid's Bill for the Total Prohibition of Vivisection*. London: VSS, 1883.
—*Controversy in a Nutshell*. London: VSS, n.d., c. 1895.
—*The Dangers of Pasteurism to Body and Soul*. London: VSS, 1889.
—*Doctor's Doctrine. A Correspondence in the 'Leicester Daily Post'*. London: VSS, 1888.
—*Doomed To Be Saved*. Preached at the Anniversary Service of the Clerkenwell Unitarian Sunday School, 5 October 1873. London: The Clerkenwell Unitarian Church, 1874.
—*The Fallacy of Restriction Applied to Vivisection*. London: VSS, 1886.
—*Friendless Girls, and How to Help Them: Being an Account of the Preventive Mission at Bristol*. A paper read at the Social Science Congress in Dublin, 1861. Published by Emily Faithfull and Company, n.d., c. 1862.
—*A Guest for Queen Victoria*. London: VSS, 1891.
—*Health and Holiness*. An address read to the Cambridge Ladies' Discussion Society, November 6th, 1891. London: George Bell and Sons, 1891.
—*Monkey's Brains*. London: VSS, 1889.
—*My Dr Tells Me That Experiments on Animals are Made to save the necessity of experimentation on human beings*. London: VSS, n.d.
—*The New Benefactor of Humanity*. London: VSS, 1884.
—*Our Policy. An Address to Women Concerning the Suffrage*. London: London National Society for Women's Suffrage, n.d.
—*The Red Flag in John Bull's Eyes*. London: Published for the Ladies' London Emancipation Society by Emily Faithfull, 1863.
—*Rejoinder to Mrs Stowe's Reply to the Address of the Women of England*. London: Emily Faithfull, 1863.
—*The Right of Tormenting*. London: VSS, 1888.
—*The Sick in Workhouses*. London: J. Nisbet and Company, 1861.
—*Somerville Hall, A Misnomer. A Correspondence with Notes*. London: VSS, 1891.
—*Why We Have Founded the British Union for the Abolition of Vivisection*. British Union for the Abolition of Vivisection, 1901. First published 1898.
—*Why Women Desire the Franchise*. London: Published for the London National Society for Women's Suffrage by Spottiswoode and Co., 1869.
—*Women's Duty to Women*. A paper read at the conference of Women Workers, held in Birmingham, November 1890. National Union of Women's Suffrage Societies Collection, M50/65.

—*Workhouse as an Hospital*. London: Emily Faithfull and Company, 1861.

Coleridge, the Hon. Stephen. *Step By Step.Being a Reply to a Pamphlet by Miss Frances Power Cobbe, entitled—'Why We Have Founded the British Union for the Abolition of Vivisection*. London: The National Anti-Vivisection Society, 1898.

Cowper, John Powys. *Anti-Vivisection*. London: British Union for the Abolition of Vivisection, n.d.

Elliot, Margaret and Cobbe, Frances Power. *Destitute Incurables in Workhouses*. A paper read at the Social Science Meeting, Glasgow, September 1860. Published 1861.

The Oubliettes of Science. Anti-Vivisection Meeting at Birmingham, November 9th, 1890. London: VSS, n.d.

Secondary Sources—Unpublished Material

Caine, Barbara. 'Frances Cobbe and the English Women's Movement'. n.d. A copy of this paper is held by Ann Robson, University of Toronto.

Caskie, Helen. 'Frances Power Cobbe: Victorian Feminist'. Unpublished Dissertation, January 1981. Fawcett Library.

Linzey, The Reverend Professor Andrew. 'Making Peace with Creation'. Paper given at Harris Manchester College, Oxford, June 1997.

Secondary Sources—Books

Adams, Carol. *The Sexual Politics of Meat. A Feminist-Vegetarian Critical Theory*. Cambridge: Polity Press, 1990.

Bebbington, D.W. *Evangelicalism in Modern Britain: A History from the 1730s to the 1980s*. London: Unwin Hyman, 1989.

Birkett, Dea. *Spinsters Abroad*. London: Basil Blackwell, 1989.

Bolt, Christine. *Feminist Ferment. 'The Woman Question' in the USA and England, 1870–1940*. London: UCL Press, 1995.

Bonner, Thomas Neville. *Becoming a Physician. Medical Education in Britain, France, Germany, and the United States, 1750–1945*. Oxford: Oxford University Press, 1995.

Bradley, Ian. *The Call to Seriousness. The Evangelical Impact on the Victorians*. London: Jonathan Cape, 1976.

Budd, Susan. *Varieties of Unbelief. Atheists and Agnostics in English Society 1850–1960*. London: Heinemann, 1977.

Burdon Sanderson, Lady Ghetal. *Sir John Burdon Sanderson. A Memoir*. Completed and edited by his nephew and niece. Oxford: The Clarendon Press, 1911.

Burke, Sir Bernard. *A Genealogical and Heraldic History of the Landed Gentry of Ireland*. London: Harrison and Sons, 1912.

Burman, Sandra (ed.). *Fit Work for Women*. London: Croom Helm, 1979.

Burn, W.L. *The Age of Equipoise. A Study of the Mid-Victorian Generation*. London: Allen and Unwin, 1964.

Burstyn, Joan. *Victorian Education and the Ideal of Womanhood*. London: Croom Helm, 1980.

Bynum, W.F., Lock, Stephen and Porter, Roy (eds). *Medical Journals and Medical Knowledge*. London: Routledge, 1992.

Bynum, W.F. *Science and the Practice of Medicine in the Nineteenth Century*. Cambridge:

Cambridge University Press, 1994.
Caine, Barbara. *Victorian Feminists*. Oxford: Oxford University Press, 1992.
—*English Feminism, 1780–1980*. Oxford: Oxford University Press, 1997.
Chapman, Alison and Jane Stabler (eds). *Unfolding the South: Nineteenth-Century British Women Writers and Artists in Italy*, Manchester: Manchester University Press, 2003.
Cockshut, A. *The Unbelievers. English Agnostic Thought, 1840–1890*. New York: New York University Press, 1966.
Connolly, Sean. *Religion and Society in Nineteenth-Century Ireland*. The Economic and Social History Society of Ireland, 1985.
Corbett, Mary Jean. *Representing Femininity. Middle-Class Subjectivity in Victorian and Edwardian Women's Autobiographies*. Oxford: Oxford University Press, 1992.
Cranshaw, Lindsay and Porter, Roy (eds). *The Hospital in History*. London: Routledge, 1989.
Crowther, M.A. *The Workhouse System, 1834–1929*. London: Batsford Academic and Educational, 1981.
Cunningham, Hugh. *The Children of the Poor. Representations of Childhood Since the Seventeenth Century*. Oxford: Blackwell, 1991.
Dale, Antony. *Fashionable Brighton, 1820–1860*. London: Ariel Press Limited, 1967.
Dally, Ann. *Women Under the Knife. A History of Surgery*. London: Hutchinson Radius, 1991.
D'Alton, John. *The History of County Dublin*. Cork: Tower Books of Cork, 1976. First published Dublin: Hodges and Smith, 1838.
Davidoff, Leonore and Hall, Catherine. *Family Fortunes. Men and Women of the English Middle Class, 1780–1850*. London: Century Hutchinson, 1987.
Davin, Anna. *Growing Up Poor. Home, School and Street in London, 1870–1914*. London: Rivers Oram, 1996.
D'Cruz, Shani (ed.). *Everyday Violence in Britain, 1850–1950*, Harlow: Longman, 2000
Delamont, S. and Duffin, L. (eds). *The Nineteenth Century Woman: Her Cultural and Physical World*. London: Croom Helm, 1978.
Desmond, Adrian and Moore, James. *Darwin: The Life of a Tormented Evolutionist*. London: Michael Joseph, 1991.
Digby, Anne. *The Poor Law in Nineteenth-Century England and Wales*. London: Historical Association, 1982.
—*Making a Medical Living. Doctors and Patients in the English Market for Medicine, 1720–1911*. Cambridge: Cambridge University Press, 1994.
Doggett, Maeve. *Marriage, Wife-Beating and the Law in Victorian England*. South Carolina: University of South Carolina Press, 1993.
Duckworth, Jeannie. *Fagin's Children; Criminal Children in Victorian England*, London: Hambledon and London, 2002.
Faderman, Lillian. *Surpassing the Love of Men. Romantic Love and Friendship Between Women from the Renaissance to the Present*. London: The Women's Press, 1981.
Finlayson, G.B.A.M. *The Seventh Earl of Shaftesbury*. London: Eyre Methuen, 1981.
Flanders, Judith. *The Victorian House: Domestic Life from Childbirth to Deathbed*, London: HarperCollins, 2003.
Fletcher, Sheila. *Feminists and Bureaucrats. A Study in the Development of Girls' Education in the Nineteenth Century*. Cambridge: Cambridge University Press, 1980.
Fraser, Derek (ed.). *The New Poor Law in the Nineteenth Century*. London: The

Macmillan Press, 1976.

French, Richard. *Antivivisection and Medical Science in Victorian Society*. New Jersey: Princeton University Press, 1975.

Gilbert, John T. *A History of the City of Dublin*. Shannon: Irish University Press, 1972. First published 1854–9. 3 volumes.

Guerrini, Anita. *Experimenting with Humans and Animals: From Galen to Animal Rights*, Baltimore: The Johns Hopkins University Press, 2003.

Hamer, Emily. *Britannia's Glory. A History of Twentieth-Century Lesbians*. London: Cassell, 1996.

Hammerton, James A. *Cruelty and Companionship. Conflict in Nineteenth-Century Married Life*. London and New York: Routledge, 1992.

Heyck, T.W. *The Transformation of Intellectual Life in Victorian England*. London: Croom Helm, 1984.

Himmelfarb, Gertrude. *Poverty and Compassion. The Moral Imagination of the Late Victorians*. New York: Vintage Books, 1992.

Hodder, E. *The Life and Work of the Seventh Earl of Shaftesbury*. London: Cassell and Company Limited, 1886. 3 volumes.

Holcombe, L. *Victorian Ladies at Work: Middle Class Working Women in England and Wales, 1850–1914*. Newton Abbot: David & Charles, 1973.

Houghton, Walter. *The Victorian Frame of Mind, 1830–1870*. New Haven: Yale University Press, 1957.

Hurt, J.S. *Elementary Schooling and the Working Classes, 1860–1918*. London: Routledge and Kegan Paul, 1979.

Johnston, Judith. *Anna Jameson. Victorian, Feminist, Woman of Letters*. Hants: Scolar Press, 1997.

Jones, E. Rosalie. *A History of Barmouth and Its Vicinity*. Barmouth: John Evans and Nephew, 1909.

Kean, Hilda. *Animal Rights: Political and Social Change in Britain Since 1800*, London: Reaktion, 2000.

Kidd, Beatrice and Richards, Edith M. *Hadwen of Gloucester. Man, Medico, Martyr*. London: John Murray, 1933.

Lansbury, Coral. *The Old Brown Dog. Women, Workers and Vivisection in Edwardian England*. Wisconsin: The University of Wisconsin Press, 1985.

Levine, Philippa. *Feminist Lives in Victorian England. Private Roles and Public Commitment*. Oxford: Blackwell, 1990.

Lewis, Gifford. *Eva Gore Booth and Esther Roper*. A Biography. London: Pandora, 1988.

Lightman, Bernard. *The Origins of Agnosticism: Victorian Unbelief and the Limits of Knowledge*. Baltimore: Johns Hopkins University Press, 1987.

McAleer, Edward C. (ed.). *Dearest Isa. Robert Browning's Letters to Isabella Blagden*. Austin: University of Texas Press, 1951.

Maitland, Edward. *Anna Kingsford. Her Life, Letters, Diary and Work*. London: George Redway, 1896. 2 volumes.

Manton, Jo. *Mary Carpenter and the Children of the Streets*. London: Heinemann Educational Books, 1975.

Murray, Janet Horowitz. *Strong Minded Women and Other Lost Voices From Nineteenth-Century England*. New York: Pantheon Books, 1982.

Myerson, Joel and Shealy, Daniel (eds). *The Journals of Louisa May Alcott*. Boston and

Toronto: Little Brown and Company, 1989.
Neeley, Kathryn A. *Mary Somerville: Science, Illumination, and the Female Mind*, Cambridge: Cambridge University Press, 2001.
O'Connor, W.J. *British Physiologists, 1885–1914. A Biographical Dictionary*. Manchester: Manchester University Press, 1991.
—*Founders of British Physiology. A Biographical Dictionary, 1820–1885*. Manchester: Manchester University Press, 1988.
Owen, David. *English Philanthropy, 1660–1960*. Cambridge: Harvard University Press, 1964.
Parson, Gerald (ed.). *Religion in Victorian Britain*. Volume 4, 'Interpretations'. Manchester: Manchester University Press, 1988.
Peacock, Sandra J. *The Theological and Ethical Writings of Frances Power Cobbe, 1822–1904*, Lewiston, NY, Lampeter: Edwin Mellen Press, 2002.
Peterson, M.J. *The Medical Profession in Mid-Victorian London*. Berkeley and Los Angeles: University of California Press, 1978.
Poovey, Mary. *Uneven Developments: The Ideological Work of Gender in Mid-Victorian England*. Chicago: University of Chicago Press, 1988.
—*Making a Social Body. British Cultural Formation 1830–1864*. Chicago, 1995.
Prochaska, F.K. *Women and Philanthropy in Nineteenth-Century England*. Oxford: Oxford University Press, 1980.
Pugh, Martin. *Votes for Women in Britain, 1865–1928*. London: Historical Association, 1995.
—*The March of the Women: a Revisionist Analysis of the Campaign for Women's Suffrace, 1866–1914*, Oxford: Oxford University Press, 2000.
Richardson, Ruth. *Death, Dissection and the Destitute*. London: Routledge and Kegan Paul, 1987.
Ritvo, Harriet. *The Animal Estate. The English and Other Creatures in the Victorian Age*. Cambridge: Harvard University Press, 1987.
Romano, Terrie M. *Making Medicine Scientific: John Burdon Sanderson and the Culture of Victorian Science*, Baltimore: The Johns Hopkins University Press, 2001.
Rose, Lionel. *Massacre of the Innocents. Infanticide in Great Britain, 1800–1939*. London: Routledge and Kegan Paul, 1986.
Rose, Michael. *The Poor and the City*. Leicester: Leicester University Press, 1985.
Rover, Constance. *Women's Suffrage and Party Politics in Britain, 1866–1914*. London: Routledge and Kegan Paul, 1967.
Rupke, Nicolaas (ed.), *Vivisection in Historical Perspective*. London: Croom Helm, 1987.
Ryder, Richard. *Animal Revolution. Changing Attitudes Towards Speciesism*. London: Basil Blackwell, 1989.
—*Victims of Science. The Use of Animals in Research*. London: Davis Poynter, 1975.
Sanders, Valerie. *The Private Lives of Victorian Women. Autobiography in Nineteenth-Century England*. Hertfordshire: Harvester Wheatsheaf, 1989.
Smith, Sidonie. *A Poetics of Women's Autobiography. Marginality and the Fictions of Self-Representation*. Bloomington: Indiana University Press, 1987.
Somerville, Martha (ed.). *Personal Recollections from Early Life to Old Age of Mary Somerville*. Boston: Roberts Brothers, 1874.
Spencer, Colin. *The Heretics Feast. A History of Vegetarianism*. London: Fourth Estate, 1993.

Spender, Dale. *Feminist Theorists*. London: The Women's Press, 1983.
—*Women of Ideas And What Men Have Done to Them*. London: Ark Paperbacks, 1983.
Sperling, Susan. *Animal Liberators. Research and Morality*. Berkeley and Los Angeles: University of California Press, 1988.
Stanton, Theodore (ed.). *Reminiscences of Rosa Bonheur*. London: Andrew Melrose, 1910.
Stedman Jones, Gareth. *Outcast London. A Study in the Relationship Between Classes in Victorian Society*. Oxford: Clarendon Press, 1971.
Sullivan, Roger J. *Immanuel Kant's Moral Theory*. New York: Cambridge University Press, 1989.
Tester, Keith. *Animals and Society. The Humanity of Animal Rights*. London: Routledge, 1991.
Thomas, Keith. *Man and the Natural World. A History of Modern Sensibility*. New York: Pantheon Books, 1983.
Turner, E. *All Heaven in a Rage*. London: Michael Joseph, 1964.
Turner, Frank. *Contesting Cultural Authority. Essays in Victorian Intellectual Life*. Cambridge: Cambridge University Press, 1993.
Turner, James. *Reckoning with the Beast. Animals, Pain, and Humanity in the Victorian Mind*. Baltimore: The Johns Hopkins University Press, 1980.
Vicinus, Martha. *Independent Women. Work and Community for Single Women. 1850–1920*. London: Virago Press 1985.
Vyvyan, John. *The Dark Face of Science*. London: Michael Joseph, 1971.
—*In Pity and In Anger*. London: Michael Joseph, 1969.
Walkowitz, Judith. *Prostitution and Victorian Society: Women, Class and the State*. Cambridge: Cambridge University Press, 1980.
Warboys, Michael. *Spreading Germs: Diseases, Theories and Medical Practice in Britain, 1865–1900*, New York: Cambridge University Press, 2000.
Webb, R.K. *Harriet Martineau. A Radical Victorian*. London: William Heinemann Ltd., 1960.
Wohl, Anthony. *Endangered Lives. Public Health in Victorian England*. London: Dent, 1983.

Secondary Sources—Articles

Bauer, Lawrence and Ritt, Carol. 'A Husband is a Beating Animal. Frances Power Cobbe Confronts the Wife Abuse Problem'. *International Journal of Women's Studies*. 6, no.2, 1983, pp.99–118.
—'Wife Abuse, Late-Victorian English Feminists, and the Legacy of Frances Power Cobbe'. *International Journal of Women's Studies*. 6, no.3, 1983, pp.195–207.
Caine, Barbara. 'Feminism, Suffrage and the Nineteenth-Century English Women's Movement'. *Women's Studies International Forum*. 5, no.6, 1982, pp.537–50.
Connolly, Peter. 'The Moral Status of Animals'. *Ethical Record*. 102, 7, July/August 1997, pp.7–15.
French, Richard. 'Some Problems and Sources in the Foundations of Modern Physiology in Great Britain'. *History of Science*. 10, 1971, pp.28–55.
Geison, Gerald L. 'Social and Institutional Factors in the Stagnancy of English Physiology, 1840–1870'. *Bulletin of the History of Medicine*. 46, 1972, pp.30–58.

Harris, Mary Corbett. 'Frances Power Cobbe (1822–1904) of Hengwrt'. *Journal of the Merioneth Historical and Record Society.* 7, part 4, 1976, pp.416–23.

Harrison, Brian. 'Animals and the State in Nineteenth-Century England'. *English Historical Review.* 88, 1973, pp.786–820.

—'Philanthropy and the Victorians'. *Victorian Studies.* 9, no.4, 1966, pp.217–59.

Kean, Hilda. 'The "Smooth Cool Men of Science": The Feminist and Socialist Response to Vivisection'. *History Workshop Journal.* 40, 1995, pp.16–38.

Lansbury, Coral. 'Gynaecology, Pornography and the Anti-Vivisection Movement'. *Victorian Studies.* 28, 1985, pp.413–38.

Lawrence, Christopher. 'Incommunicable Knowledge. Science, Technology and the Clinical Art in Britain, 1850–1914'. *Journal of Contemporary History.* 20, 1985, pp.503–20.

Ozer, Mark. 'The British Vivisection Controversy'. *Bulletin of the History of Medicine.* 40, 1966, pp.158–67.

Passmore, J.H. 'The Treatment of Animals'. *Journal of the History of Ideas.* 36, 1975, pp.195–218.

Porter, Dorothy and Porter, Roy. 'The Politics of Prevention: Anti-Vaccinationism and Public Health in Nineteenth-Century England'. *Medical History.* 32, no.3, 1988, pp.231–52.

Prochaska, F.K. 'Body and Soul: Bible Nurses and the Poor in Victorian London'. *Historical Research.* 60, 1987, pp.337–48.

Robson, A.P.W. 'The Founding of the National Society for Women's Suffrage, 1866–1867'. *Canadian Journal of History.* 8, 1973, pp.1–22.

Ryan, Andrew. 'History of the British Act of 1876. An Act to Amend the Law Relating to Cruelty to Animals'. *Journal of Medical Education.* 38(1), 1963, pp.182–94.

Schiller, Joseph. 'Claude Bernard and Vivisection'. *Journal of the History of Medicine.* 22, 1967, pp.246–60.

Schumpf, Harriet Warm. 'Single Women and Social Reform in Mid-Nineteenth Century England: The Case of Mary Carpenter'. *Victorian Studies.* 17, 1974, pp.301–17.

Shugg, Wallace. 'The Cartesian Beast Machine in English Literature, (1663–1750)'. *Journal of the History of Ideas.* 29, 1968, pp.279–92.

—'Humanitarian Attitudes in the Early Animal Experiments of the Royal Society'. *Annals of Science.* 24, no.3, 1968, pp.227–38.

Smith-Rosenberg, Carroll. 'The Female World of Love and Ritual. Relations Between Women in Nineteenth-Century America'. *Signs.* 1, 1, 1975, pp.1–29

Stanley, Liz. 'Romantic Friendship? Some Issues in Researching Lesbian History and Biography'. *Women's History Review.* 1, 2, 1992, pp.193–216.

Stevenson, L.G. 'Religious Elements in the Background of the British Anti-Vivisection Movement'. *Yale Journal of Biology and Medicine.* 24, 1956, pp.125–57.

Tansey, E.M. 'The Wellcome Physiological Research Laboratories, 1894–1904: The Home Office, Pharmaceutical Firms, and Animal Experiments'. *Medical History.* 33, no.1, 1989, pp.1–41.

Tomes, Nancy. 'A Torrent of Abuse. Crimes of Violence Between Working-Class Men and Women in London, 1840–1875'. *Journal of Social History.* 11, 1977–8, pp.328–45.

Vicinus, Martha. 'Distance and Desire: English Boarding School Friendships, 1870–1920'. Duberman, Martin Bauml, Vicinus, Martha and Chauncy, George Jr. (ed.) *Hidden From History. Reclaiming the Gay and Lesbian Past.* New York: New American Library, 1989.
—'They Wonder to Which Sex I Belong: The Historical Roots of the Modern Lesbian Identity'. Altman, Denis, et al. (eds), *Homosexuality: Which Homosexuality?* London: Gay Men's Press, 1989.
Yeo, Eileen Janes. 'Social Motherhood and the Sexual Communion of Labour in British Social Science, 1850–1950'. *Women's History Review*, 1, no.1, 1992, pp.63–87.

INDEX

Abercromby, Lord, 199
Abolitionist, the, founding of, 202
abolitionists, on Carnarvon's bill, 128
Acland, Henry, 150
Act for the Better Prevention and Punishment of Aggravated Assaults Upon Women and Children and for Preventing Delay and Expense in the Administration of the Criminal Law (1853), 82
Act to Amend the Law Relating to Cruelty to Animals (1876): provisions of, 131; response to, 131–2; Cobbe's reaction to, 211
Adams, Charles Warren, 136; and Mildred Coleridge, 178–9, 248 *n*14; on Cobbe and anti-vivisection, 211; sues Cobbe, 180; and VSS, 178, 179
Addison, Joseph, 104
Adlam, Mr and Mrs, 199
Agnosticism, 22
Alcott, Louisa, 1–2
Aldrich, Thomas B., 209
Alfort, 97, 100, 101, 105
Amberleys, 90
America, and Cobbe's autobiography, 193; New England Anti-Vivisection Society, 183; vivisection in, 118; women's education and vivisection, 155; women's rights, 76
anaesthetics, 101, 111, 120–2, 125, 127, 131, 138, 145, 162, 189
Animal Defence and Anti-Vivisection Society, 215
Animal Psychology Bureau, 188
animal welfare, Cobbe on, 99, 103; development of, 101, 102, 105; extent of 105; nature of arguments supporting, 102, 103
animals: attitudes towards, in France, 97, 120; in Italy, 106; and Bible, 103; and children, 50; as children, 101; Cobbe begins to write on, 94; Cobbe on duties of man towards, 99, 103, 104, 212, 218, 219; Cobbe's relationship with, 99, 204; cruelty towards, 97, 100, 218; eighteenth-century ethicists on, 101, 104, 105; as food, Cobbe on, 104, 218; and happiness, 99; and humans, 101–4; Jesuits on, 188; (lack of) moral sense of, 101; possession of souls, 105; protection societies, 97; and rights, 102; in science, Cobbe's arguments for, 104; in sport, Cobbe's arguments defending 102, 219; subordination to man, Cobbe on, 103; and suffering, 99, 100, 101, 104, 120, 137, 138, 145, 152; as 'unmoral' creatures, 103; and working classes, 102, 114; and women, 109–10, 134
anthropocentrism, 102, 103, 105, 106, 188; influences VSS policy, 135; and 'Rights of Man', 100; and Royal Commission, 124
anti-Semitism, Cobbe accused of, 187; and anti-vivisection, 187, 250 *n*36
anti-slavery, and anti-vivisection, 202; Cobbe's involvement in 92, 202
anti-vaccination, 171–2; and Cobbe, 172; Walter Hadwen on, 204
anti-vivisection: and anti-Semitism, 187; and anti-slavery, 202; current movement, 147, 215, 216, 219; early sentiments, 105; propaganda, 133; propaganda and Cobbe, 133, 134, 147,

148, 149, 151–2, 152; propaganda, response to, 134, 152; propaganda, Shaftesbury's response to Cobbe's zeal for, 147–8; women in, 243 *n*89; women in, Cobbe on, 152–3
anti-vivisectionists, criticised, 143, 174, 177; female, treatment of, 191; and misanthropy, 173; today, 215, 216, 219
Appleton, Dr, 107
Arbrath, Dr Gustav Adolph, 141
Armour, Sara, 75
Association for the Advancement of Medical Research, 149, 215
Atkinson, Blanche, 194, 199, 211
autobiography: female, 6, 10; Cobbe writes hers (1894), 193; inadequacy of, 6, 13, 144, 194; creation of 'self', 6; revised (1904), 194

Balfour, Arthur J., 201
Barmouth Library, 211
Barnardo, Dr, 68
Battersea, Constance, 90, 211
Becker, Lydia, 94–5; and wife abuse, 82
Bell, Ernest, 197, 203
Bentham, Jeremy, 103; Cobbe critical of, 31
Berdoe, Edward, 161; defends Cobbe, 190; and *Nine Circles*, 189
Bernard, Claude, 111, 120, 135; Cobbe attacks, 137–8; equipment used by, 139–40
Besant, Annie, 193; criticises Cobbe, 32, 34, 174
Bible, and animals, 103; and Cobbe, 20, 21, 23, 24, 30
bills, animal cruelty, 102; vivisection: Carnarvon's (1876 Act), 127–32; abolitionists on, 128, physiologists on, 128, 129, 131–2, ; VSS on 128; Henniker's (1875), 12–2; Holt's (1879), 133, 135, 197; Playfair's (1875), 122, Cobbe criticises, 123; Reid's (1881), 136; Truro's (1879), 135, defeated, 136
biography, Cobbe on purposes of, 6
Blackstone, William, 78
Blackwell, Elizabeth, 117, 162
Blagden, Isa, 44, 53, 55, 93, 105
Blake, Matilda, 84
Bodichon, Barbara, 75–6
Boer War, 207
Bolton, Duke of, 7

Bonheur, Rosa, 44, 85
Bonner, Thomas Neville, 110
Boucherett, Jessie, 76, 83
Boyle, Eleanor Vere, 152, 153
Bridgewater Treatises, influence on Cobbe, 23
Bright, Jacob, 199
Bright, John, 115
Bristol, Cobbe in, 47–55, 55–69; slums, 50–1
Bristol, Dean of, 56
Bristol and West of England Anti-Vivisection Society, 199
British Association for the Advancement of Science, 111
British Institute for Preventive Medicine, 175
British Medical Association, 112–13
British Union for the Abolition of Vivisection, 4, 211, 212, 213; branches, 209; Cobbe founds, 198; membership, 199; relationship with NAVS, 204–5, 215; *Zoophilist* on, 202–3
Brown dog controversy, 215
Brown-Séquard, Charles-Edouard, 145
Browning, Robert, 93
Bryan, Benjamin, 163, 181, 183
Burdett-Coutts, Baroness, 117
Burdon Sanderson, Mrs, 153–4
Burdon Sanderson, John Scott, 135, 149; and Physiological Society, 132; and *Handbook for the Physiological Library*, 112; and medical education, 111; at Oxford, 150; at University College, 111
Buss, Frances, 75
Bute, Marquis of, 126
Butler, Bishop, 103
Butler, Josephine, 6, 206, 209, 244 *n*4
Byron, Lady, 47

Caine, Barbara, 3
Cambridge, and vivisection, 154–5
Canterbury, Archbishop of, 115, 206
Canterbury, Dean of, 209
Cardwell, Edward, 122, 123
Carlyle, Thomas, 115
Carnarvon, Lord, 127, 128
Carpenter, Mary, 47, 48; on boarding out, 68; and children, 48, 54; Cobbe criticises, 50–1; on discipline, 49; relationship with Cobbe, 47, 49, 50, 52–3, 54–5; and Rosanna, 54

Carpenter, the Reverend Estlin, 90, 209, 211
Carrington, Edith, 204
Central Committee for Women's Suffrage (London), 209
Chadwick, Edwin, 61, 166
Chauveau, Auguste, 145, 175
Chelsea Hospital, 164
children: and animals, 50; boarding out, failure of, 5; Cobbe on, 48–50, 67, 84; Mary Carpenter on, 48; at Red Lodge, 49, 54; street children, 47–8; workhouse children, Cobbe on, 63–6, Ellice Hopkins on, 67, statistics, 66; working-class education, 47
Childs, A.P., 126, 135
Chronology of the Anti-Vivisection Movement, 200
churches and vivisection, 138
Clancarty, Earl of, 8
Cobbe, Charles, Archbishop of Dublin, 7, 19
Cobbe, Charles (father), as absentee landlord, 8; attacked by Irish, 8; birth of, 7; death of, 34; inherits Newbridge, 8; marries Frances Conway, 7; portraits, 33; relationship with Cobbe, 15, 17, 20, 23, 25, 28, 32, 34–5; serves under Wellesley, 7
Cobbe, Charles (brother), 14, 36, 44; birth of, 8; death of, 182
Cobbe family, background, 7, 15, 17; family tree, 9; seat, 18
Cobbe, Frances (*née* Conway), 8; death of, 24; marries Charles Cobbe, 7; and physicians, 10, 157; relationship with Cobbe, 10, 11, 15, 16, 19, 25, 89
Cobbe, Frances Conway (niece), 213
Cobbe, Frances Power, achievements, 211–12; and animals, 100–5, 128, 129, 205, 212, 214, 219; accused of cruelty to animals, 206; accused of anti-Semitism, 187; involvement in anti-slavery, 202; and anti-vaccination, 172; appearance, 1, 16, 87, 91–2; autobiography, 6, 13–14, 144, 193–4; background and childhood, 7–13; beliefs, ethical basis of, 2; on biography, purposes of, 6; birth of, 7, 8; on Boer War, 207; on Britishness, 39; relationship with Mary Carpenter, 47–50, 52–3; character of, 1–2, 4, 10, 16, 20–22, 40, 41, 53, 89, 90–1, 142, 143, 144, 147, 156, 173, 176, 186, 196, 201, 202, 203, 207–8, 216, 219; on children, 48–50, 50, 67; Coleridge Libel Case, 209; conflict with individuals (Charles Warren Adams and Mildred Coleridge), 178–9, 180, (Stephen Coleridge), 182, 197–8, 204–5, (Fanny Kemble), 184, (Anna Kingsford), 143–3; conservatism, 3; on Conservatives, 95, 201; involvement in controversy, 185–93; supports cremation, 211; criticism of, 4, 115, 117, 134, 146–7, 151–2, 173–4, 177–8, 187–91, 201–2, 203, 211–12; *Daily News*, 69, 105–6; and Darwin, 90, 94, 116; death of, 210; on democracy, 4, 77, 216, 217; depression, 208–9, 214; on discipline, 49–50; and dress reform, 92; *Echo*, 80; on Edward VII, 207; education 11–13, 15, 45–6, 70–5, 94, 151, 153–6; on exploitation, 3, 4, 69, 109, 212; on field sports, 145, 205, 219; in France, 97–9; funeral of, 211; on gender differences, 30–1, 72–3, 81, 217; and germs, 165, 171; on Gladstone, 95; government, 5, 83, 158, 169, 216; Grand Tour, 36–44; heteropathy, 49, 62; and indigenous peoples, 38, 40, 41; on health and medicine, 157–75, 219; on Home Rule, 95; ill-health, 97, 182, 188, 190, 194–5, 206–7; Italy, 38, 42, 53, 55, 105–7; journalism, 92–4; Jews, 180–2; Jesuits, 188; lesbianism, 48, 85–7; on Liberals, 94–5; on love, 87; relationship with Mary Lloyd, 44, 74, 85–90, 185, 195–6, 218; on marriage, 2, 78–84, 214; medical education, 160–1; memorial to RSPCA, 114–17; on men, 2, 16, 58, 64, 79, 90; notification and isolation, 170; on paupers, 59–67; portraits, 98, 214; poverty, 67–8, and (her perceived), 36, 185; philanthropy, 31, 46, 70, 217; on physicians, 157–61, 167–8; premature burial, 210; questions direction of life, 44–5; Red Lodge, 47–55; relationships, theories on, 84, 103; religion, 19–34; on sanitation, 167; on Schadenfreude, 49; on science, 90, 112; on separate spheres, 44, 45, 66, 74; relationship with Lord Shaftesbury, 126, 133, 141–2, 147–9,

178–80, 181; shortcomings, 4, 63, 82, 109, 146, 147, 156, 159, 186, 200; on slaughter, 104, 218; on slavery, 202; social life (Dublin), 15–16, (Bristol), 56, (London), 90–7; suffering, 4, 104, 145, 172, 173, 195; on sympathy, 63, 71; on vaccination, 171–2; vivisection, 97, 105–10, 114–56: abolition, 132, 135; attitudes towards, 100, 112, 115; bill (1875), 121–2; founds BUAV, 198; on Carnarvon's bill, 130; Ferrier prosecution, 141–2; Hadwen as successor, 204; human vivisection, 161–2, 164; introduced to vivisection, 97; Italian memorial, 106; Louis Pasteur, 138; Playfair bill, 123; propaganda, 133, 147–9, 151, 152; restriction, 200–1; role in movement, 211–12, 215; and RSPCA, 114, 118–19; Moritz Schiff, 106–7; SPALV, 125; Somerville Hall, 153–4; and VSS, 181, 202; on 'vivisecting spirit', 137; women and, 152–3; edits *Zoophilist*, 180; wife abuse, 80–4; on women, 73–4, 83–4, 110; duties of women, 28, 217, 218; education 45, 72–3, 75, 94; employment, 46, 63, 70; and medicine, 71, 160; moral superiority, 46, 68, 96, 110, 208, 217, 218; philanthropy, 46, 54, 143; in workhouses, 58, 61; unmarried women, 2, 44, 46, 70, 72; vivisection, 151, 153–6; women's rights: 3, 4, 70–78; 'over-exposure' in movement, 76; radicalism, 77; workhouses, 57–61

Publications: *Alone to the Alone*, 183; 'Animals in Fable and in Art', 94; *An Appeal to the Human Jews of England*, 186; *Bernard's Martyrs*, 137–8; *Broken Lights*, 93; *Cancer Experiments on Human Beings*, 164; 'Celibacy v Marriage', 70; *Confessions of a Lost Dog Reported by Her Mistress*, 93; 'Consciousness of Dogs', 93; 'Criminals, Idiots, Women, and Minors; Is the Classification Sound?', 78–9, 109; *Dawning Lights*, 93, 171; 'Dogs Whom I Have Met', 94; *Duties of Women*, 28, 138, 183; 'Essay on True Religion', 26; 'Ethics of Zoophily', 188; *Fallacy of Restriction*, 182, 198; 'Female Charity-Lay and Monastic', 46; *The Friend of Man; and His Friends,—the Poets*, 183; *A Guest for Queen Victoria*, 175; 'Hades', 108; *Health and Holiness*, 175; *Hopes of the Human Race, Hereafter and Here*, 49; *Italics. Brief Notes on Politics, People, and Places in Italy in 1864*, 93; 'The Janus of Science', 172; *Life of Frances Power Cobbe. By Herself* (1894), 193–4; *Life of Frances Power Cobbe as Told by Herself* (1904), 194; 'The Medical Profession and its Morality', 158, 160, 162, 218; *The Modern Rack, Papers on Vivisection*, 183, 183; 'The Moral Aspects of Vivisection', 183; 'The Morals of Literature', 108–9; *Need of a Bill*, 114; *The Nine Circles. Or the Torture of the Innocent*, 189–8; *Our Policy*, 183; *Physiology as a Branch of Education*, 150–1, 161, 183; *The Red Flag in John Bull's Eyes*, 92, 202; *Rejoinder to Mrs Stowe's Reply to the Address of the Women of England*, 93, 202; *Reasons for Interference*, 114; *Religious Duty*, 34; 'The Rights of Man and the Claims of Brutes', 100, 104; 'Schadenfreude', 208; *Science in Excelsis*, 183; *The Scientific Spirit of the Age and Other Pleas and Discussions*, 183; 'Social Science Congresses and Women's Part in Them', 70; *Somerville Hall. A Misnomer*, 154; *The Theory of Intuitive Morals*, 1, 29, 31–2, 34, 46, 58, 99; 'Vivisection-Four Replies', 145; *Vivisection in America*, 183; *Why Women Desire the Franchise*, 69; *Why We Have Founded the British Union for the Abolition of Vivisection*, 200; 'Wife Torture in England', 83; 'Woman Suffrage. Justice for the Gander—Justice for the Goose', 208; *Women's Duty to Women*, 95; *Workhouse as an Hospital*, 62; publications, new editions, 183

Cobbe, Helen Louisa, 206, 210, 215
Cobbe, Henry, birth of, 8
Cobbe, Thomas, 215; birth of, 8; and literary vivisector, 109
Cobbe, William, birth of, 8
cock-fighting, 102
Colam, John, 118; and Norwich incident, 113; and Royal Commission, 124
Coleridge, Bernard and Ferrier prosecution, 142; and restriction, 182, 197, 198
Coleridge libel case, 209, 252 n41
Coleridge, Lord Chief Justice, 126, 178
Coleridge, Mildred, 178, 248 n14
Coleridge, Stephen, 2, 144, 197, 203,

204, 220; purported leader of anti-vivisection movement, 215; and Cobbe, 181, 200, 201–2, 204–5, 219; and restriction, 182, 197, 198; and VSS fissure, 202; Walter Hadwen on, 205
Collins, Wilkie, 163
Conservatives, and vivisection, 133, Cobbe criticises, 201; and women's suffrage, 95
Crawford, Mabel Sharman, 84
cremation, Cobbe on, 211
Cross, Richard, announces Royal Commission, 123; and BMA deputation, 130, 158; and VSS deputation, 127
curare, 121, 122, 131
Cushman, Charlotte, 44, 85

Darwin, Charles, 2, 94, 112; Cobbe on, 90; 94; on Playfair bill, 122; on R.H. Hutton, 119; and vivisection, 116
David-Neel, Alexandra, 40
Davies, Emily, 2, 72, 73, 76, 85; and *Englishwomen's Journal*, 75–6; on Cobbe, 75–6; and vivisection, 154
Davis, the Reverend David, 97
democracy, Cobbe on, 4, 77, 216, 217
Descartes, René, 101
The Discourse of Religion, 23–4
Disraeli, Benjamin, 185; and vivisection, 127
dissection, and female education, 155
dogs, 94, 128, 129, 138; favoured in vivisections, 128
Durham, Dean of, 209
Durham, Edith, 40
Dyke, Sir William Hart, 121

Eastlake, Elizabeth, 5
Echo, 93
education: Cobbe on, 15, 150–1; Cobbe's lack of, 46; education for servants, 66; in workhouses, 64; working-class, 47; and vivisection, 110–12; women's, 70–5, 94, and vivisection, 154–6
Edward VII, Cobbe on, 207; and vivisection, 175, 176
Edwards, Amelia, 40
Egerton, Louisa, 91
Egyptology, 108
Electoral Anti-Vivisection League (London), 199

Eliot, George (Mary Ann Evans), 20, 23
Elliot, Margaret, 56–7, 65
Elmy, Elizabeth Wolstenholme, 75, 84
Ely, Dean of, 209
employment, for women, Cobbe on, 46, 63, 71
enfranchisement: female, Cobbe on, 83, 94, 208–9; and social improvement, 208; Conservatives on, 95; Liberals on, 95; working-class enfranchisement, Cobbe on, 77
Englishwomen's Journal, 75–6
Englishwomen's movement, 75–6
equalisation of poor rates, 60
Erichsen, John Eric, 123
Essays and Reviews, 21
evangelicalism, and animal welfare, 101; and Cobbe family, 17–19; in Ireland, 19
Exeter, Bishop of, 209

Faderman, Lilian, 86
Fawcett, Henry, 115
Fawcett, Millicent Garrett, 8, 95, 195, 196, 209; and vivisection, 152, 154–5
feminism, 70, 74, 208, 217; and anti-vivisection, 152
Ferrier, David, 141–2
Ferrier prosecution, 141–2
field sports, Cobbe defends, 145, 219; Cobbe opposes, 205
food and vital force, 51, 92
Forster, W.E., 123
Foster, Michael, 110–11, 124, 132, 135, 149, 154
France, and animals, 97, 120; Cobbe in, 97
French Anti-Vivisection Society, 192
French, Richard, 124, 198
Froude, J.A., 100, 115
Fuller, Margaret, 87
Furness, Horace H., 209

Galton, Francis, 90
Garrett, Elizabeth, 4, 70, 73, 75, 160
gender difference, 72–4, 208, 217; and legal system, 81; and sin, 30–1; and vivisection, 156
germ theory, 165, 166, 204
Gibbon, Edward, 23
Girton College, 154–5
Gladstone, William Ewart, 90, 127;

Cobbe's opinion of, 95; and vivisection, 136; and women's suffrage, 95
Gloucester, small-pox epidemic, 204
God, and animals, 101, 104, 218–19; and Cobbe, 19, 22, 23, 25, 28, 30–1, 49, 58, 64, 99, 106, 219; and feminism, 46, 58, 73; and gender difference, 73; and love, 87; and patients, 157; and philanthropy, 64; and women, 217; and workhouses, 58
Goltz, Friedrich, 141, 186
government: Cobbe criticises, 5, 83, 158, 216; in Boer War, 207; and public health, 169; and vivisection, 201; and wife abuse, 83
Greg, William Rathbone, 2
Grey, Mrs, 75
Guarnieri, Patrizia, 106
Gull, William, 115, 124, 149

Hadwen, Dr Walter, 204, 205, 211, 215; post-death operation on Cobbe, 210
Hall, Marshall, 111
Hamer, Emily, 86
Hammerton, James, 80, 84
Hampson, Jane, 77
Handbook for the Physiological Laboratory, The, 112
happiness, Cobbe on, 31; and animals, 99; and workhouse inmates, 58–9
Harcourt, Mrs. Vernon, 153
Harcourt, William, 149
Harrison, Frederic, 209
Hart, Ernest, 61, 129, 135; criticised by Cobbe, 118; criticises Cobbe, 117, 191; criticises RSPCA, 118
Hartley, David, 101
Hayes, Matilda, 85
health, Cobbe's holistic understanding of, 166, 167
Hengwrt, 87, 181–2, 185, 205–7
Henniker, Lord, 121
Hereford, Bishop of, 209
Hereford, Dean of, 209
heteropathy, 49, 62
Hill, Alfred, 83
Hill, Florence, 68
Hill, Recorder, 56
Hogarth, William, 105
Hoggan, Dr Frances, 135, 210
Hoggan, Dr George, 124, 133; on anaesthetics, 120–1; co-founds SPALV, 125;

on vivisection, 120; leaves VSS, 135
Holden, Mrs Luther, 114
Holt, J.M., 133
Home Chronicler, founding of, 126
Home Rule, 95
Homo noumenon, 30, 31
Homo phenomenon, 30
Hopkins, Ellice, 5, 67
Horsley, Victor, 203, 211; on Cobbe as anti-Semite, 187; Nine Circles incident, 189–91
Hosmer, Harriet, 44
Howe, Julia Ward, 209
Hughes, Dr Arthur, 210
human vivisection, 105, 128, 163–4, 219; poets and novelists on, 163
humanitarianism, development of, 101
Hume, David, 23
Hutchinson, Jonathan, 162
Hutton, R.H., 95, 123; on Cobbe's resignation, 181; criticises RSPCA, 119; on domestic pets, 125; on human suffering, 173
Huxley, T.H., 134; on Playfair bill, 122, 123; on Royal Commission, 123
Hyde Park Riots, 77
Hygeiolatry, 166, 167

ill-health, Cobbe and, 68–9, 182, 188, 190, 194, 206–7; at Red Lodge, 53–5
Imperial Research Fund, 176
International Association for the Suppression of Vivisection, 126, 132, 133, 135, 144, 199; and Anna Kingsford, 144; draws up abolition bill, 133
International Congress of Hygiene and Demography (1891), 175, 207
International Medical Congress (1881), 141
Italy, and animals, 106; Cobbe on, 38; Cobbe visits, 42, 44, 53, 55, 105; and Theodore Parker, 55; and vivisection, 105–6

Jack the Ripper, as vivisector, 163
James, Henry, 209
Jameson, Anna, 69
Jesse, George, 121, 133–4, 187
Jesuits, 188
Jews, 185–7
Johnson, Samuel, 105

Jowett, Benjamin, 56

Kant, Immanuel, 29; on happiness, 31; on moral nature, 50; on relationships, 103
Karslake, Sir John Burgess, 123
Kelly, Sir Fitzroy, 126
Kemble, Frances, 107, 126–7; autobiographical 'self', 6; and Hereford Square, 184–5
Kensington Discussion Society, 73, 75
'kicking districts', 82
Kidd, Beatrice, 215
Kingsford, Anna, 143–3 146, 198, 218; conflict with Cobbe, 143
Koch, Robert, 163–4

Ladies London Emancipation Society, 202
Lansdowne, Lord, 56
Legal and Illegal Cruelty, 204
Leigh, Colonel Egerton, 82
lesbianism, 48, 85–6
Levine, Philippa, 76
Liberals, and vivisection, 201; and women's suffrage, 95
Lind-af-Hageby, Louise, 215, 252 *n*41
Linzey, Andrew, 3
Lister, Joseph, 124, 149, 176
literature, Cobbe on purposes of, 6, 37; morals in, 108–9
Liverpool and District Anti-Vivisection Society, 199
Llangollen, Ladies of, 182
Lloyd, Mary, 44, 87, 130, 207, 209; death of, 195; and Hengwrt, 182; ill-health, 4, 194–5; relationship with Cobbe, 44, 74, 85–90, 181; and SPALV, 126
Locke, John, 60, 116
Locket, Jeannie, 84
London Anti-Vivisection Society, 126, 132, 135, 199
London Ladies Emancipation Society, 93
London National Society for Women's Suffrage, 75–7, 183
London School Board, 75
London School of Tropical Medicine, 176
London University, 94
Longman, William, 32
Lowe, Robert, 121
Lyell, Charles, 90, 112

Macclesfield Anti-Vivisection Society, 199
Magnan, Eugene, 113
Maitland, Edward, 218; and Anna Kingsford, 143–3, 146
Manchester, Bishop of, 209
Manning, Cardinal, 126, 199
Manton, Jo, 48
marriage, Cobbe and Lloyd's relationship as, 86, 89, 90; Cobbe on, 2, 78–84, 218; women victimised in, 81
Married Women's Property Committee, 75
Martin, Richard, 7, 102
Martineau, James, 90, 91, 134, 192; and vivisection, 115
Martin's Act (1822), 7, 102, 113, 211; Cobbe's opinion of, 114
Matriomonial Causes Act (Divorce Act) (1857), 80
Matrimonial Causes Act (1878), 5, 83–4
medical education, 112, Dr Edward Berdoe on, 161; brutalising effect of, 161; Cobbe on, 160–1; reform of, 110–11
medical research, 164, 175, 176
Medical Research Committee (Medical Research Council), 176
medicine: changes in, 219; Elizabeth Blackwell on, 162; Cobbe on, 151, 159–60, 219; lack of womanly qualities in, 71; women and, 70–2, 160
men, Cobbe criticises, 58, 64, 66, 79, 110
Metropolitan Association for Befriending Young Servants, 65
Metropolitan Poor Law Amendment Act (1867), 61–2
Mica, Natalie, 85
Mill, John Stuart, 2, 90; Cobbe praises, 90; and wife abuse, 82; and women's rights, 76
misanthropy and anti-vivisection, 173
Montague, Mary Wortley, 36
Moodie, Susanna, 36
Moral Law, 29, 31, 48, 218, 219; and disinterested behaviour, 64; and health, 166; and philanthropy, 31, 46; and sympathy, 63; violated by slave owners, 202; violated by vivisectors, 106, 141, 202
morals, 108; and animals, 101; in literature, 108–9; and Prince of Wales, 207; in workhouses, 67; and vivisection, 151;

and working class, 102
More, Hannah, 17
Morelli, J.D., 90
Morris, Lewis, 199
'muff' incident, 177
Mumby, Arthur, 16, 91

Napoleon III, and animals, 97
National Anti-Vivisection Society (formerly Victoria Street Society), 197–9, 204; and Cobbe's funeral, 211; membership, 199; relationship with BUAV, 204–5, 215; and restriction, 198, 200, 203; and subscriptions, 203
New Woman, and vivisection, 191
Newbridge, 7, 8, 27, 44
Newman, F.W., 28
Nightingale, Florence, 20, 61, 166, 209
Nine Circles incident, 189–93
Noailles, Comtess de, 199
Norris, John, 199
Norwich, Dean of, 209
Norwich incident, 113
notification and isolation, Cobbe criticises, 170
nurses, workhouse, 46, 62–3, 67; Cobbe on, 62–3; Louisa Twining on, 62

orphans, in workhouse, 67
Ossory, Bishop of, 209
Ouida (Marie Louise De la Ramée), 32
Owen, Richard, 136, 145
Oxford, anti-vivisection protest, 149–50; J.S. Burdon Sanderson at, 149–50; plaque commemorating Cobbe, 3; Ruskin resigns Slade professorship, 150; vivisection at, 150

Paget, James, 124, 135, 136, 145, 149
Paget, Walburga, 91
pain: and animals, 100, 101, 103, 121; Cobbe on, 104, 108, 145, 147; and Lloyd, Cobbe on, 195; humans, 172, 173, 174; R.H. Hutton on, 173
Paley, William, 23
Palmer, Susanna, 80–1
Parker, Theodore, and anti-slavery, 202; and Cobbe's religious sympathies, 24, 26, 28; and Cobbe and Red Lodge, 51–2, 55
Parkes, Bessie Rayner, 75; on Cobbe, 76
Parminter, Jane, 36

Pasteur, Louis, 164; attacked by Cobbe, 138
patients, Cobbe on, and doctors, 157, 162, 165, 167, 170, 219; female, 71, 157, 167; and God, 157; victims, 105, 162, 163, 164; vivisection on, 162–3
paupers, Cobbe on, aged, 63; children, 64, 66; curables, 59; incurables, 59-61; orphans, 67
Penzance, Lord, 83
pet-keeping, 101
petitions, anti-vivisection, 106, 114, 115, 116, 130, 135, 211; pro-vivisection, 130
philanthropy, Cobbe's understanding of, 31, 46, 217; and feminism, 70; and women, 46, 70
Phillipson, Caroline Giffard, 133
physicians, Cobbe mistreated by, 68–9; Cobbe on, 157–61, 168; education of, 110–11, 160–3; as entrepreneurs, 159; and Frances Cobbe (mother), 10, 157; and patients, 157, 162, 165, 167, 170, 219; social origins of, 159, 244 *n*4; support physiologists, 130, 158; and vivisection, 158, 164; as vivisectors, 105, 116–17, 157, 164; and women, 11, 157, 167
Physiological Association, 149
Physiological Society, 132
physiologists, on Carnarvon's bill, 128, 129, 131–2; Cobbe on, 113–14, 116, 121, 123, 137, 145, 146, 152; assist Home Secretary, 149, petition, 130; Playfair bill, 122; supported by physicians, 130, 158; violate Moral Law, 106, 141, 202
Playfair, Lyon, 122
Ponsonby, Henry, 182
Poor Law Amendment Act (1834), 60–1; Cobbe criticises, 60
Poor Law Guardians, Cobbe criticises, 64–5
Pope, Alexander, 104
Portland, Duke and Duchess of, 199
poverty, Cobbe on, 56–68; on her own, 36, 55, 185
Prayer Gauge Debate, 93, 234 *n*75
premature burial, Cobbe's fear of, 210
press, on 1876 Act, 131–2; on Carnarvon's bill, 129; on Cobbe's death, 210; on cruelty to animals, 97; on Henniker's and Playfair's bills, 122;

and medical reporting, 151; and *Nine Circles* controversy, 189–92; and Norwich incident, 113; on Royal Commission, 124; on vivisection and anti-vivisection, 97, 114, 117, 123, 130, 134, 146, 150, 173, 174; on women's rights, 73; on Cobbe's recommendations for workhouses, 62
Primrose League, 95, 207

Queen Victoria, and animals, 97; death of, 207; and vivisection, 127, 175

Ragged School Union (London), 209
Red Lodge (Bristol), 47–55; Cobbe and, 47, 50, 52, 55; lack of physical comfort at, 51; teachers suffer at, 51
relationships, Cobbe on, 218; Kant on, 103; between God, man and animals, 104; humans and animals, 99, 101; men and women, 84–5; women, 84–7
religion, Cobbe family and, 17–20; Cobbe and, 17–34; crisis of faith, 20–22; in Ireland, 19
Rhodes, Georgine, 188, 190–1
rights, animals, 102; humans, 102; violated, 169–70, 172
Ripon, Dean of, 209
Ritchie, Anne Thackeray, 209
Roman Catholic church, and anthropocentricism, 106
Romanes, George J., 134
Roscoe, Muriel, 199, 200, 215
Rothschild, Lady, 209
Royal Commission on Vivisection (1875), 123–5; anthropocentrism of, 124
Royal Commission on Vivisection (1906), 215
Royal Society for the Prevention of Cruelty to Animals, 97, 102, 148; Cobbe criticises, 119; Cobbe's memorial presented to, 116; criticised by Ernest Hart, 118; opposes Truro's bill, 136; prosecutions, 102; and vivisection, 114, 115, 116–19, 128, 238 n44
Ruskin, John, 115, 150
Russell, George, 192
Ryan, Andrew, 119
Rye, Maria, 68

St Davids, Dean of, 209
St Leger, Harriet, 15, 34, 37, 85, 184

Salisbury, Lord, 201
Sanders, Valerie, 10
sanitation, 166–9
Schadenfreude, 49, 208
Schäfer, E.A., 110–11
Schiff, Moritz, 105, 186; attacked by Cobbe, 106–7
Schuyler, Louisa Lee, 211
science, animals in, Cobbe's arguments for, 104; Cobbe on, 90, 112–8, 219; Cobbe's ignorance of, 90
Scottish Anti-Vivisection Society, 192
self-help, 31, 217
Sen, Kesub Chunder, 90
separate spheres, 41, 44, 66; Cobbe on, 44, 45, 74
servants, Cobbe criticises training of, 66
Shaftesbury, Lord, 3, 125–6, 133, 135, 137, 145, 148, 162, 173, 180, 199; on Charles Warren Adams and Mildred Coleridge, 178–9; and Cobbe, 141–2, 147–9, 178–80; on Cobbe's resignation, 181; death of, 182; on Ferrier prosecution, 141, 142; on human vivisection, 128; President of VSS, 126; supports Truro's bill, 136
Shambles of Science, The, 215, 252 n41
Sharpey, William, 111
Shaw, George Bernard, defends Cobbe, 190; on doctors, 159
Shirreff, Emily, 75
Sidgwick, Eleanor, 29; and vivisection, 152, 155
Simcoe, Elizabeth, 36, 41
Simon, John, 124
sin, Cobbe on: 30; and gender inequality, 30–1; and health, 166, 172
slaughter, Cobbe on, 104, 219; and spontaneous generation, 165
slavery and Moral Law, Cobbe on, 202
small-pox, 204
Society for the Abolition of Vivisection, 121, 132
Society for the Protection of Animals Liable to Vivisection, 4; founding 125; membership, 126; changes to VSS, 126; and women, 125
Somerset, Duchess of, 199
Somerville Hall, and vivisection, 153–4
Somerville, Mary, 44, 77, 87, 89–90, 93; and vivisection, 106, 153
Sorosis Club, 76

speciesism, 216
spiritualism, 144
Stanley, Liz, 85
Stanley, Maude Althea, 68
Stanton, Theodore, 94
state intervention, Cobbe supports, 216
Step by Step, 200
Stuart-Wortley, Jane, 68
Summary Jurisdiction Act (1895), 84
Swanwick, Anna, 199
sympathy, Cobbe on lack of in workhouses, 63

Tait, Lawson, 199
Taylor, Clementia, 1, 75
Taylor, Harriet, 82
Taylor, Helen, 77, 84
Taylor, Peter, 1, 172
teaching hospitals, 162, 207
Tennyson, Alfred, 163
Theism, 216; Cobbe discovers, 24; as 'religion of the future', 29; and Theodore Parker, 23–4
Thring, the Reverend Edward, 161
Traill, Catherine Parr, 36
transcendentalism, 24
Trench, Anne Power, 8
Trist, Sidney, 204, 213
Truro, Lord, 135
Tufnell, T. Joliffe, 113
Twain, Mark, 209
Twining, Louisa, 58, 68; meets Cobbe, 61; on workhouses, 62, 64, lack of womanly influence in, 5
Tyndall, Professor, 90

Unitarianism, 23

vaccination, 171
van Manen-Thesingh, Madam, 136
Vaughan Yates, Mrs Richard, 185
vegetarianism, 143, 144, 218
veterinary colleges, 111
Vicegerent of God, 104, 106
Victoria Magazine, 76
Victoria Street Society: and abolition, 135; changes name to NAVS, 197; on Carnarvon's bill, 128; Cobbe leaves, 181; Cobbe and, 212; criticism of, 135; draws up bill, 127; endorses Holt's bill, 133; fissure, 197; founding of, 125; membership, 125–6; and restriction, 197

Virchow, Professor, 174
vital force, Cobbe on, 51, 92, 168
'vivisecting spirit', 137
vivisection: in America, 118, 155–6; and BAAS, 111; Cobbe's early understanding of, 112; Cobbe's introduction to, 97; in Cobbe's writings, 108–9; destroys womanliness, 155; in England, 104, 110–13, 124; in Europe, 104, 124; and female education, 153–6; guidelines for (1870), 111; human, 105, 128, 163–4, 219; in Italy, 105–6; literary, Cobbe on, 109; and Moral Law, 202; at Oxford, 150; and physicians, 158, 164; press on, 117, 123, 130, 134, 146, 150, 173, 174; and RSPCA, 114–15, 118, 119; and Somerville Hall, 153–4; statistics, 144, 213; and women, 152–3; and women's rights, Cobbe on, 109–10
vivisector, 137; literary, 109; violates Moral Law, 106, 141, 202
von Schartau, Liesa, 215, 254 *n*41

Wales, Cobbe and Lloyd in, 182–96
Ward, Mrs Humphrey, 29, 192
Wellcome Physiological Research Laboratories, 175
Wesley, John, 104
White, Blanco, 23
wife abuse, 8, 134; Cobbe and, 80–4
Wilberforce, Archdeacon, 209
Wilberforce, Canon, 189
Wilberforce, William, 17
Wilks, Samuel, 129, 136, 145, 149
Williams, Dr Evans, 210
Wilmont, J.E. Eardley, 136
Wilson, Archdeacon, 209
Winchester, Dean of, 209
Winmarleigh, Lord, 123
Wister, Sarah, Cobbe's letters to, 4, 66, 73, 74, 77, 87, 89, 90, 118, 121, 179, 184, 188, 193, 194, 195, 196, 199, 200, 202, 206, 207, 209
Wollstonecraft, Mary, 219
women: Cobbe on, 45–6, 74, 83–4; and animals, exploitation of, 109–10, 134; in anti-vivisection, 152–3, 243 *n*89; duties of, 28, 217, 214; education, 45, 715, 94; employment of, 63; experiments on, 164; and God, 217; and medicine, 70–1, 160; moral superiority of, 46, 68, 96, 105, 208, 217, 214; as

patients, 71, 157, 167; and philanthropy, 46, 54, 143; and SPALV, 125; unmarried women: Louisa May Alcott on, 2; Cobbe on, 2, 70, and education, 72, and philanthropy, 46; women travellers, 36, 39, 40; victimised, in marriage, 81, in workhouses, 58, 62; and vivisection, 150–6; as workhouse visitors, 5, 58
Women's Liberal Federation, 207, 211
women's rights, 138, 217; in America, 76; Cobbe introduced to, 70; Cobbe on, 3, 70–78; in medicine, 70–1; in publishing, 32; in workhouse visiting, 58; and vivisection, 109–10
workhouses: Cobbe's impressions of, 56; Cobbe visits, 57–68; conditions within, 57–8; 'curables', 59; Anna Jameson on, 69; Ellice Hopkins on, 67; workhouse hospitals, 5, 61–2; workhouse hospitals, Louisa Twining on, 62; 'incurables', 59–61; moral contagion in, 67; orphans in, 67; and physicians, 157; womanly influence in, 5, 58, 64
working class, and animals, 102; education, 47; enfranchisement, 77; health and workhouses, 60; lack of moral awareness, 102
World League Against Vivisection, 215

Xenotransplantation, 219

Yeo, Gerald, 135, 142, 149; criticises Cobbe, 146–7
York Anti-Vivisection Society, 199
York, Archbishop of, 126, 133, 135

Zola, Emile, criticises anti-vivisectionists, 174
Zoophilist, founded, 136; on BUAV, 202–3